THE UNITED STATES
IN VIETNAM
REVISED EDITION

by

George McTurnan Kahin
and
John W. Lewis

A DELTA BOOK

BY GEORGE McT. KAHIN

Nationalism and Revolution in Indonesia
The Asian-African Conference
Major Governments of Asia (editor)
Governments and Politics of Southeast Asia (editor)

BY JOHN W. LEWIS

Chinese Communist Leadership and the Succession
to Mao Tse-tung: Appraisal of Tensions
Leadership in Communist China
Major Doctrines of Communist China
Education and Political Development (contributor)

A DELTA BOOK

Published by
Dell Publishing Co., Inc.
750 Third Avenue
New York, N.Y. 10017

Delta ® TM 755118, Dell Publishing Co., Inc.
Reprinted by arrangement with The Dial Press, Inc.
Library of Congress Catalog Card Number: 79-78461
Printed in the United States of America
Revised edition
Seventh Printing

Acknowledgments for copyrighted material appear on page VI
and constitute an extension of this page.

for our children:

Brian and Sharon

AND

Amy, Cynthia, and Stephen

Acknowledgments

The following maps are reproduced by permission of their publishers:

Map 1: Vietnam in Continental Southeast Asia. © 1959 and 1964 by Cornell University Press. Used by permission of Cornell University Press.

Map 4: The Situation in May 1953. Reprinted from *Agonie de l'Indochine* by Henri Navarre by permission of Librarie Plon, Paris.

Map 6: South Vietnam, Areas of Control and Influence as of 30 January 1966. © 1966 by The New York Times Company. Reprinted by permission. Demarcations showing area of country controlled by each division of South Vietnamese Army added by authors.

*　　*　　*

Part of the material on which this book is based first appeared as an article entitled "The United States in Vietnam" in the June 1965 issue of *Bulletin of the Atomic Scientists,* published by the Educational Foundation for Nuclear Science, 935 East 60 Street, Chicago, Illinois.

Preface

For most Americans the word "Vietnam" spells confusion and complexity. It had never been an area of significant interest to them before, and they awoke rather suddenly to its very existence only after their government had made what they were told were irrevocable commitments there. While confronted with the disparity between the depth of the United States involvement in Vietnam and the shallowness of their own knowledge of that country, Americans have found themselves called upon to rally behind the President without having sufficient understanding of the situation to evaluate his Administration's policies. Lacking this knowledge, those who are inclined to question these policies in terms of political realism are often inhibited from challenging the Administration's assertion that it knows what is best for Vietnam and the United States. For the same reason, even many of those whose disposition has been to dispute this contention primarily on the basis of humanitarian and moral considerations have been led to mute their reactions.

Having gone so far in committing the United States and insisting that the American people close ranks behind its war effort, the Administration would seem to bear a responsibility for providing the information necessary for them to comprehend the situation that has actually developed in Vietnam. This it has not done. Much that is necessary for such an understanding has been withheld or rendered out of context. And the more deeply one probes into the history of the U.S. involvement in Vietnam, the more evident it becomes that a seriously distorted picture has been presented.

In this book we have tried to describe the record as fully

as possible and to make available the essential facts—including many that would normally remain difficult or impossible of access to the reader. In the course of our work we have talked to Vietnamese and Westerners knowledgeable about Vietnam, and we have analyzed relevant documentary material, much of which has not previously been utilized in published studies dealing with the country. Since our own professional careers have focused on research related to China and Southeast Asia, we drew upon our knowledge of these areas in an endeavor to clarify important parts of the context in which American policies in Vietnam are set.

It is our hope that this book will help provide a better understanding of how the Vietnam problem developed and of the fundamental issues that underlie it. We realize that events significantly affecting the situation may soon overtake our study. But whatever importance they may have, most or all of the basic elements of the problem as of November 1966 (when our manuscript was completed) are likely, we believe, to remain basic for some time.

We could not have written this study without the generous assistance and advice that a great many people have given us. We are especially indebted to Audrey Richey. Her contributions have ranged from research to editorial guidance, and without her help this book might well have never been finished. In our research we owe a special debt to Franklin B. Weinstein and Christine Pelzer White. In this respect, we are also appreciative of the assistance of Miriam Berkley, Brian Sean Brady, Barry Michael Casper, Sandra Hamilton, Mary V. Loosbrock, Peggy Meyer, Milton E. Osborne, Michael A. Nolte, Michael L. Sherard, and Donald Voth. We wish, too, to thank the numerous Vietnamese who were helpful to us in many aspects of our research.

Our study has profited from the suggestions of criticisms of specialists in various fields relevant to our discussion. We are particularly grateful to these colleagues who have read all or parts of the manuscript and have given us the benefit of their advice: Benedict Anderson, Herbert W. Briggs, Frederick P. Bunnell, Philippe Devillers, R. B. Jones, David P. Mozingo, Clinton Rossiter, and O. W. Wolters. We should also like to acknowledge with gratitude the similar contributions of Ruth Adams, Joseph Kraft, Daniel S. Lev, Theodore J. Lowi, Franz Schurmann, Josef Silverstein, and Constance M. Wilson.

In preparing the manuscript we were crucially dependent upon the unfailing assistance of Gerry Bowman of the London-Cornell Project. In this respect, we are further indebted to Katrina Morse, Rita J. Marsland, Laurie Sieverts, and Carrie Ricklefs.

The views expressed in this book are those of the authors alone, and only the authors, of course, share the responsibility for the facts and opinions presented.

Finally, we wish to express our thanks to Cornell University's Southeast Asia Program, which provided funds for preparing the manuscript. Our gratitude also goes to the staff of The Dial Press for their patience and understanding assistance in readying our manuscript for publication.

G. McT. K.
J. W. L.

Ithaca, New York
November 15, 1966

Note to the Second Edition

Because we consider that the material and analysis presented in the first edition of this book remain valid, we have restricted changes in the original chapters to the correction of typographical errors. This second edition adds a substantial section on developments since November 1966 that undertakes to bring the story of the United States in Vietnam up through mid-1969. The material for this section reflects a further visit of one of the authors to South Vietnam, as well as his discussions with a high official of the National Liberation Front in Cambodia in mid-August 1967 and with members of the American, North Vietnamese and NLF delegations in Paris in September 1968 and May 1969. We have also replaced the last two appendices of the first edition with documents currently more relevant.

As before, we are grateful to many individuals for their generous assistance—especially to David P. Mozingo. We are also indebted to the late Bernard B. Fall; to Stanley Bedlington, Don Luce, David Marr, Jayne S. Werner; to American and Vietnamese officials in Paris, South Vietnam and Washington; and especially to those courageous and candid Vietnamese citizens whose names we would like to list, but which we withhold in order not to risk making their troubled lives more difficult. We also wish to thank Marion Bieber, Gerry Bowman, Emily Nelson, and Dorothy Neumann for their help in the preparation of the manuscript. We wish to acknowledge with thanks the financial assistance of Cornell's Project on the International Relations of East Asia, its Southeast Asia Program and Stanford University's Center for Research in International Studies.

Finally, our wives have been a special source of support and encouragement in the writing of this edition. As with the first edition, the contribution of Audrey Richey Kahin has been invaluable, both with respect to research and editorial guidance.

G. McT. K.
J. W. L.

June 15, 1969

Table of Contents

MAPS

TABLES

APPENDICES

THE UNITED STATES IN VIETNAM

CHAPTER I

Historical Background

1 : **The coastline of Vietnam** describes a mighty "S" running from the southern border of China to the tip of the Indochina peninsula. Stretching for more than 1,200 miles, it nearly equals the length of the entire Pacific coast of continental United States. The country's area of 127,000 square miles reaches back unevenly from the coast for distances of as little as 33 to as much as 300 miles.

The rich, alluvial deltas of the Red River in the North and the Mekong River in the South have often been likened to two rice baskets suspended at the ends of a peasant's carrying pole, for along with the generally narrow coastal plains they produce nearly all of Vietnam's rice. Although these regions constitute well under a quarter of the country's area, they support almost all of that five-sixths of its population who are ethnically Vietnamese. In the extensive arc of hill and mountain country to the north and west of the Red River delta live several groups of Tai who speak languages closely allied to those of Thailand and much of Laos and very different from Vietnamese. The vast plateau and hill areas of central Vietnam are inhabited by other, distinctly non-Vietnamese peoples. These Malayo-Polynesian and Mon-Khmer speaking groups were displaced from the more fertile coastal areas by the Vietnamese as they pushed south from their original home in the Red River delta. Along with the Tai tribes in the North and several smaller non-Vietnamese groups scattered through the interior, they constitute what the French collectively termed the *Montagnards,*—mountain people living almost exclusively in the hill, mountain, and plateau areas that make up three-quarters of the country. Altogether there are

3

approximately 3½ million of these Montagnards with more than twice as many living north as south of the 17th parallel. Not far west of Saigon, and also to the south of the Mekong, reside about 700,000 Cambodians, in what were once districts of the Kingdom of Cambodia. In addition, there are over a million Chinese in Vietnam, living mostly in the South and particularly in Saigon and its twin city, Cholon. Today the total population of Vietnam numbers about 34 million, with about 18 million living north of the 17th parallel and 16 million to the south.

2 : **In all Southeast Asia,** Vietnam has stood unique as the one country with close cultural and political ties to China. This relationship seems to have existed as early as 221 B.C., when Chinese garrisons were sent to the Red River delta. A Sino-Vietnamese kingdom existed there from 207 B.C. until 111 B.C., when this territory was annexed by China. For the next thousand years, until 939 A.D., most of the area of present-day North Vietnam was governed as a Chinese province, though Chinese control was often relaxed. During this long period many features of Chinese culture spread through at least the upper levels of Vietnamese society, imbuing it with Confucian social and political values. The Vietnamese adopted the hierarchical system of Mandarin bureaucracy, including a civil-service examination system and the study of Chinese classics, upon which the system was based. As in China, the whole Mandarin system was ill suited to cope with rapid change.

The Vietnamese admired many aspects of Chinese civilization, but their own culture remained sufficiently distinct for them to resent China's long-continuing political domination. Vietnamese restiveness grew, until in 939 they revolted and secured their freedom from China.[1] They successfully resisted Kublai Khan's invasion in the 13th century, and continued to keep free of China's control except for a brief reassertion of its political authority during the early 15th century. The Vietnamese remained jealous of their independence and effectively repelled the subsequent efforts of their powerful northern neighbor to reestablish its former overlordship.[2] Consequently, for many centuries a basic and constant theme of their nationalism was freedom from China's domination. When after a century of French colonial rule, freedom was again won, this theme reasserted itself with traditional vigor. Thus in July 1963, in celebrating the ninth anniversary of independence from France, Hanoi radio illustrated Vietnam's "triumphal struggle for independence" by bracketing three victories over Chinese invaders, (beginning in 939 A.D.) with the 1954 defeat of the French at Dienbienphu.[3] In Hanoi's Historical Museum today, a large room is devoted to "The Heroic Struggle of the Vietnamese People Against Chinese Feudal Invaders." [4]

3 : The penetration of the Vietnamese south of the center coastal littoral was barred initially by the Indonesian kingdom of Champa. After a long struggle, the Vietnamese defeated and largely destroyed this kingdom in 1471, but it was not until the 17th century that they pushed as far as the then Cambodian-controlled Mekong River delta. Vietnamese occupation of this relatively underpopulated area was not far advanced until the 18th century and was still in progress when the French arrived in the mid-19th century. In the 17th and 18th centuries Vietnam was under separate and bitterly hostile governments in Hanoi and Hué. The Hué government was able only gradually to exercise effective centralized administration in the newly settled southern areas.

For the first half of the 19th century, however, the Emperor Gia-long and his successors governed the whole of Vietnam from their court at Hué. But this brief period of unification was brought to an end by the coming of the French. Aware of China's recent defeats at the hands of British and French forces, Gia-long's successors attempted to keep out the Westerners and Western commerce. Fearing the political activities

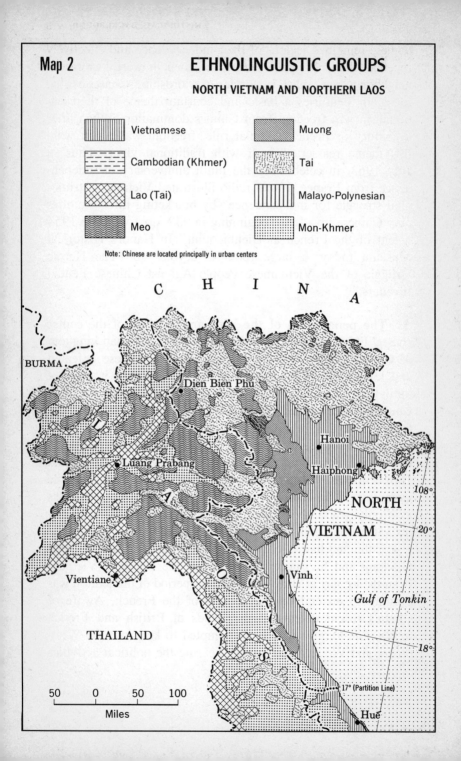

Map 2

ETHNOLINGUISTIC GROUPS

NORTH VIETNAM AND NORTHERN LAOS

Vietnamese		Muong	
Cambodian (Khmer)		Tai	
Lao (Tai)		Malayo-Polynesian	
Meo		Mon-Khmer	

Note: Chinese are located principally in urban centers

C H I N A

BURMA

Dien Bien Phu

Hanoi

Luang Prabang

Haiphong

NORTH

VIETNAM

108°

20°

Vinh

Vientiane

Gulf of Tonkin

THAILAND

18°

17° (Partition Line)

Hué

50   0   50   100

Miles

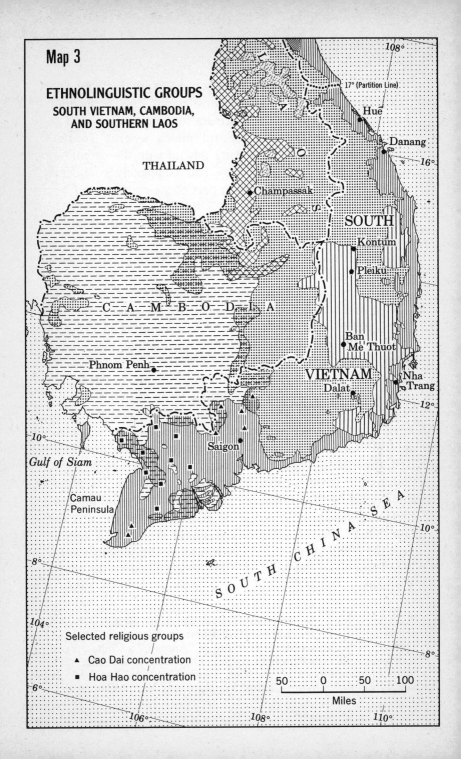

Map 3

ETHNOLINGUISTIC GROUPS
SOUTH VIETNAM, CAMBODIA,
AND SOUTHERN LAOS

THAILAND

17° (Partition Line)

Hué

Danang

16°

Champassak

SOUTH

Kontum

Pleiku

C A M B O D I A

Ban
Me Thuot

Nha
Trang

Phnom Penh

VIETNAM

Dalat

12°

10°

Saigon

Gulf of Siam

Camau
Peninsula

10°

8°

SOUTH CHINA SEA

104°

Selected religious groups

▲ Cao Dai concentration

■ Hoa Hao concentration

50   0   50   100

Miles

6°

106°   108°   110°

of the French missionaries already resident in Vietnam, they carried out strong measures against them. This persecution provided the French with a pretext for intervention, and in 1857 they launched a successful attack against Tourane (present-day Danang), following this up with the capture of Saigon in 1859. By 1867 they had completely conquered Cochin China, the southernmost part of the country, and had made it a French colony.[5] In 1883 the French moved against the remainder of the Vietnamese state and in the following year took over Annam and Tonkin as protectorates.* But it was another twelve years before the French could pacify these areas, and armed opposition did not cease until 1917.

The unity that Emperor Gia-long and his successors were seeking to establish throughout the (by then) greatly enlarged Vietnamese kingdom was undercut by the nature of France's colonial government. In Cochin China, where the French ruled directly, no remnants of the imperial administration remained. In Annam and Tonkin, France maintained a facade of Vietnamese authority, permitting some members of the Mandarin bureaucracy to carry out a decreasing range of administrative functions under the supervision and effective control of French officials. A consequence of this decentralized, tripartite, French colonial administration was to preserve, and in some respects enhance, regional distinctions. The minor role played by the Mandarins in the government and the continued existence of the old court at Hué did not disguise the fact that by the time of the First World War French control over the Vietnamese was unchallengeable and all-encompassing. Throughout the areas of Vietnam inhabited by the ethnic Vietnamese, the exercise of French authority became increas-

---

* Cochin China, Annam, and Tonkin are Chinese and Western terms applied to the territorial divisions in Vietnam. The Vietnamese particularly object to the use of "Annam," a Chinese word that means literally "pacified south." They refer to the three divisions of their land as Nam Viet, Trung Viet, and Bac Viet, or simply South Vietnam, Central Vietnam, and North Vietnam.

ingly direct and widespread, and the Emperor and his court at Hué came to perform little more than ceremonial functions.

But the situation was very different for the non-Vietnamese, highland-dwelling peoples. Most of the Montagnards, especially in the South, were left relatively undisturbed by the French; they were able to maintain a large degree of autonomy, and some groups remained free of French control until as late as 1940.

The French colonial administration in Vietnam was headed by a Governor-General * directly responsible to the Ministry of Colonies in Paris. French rule of the Vietnamese was strongly authoritarian and widely pervasive, more Western personnel being used at lower administrative levels than in any other Southeast Asian colony. By 1930 there were approximately as many French civil servants administering Vietnam as there were British colonial officials in India, where the population was at least twelve times as large. Cochin China was for the French the most profitable of the three components of Vietnam. Here they invested most of their capital, and here their administration penetrated deepest—down to the district and sometimes even to the village level.

Under French rule the Vietnamese economy remained predominantly agrarian, and as elsewhere in Southeast Asia the peasantry constituted over 80 per cent of the population. Most of the lowland Vietnamese-settled areas of Tonkin and Annam were characterized by small holdings, where the large majority of peasants cultivated their own land; but as the population expanded, especially in Tonkin, plots became increasingly inadequate. In contrast, arable land in Cochin China was relatively abundant. Much of it was covered by the holdings of French and wealthy Vietnamese, where a large part of the

---

* The Governor-General concurrently headed the colonial governments in Cambodia and Laos, in both of which French administration was much less pervasive than in Vietnam; it was also more indirect, relying heavily on the cooperation of the more amenable members of the traditional local aristocracies.

peasantry worked as laborers and tenants. Throughout most of Vietnam the weight of taxation on the peasantry was heavy and was one of the factors leading to their increasingly widespread indebtedness. Although France as a whole received little economic benefit from Vietnam and certainly by 1954 had sustained a considerable overall loss, a minority of French investors, working through a small but potent lobby in the French Parliament, made very considerable profits out of the colonial relationship.

Although colonial rule insured Vietnam greater political stability, and under the French public health, flood control, and communications were improved, Western education was brought to only a handful of Vietnamese. Facilities provided by the French for secondary and technological education in Vietnam were of high quality, but very few qualified Vietnamese were given the opportunity to attend either these schools or those in France. By 1940 there were only fourteen secondary schools in all Vietnam, and there was only a single university, founded in Hanoi in 1917. Those who did manage to acquire a higher education were faced with heavy discrimination when they sought positions either in the civil service or in French business firms in Vietnam; decided preference was given to the French even when they were less educated and less qualified than Vietnamese applicants. This treatment antagonized the small but expanding group of Western-educated Vietnamese, particularly those who had been exposed to egalitarian ideas while studying in France. Their consequent embitterment provided an important impulse in the development of a modern Vietnamese-nationalist movement. Additional recruits for the movement came from some of the 100,000 Vietnamese soldiers and workers sent to France in 1915 to support the French war effort against Germany. Many of these Vietnamese came into contact with social and political ideas that were quite inconsistent with the colonial system existing at home. Upon their return to Vietnam, some naturally gravitated towards those Vietnamese leaders who were dedicated to the overthrow of French colonial rule.

Most efforts by the Vietnamese to achieve even moderate reforms by working through the colonial administration were frustrated. Those nationalists who attempted to work for independence through legal political activity soon found themselves in jail. French repression of such activity became so severe that it was usually only through clandestine, underground organizations that the nationalists could operate with any real chance of political effectiveness. During the 1920's, the major underground nationalist organization was the Vietnam Quoc Dan Dang (VNQDD) or the Vietnamese Nationalist Party. Its major objectives were the overthrow of French rule and the establishment of a republican government. Its members looked to the Chinese Nationalist Party (Kuomintang) as their model for organization. In early February 1930, the VNQDD led a revolt of the Vietnamese soldiers garrisoned at Yen Bay in north central Tonkin. It was hoped that this would set in motion uprisings throughout the country, leading to a general revolution. But the French were informed of the plans and quickly suppressed the rebellion. The VNQDD as an organization was effectively destroyed. Some of its leaders fled to China and did not appear again until some fifteen years later, when with Japan's capitulation they reentered Tonkin in the train of Chiang Kai-shek's occupation forces.

4: **After the destruction of the VNQDD,** the major anti-French underground activity in Vietnam was undertaken by Communist organizations. Three such groups were united in 1930 into the Indochinese Communist Party by Ho Chi Minh, who then bore the name of Nguyen Ai Quoc (Nguyen the Patriot).[6]

Ho had been born in 1890 in northern Annam, son of a Mandarin official whose career had been arrested because of anti-French nationalist activity. In 1911, at the age of nineteen, Ho left Vietnam on a French merchant ship.[7] He lived in London for several years, working for a time as assistant to the chef of the Carlton Hotel.[8] Following this, Ho is reported by one of his top associates to have visited the United States and lived in Harlem. On the basis of this, writes Bernard Fall, "He was sufficiently impressed by what he saw (or said he saw) to write, during his stay in Moscow in 1924, a pamphlet entitled *La Race Noire (The Black Race)* which was bitterly critical of American and European racial practices." [9] Returning to France in 1917 or 1918, Ho supported himself as a photographer's assistant and soon became politically active in the Vietnamese community there. In 1919, at the Versailles Conference, he addressed a memorandum to the Great Powers demanding that the principles of Woodrow Wilson be applied to Indochina.[10] Although his memorandum went unheeded, the editor of the socialist newspaper, *Le Populaire,* published it and thereafter accepted a number of Ho's articles. Ho joined the French Socialist Party and was a member of the majority group, which split off and formed the French Communist Party in 1920.[11] He became the Party's specialist on colonial matters and in 1923 was sent to the Krestintern (Peasants' International) in Moscow as the delegate representing the French colonial territories. He was elected to the Krestintern's ten-man Executive Committee and in mid-1924 was a delegate to the Fifth Congress of the Comintern.[12]

In January 1925 Ho was sent to Canton as secretary-translator for Borodin, the Comintern's advisor to Sun Yat-sen's Kuomintang. This was the period when the Russians had been asked to reorganize and strengthen the Kuomintang's political organization and armed forces and when noncommunist Chinese, such as Chiang Kai-shek, as well as Chinese communists welcomed and worked with the Russians. It was in Canton, in June 1925, that Ho organized Vietnamese political refugees into an association of Vietnamese Revolutionary Youth, the precursor of the Indochinese Communist Party. He arranged for several members of this group to be trained in

Canton at the Whampoa Military Academy, which was then led by Chiang Kai-shek with the aid of Chou En-lai and with the advice of Russian General Vassily Bluecher.[13] Fall notes that "one of the most brilliant" of the Vietnamese graduates of Whampoa was Pham Van Dong, whose father—a high-ranking Mandarin—had been involved in an anti-French rebellion in 1917. (In 1955 Pham Van Dong was to become Prime Minister of the Democratic Republic of Vietnam.) [14] In the spring of 1927, following the rupture within the Kuomintang between Chiang Kai-shek's followers and the communists, Ho, along with Borodin and his mission, was obliged to leave Canton. He travelled first to Hankow and then to Moscow, where he remained until 1928.[15]

After working briefly among the Vietnamese colony in Siam, Ho arrived in Hong Kong in January 1930. It was here that he undertook to reconcile the several competing Vietnamese communist groups and by the end of February had arranged for their amalgamation into one organization, the Vietnam Communist Party (later named the Indochinese Communist Party). Headquarters for this new party were set up in Haiphong, in northern Vietnam. In June 1931 British authorities in Hong Kong arrested Ho and detained him for eighteen months. Upon his release he went to Shanghai and soon afterwards returned to Russia.[16] He appears to have remained in Moscow during the mid-1930's, reportedly visiting communist bases in northwest China in 1937 or 1938.[17]

In the meantime, from May 1930 to September 1931, acute agrarian discontent gave rise to a series of peasant rebellions in northern Annam, especially in Ho's native province of Nghe An. Members of Ho's recently established Communist Party undertook, without notable success, to provide leadership to the rebels. Several of these leaders were later to emerge among the most prominent of Ho's lieutenants—Pham Van Dong, Vo Nguyen Giap, and Truong Chinh. The rebellion was quickly and brutally suppressed by the French, and these three, together with many other communists and noncommunists, were arrested. During the 1930's several thousand such political prisoners were held in Vietnamese jails and penal settlements. Following a period of amnesty from 1936 to 1939, made possible because of a Popular Front government in France, the communists were again subjected to heavy repression from which they were unable to recover until well into the Japanese occupation.[18]

Despite these reversals, on the eve of World War II the communists still controlled by far the best organized and strongest of the anti-French underground groups. Being the most effective nationalist organization, the Communist Party attracted many Vietnamese patriots who had no particular interest in communism. Here, then, were the beginnings of a fusion of nationalism and communism that was to develop much further under the particular circumstances of the Japanese occupation and the subsequent nine-year French effort to destroy the independence forces and to reassert French authority.

5: **Soon after the Japanese entry into Indochina,** Ho Chi Minh, already in China, moved to its southern border area, just north of Tonkin.[19] Now that the Japanese occupied Vietnam, Chiang Kai-shek and his southern generals had an important objective in common with Ho and his Vietnamese communist organization—the undermining of the newly-established Japanese power on China's southern flank.

Following the Nazi invasion of France in 1940, the Japanese served a series of ultimata upon the French in Indochina. After unsuccessful appeals for Allied support, the French capitulated. Under agreements of September 22, 1940 and May 1941, Japan, in effect, recognized French sovereignty and left local administration and security functions in French hands. In return, the French gave the Japanese the right of transit through Indochina, as well as control over local military facilities and the country's economic resources.

Japan's role in Indochina was radically different from her

occupation of any other Southeast Asian country. In the rest of the colonies there, the Japanese realized the advantage of working through the native elites, whom they regarded as more satisfactory instruments of administration than Western colonial civil servants. In order to secure the support of the educated indigenous groups in these other areas, the Japanese were obliged to grant them concessions. Thus, in addition to promoting native officials to considerably higher administrative posts than they had previously held, the Japanese also gave local leaders greater scope for promoting nationalist movements and, in nearly every case, promised independence. Most active nationalists in Southeast Asia, therefore, found it more to their interest to operate openly through some sort of marriage of convenience with the Japanese rather than to continue their struggle underground.

The one great exception was in Indochina. There the pro-Vichy French administration was willing to come to terms with the Japanese, and consequently its officials were permitted to retain their previous positions under the general control and supervision of the Japanese. Being able to rely upon the French bureaucracy in Vietnam, the Japanese did not need to make concessions to Vietnamese nationalists. Vietnamese patriots had no opportunity to work towards independence openly and were still obligated to operate underground. Thus, during the war the major channel open to those Vietnamese who wished to free their country from Japanese, and ultimately French, control was an underground movement where Vietnamese communists already had a strong and entrenched position. Inasmuch as Ho and his party were operating under a national-front policy and emphasizing nationalism well above communism, they secured significant backing even from noncommunist Vietnamese, particularly in Tonkin.

Had Ho been closely identified with Chinese communism, Vietnamese sensitivity to the possible reassertion of Chinese domination might have weakened his chances for attracting the support of noncommunists. However, his ideological development had taken place largely in France and in the Soviet Union, and he was (and still is) generally regarded as more sympathetic to the communist leaders in Russia than to those in China. He had, moreover, established himself as a leading Asian communist leader before Mao Tse-tung became prominent. Jean Lacouture, who probably knows as much about Ho's career as any noncommunist Westerner, puts the matter this way:

> . . . for Ho Chi Minh, a Bolshevik since the earliest days, who was one of the founders of the Comintern and who even seemed to be the possible leader of Asiatic communism in the years 1925–1928, Mao Tse-tung is not as fabulous a personage as he is in the eyes of almost all Far Eastern revolutionaries. Certainly, Ho credits his Chinese colleague with a great preeminence in matters of strategic invention and doctrinal competence; but he regards him only as one of his peers who has more means at his command rather than more constancy or revolutionary merit.[20]

Moreover, for Ho Vietnam always took first place over communism, and even Ngo Dinh Diem openly admitted that it was because of Ho's leadership as a nationalist that he was ultimately able to rally such wide Vietnamese support.[21]

The Indochinese Communist Party became the focal point for nationalist resistance against the Japanese occupation. At the outset, on November 22, 1940, Tran Van Giau, a southern communist leader, organized an abortive uprising in western Cochin China, which French troops and planes quashed within two weeks.[22] Giau had apparently organized this revolt independently, but thereafter communist efforts were more cautious and realistic and usually carried out in closer liaison with Ho and his senior lieutenants.

The remnants of the Central Committee of the Indochinese Communist Party met with Ho Chi Minh in May of 1941 in South China near the border of Tonkin. Here they established the Viet Nam Doc Lap Dong Minh Hoi (Vietnamese Independence League), or Vietminh as it was generally called. This was, in effect, a national-front organization, led primarily by the Indochinese Communist Party but attempting to attract Vietnamese patriots of all political hues in a common struggle against the Japanese and the French.[23] The Vietminh, under Ho's leadership, was to become the principal vehicle of Vietnamese nationalism in the thirteen-year struggle that ended in France's defeat and the Geneva Conference of 1954.

The nature of Kuomintang Chinese support to the Vietminh was vacillating, and they placed Ho under arrest from August 1942 to September 1943. Nevertheless, the Vietminh made good use of the limited facilities that the Kuomintang granted it, and until late 1944 or early 1945 its major training and base area was in the southern border region of China's Kuomintang-controlled Kwangsi province.

Towards the end of 1943 small groups of Vietminh commandos penetrated into Tonkin led by Vo Nguyen Giap,[24] the future strategist at Dienbienphu and today Commander in Chief of the armies of North Vietnam. On November 8, 1944, a larger unit crossed the frontier and launched the first of a series of attacks against border-guard posts. During the course of the winter of 1944–45 Vietminh forces gained control over wide regions of three of the northernmost Vietnamese provinces and of adjacent border areas.[25] According to Harold Isaacs, a veteran *Newsweek* correspondent who was among the first American writers to visit Vietnam after Japan's capitulation: "Between March and August [1945] the Viet Minh guerrillas cleared large sections of five of the northern provinces of Tonkin and engaged the full attention of the bulk of the Japanese 21st Division."[26]

As it became widely recognized as the only strong force opposing the Japanese, the Vietminh received support from the American Office of Strategic Services (O.S.S.). The Vietminh helped rescue downed American pilots and provided important intelligence concerning the movement of Japanese armed forces to O.S.S. agents. A number of the O.S.S. officers did not conceal their admiration and enthusiasm for the Vietminh guerrillas and helped convince its leaders that the United States backed them in their struggle for independence.[27] These Vietnamese were already prepared to expect American support because of President Roosevelt's Atlantic Charter, with its emphasis upon self-determination of all peoples—not merely Europeans. Undoubtedly this expectation had also been strengthened by persistent United States Office of War Information broadcasts across the Pacific that emphasized the United States' dedication to freedom for colonial peoples.

6: During the early months of 1945, as an Allied victory appeared imminent, Gaullist influence spread among the previously pro-Vichy French, who had been administering Indochina. Increasingly worried over this change, the Japanese suddenly interned almost all French troops and civil servants in Indochina on March 9, 1945, and themselves took over the positions of higher and intermediate authority previously left to the French. Concurrently, the Japanese made some rather tentative and ineffective moves towards establishing a national Vietnamese government, and in an endeavor to secure some measure of Vietnamese support they made a nominal grant of independence to the country on March 11. As head of this "independent" state embracing all of Vietnam, they appointed Bao Dai, who for a decade prior to the war had been the French-controlled emperor of Annam. The Japanese, however, had insufficient time and probably little inclination to build any substance for his administration, whose authority was in any case confined to the cities and towns garrisoned by their troops.

After the internment of French officials, the Japanese were unable to control the countryside, and Vietminh forces moved closer to Hanoi. Ho apparently anticipated the Japanese collapse and was prepared to strike when it occurred. Two days after Japan's surrender to the Allies, pro-Vietminh elements in Hanoi staged an uprising, and the next day armed Vietminh forces entered and seized the city without resistance. Bao Dai abdicated a few days later, turning the Imperial Great Seal over to the Vietminh and offering to serve Ho's government. On August 29 the Vietminh formed a "Provisional Government of the Democratic Republic of Vietnam," with its capital in Hanoi. On September 2, 1945, Ho Chi Minh formally proclaimed Vietnam's independence.[28]

Meanwhile, Vietminh elements in the south, under the leadership of Tran Van Giau, took over Saigon and then moved to consolidate control over adjacent areas of Cochin China. Although they had some success in building Vietminh support in the region, their methods were sometimes harsh and politically clumsy. Consequently, several important groups were alienated from the Vietminh. At the very outset there was a recrudescence of prewar friction with the locally powerful Trotskyite communists, which ended in Giau's harsh repression of this group. In addition, Giau and his followers were held responsible for the deaths of several leaders of the large and cohesive religious sects known as the Cao Dai and the Hoa Hao, and this undoubtedly contributed to the sects' antagonism towards the Vietminh.[29] These were substantial losses because both religious sects, the Cao Dai in particular, were well organized and possessed substantial, clearly defined territorial bases; moreover, the Japanese had provided the two groups with some military training and arms. The French were later able to take advantage of the sects' hostility to the Vietminh and, by paying their leaders regular subsidies, helped further insure that most of their following would remain out of the Vietminh camp.*

---

* The Cao Dai, launched in the late 1920's by Vietnamese claiming mystical, religious insights, is regarded by its adherents as a synthesis of the world's major religions (with the exception of Islam) wherein their common denominators are readily apparent. Its closely organized membership, variously estimated at between 300,000 and 2,000,000, is primarily based a short distance from Saigon—to the north, and especially northwest adjacent to the

From the outset in Tonkin and Annam, and subsequently in Cochin China, Ho's other lieutenants showed greater ability and wisdom than Tran Van Giau in their dealings with the population, and generally they were successful in winning adherents. Ho was anxious to secure a wide spectrum of support from nationalists of all political viewpoints. This objective undoubtedly weighed more heavily with him than the wish to court noncommunist international backing when, in November 1945, he decided to dissolve the Indochinese Communist Party. Communists and procommunists close to Ho Chi Minh retained key positions in the government, but noncommunists were given sufficient scope to insure their continued support. Ho Chi Minh soon came to be acknowledged by most noncommunists as well as by procommunists as their outstanding leader in Vietnam's struggle for independence against the French and the principal symbol of the new Vietnamese nationalism.

Cambodian border. The Hoa Hao, less centrally organized than the Cao Dai, according to Bernard Fall, claimed in 1955 nearly 1,500,000 adherents, "mostly concentrated in the highly fertile rice-bowl of the Mekong Delta, particularly in the . . . Trans Bassac." Its mystical founder began preaching in 1939 a sort of "Buddhist Protestantism," which by 1940 had drawn more than 100,000 followers into a socio-religious movement with a decidedly anti-French posture. Bernard Fall, "The Political-Religious Sects of Viet Nam," *Pacific Affairs,* Vol. 28, No. 3, September 1955, pp. 235–253; see also Donald Lancaster, *The Emancipation of French Indochina* (London: Oxford University Press, 1961), pp. 86–90.

Notes to Chapter I

1. This was after the collapse of the Tang Dynasty, and it was from Nan Han, a small successor kingdom confined to South China, that the Vietnamese won their independence.

2. For fuller accounts of this early period, see D. G. E. Hall, *A History of Southeast Asia,* 2nd ed. (London: Macmillan, 1963); John F. Cady, *Southeast Asia: Its Historical Development* (New York: McGraw-Hill, 1964); Joseph Buttinger, *The Smaller Dragon* (New York: Praeger, 1958).

3. Hanoi Radio, July 15, 1963.

4. Bernard Fall, "A Straight Zig-Zag: The Road to Socialism in North Vietnam," in *Communist Strategies in Asia,* ed. by A. Doak Barnett (New York: Praeger, 1963), p. 214.

5. For a scholarly treatment of the period 1840–1860, see John F. Cady, *The Roots of French Imperialism in Eastern Asia* (Ithaca, N.Y.: Cornell University Press, 1954).

6. The most comprehensive biography of Ho Chi Minh available in English is to be found in Bernard B. Fall, *The Two Viet-Nams* (New York: Praeger, 1964), especially pp. 81–103. All subsequent citations from Fall's work in this chapter refer to this book. Another substantial account is to be found in Jean Lacouture, *Cinq hommes et la France* (Paris: Editions du Seuil, 1961), pp. 11–108. A large part of Ho Chi Minh's writings for the period May 25, 1922 through September 10, 1960 are available in a four-volume edition (Ho Chi Minh, *Selected Works* [Hanoi: Foreign Languages Publishing House, 1960–62]).

7. Philippe Devillers, *Histoire du Vietnam* (Paris: Editions du Seuil, 1952), p. 57; Fall, *op. cit.,* pp. 83–84.

8. Fall, *op. cit.,* p. 87; Donald Lancaster, *The Emancipation of French Indochina* (London: Oxford University Press, 1961), p. 79.

9. Fall, *op. cit.,* pp. 87–88. This pamphlet is not included in Ho's *Selected Works.* For his ideas on race relations in the United States, see in Volume I of this series, "Lynching, a Little Known Aspect of American Civilization," pp. 99–105, and "The Ku-Klux-Klan," pp. 127–132.

10. Devillers, *op. cit.,* p. 57.

11. Lancaster, *op. cit.,* p. 80; Fall, *op. cit.,* p. 90.

12. Devillers, *op. cit.,* p. 57; Lancaster, *op. cit.,* p. 80; Fall, *op. cit.,* pp. 91–92; I. Milton Sacks, "Marxism in Vietnam," in *Marxism in Southeast Asia,* ed. by Frank N. Trager (Stanford, Cal.: Stanford University Press, 1959), p. 109.

13. Lacouture, *op. cit.,* pp. 30–31; Devillers, *op. cit.,* pp. 57–58; Fall, *op. cit.,* pp. 93–94; Sacks, *op. cit.,* p. 117; Lancaster, *op. cit.,* pp. 80–81.

14. Fall, *op. cit.,* p. 94.

15. Lacouture, *op. cit.,* p. 31; Devillers, *op. cit.,* p. 59.

16. Fall, *op cit.,* p. 96; Devillers, *op. cit.,* p. 60; Sacks, *op. cit.,* pp. 123–133; Lancaster, *op. cit.,* pp. 82–83.

17. Fall, *op. cit.,* p. 97. There is considerable agreement that Ho spent this period in Moscow. Fall appears to be the only writer who feels sure he visited communist-held areas of Northwest China.

18. Devillers, *op. cit.,* pp. 60–61; Fall, *op. cit.,* p. 96; Lancaster, *op. cit.,* pp. 82–83.

19. Lacouture, *op. cit.,* p. 36; Fall, *op. cit.,* pp. 97–98.

20. Jean Lacouture, *Vietnam: Between Two Truces* (New York: Random House, 1966), p. 47.

21. Statement of Diem to Southeast Asia Seminar, Cornell University, February 20, 1953.

22. Lancaster, *op. cit.,* p. 85.

23. The fullest accounts of the establishment and early development of the Vietminh are to be found in Devillers, *op. cit.,* pp. 96–113; and in Ellen J. Hammer, *The Struggle for Indochina* (Stanford, Cal.: Stanford University Press, 1954), pp. 94–105. See also Lacouture, *Cinq hommes et la France,* pp. 36–37.

24. *Ibid.,* p. 37.

25. Devillers, *op. cit.,* pp. 112–113.

26. Harold Isaacs, *No Peace for Asia* (New York: Macmillan, 1947), pp. 148–149.

27. Devillers, *op. cit.,* p. 152; Fall, *op. cit.,* pp. 100–101; Lancaster, *op. cit.,* p. 143; Hammer, *op. cit.,* pp. 130–151; Isaacs, *op. cit.,* pp. 148, 164.

28. See Appendix 1.

29. With respect to the alienation of the Cao Dai, Hoa Hao, and the Southern Trotskyites, see Lancaster, *op. cit.,* p. 137, footnote 20; Fall, *op. cit.,* p. 66.

CHAPTER II

France and the Vietminh

1: **On the eve of Japan's defeat in World War II,** the Vietminh confidently looked forward to Allied support in any future struggle against French colonialism. Because of the assistance they had given to his resistance movement against the Japanese, Ho Chi Minh apparently anticipated ultimate Allied recognition of his newly-established government, the Democratic Republic of Vietnam. This expectation was clearly reflected in his government's Declaration of Independence of September 2, 1945,[1] which stated: "We are convinced that the Allied nations . . . will not refuse to acknowledge the independence of Viet Nam." But France's postwar government was determined to reassert French control in Indochina; and in the years immediately after the war the other Allies—the U.S. and Russia included—were more concerned with maintaining good relations with France than with any effective support of the principle of self-determination in Vietnam.

The first hint of Allied plans for postwar Vietnam came at Potsdam. The Agreement reached there in July 1945 stipulated that, following the defeat of Japan, British forces were to occupy the southern half of Vietnam up to the 16th parallel, and Chiang Kai-shek's Chinese forces were to take over the country north of that parallel. Under this Agreement the mandate of both the British and Chinese forces was restricted to "the round-up and disarming of the Japanese, and the Recovery of Allied Prisoners of War and Internees."[2]

The conduct of the Allied occupation in fact went far beyond this limited assignment. The Commander of the British occupation forces, Major-General Douglas Gracey, exceeded both the Potsdam mandate and the orders of his superior,

Admiral Louis Mountbatten, who had admonished him to "confine operations of British/Indian troops to those limited tasks which he had been set." [3] Short of troops of his own, Gracey relied heavily upon Japanese forces to keep Saigon and the surrounding areas under his control and out of the hands of the Vietminh.* He rearmed the bulk of the 5,000 French troops interned in the Saigon area and permitted the French to launch a coup d'état on September 23, by which they seized control of the Saigon government from the Vietminh. Combined British-Indian and Japanese forces joined battle against Vietminh units in the areas around Saigon until sufficient French reinforcements were available to take over from them.[4] By that time, General Gracey had enabled the French to eliminate the nascent Vietminh administration, not only in Saigon, but also in several other districts. In December of 1945, French forces in the British occupation zone of the South had reached approximately 50,000, and General Gracey completed preparations to withdraw, having fulfilled what he regarded as his mission.[5]

The Kuomintang Chinese army, in the northern half of Vietnam, deviated from the Potsdam mandate in a rather different way. Their force of 180,000 men, which was far larger than required, displayed more interest in systematically looting the country than in repatriating the Japanese. In parts of Northern Tonkin, the Chinese replaced the Vietminh with their own protégés. However, despite attempts to influence the Vietminh's activities, the Chinese commanders recognized Ho Chi Minh's regime in Hanoi as the de facto government and allowed it to function with considerable freedom. Nevertheless,

---

* These British actions, coupled with the similar use of Japanese troops in Java, reportedly prompted General Douglas MacArthur to exclaim: "If there is anything that makes my blood boil it is to see our Allies in Indochina and Java deploying Japanese troops to reconquer the little people we promised to liberate. It is the most ignoble kind of betrayal." Edgar Snow, *The Other Side of the River: Red China Today* (New York: Random House, 1961), p. 686.

the weight of the Chinese occupation, politically as well as economically, was sufficiently onerous to dispose the Vietminh to meet some of France's demands in order to secure the evacuation of Chiang's troops from the area. On February 28, 1946, in return for substantial French concessions,* Chiang Kai-shek agreed to withdraw his forces within three months from the northern half of the country.

The departure of the British and Chinese forces brought the Vietminh government under direct pressure from France. By this time it was evident to Ho that no support would be forthcoming from either the United States or Soviet Russia; from his perspective, the Vietminh had been deserted by the international community and left alone to deal with France. Within the country the depredations of the Chinese occupation forces had further weakened an already war-ravaged economy. In addition, wartime neglect and Allied air bombardment of the North's river-control systems had led to the flooding of some eight provinces, causing many deaths and widespread starvation. These near catastrophic economic conditions strengthened France's bargaining position, and on March 6, 1946, Ho Chi Minh felt compelled to reach a compromise settlement. Under this agreement he made the maximum concessions possible without risking forfeiture of his dominant position in the nationalist movement. Even so, strong dissatisfaction with the settlement was expressed by various political groups, and Ho had to exert all his influence to secure their final acquiescence.

---

* The French agreed to give up all extraterritorial rights they had held in China and to transfer to China their concessions in Canton, Hankow and Shanghai. They also agreed to relinquish that part of the Haiphong-Yunnan railroad that was in China and to permit freight to be transported over it duty free in either direction between China and Haiphong. Allan B. Cole, ed., *Conflict in Indochina and International Repercussions: A Documentary History, 1945–1955* (Ithaca, N.Y.: Cornell University Press, 1956), pp. 7–9. See also Donald Lancaster, *The Emancipation of French Indochina* (London: Oxford University Press, 1961), pp. 144–145.

Under the March 1946 agreement, France could introduce 15,000 troops into the northern part of Vietnam to relieve the Chinese occupation forces. This was on the understanding that each year thereafter 3,000 of these French troops would be withdrawn, until by the end of 1951 none would remain. In return for the Vietminh's consent to the reentry of French forces into the North, Paris recognized Ho's Democratic Republic of Vietnam as "a free state, having its own government, parliament, army and treasury, forming part of the Indochinese Federation and the French Union." The French further pledged to abide by the results of a referendum in Cochin China, which was to determine whether it should be reunified with Annam and Tonkin.[6]

Although this agreement resulted in an uneasy truce, France soon made it clear that it had no intention of allowing Cochin China to unite with the rest of Vietnam.* On June 1, 1946, Admiral G. Thierry D'Argenlieu, the new French Viceroy in Indochina, set up a separate puppet government in Cochin China and recognized it as a "free Republic." Concerning this French effort to detach the South, Donald Lancaster observed: " . . . [I]n spite of some local hostility towards the Tongkingese the population, who were conscious of their ethnic identity with the inhabitants of North and Central Vietnam, for the most part refused to support a movement considered to represent a French manoeuvre designed to split the nation in its struggle for independence." [7] Moreover, in recognizing the Vietminh's territories of Annam and Tonkin as "a free state" within the French Union, it was evident that the French had in mind something short of independence. Effective control of the whole of Vietnam was to be retained in Paris. Ho had entered into an armistice on the basis of promises that were not fulfilled.

---

* By retaining control of this southern region the French could safeguard most of their economic interests in the country (60 per cent of all French holdings in Indochina were in Cochin China).

During the summer of 1946 further attempts at negotiations between France and the Vietminh proved fruitless. Relations between the two sides worsened rapidly, while actions by both resulted in increasing friction and numerous small-scale incidents. The mounting tension culminated on November 23 with the French naval bombardment of Haiphong, where at least 6,000 Vietnamese civilians were killed.[8] The Vietminh retaliated by launching coordinated attacks against the French in Hanoi, which touched off major hostilities. These events marked the beginning of a war that was soon to spread throughout most of Vietnam.

For the next eight years France fought unsuccessfully to defeat the Vietminh. Its generals mounted major and sustained military campaigns that sometimes cut deeply into Vietminh-controlled areas, but as soon as the French regrouped their troops to attack elsewhere the Vietminh was able to reassert its authority. With their superior fire power the French could hold the cities and the majority of the towns, while the Vietminh managed to dominate most of the countryside—more and more of it as the years went by.

The scope and intensity of her military campaigns raises the question of why France should have made such a long and costly effort. Certainly her major reason was not economic. As early as 1950, France's military expenditure in Vietnam surpassed the total of all French investments in the whole of Indochina, and, despite their disproportionate influence, the small group of Frenchmen with a favored position and a valuable stake in Vietnam could not alone have determined French policy.

The official attitude in Paris toward Indochina was conditioned by considerations that were more political and psychological than economic. One strong emotion affecting France's Vietnam policy stemmed from her defeat in World War II. Many Frenchmen would have regarded France's ouster from her colonies as a further loss in national dignity. Moreover, the French saw Vietnam in terms of their empire as a whole, particularly with relation to their North African territories. They were apprehensive that if the Vietnamese were successful in wresting their independence from France, the already-restive nationalists in Algeria, Morocco, and Tunisia would be inspired to follow their example.

2 : By the end of 1947 the increase in the popularity of Ho Chi Minh and his Vietminh throughout most of Vietnam had convinced the French that victory could not be achieved through purely military means. Therefore, Paris complemented its persistent military campaigns with an attempt to establish an amenable indigenous Vietnamese regime as a competitor of the Vietminh. France would hold the ultimate power strings, but she hoped that by endowing the regime she sponsored with a semblance of autonomy it would attract substantial nationalist support away from the Vietminh. The man chosen to head the new regime was Bao Dai, the former Emperor of Annam whom the Japanese had also endeavored to exploit in their eleventh hour. After a lengthy process of bargaining, by June 1948 Bao Dai was induced to cooperate on condition that, under his leadership, the State of Vietnam, incorporating Cochin China together with Tonkin and Annam, would be "independent . . . within the French Union." An additional year of negotiations over the meaning of this terminology concluded with the Elysée Agreements of March 1949, which the French Chamber of Deputies ratified only on January 29, 1950.[9]

Since, under the French Constitution, Paris would dominate the envisaged French Union, negotiations could not lead to any genuine independence for the Union's members.[10] Thus the Elysée Agreements, if implemented, would have provided only for a limited autonomy, not real independence. Under them France retained actual control of the foreign relations and armed forces of Vietnam, Cambodia, and Laos. Although these states could maintain their own armies, separate French Union forces were to be stationed in each country, with complete freedom to operate between their bases and garrisons.

Moreover, France was empowered to assume authority over the armies of the three Indochina states in time of war, a condition that in fact prevailed right up to the Geneva Conference of 1954. Without the specific permission of Paris, the governments of the three states were forbidden to interfere in any way with French property and enterprises within their borders. Furthermore, they lacked specific and unfettered rights to manage their own treasuries, economic planning, foreign trade, customs, and communications. It was stipulated that the details concerning such "rights" were to be worked out at a future conference, which took place in the fall of 1950.

So many of the substantive attributes of power were reserved to France that even on paper the new State of Vietnam was effectively and directly under French dominion. And, in fact, most of the very modest concessions granted under the agreements were never actually transferred to Bao Dai's "government," which continued to lack the attributes of independence necessary to attract nationalist support. Bao Dai emerged from the long process of negotiations with no increase in political prestige among the nationalist elements in Vietnam. Obviously dependent on France, his regime remained an unconvincing facade for a continuing French military and civil control that allowed few significant roles for Vietnamese. The only conclusion Vietnamese patriots could reach was that France, with Bao Dai as its agent, continued to run that part of the country not under the Vietminh. The effective range of political alternatives for these patriots remained quite as narrow as before—the Vietminh or the French—and this polarization grew more pronounced as the French now regularly labeled all those who resisted them or opposed Bao Dai as "communist." For more and more Vietnamese that word came to connote something good—a badge of honor, representing patriotic nationalism and courageous opposition to French rule. Thus did French intransigence in Vietnam further strengthen the ties between nationalism and communism there—a circumstance unique in Southeast Asia.

Meanwhile, France had failed in her military efforts, despite the fact that by the end of 1949, approximately $1.5 billion had been poured into the war. Well before this time the French forces were being pushed back and the military initiative had passed to the Vietminh.[11] The success of Ho's battalions, moreover, had been achieved with arms far inferior in both quantity and quality to the relatively modern American equipment employed by the French. Initially, the Vietminh had depended upon a wartime stock of light and often obsolete arms secured from Chiang Kai-shek, the O.S.S. and the Japanese; after 1946 these weapons were supplemented by United States equipment captured from the French forces. Any disparity in military equipment, however, was more than compensated for by the Vietminh's popular backing, the essential attribute of power that the French were never able to develop.*

3: **Until the end of 1949** the United States displayed little, if any, real interest in Indochina. It occasionally urged the French to take steps toward granting independence to these areas, but its urging was mild and restrained. Washington was apprehensive lest any pressures it exerted in this regard might adversely affect France's attitude toward cooperating with it in the formation of European defense alliances, which in the postwar years received the highest priority among the United States' strategic objectives.

Yet, other priorities in Asia and the underdeveloped world as well as the American public's attachment to the principle of self-determination dictated against overt American backing

---

* The Vietminh had gained the military initiative well before the communists came into power in China. Their military strength against the French was already clearly established before they were able to secure even modest military assistance from Communist China, although during the final phases of the war materiel supplied by the Chinese was to help considerably in major battles. The French did not allege a military-assistance agreement between the Vietminh and the Chinese communists until April 1950. See Ambassade de France, *Service de Presse et d'Information,* Document No. 26 (New York, November 10, 1950).

of French interests in Vietnam. Major support for the French was not given until mid-1949, when communist rule was established in China. Later, when Peking sent its armies into the Korean War, this disposition to aid the French effort was further reinforced. A policy leading to the containment of China increasingly preoccupied the Truman Administration, and, during the Korean War, Paris endeavored with considerable success to convince Washington that the French campaign in Vietnam basically sustained that policy. Thus President Truman linked his decision to send American forces to Korea with the announcement of increased arms shipments to the French in Indochina and the interposition of American power between Communist and Nationalist China in the Formosa Straits.[12] In accordance with these new American priorities, France's position in Vietnam was now described in terms of the Free World's stand against communist expansionism, and Washington ceased to perceive the war in Vietnam as primarily a local colonial conflict. Now linked to the Cold War, Vietnam was regarded as an area of strategic importance to the United States.

The communists' victory in China also led Washington to exhibit less circumspection in assessing the nature of the political struggle within Vietnam. In this approach, anticommunism preempted anticolonialism or pronationalism in importance. Until this time, Washington had never viewed Bao Dai as a man capable of mobilizing substantial support from the Vietnamese people. In mid-1949, however, the Truman Administration began to depict him as a staunch patriot, capable of successfully challenging Ho Chi Minh for the allegiance of Vietnamese nationalists and worthy of American respect and aid. The United States thus indicated its backing of Bao Dai's regime seven months before the French Parliament ratified the Elysée Agreements,[13] and on February 7, 1950, a week after this ratification, the U.S. extended diplomatic recognition to his government. Thirty other states soon followed suit.[14]

Only when the French Parliament finally made clear its intention to ratify the Elysée Agreements and when international backing of Bao Dai seemed imminent did Ho Chi Minh request diplomatic recognition from Peking and Moscow. They responded promptly, establishing formal relations on January 18 and 31, respectively. The Cold War had decisively entered the Vietminh–French dispute. Within this context, the policies of France in Indochina took on a greater legitimacy in the eyes of Washington and gave her the right to substantial U.S. aid.

Washington's recognition of Bao Dai sparked economic- and military-assistance programs, which began in mid-1950.[15] The dollar flow to back up the French military campaign in Vietnam grew rapidly from approximately $150 million per year in 1950 to over $1 billion in the fiscal year of 1954, when the United States was underwriting 80 per cent of the cost of the war. On April 6, 1954, the U.S. announced that its aid to Indochina for the subsequent fiscal year would run to $1.33 billion. This equalled one-third of the entire American foreign-aid program and was by far its largest single component. Of this amount $800 million was "allocated through France" for "direct support" of French Union forces fighting in the Indochina theater, $300 million was for equipment to be supplied to them, and $33 million was for economic and technical assistance.[16] In comparison, this totaled more than eleven times the entire United States' economic-aid program budgeted that year for India. By so underwriting the French military endeavor, the United States took a long step towards making Vietnamese nationalists cynical about America's protestations of its commitment to national self-determination and political freedom.

The United States had initially intended its assistance to flow directly to Bao Dai's government, but the French adamantly insisted that all aid be channeled through their own officials. The Administration's previous hopes of bolstering Bao Dai's independence of the French through American aid supplied directly to him were frustrated, and total French governance of his regime continued. Although the French established a Vietnamese National Army in 1951, this remained effectively under their control.

While continuing to urge the French to grant genuine independence to Bao Dai's government, both the Truman and Eisenhower Administrations kept assuring the American public that actual authority had already been transferred. However ineffective Bao Dai was in wooing Vietnamese nationalists away from the Vietminh leadership, he was represented to American congressmen and the public at large as a popular figure with substantial power and a sizeable nationalist following. During this period Washington continued to credit the frequently unreliable French war communiqués and, almost on the eve of the fall of Dienbienphu, encouraged the American public to believe that the Vietminh would soon be defeated. In the context of the American preoccupation with communism, the fact that Ho Chi Minh was a communist made Congress and the American public more susceptible to the Administration's myth about Bao Dai and less inclined to question the United States' assumption of most of the costs of France's war effort in Vietnam.

Some few did dispute these claims, but their impact on American policy was slight. Among them was Senator John F. Kennedy, who declared as early as November 1951: "In Indochina we have allied ourselves to the desperate effort of the French regime to hang on to the remnants of empire. There is no broad, general support of the native [Bao Dai] Vietnam Government among the people of that area." [17] More than two years later he was still able to say:

> Every year we are given three sets of assurances: first, that the independence of the associated states is now complete; second, that the independence of the associated states will soon be completed under steps "now" being taken; and, third, that military victory for the French Union forces in Indochina is assured, or is just around the corner.[18]

But the skepticism of Kennedy and others had little or no

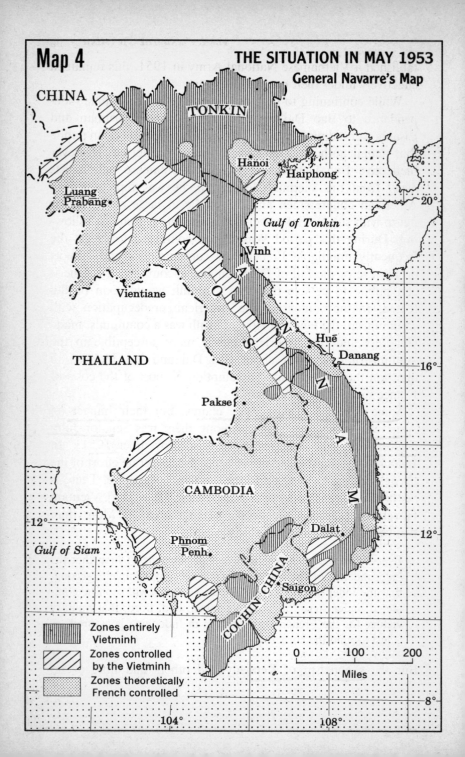

effect upon Washington's determination to back the French.

Despite the continuing deterioration of the situation during 1953, the French were unwilling to make the bold political moves necessary to win any significant measure of Vietnamese backing. The most Paris was then willing to concede was that there were grounds to complete the independence and sovereignty of the Indochinese states—within the French Union, and on July 3 she announced plans to enter into negotiations with a view to redefining the full range of her relations with them.[19] The resultant bargaining between Bao Dai's representative and Paris, however, yielded little of significance, and the French continued to dominate the State of Vietnam right down to the Geneva Conference.*

4: By mid-1953, despite the substantial aid she was getting from the United States, France had lost to the Vietminh her authority over all but a minor portion of the country. In the North by far the major part of Tonkin was in Vietminh hands. Most of Annam was solidly under the Vietminh, as were the northern districts of Cochin China almost as far south as Saigon itself, with the Camau peninsula as well as much of the

---

* Thus the situation obtaining on the eve of the Geneva Conference was accurately described by Senator John F. Kennedy in a speech to the Senate on April 6, 1954: "Politically, French control was and is extensive and paramount. . . . Although the Associated States are said to be 'independent within the French Union,' the French always have a permanent control in the high council and in the Assembly of the Union and the Government of France guides its actions. . . . Militarily, French control is nearly complete. . . . Economically French control of the country's basic resources, transportation, trade and economic life in general is extensive. In Vietnam, estimated French control is nearly 100% in the field of foreign commerce, international and coastal shipping, and rubber and other export products. . . . All of this flies in the face of repeated assurances to the American people by our own officials that complete independence has been or will be granted." *The War in Indochina* (Washington: U.S. Government Printing Office, 1954), p. 6.

Mekong delta administered by the Vietminh. The map prepared by the Commander in Chief of French Union forces in Indochina, General Henri Navarre, described graphically the actual position of the French in May of 1953, a position that was to worsen rapidly during the course of the next twelve months. (See map, p. 34.)

In September of 1953 France, with strong American encouragement, essayed one final and disastrous effort to recoup her military defeats and achieve a position of strength from which to negotiate with the Vietminh. This last major military bid, termed the "Navarre Plan," was undertaken at a time when France had lost any chance of gaining the political support necessary for it to succeed. When they mounted this campaign the French were able to draw on a total of 517,000 men. Of these, 369,000 were Indochinese, for the most part Vietnamese; 48,000 were soldiers from France's North African colonies; 20,000 were members of the French Foreign Legion; and a total of 80,000 were French. These last comprised 52,300 commissioned or noncommissioned officers, representing 26 per cent of all officers and 42 per cent of all noncommissioned officers in the French army. This was a substantial portion of overall French cadre strength, the equivalent of ten French divisions as compared to the twelve in Europe.*

General Navarre's offensive soon gave way to a continuing series of French military reverses and a further yielding of territory to the Vietminh. The culminating and most dramatic battle that presaged the collapse of the French position came in the spring of 1954 at Dienbienphu, a fortress situated in a valley on the former Vietminh invasion route into Laos, at the western extremity of Tonkin. Here, the French constructed a complex of supporting fortresses, defended by heavy artillery

---

* Only 27,700 of the 80,000 French troops were rank-and-file soldiers, because French public opinion would allow Paris to commit only France's professional army to the battle for Indochina. Because of this heavy commitment from her professional army, France had fallen seriously behind in her commitments to NATO.

that they believed to be much more powerful than anything available to the Vietminh. Navarre's strategy was to encourage large Vietminh units to attack these supposedly impregnable positions. The overwhelming fire power that could then be concentrated against the massed Vietminh was expected to destroy them. French calculations were correct in that the Vietminh accepted the challenge offered by the exposed fortress; but the French had completely underestimated the fervor of the attackers and the caliber of the artillery that they trained against the fortress from the surrounding hills. Despite a grueling and heroic defense, the French garrison was overrun, and not only Paris but a worldwide audience realized that France's military power in Vietnam had sustained its decisive defeat at Dienbienphu.

5: With the collapse of Navarre's strategy and the rapid disintegration of his military position, both Paris and Washington faced some important and basic decisions. On March 20, 1954, the French Chief of Staff, General Paul Ely, informed President Eisenhower that only by massive American intervention could France hope to prevent a defeat at Dienbienphu. He apparently intimated that without such intervention France would be obliged to negotiate a settlement with the Vietminh. This prospect of a communist victory in Vietnam precipitated a major debate within Administration circles in Washington. Admiral Radford, Chairman of the Joint Chiefs of Staff, took a hard-line stand in favor of prompt U.S. military action. Other powerful elements in the Administration, including Vice-President Richard Nixon and, somewhat more circumspectly, Secretary of State John Foster Dulles, joined Radford in advocating American armed intervention in an attempt to stave off a French defeat. This debate had been preceded by weeks of discussion on the feasibility of an American air strike to relieve the beleaguered French garrison at Dienbienphu. Plans were also underway to ship U.S. military personnel from Korea to Vietnam should Washington finally decide to provide the French with ground support. Two U.S. aircraft carriers were ordered to take station off the Indochina coast, and it was rumored that their planes were fitted with atomic bombs. The atmosphere of war preparations set the stage for the climax of the debate on April 3, 1954, as to whether the U.S. should intervene in the war.[20]

Despite the urgency of the situation and the sizable U.S. commitment of military-assistance funds to France, the Administration feared the problems that could arise from outright American intervention in support of an unpopular war. There was considerable appreciation at the time that the introduction of American troops would run counter to the nationalist aspirations of the Vietnamese people. Dulles and Eisenhower concurred in the belief that, without a prior grant of full independence by France, the United States could not appropriately enter the Vietnam war. In reaching this conclusion, they were not without guidance from the State Department's Policy Planning Staff, one of whose members, Louis J. Halle, Jr., had written:

> A possible variant to the policy of gaining national objectives by eliciting the consent of those who have jurisdiction is to assure jurisdiction for a regime which accords its consent. Such an undertaking may, on rare occasions, be valid and feasible; but all modern history warns that it is likely to be an enticement into quicksands. The only way one can assure jurisdiction, abroad, for a regime that cannot assure jurisdiction for itself is by a species of intervention that, in addition to dissipating the popular consent which the intervening nation might otherwise enjoy, dissipates the consent on which the imposed regime must base itself if it is to establish a tolerable government. When a nation intervenes in a foreign country, it not only tends to turn the people of that country against it, but it also discredits the regime that accepts its support.[21]

It was apparently with these basic tenets in mind that the Eisenhower Administration refused to countenance the dispatch of U.S. fighting men to Vietnam unless the French first granted a greater measure of genuine independence to the Vietnamese. President Eisenhower, in particular, was conscious that the French had engendered too much popular antagonism among the Vietnamese to win the war and that the large majority of the population supported Ho Chi Minh against them.[22]

Also militating against any decision to intervene was Eisenhower's belief that such action should not be undertaken without a clear endorsement from a majority of the Congress, and unless America's Allies, particularly Great Britain, indicated their willingness to become involved along with it. The President felt that even token forces from other nations "would lend real moral standing to a venture that otherwise could be made to appear as a brutal example of imperialism." Eisenhower concluded that: "This need was particularly acute because there was no incontrovertible evidence of overt Red Chinese participation in the Indochina conflict."[23]

As the debate developed, it became evident that a sufficient degree of congressional backing would not be forthcoming, and the British remained adamantly opposed to joining in even a limited military intervention confined to air action. Referring afterwards to his government's stand, Eden stated to the House of Commons:

> The United Kingdom Government has been reproached in some unofficial quarters [probably a polite reference to the American Secretary of State] for their failure to support armed intervention to try to save Dien Bien Phu. It was quite true that we were not willing to support such action. This was for three reasons which then seemed to be good and still seem to be good: firstly, we were advised that air action alone could not have been effective; secondly, any such military intervention could have destroyed the chances of a settlement at Geneva; thirdly, it might well have led to a general war in Asia.[24]

In view of the lack of support from Congress and the British and because of France's continuing unwillingness to grant full independence for the states of Indochina, President Eisenhower held his ground against his more militant advisers. Probably his conviction in the matter was reinforced by the view of his Army Chief of Staff, General Matthew B. Ridgway, who later wrote:

> . . . when the day comes for me to face my Maker and account for my actions, the thing I would be most humbly proud of was the fact that I fought against, and perhaps contributed to preventing, the carrying out of some harebrained tactical schemes which would have cost the lives of some thousands of men. To that list of tragic accidents that fortunately never happened I would add the Indochina intervention.[25]

Notes to Chapter II

1. See Appendix 1.

2. "Extract from the Report to the Combined Chiefs of Staff by the Supreme Allied Commander, South-East Asia, 30 June, 1947," *Documents Relating to British Involvement in the Indo-China Conflict,* Command 2834 (London: Her Majesty's Stationery Office, 1965), p. 47.

3. *Ibid.,* p. 49.

4. See Harold Isaacs, *No Peace for Asia* (New York: Macmillan, 1947), pp. 152–180.

5. According to Harold Isaacs, General Gracey stated to him: "We have discharged our obligation to them. Now its up to them to carry on." Isaacs, *op. cit.,* p. 162.

6. For the only comprehensive treatment of the March 6 agreement and its background, see Philippe Devillers, *Histoire du Vietnam* (Paris: Editions du Seuil, 1952), Ch. 11–13. See also Allan B. Cole, ed., *Conflict in Indo-China and International Repercussions: A Documentary History, 1945–55* (Ithaca, N.Y.: Cornell University Press, 1956), pp. 40–42; Ellen J. Hammer, *The Struggle for Indochina* (Stanford, Cal.: Stanford University Press, 1954), p. 153; Donald Lancaster, *The Emancipation of French Indochina* (London: Oxford University Press, 1961), p. 147.

7. Lancaster, *op. cit.,* p. 154.

8. Estimate of the French naval officer who assumed command in the area in December 1946. Devillers, *op. cit.,* p. 337.

9. For the full text of these agreements, see Cole, *op. cit.,* pp. 72–79. A detailed account of the establishment of Bao Dai's regime can be found in Devillers, *op. cit.,* Ch. 23–25.

10. Article 62 of the French Constitution (Title 8, Section 1), October 27, 1946, reads: "The members of the French Union shall place in common all their resources so as to guarantee the defense of the whole Union. The Government of the Republic shall coordinate these resources and direct such policies as will prepare and ensure this defense."

11. See Bernard Fall, *The Two Viet-Nams* (New York: Praeger, 1964), p. 108. Fall notes that by May 1949, the French army's chief of staff, General Revers, was recommending "the immediate withdrawal of all French forces from the outlying border areas and their concentration upon the low-lying fertile rice deltas."

12. For the text of President Truman's statement, see *Department of State Bulletin* (Washington, July 3, 1950), p. 5.

13. On June 21, 1949, the Department of State had officially welcomed the forthcoming formation of Bao Dai's "new unified State of Vietnam." *Department of State Bulletin* (Washington, July 18, 1949), p. 75.

14. *Major Problems of United States Foreign Policy, 1950–1951*, prepared by the staff of the International Studies Group (Washington: Brookings Institution, 1950), p. 313.

15. *Department of State Bulletin* (Washington, June 12, 1950), pp. 977, 978.

16. *New York Times,* April 7, 1954.

17. John F. Kennedy, *The Strategy of Peace* (New York: Harper, 1960), p. 60.

18. *Ibid.*

19. See Lancaster, *op. cit.,* p. 275, for a fuller discussion of the July 3 note.

20. Probably the fullest account of this debate is Chalmers Roberts' article "The Day We Didn't Go To War," *The Reporter,* September 14, 1954, pp. 31–35. The reliability of Roberts' account was attested to by Senator Mansfield in the Senate on July 9, 1954. See U.S. Congress, *Congressional Record,* Vol. 100 (Washington: U.S. Government Printing Office, July 9, 1954), p. 1037. See also Miriam S. Farley, *United States Relations with Southeast Asia* (New York: American Institute of Pacific Relations, 1955). British Foreign Secretary Anthony Eden states that at this time the United States was considering sending three full divisions to Vietnam. Anthony Eden, *Full Circle* (London: Cassell, 1960), p. 143.

21. *Department of State Bulletin* (Washington, September 21, 1953), p. 379.

22. See Dwight D. Eisenhower, *Mandate for Change: The White House Years, 1953–1956* (New York: Signet, 1963), pp. 409, 449.

23. *Ibid.,* p. 412.

24. Great Britain, 5 *Parliamentary Debates* (Commons), Vol. 529, Cols. 434–435.

25. Matthew B. Ridgway, *Soldier: The Memoirs of Matthew B. Ridgway* (New York: Harper and Bros., 1956), p. 278. For a full account of the French position and of the policy debate in Paris, see Jean Lacouture and Philippe Devillers, *La Fin d'une Guerre, Indochine 1954* (Paris: Editions du Seuil, 1960), Ch. 5–7.

CHAPTER III

The Geneva Conference

1: The Geneva Conference,* held from April 26 to July 21, 1954, officially registered France's defeat by the Vietminh and provided her with a face-saving means of disengagement. The agreements reached were designed to end the nine-year-old war and open the way for internationally supported accords by which outstanding problems between the contending parties could be peacefully resolved.

On the eve of the conference France confronted a domestic political crisis as public sympathy mounted for peace in Indochina at almost any price. The fall of Dienbienphu on May 7, the day before the opening of the Indochina phase of the conference, had underlined and dramatized the frailty of France's position. Midway through the conference, when Joseph Laniel was replaced as Prime Minister by Pierre Mendès-France, it was obvious that the French wished only to disengage from the war as gracefully and rapidly as possible. The new Prime Minister's stipulation that he would resign if a peaceful agreement minimally acceptable to France were not reached by July 20 reflected the mounting domestic pressure for a settlement.

---

* This conference had been planned by the American, British, French, and Russian foreign ministers, meeting in Berlin during the previous January and February, at which time it was agreed to invite Communist China in addition to other interested states, with a view to effecting "a political settlement of the Korean question," as well as discussing "the problem of restoring peace in Indochina." Almost at the outset it was clear that no progress would be made with respect to Korea. But the conference was able to move forward on the Indochina issue, especially after June 17, when Mendès-France replaced Joseph Laniel as Prime Minister of France.

Meanwhile Washington adopted a highly ambiguous stand on the conference. To some degree this ambiguity mirrored the dilemma facing President Eisenhower on the home front. The Geneva Conference convened just when the campaign for the 1954 congressional elections was gaining momentum. On the one hand, the Administration realized that its earlier electoral successes were partially the result of Eisenhower's image as a peacemaker in Korea. The unpopularity of the Korean War carried over into a general public desire to avoid becoming entangled in another military involvement on the continent of Asia. Only a year after the Korean truce the American public would hardly have welcomed a new war on China's southern flank. On the other hand, the administration could not countenance an Indochina settlement that abandoned a part of "free Asia," even a French colony, to conquest by communist-led forces. This would have exposed the Republican Administration to the same charges it had leveled against the Democrats in the 1952 presidential campaign where the issue of the "loss of China to communism" was so prominent. The situation for Washington was further complicated by strategic considerations involving France's role in Europe. In its efforts to strengthen the defense of Europe the U.S. needed support from the same French leaders who were so determined to reach a political solution at Geneva. Had Washington blocked the peaceful settlement of the Indochina dispute, it would have lost any chance of enlisting French participation in its European defense plans.*

Thus the Eisenhower Administration, endeavoring to balance international objectives with domestic political pressures, elected to follow an uncomfortable middle course in the Geneva negotiations. In essence it disassociated itself to the

---

* One of Washington's top strategic priorities at the time was the formation of a European Defense Community (EDC) that would include Germany. The United States envisaged the proposed EDC structure as a stronger and more comprehensive organization than NATO and one wherein France would also play a strategically central role.

extent possible from the conference proceedings and, in the end, neither gave its full approval to the agreements nor registered outright opposition to them.

The major communist countries exerted a restraining influence at Geneva, their attitudes for the most part paralleling the French position, but markedly at variance with that of the United States. The Soviet Union and Communist China appeared anxious that a peaceful settlement be concluded and reportedly applied behind-the-scenes persuasion, if not pressure, on the Vietminh delegation. Both of the communist powers sought to insure that the Vietminh would moderate its negotiating demands sufficiently to make them minimally acceptable to France.* Their restraint undoubtedly reflected their recently adopted line of "peaceful coexistence," which aimed at a reduction in international tension. They were uneasy over the possibility that the United States might extend massive military assistance to the beleaguered French, with consequences that would extend beyond Indochina. They presumably realized that overly severe demands on the French would play into the hands of that minority of American leaders who had earlier advocated the atomic bombing of Vietminh positions around Dienbienphu. Apparently Chinese and Russian

---

* As *New York Times* correspondent Tillman Durdin cabled from Geneva: "Vietminh leaders are not entirely happy about the peace settlement in Vietnam. A number of members of the Vietminh delegation have declared openly that pressure from Chinese Communist premier Chou En Lai and Soviet Foreign Minister Vyacheslav M. Molotov forced their regime to accept less than it rightfully should have obtained here." These Vietminh officials contended, according to Durdin, that the military situation in Vietnam would have given the Vietminh almost full control within a year and that Cambodia and Laos could have been taken over eventually. They saw the settlement as a sort of appeasement "in the interests of Soviet and Chinese Communist international relations," and felt "their revolution has been slowed down, if not halted, right on the verge of complete success." (*New York Times,* July 25, 1954.) See also Jean Lacouture and Philippe Devillers, *La Fin d'une Guerre, Indochine 1954* (Paris: Editions du Seuil, 1960), pp. 282–285.

leaders were no more confident than President Eisenhower and other opponents of this course that nuclear warfare begun in one corner of Asia could be confined there.

The problem of Germany was also uppermost in Russian strategic planning in 1954.[1] The Soviet Union reportedly believed that by moderating Vietminh demands and upholding some of France's proposals she might induce the French to stay out of the projected United States–sponsored European Defense Community.[2] It must have been clear to Moscow that the EDC proposal had more chance of being defeated in the French Parliament if Mendès-France remained Prime Minister than if a failure of the conference led to his resignation. And, defeat of EDC, it seemed then, would prevent the inclusion of Germany in the collective-security arrangements in Europe.*

As for China, both the demands of her domestic program for economic development and her newly-embarked-upon moderation in foreign policy (which reached full flower a year later at the Bandung Conference) made her oppose any spread of the fighting in Indochina. Recalling the vivid lessons of Korea, Peking's leaders wished to avoid giving the U.S. any pretext for introducing forces on her southern flank.[3] These reasons explain in part why the Chinese joined the Russians in advising the Vietminh to settle for an incomplete victory over France.

But the terms "advice" and "pressure" probably give a misleading impression of Ho Chi Minh's true position, for the Vietminh leaders had good reasons of their own to make concessions at Geneva. Most important, by negotiating a settlement the Vietminh could avoid further deaths and material destruction. Though their ultimate victory seemed assured, the further campaigns needed to oust the French militarily would have been very costly indeed, particularly if the U.S. were to

---

* After the French Parliament defeated EDC, the NATO partners resurrected the Brussels Pact and modified it to bring Germany into the alliance in such a way that approval of the French Parliament was not necessary.

enter the conflict. Vietminh leaders were quite unwilling to assume responsibility for refusing a settlement that could avoid further destruction.

Within Vietnam, the eight-year struggle with France had spawned a feeling of sheer exhaustion. The war weariness of the Vietnamese people now became a factor in the calculations of the Vietminh, whose conduct of successful guerrilla warfare depended on a close rapport with the populace. This undoubtedly inclined the Vietminh to respond sympathetically to the mood of the people, and it thus felt obliged to end the bloodshed as soon as possible—or at least as soon as its most important political objectives had been attained.

The agreements concluded at Geneva, if fully implemented, did appear to meet these essential objectives. Under them the Vietminh could expect to win on a political plane the struggle that it was already winning militarily. It could look forward not only to reestablishing its authority in those southern areas that its troops had evacuated, but also to extending its rule over previously French-controlled areas of the South. The firm pledge of nationwide elections was of key importance in the Vietminh's agreement to the temporary surrender of such extensive areas south of the 17th parallel. Without this promise, its leaders would naturally have opposed a withdrawal of their forces into less than half of the country's territory.

When the Geneva Conference opened the Vietminh was already dominant in more than three-quarters of Vietnam and was poised to overrun considerably more. In Tonkin the French controlled scarcely more than the cities of Hanoi and Haiphong—almost all the villages in the surrounding Red River delta had come under effective Vietminh control.* In

---

* It will be recalled that a full year earlier the Vietminh already controlled more villages in the Red River delta than did the French. Bernard Fall concluded that in May 1953 the French controlled only "1,803 villages and towns out of a total of approximately 5,780; another 1,843 were considered 'unsafe,' and the remaining 2,143 were under effective Communist control." Fall, *Viet-Nam Witness, 1953–66* (New York: Praeger, 1966), p. 281.

fact, prior to the conference the French had already planned the evacuation of the delta, and, a month before it concluded, their hard-pressed forces had begun their withdrawal from the southern part of Tonkin.[4] The Vietminh at Geneva agreed to evacuate not only the rich rice-growing areas in the Mekong delta south of Saigon, but also the vast stretch of land between the 13th and 17th parallels that had constituted one of its major political bastions. As Prime Minister Mendès-France stated to the French Parliament, just after the conclusion of the Geneva Conference:

> So far as the demarcation line is concerned, the enemy was asking for the thirteenth parallel; and today we have the seventeenth. Now between the thirteenth and seventeenth parallel, Tourane [now Danang] and Hué are located, and there are three provinces which have always shown allegiance to the Vietminh and which the Vietminh is now going to evacuate so that they may pass under our control.[5]

Any indication to the Vietminh that its evacuation might be permanent would have destroyed any basis for a negotiated settlement. But in evacuating its military units from the South, the Vietminh was not being called upon to abandon its struggle for power, but only to transfer the competition from the military to the political plane. And whether in a military or an exclusively political contest, the Vietminh confidently expected victory. This expectation, moreover, was not confined to the Vietminh and was generally shared by Western observers at the conference.

2: **The importance of the Geneva Agreements** is such as to warrant a close scrutiny of their most important features.

Two agreements on Vietnam were reached at Geneva: the bilateral armistice agreement between France and the Vietminh and the later and more publicized multilateral Final Declaration.[6] The bilateral armistice agreement provided the prerequisite foundation upon which the multilateral Geneva Declaration rests. As the antecedent and basic agreement be-

tween the two military protagonists, it should be considered
first.

This "Agreement on the Cessation of Hostilities in Viet
Nam" was signed on July 20, 1954, by Brigadier General
Henri Delteil, acting for the "Commander in Chief of the
French Union forces in Indo-China" and by Ta Quang Buu,
Vice-Minister of National Defense of the Democratic Republic
of Vietnam, in behalf of the "Commander in Chief of the
People's Army of Vietnam." It incorporated the following
essential features. First, there was to be established a "provisional military demarcation line" (fixed at the 17th parallel)
"on either side of which the forces of the two parties shall be
regrouped after their withdrawal, the forces of the People's
Army of Viet Nam [Vietminh] to the north of the line and the
forces of the French Union to the south" (Article 1). The
maximum period of this regrouping was not to exceed 300
days from the date the armistice entered into force (Article 2).
Civil administration in the regroupment zone to the north of
the 17th parallel was to be in the hands of the Vietminh, and
the area to the south of the parallel was to be in the hands of
the French (Article 8).

Article 14 detailed the provisions for political and administrative control in the two regrouping zones pending the general elections. Paragraph (a) states in full: "Pending the
general elections which will bring about the unification of Viet
Nam, the conduct of civil administration in each regrouping
zone shall be in the hands of the party whose forces are to be
regrouped there in virtue of the present Agreement." Paragraph (b) of Article 14 specified that following the evacuation
of Vietminh troops from south of the parallel, the French
would assume responsibility for administration there. Paragraphs (c) and (d) of Article 14 provided that during the
300-day period allotted for regroupment of troops, civilians
residing north or south of the parallel were to be "permitted
and helped" to cross the parallel if they so desired. As discussed above, both parties to the agreement promised "to
refrain from any reprisals or discrimination against persons or

organizations on account of their activities during the hostilities and to guarantee their democratic liberties."

A group of four articles in the armistice pact provided for the insulation of Vietnam from the international pressures of the Cold War. Article 16 banned the introduction into the whole of Vietnam, north and south, of "any troop reinforcements and additional military personnel" from the outside. Article 17 banned "the introduction into Viet Nam of any reinforcements in the form of all types of arms, munitions and other war matériel, such as combat aircraft, naval craft, pieces of ordnance, jet engines and jet weapons, and armoured vehicles." Article 18 forbade the establishment of "new military bases." The purpose of Article 19 was the neutralization of all of Vietnam. It stated: "[N]o military base under the control of a foreign State may be established in the re-grouping zone of either party; the two parties shall ensure that the zones assigned to them do not adhere to any military alliance and are not used for the resumption of military hostilities or to further an aggressive policy."

Article 29 and most of the subsequent articles in the agreement provided for the establishment of an International Commission for Supervision and Control,* which was to be "responsible for supervising the proper execution by the parties of the provisions of the agreement" (Article 36). This commission was to be composed of representatives of Canada, India, and Poland, with the representative of India serving as chairman (Article 34). Although the recommendations of the International Commission were to be made on the basis of a majority vote, its powers with regard to some important matters were limited by the requirement of unanimity in such cases. This was the case with respect to "questions concerning violations, or threats of violations, which might lead to resumption of hostilities, namely: a) Refusal by the armed forces of one party to effect the movements provided for in the

---

* Later usually referred to as the International Control Commission, or ICC.

regroupment plan; b) Violation by the armed forces of one of the parties of the regrouping zones, territorial waters, or air space of the other party" (Article 42). Finally, it was stipulated in Article 43: "If one of the parties refuses to put into effect a recommendation of the International Commission, the parties concerned or the commission itself shall inform the members of the Geneva Conference." It was also required that, in those cases under Article 42 (violations or threats of violations, which might lead to a resumption of hostilities) where the International Commission could not reach unanimity, "it shall submit a majority report and one or more minority reports to the members of the Conference."

It was the day after the signing of the above-described armistice agreement that the Final Declaration was brought before the delegates. This declaration was endorsed by the recorded oral assent of the representatives of the United Kingdom, the People's Republic of China, the U.S.S.R., Cambodia, and Laos, as well as by France and the Vietminh.[7] At the last minute the delegates had agreed to substitute the oral declaration for signatures because U.S. Secretary of State Dulles had declined to affix an American name to the settlement.[8] Nonetheless, the representatives of the United States and Bao Dai's State of Vietnam refused to register even their oral assents.

The Final Declaration of the conference endorsed the preceding armistice agreement for Vietnam, together with those for Laos and Cambodia. With respect to Vietnam, it also sanctioned and even further detailed some of the political and administrative arrangements outlined in the armistice agreement. Two of the most important of these paragraphs had a decided bearing on the Vietminh's expectations concerning Vietnam's political future, and they deserve quotation in full. Paragraph 6 read:

> The Conference recognizes that the essential purpose of the agreement relating to Viet Nam is to settle military questions with a view to ending hostilities and that the military demarcation line is provisional and should not in any way be interpreted as constituting a political or territorial boundary. The Confer-

ence expresses its conviction that the execution of the provisions set out in the present declaration and in the agreement on the cessation of hostilities creates the necessary basis for the achievement in the near future of a political settlement in Viet Nam.

Paragraph 7, focused on the elections and unification, stated:

The Conference declares that, so far as Viet Nam is concerned, the settlement of political problems, effected on the basis of respect for the principles of independence, unity and territorial integrity, shall permit the Vietnamese people to enjoy the fundamental freedoms, guaranteed by democratic institutions established as a result of free general elections by secret ballot. In order to ensure that sufficient progress in the restoration of peace has been made, and that all the necessary conditions obtain for free expression of the national will, general elections shall be held in July 1956, under the supervision of an international commission composed of representatives of the Member States of the International Supervisory Commission, referred to in the agreement on the cessation of hostilities. Consultations will be held on this subject between the competent representative authorities of the two zones from July 20, 1955, onwards.

This last paragraph has often been misrepresented, and it should be emphasized that it did not render the internationally supervised elections dependent upon the prior establishment of "fundamental freedoms and democratic institutions" in either of the regroupment areas. Consistent with Article 14a of the armistice, it stated rather that these freedoms and institutions were the anticipated attributes of a unified Vietnamese nation to be established *as a result of* the nationwide elections.

Further, the parties at Geneva provided for a period of two years within which to complete military regroupment and prepare for the elections. Following the regroupment (expected to last a maximum of ten months), the consultations (scheduled to begin on July 20, 1955, two months after the regroupment deadline) could be carried through for working out the modalities of the elections and the system for conducting and supervising them. To ensure that the necessary conditions prevailed for the "free expression of the national will," it was explicitly stipulated that the elections were to be carried out under the supervision of an international commission.* Any interpretation of the Final Declaration's paragraph 7, quoted above, must also take into account the relevant provisions of the armistice agreement, whereby, until the elections were held, administration north of the 17th parallel was placed in the hands of the Vietminh and administration to the south of it in the hands of the French. Because of this stipulation the Vietminh justifiably expected that the international commissions would be backed by France, both in arranging for the preelection consultations and in supervising the actual balloting in mid-1956. The Vietminh's interests were further safeguarded by the provision that any administration succeeding the French prior to the 1956 elections would legally assume France's obligations and be "responsible for ensuring the observance and enforcement of the terms and provisions" of the agreements entered into between the Vietminh and France.[9]

The fact that in the Final Declaration the Soviet Union and China as well as Great Britain supported the basic provisions of the armistice undoubtedly further strengthened the Vietminh's belief that so central a feature as the promised elections would actually be honored. And even though the United States refused to endorse the agreements, it did make a unilateral declaration directly relevant to the matter of elections, wherein Under-Secretary of State Walter Bedell Smith stated:

> In connection with the statement in the Declaration concerning free elections in Viet Nam, my government wishes to make clear its position which it has expressed in a Declaration made in Washington on June 29, 1954, as follows: "In the case of nations now divided against their will, we shall continue to seek to achieve unity through free elections, supervised by the United Nations to ensure that they are conducted fairly."

---

* This commission would be composed of representatives from the three states comprising the ICC—but not necessarily the same men or with the same-sized staff.

With even the United States giving no indication that it would oppose elections, the Vietminh had reason to assume that they would indeed be held. In its unilateral declaration the United States also "took note" of the armistice agreement and the Final Declaration and "declared" that the United States "will refrain from the threat or the use of force to disturb them" and "would view any renewal of the aggression in violation of the aforesaid agreements with grave concern and as seriously threatening international peace and security." Nowhere in its declaration did the United States speak of a "South" or "North" Vietnam. Every reference of the American representative was to a single Vietnam. Indeed, there was as yet no such thing as a state of South Vietnam, and even today there is no nation limited constitutionally to either the South or the North. Thus the terminology used by the American delegate was consistent with the fact that the Geneva Agreements only created temporary regroupment areas south and north of the 17th parallel.

3: Geneva did not, then, leave two separate states, but, rather, it left two contesting parties within a *single* national state. Both these rivals—the Vietminh (the Democratic Republic of Vietnam) on the one hand and the French-supported Bao Dai regime (the State of Vietnam) on the other—continued after Geneva, just as each had before, to lay claim to the whole country. The difference was that before Geneva the contending parties sought to enforce that claim through military means, but by agreement at Geneva their contest was transferred to the political level, with the resolution dependent upon the outcome of the scheduled national elections.

However, there was an essential and clearly understood disparity in the positions of the contestants: the Agreements authorized the Vietminh to administer one of the two regroupment zones while preparing for elections in both; on the other hand, in the southern regroupment zone the responsibility for administration lay with the French and not with the Vietnamese party, headed by Bao Dai, that was to compete in the elections. While each party was free to prepare for and contest the elections in both zones, the Vietminh alone would be administering the northern regroupment zone for the two-year period before elections, while it could expect that its southern-based political opponent would be disadvantaged in the elections by its popular image as a semicolonial subordinate of the French administration.

The armistice prescribed only a military disengagement, not a physical dismemberment of the country. During the period of the required regroupment of the French and Vietminh armies, civilians were free to relocate in either the North or the South, but their movement was to be entirely voluntary, and there was absolutely no obligation for them to accompany their armed forces. The political adherents of the Vietminh or any other party—whether leaders, functionaries, or followers—were in no sense called upon to leave their home areas. Their safety was to be guaranteed by the provision prohibiting "any reprisals or discrimination against persons or organizations on account of their activities during the hostilities" (Article 14c), and the International Commission appointed at Geneva was charged with ensuring that this injunction was fully respected. There was nothing in the Geneva provisions limiting peaceful political activity by the Vietminh in either of the two zones. In fact, the scheduling of the elections was the clearest evidence that political campaigning was to be anticipated. Without the expectation of freedom of political action culminating in elections the Vietminh would, of course, have hardly been disposed to make the military and territorial concessions that it did. For the Vietminh the military truce would otherwise have been fruitless, and it would have regarded the agreements as a whole as ones wherein it alone had made significant concessions.

The armistice at Geneva was signed by the French command in behalf of all Vietnamese in the areas it still controlled, including the 369,000 of the Vietnamese National Army that constituted part of the French Union forces. Since the troops actually commanded by Bao Dai were confined to a personal bodyguard, his "government" could hardly have been a party to these military agreements. While nothing in the Geneva Agreements restrained France from transferring political power in the South to Bao Dai or any other Vietnamese leadership, it will be recalled that the armistice agreement already provided that any such successor to the French would be "responsible for ensuring the observance and enforcement of the terms and provisions" of those agreements.[10] Failure of the successor to honor those agreements would, then, destroy the legal basis of the truce and thus open the way for a resumption of military hostilities.

In the years since Geneva much has been made of the fact that Bao Dai's representatives there did not assent to the Final Declaration of the conference. This has provided one of the principal rationalizations for Saigon's repudiation of selected aspects of the agreements that it found contrary to its own interests, notably the elections. But in the context of Geneva, the refusal of Bao Dai's Foreign Minister to subscribe to this declaration was meaningless. How real a political entity did he represent? In fact, the "State of Vietnam" remained an artificial construction of France, headed by a Bao Dai quite as devoid of popular following as at the time of the abortive Elysée Agreements of 1950. There was, to be sure, a new French pledge, initialed on June 4 midway through the Geneva discussions, which promised a fuller measure of independence. However, Bao Dai did not actually receive some of the most important attributes of power until well after the Geneva Conference had ended. Indeed, it was not until January 1, 1955, that Bao Dai's Prime Minister Ngo Dinh Diem could proclaim the reality of independence from France; [11] and not until two months after that did France transfer to the Saigon government control over the Vietnamese elements of the French Union forces stationed in Vietnam. Thus the State of Vietnam did not and could not play any real role at the Geneva Conference, and its delegate, Tran Van Do, was "left to wander disconsolately on the fringes of the Conference." [12] The most that he could do was to register dissent.

Since Bao Dai's entourage owed their positions primarily to the French and lacked genuine authority among the Vietnamese, it is understandable that they should have opposed an agreement whose political keystone was the promised elections. As they could easily foresee, elections would quickly expose the meagerness of their following and demonstrate all the more clearly that their State of Vietnam owed its existence primarily to French military power rather than to the will of the Vietnamese people. Those Vietnamese whose political positions had been so badly compromised by their collaboration with French colonialists could hardly relish the prospect of risking their political future in a contest with men who were regarded by all their countrymen as the victorious leaders of Vietnam's independence struggle. Nevertheless, it was this promise of elections that constituted an essential condition insisted upon by the Vietminh at Geneva. France was prepared to pay the political price of that condition in order to get the armistice that she so urgently wanted. Her successor would be obliged to abide by that condition or face the certain resumption of hostilities. The reason for this is patent: when a military struggle for power ends on the agreed condition that the competition will be transferred to the political plane, the side that violates the agreed condition cannot legitimately expect that the military struggle will not be resumed.

4: There were mixed feelings in Washington as the conference in Geneva drew to a close. The Under-Secretary of State, General Walter Bedell Smith, upon returning from Geneva, characterized the agreements as "the best which we could have possibly obtained under the circumstances." When confronted by critical members of Congress he stated: "I would like to point out, too, that when we analyze and discuss the results of Geneva it will be well to remember that diplomacy has rarely been able to gain at the conference table what cannot be gained or held on the battlefield." [13]

However, for the Eisenhower Administration, the Geneva Agreements—if allowed to work to their final conclusion in the 1956 elections—generally were seen as potentially disastrous. A high-ranking State Department official said: "It would be an understatement to say we do not like the terms of the ceasefire agreement just concluded." [14] A year earlier Washington had begun to speak of the effect on Southeast Asia of the possible fall of Indochina in terms of a "row of dominoes." Under the Geneva Agreements the Administration could foresee the toppling of the first domino in the forthcoming Vietnamese elections. As the State Department "White Paper" of 1961 was to declare:

> It was the Communists' calculation that nationwide elections scheduled in the Accords for 1956 would turn all of Viet-Nam over to them. With total control over the more populous North in their hands, the Communists assumed they would be able to promote enough support in the South for their cause to win in any balloting. The primary focus of the Communists' activity during the post-Geneva period was on political action—promoting discontent with the Government in Saigon and seeking to win supporters for Hanoi. The authorities in South Viet-Nam refused to fall into this well-laid trap. [15]

What the White Paper referred to as a "trap" in fact constituted an essential provision of the Geneva Agreements, the major reason the Vietminh had accepted the armistice.

The American response to the post-Geneva developments was foreshadowed in the unilateral declaration made by its delegate at the conference's concluding plenary session on July 21. He said: "With respect to the statement [of nonagreement with the Geneva settlement] made by the Representative of the State of Viet Nam, the United States reiterates its traditional position that peoples are entitled to determine their own future and that it will not join in an arrangement which would hinder this." [16] Though the United States said it would "refrain from the threat or the use of force to disturb" the agreements, it soon became evident that it was prepared to use every other means to back up the Saigon regime in its departure from their central provisions.

For more than a year before Geneva, as it had become increasingly clear that France was unable to stem the Vietminh's power, the United States had begun to develop a new strategy for Southeast Asia. In general Secretary of State Dulles hoped to form a cooperative alliance of anticommunist states that would respond in unison to indigenous or external communist threats in the area.

Prior to Geneva, French colonial rule had hampered these plans, for it was difficult to persuade potential allies that the colonies in Indochina should serve as the rallying point of an alliance of "free states." A further cause for delay was that America's principal Western Allies preferred a peaceful settlement and neutralization of Vietnam to the militant "united action" advocated by the United States. In advance of the Geneva Conference the British acquiesced in principle to American plans for a Pacific alliance but stipulated that these be postponed until after the conference had concluded. The United States thus had to wait until the end of the Geneva meetings before establishing its envisaged alliance system in Southeast Asia. But in view of the moderate stance adopted by the communist powers at the conference and their proposal to neutralize the countries of Indochina, America's Western allies had lost any sense of urgency in meeting the "communist threat" to the area.

The agreements approved at Geneva had diverged widely from Washington's concept of an acceptable settlement. For the United States, one of the most crucial points in such a settlement was that it should "not contain political provisions which would risk loss of the retained area to Communist control." * The French, however, in order to secure an armistice, had felt obliged to give in to the Vietminh's insistence that nationwide elections be guaranteed.[17] As it became clear that the solution that was being arrived at in Geneva would not accord with the American concept of an acceptable settlement, Dulles insisted upon withdrawing from the proceedings and turned over representation of the United States to Walter Bedell Smith. Despite the efforts of British Foreign Minister Anthony Eden to persuade Dulles "to join us in a final all-out diplomatic effort," he refused to return for the concluding sessions, stating that he did not want to be in the position of having to say "no" in public. He said that he was in this way dissociating the United States from the agreements because "American public opinion would never tolerate 'the guaranteeing of the subjection of millions of Vietnamese to Communist rule.' " [18] He thus instructed his delegation at Geneva

---

* The U.S. position concerning an acceptable settlement was incorporated in a seven-point communiqué sent to the French Prime Minister during the course of the conference. These points were that the United States and the United Kingdom would abide by an armistice agreement that: "1. Preserves the integrity and independence of Laos and Cambodia and assures the withdrawal of Vietminh forces therefrom. 2. Preserves at least the southern half of Vietnam, and if possible an enclave in the delta; in this connection we would be unwilling to see the line of division of responsibility drawn further south than a line running generally west from Dong Hoi. 3. Does not impose on Laos, Cambodia, or retained Vietnam any restrictions materially impairing their capacity to maintain stable non-communist regimes; and especially restrictions impairing their right to maintain adequate forces for internal security, to import arms and to employ foreign advisers. 4. Does not contain political provisions which would risk loss of the retained area to communist control. 5. Does not exclude the possibility of the ultimate reunification of Vietnam by peaceful means. 6. Provides for the peaceful and humane transfer, under international supervision, of those people desiring to be moved from one zone to another of Vietnam; and 7. Provides effective machinery for international supervision of the agreement." Anthony Eden, *Full Circle* (London: Cassell, 1960), pp. 132–133.

to support the stand of Bao Dai's still French-controlled State of Vietnam.

Having dissociated the United States from the Geneva Agreements, Dulles indicated in his press statement on the conference that its outcome had not changed his plans for a Southeast Asian pact. "The important thing from now on," he said, "is not to mourn the past but to face the future opportunity to prevent the loss in northern Viet-Nam from leading to the extension of communism throughout Southeast Asia and the Southwest Pacific." [19] Now that the war had ended, he implied, the United States could make arrangements for collective defense in advance of aggression and build up "the truly independent states of Cambodia, Laos and southern Vietnam." [20]

The Secretary of State intended this Southeast Asia Collective Defense Treaty and Protocol (signed at Manila, September 8, 1954)—which came to be known as the Southeast Asia Treaty Organization (SEATO) [21] —to offset the weakened position of the West in Indochina and to serve as a major barrier against any further spread of communist political power. He saw it as an international agreement providing a cloak of protection for Cambodia and Laos against aggression by communist powers and for insuring that the Vietminh be inhibited from establishing control over the rest of Vietnam, with its authority permanently confined north of the 17th parallel. This would be achieved, Dulles presumably believed, under the specific antisubversive provisions of the Southeast Asia Treaty. In presenting the treaty to the United States Senate in late 1954, he argued that the treaty was designed to meet subversion, which was "most acute at the moment in Vietnam," and to build up in that country "a strong government which commands the loyalty of the people, and which has an effective police and constabulary at its command to detect and run down subversive activities." [22]

In fact SEATO registered United States' objectives in Southeast Asia without actually providing an effective collective means for attaining them. The agreement provided merely that in cases of aggression by armed attack from outside each SEATO power was "to meet the common danger in accordance with its constitutional processes" and that in cases of subversion each SEATO party was to "consult" with the other signatories "in order to agree on the measures to be taken for common defense." * Support for the envisaged security pact was never obtained from the major neutralist states of South and Southeast Asia—Burma, India, and Indonesia. What eventuated was an arrangement dominated by the United States and its Western allies. It attracted as Asian members only Thailand, the Philippines, and Pakistan (which saw the pact primarily as a means for strengthening itself against India, rather than as support of American purposes in Southeast Asia). The other signatories to the Southeast Asia Treaty Organization were the United States, the United Kingdom, France, Australia, and New Zealand.

On the day the treaty was signed, the same parties, by an additional protocol unanimously designated the states of Cambodia and Laos and "the free territory under the jurisdiction of the State of Vietnam" for the purposes of Article IV of the treaty. Neither the treaty nor the additional protocol constituted a commitment by the United States (or any other SEATO powers) to any government or state of South Vietnam. Any such obvious commitment would have directly

---

* By paragraph 1 of Article IV of the treaty: "1. Each Party recognizes that aggression by means of armed attack in the treaty area against any of the Parties or against any State or territory which the Parties by unanimous agreement may hereafter designate, would endanger its own peace and safety, and agrees that it will in that event act to meet the common danger in accordance with its constitutional processes. Measures taken under this paragraph shall be immediately reported to the Security Council of the United Nations." By paragraph 2, the parties agreed to "consult immediately in order to agree on the measures which should be taken for the common defense" in certain cases where, in the opinion of any of the parties, the threat to the parties or the territories designated under paragraph 1 is "other than by armed attack."

violated the Geneva Agreements, and for at least a good many years the United States wished to avoid the appearance of frontally contradicting the military provisions of those agreements.

But if SEATO did not violate the letter of the Geneva Agreements, it clearly violated their spirit, both by implying that the 17th parallel had a political character and by its inconsistency with the neutral status of the southern regroupment zone. At the very least its provisions signalled the American intent to underwrite a separate state in southern Vietnam if, despite the inadmissibility of this under the Geneva Agreements, one could be established. Paragraph 3 of Article IV of the treaty and the protocol stipulated that, should the states of Cambodia and Laos or "the free territory under the jurisdiction of the State of Vietnam" so request, they could be recipients of the same protection by the SEATO powers as was accorded to the non-Indochina areas covered in the body of the agreement.

Washington thus utilized the SEATO negotiations to offset the results of the accords reached at Geneva. Through SEATO it helped provide statehood for a territory that was in fact nothing more than one of two temporary regrouping zones, thereby ignoring the stipulation that the country was to be unified in two years' time. It enforced this action by granting protection in advance to the southern regrouping area against any attack by indigenous forces based in the other half of the same country. Vietnamese with a vested interest in this artificial division were, thereby, encouraged in their attempts to maintain this protected southern area separate from the rest of the nation and to transform the 17th parallel into a permanent political boundary.

SEATO constituted in effect one half of a two-pronged American riposte to the military armistice upon which the Geneva Agreements were based. The other prong was the United States' effort to inject sufficient power into the regime of Bao Dai and Ngo Dinh Diem to render it politically viable and able to stand as a separate state.

Notes to Chapter III

1. For the relevant documents see U.S. Congress, Senate, *Documents on Germany, 1944–1961,* 87th Congress, 1st Session (Washington: U.S. Government Printing Office, 1961), pp. 149–154.

2. See Donald Lancaster, *The Emancipation of French Indochina* (London: Oxford University Press, 1961), pp. 336–337; Daniel Lerner and Raymond Aron, eds., *France Defeats the E.D.C.* (New York: Praeger, 1957), pp. 16, 17.

3. For further development of this point, see the chapter on China, pp. 269–270 in particular.

4. Alexander Werth, *France 1940–1955* (New York: Holt, 1956), p. 683. See also Lancaster, *op. cit.,* pp. 329–330.

5. Mendès-France, *Journal Officiel de la République Française, Débats Parlementaires Assemblée Nationale, Séance du vendredi 23 juillet 1954* (Paris: Imprimerie des journaux officiels, 1954), p. 3580.

6. See Appendix 2 for texts of both.

7. See Appendix 2-C for the final ceremonies. An oral agreement, for which there is proof, can be as binding as a treaty. The World Court has held that an oral agreement between authorized representatives of countries is legally binding. (Case of Denmark and Norway with regard to Eastern Greenland, Permanent Court of International Justice, A/b No. 53 (1933), p. 71.) See also Herbert Briggs, *The Law of Nations,* 2nd ed. (New York: Appleton-Century-Crofts, 1952), p. 838, wherein he indicates that oral agreements may be binding under international law. See also *Report of the International Law Commission on the Work of its 18th Session, 1966,* A/6309, *Draft Articles on the Law of Treaties,* Article 3(b) and commentary thereon.

8. See Anthony Eden, *Full Circle* (London: Cassell, 1960), p. 142.

9. Article 27 of the Franco-Vietnamese Armistice Agreement. See also the treaty of June 4, 1954, between France and Bao Dai's State of Vietnam, which made clear that the latter's independence was to entail assumption of all obligations "resulting from international treaties or conventions contracted by France in the name of the State of Vietnam, and all other treaties and conventions concluded by France in the name of French Indochina insofar as these affect Vietnam." Secretariat of State for Foreign Affairs of the Republic of Vietnam, Bureau of Archives, *Treaties on Viet-*

namese Independence and Franco-Vietnamese Association, cited in Ngo Ton Dat, "The Geneva Partition of Vietnam and the Question of Reunification during the First Two Years (August 1954 to July 1956)" (unpublished Ph.D. dissertation, Cornell University, 1963), pp. 452–453. The writer of this dissertation served at the Geneva Conference as aide to Prince Buu Loc, who was Bao Dai's Prime Minister prior to Ngo Dinh Diem.

10. See footnote 9.

11. See Allan B. Cole, ed., *Conflict in Indo-China and International Repercussions: A Documentary History, 1945–1955* (Ithaca, N.Y.: Cornell University Press, 1956), p. 211.

12. Lancaster, *op. cit.,* p. 334.

13. Council on Foreign Relations, *The United States in World Affairs, 1954* (New York: Harper and Bros., 1956), p. 255.

14. Statement by Assistant Secretary Walter S. Robertson, *Department of State Bulletin* (Washington, August 23, 1954), p. 261.

15. *A Threat to the Peace* (Washington: Department of State, December 1961), p. 3.

16. See Appendix 2.

17. Early in the conference Pham Van Dong, the Vietminh's representative, had made clear that a cessation of hostilities was dependent upon the simultaneous acceptance of nationwide elections that would give the Vietminh the opportunity to win control of the South. *New York Times,* May 16, 1954.

18. Eden, *op. cit.,* pp. 138–139.

19. *Department of State Bulletin* (Washington, August 2, 1954), p. 163.

20. *Ibid.*

21. For the text, see Appendix 3. For an additional discussion of the Treaty, see below pp. 300–302.

22. U.S. Senate, *The Southeast Asia Collective Defense Treaty,* 83rd Congress, 2nd Session (Washington: U.S. Government Printing Office, 1954), Vol. 1, pp. 14, 24.

CHAPTER IV

The Emergence of Two Vietnams

1: During the two-year reprieve from military activity secured by the Geneva Conference, a separate state was created out of the temporary regroupment zone in the southern half of Vietnam, and the 17th parallel was transformed into the political, territorial boundary explicitly forbidden under the terms of the agreements. And as the French political and military presence was withdrawn from the South, the American attempt to build up an anticommunist state was no longer impeded by a colonial intermediary. By early 1955 the United States could deal directly with the new Prime Minister, Ngo Dinh Diem,* rather than through the French.

In the struggle for power that almost immediately arose in Saigon, the U.S. backed Ngo Dinh Diem—at first cautiously but increasingly without limit or qualification. This gave him a decisive edge over his chief rivals—the now badly dis-

---

* Diem was from a Roman Catholic Mandarin family that had served the vestigial and effectively French-controlled imperial Annamese court at Hué. After working in the imperial administration for four years, Diem resigned in 1933 because of a dispute with Emperor Bao Dai. In 1946, following a long period of political retirement and study, Diem was offered the premiership by Ho Chi Minh. He turned it down in part because he held the Vietminh responsible for the murder of his brother. After an unsuccessful attempt to develop a rival political force, he left Vietnam in August 1950. He spent the next four years abroad, mostly in the United States, where he lobbied for support among religious, political, and academic leaders. The influence of Cardinal Spellman and of the American Friends of Vietnam, a group that has often been referred to as the "Vietnam lobby," is difficult to gauge, but it was probably significant in gaining support for Diem in the United States.

credited Chief of State Bao Dai and the Commander in Chief of Bao Dai's army, General Nguyen Van Hinh. Although Diem's stature as a nationalist was somewhat reduced by his absence from the country during the final years of the independence struggle, his nationalist escutcheon was untarnished by any collaboration with the French. Moreover, as a Catholic, he undoubtedly had appeal for the country's small but generally well-educated and politically conscious Catholic minority, now greatly strengthened by the large contingent of northern Catholics who moved to the South under the terms of the Geneva Agreements.

Appointed by Bao Dai midway through the Geneva Conference, Diem became Prime Minister of the still French-controlled regime. It was not until almost six months later that France finally transferred the remaining attributes of government to the administration led by Bao Dai and Ngo Dinh Diem. The United States had, however, made manifest its support of Diem well before this transfer of authority was completed.

A personal letter from President Eisenhower to Diem of October 1, 1954 [1] (actually delivered to him three weeks later) inaugurated a series of U.S. moves to strengthen his hand against Bao Dai and General Hinh. Although Washington by then diagnosed Diem's prospects as more promising than those of his principal rivals, * the precariousness of his position probably accounts for the note of hesitancy in the Eisenhower letter. Its pledge of assistance was made condi-

---

* There was an initial period of indecision on the part of the United States before it put its full weight behind Diem. Some influential Americans inclined towards continuing support of Bao Dai, along with his military Commander in Chief, General Nguyen Van Hinh. President Eisenhower's personal representative, General J. Lawton Collins, argued against supporting Diem; but Colonel Edward G. Lansdale, a principal U.S. intelligence agent in Saigon, apparently prevailed upon Allen Dulles, then Director of the CIA, to persuade Secretary of State Dulles that Diem was a better bet. See *New York Times,* July 25, 1962.

tional on Diem's "assurances as to the standards of performance . . . in undertaking needed reforms." This aid, Eisenhower indicated, "combined with your own continuing efforts will contribute effectively toward an independent Vietnam endowed with a strong government. Such a government would, I hope, be so responsive to the nationalist aspirations of its people" as to attract domestic and international respect. Even Senator Mike Mansfield, one of Diem's most outspoken supporters, acknowledged that he as yet lacked real authority. In his report to the Senate Foreign Relations Committee on October 15, Mansfield stated:

> He has a theoretical mandate of full powers from the Chief of State Bao Dai, who in turn derives his authority from a combination of a French grant and the persistence of the symbolic power of his former role as Emperor.[2]

In this report, however, Mansfield urged that "in the event that the Diem government falls . . . the United States should consider an immediate suspension of all aid to Vietnam and the French Union forces there. . . ."

Washington translated its tentative attachment to Diem into more decisive actions shortly after Eisenhower's letter was handed to him. In mid-November, the President's special ambassador, General J. Lawton Collins, announced in Saigon that the United States would give "every possible aid to the Government of Diem and to his Government only."[3] It would not consider "training or otherwise aiding a Vietnamese army that does not give complete and implicit obedience to its premier."[4] Clearly, this move was aimed primarily at General Hinh, who as Commander of the army was the most powerful figure in Saigon standing out against Diem. As General Hinh was unwilling to respond to this pressure and refused to yield control of the army, "American representations were made to Bao Dai," who then summoned Hinh to Paris and dismissed him from his post on November 29.[5] The General himself re-

marked shortly afterwards that if he had initiated a coup
against Diem:

> Nothing could have opposed the army. But the Americans let
> me know that if that happened, dollar help would be cut off.
> That would not matter to the military. If necessary, we soldiers
> could go barefoot and eat rice, but the country cannot survive
> without American help.[6]

The dismissal of General Hinh opened the way for Diem to
establish his own authority over the army. With Hinh's removal other army leaders fell into line.*

Meanwhile the Vietminh troops were progressively withdrawing to the North. Apart from a few areas turned over to
him directly by the French, Diem established his authority
most easily in those more extensive territories evacuated by
the Vietminh. By the spring of 1955, in conformity with the
schedule laid down in the Geneva armistice agreement, the
Vietminh had removed from the South all of its army (approximately 100,000 men) and regrouped them north of the
17th parallel. The Vietminh turned over its areas in the South
to the French Union forces, which soon passed them to Diem's
Saigon administration. Since the Vietminh enjoined its political adherents who remained to conduct themselves peacefully
and prepare for the anticipated elections, Diem initially encountered little resistance in extending his administration to
these areas.

Throughout other large regions Diem had to maneuver and
battle to impose his rule over territories dominated by the Cao
Dai and Hoa Hao. In March and April 1955, Diem moved
against these militarily powerful and politically autonomous
sects, as well as against the Binh Xuyen, a Saigon-based band
of gangsters that had previously run the city's police and that
maintained its own well-equipped militia.[7] From the outset

---

* This National Army was composed of the Vietnamese components of the still partially French-officered French Union forces.

Diem could exert considerable political leverage against the sects because their previous well-subsidized marriage of convenience with the French rendered them financially dependent upon Saigon. When the French terminated their subventions to the Hoa Hao and Cao Dai in February of 1955, Diem had sufficient American funds to buy their loyalty and amalgamate them into his state had he so elected. Previously, American advisors had urged him to reach a compromise agreement with the sect leaders whereby they would assume significant positions in his cabinet. Diem, however, displaying the same resoluteness of purpose that characterized his entire consolidation of power, rejected any such compromise. For their part, the sect leaders laid down three main conditions for the merger of their troops into Diem's army: that he take over and continue France's financial subvention; that he recognize their existing territorial autonomy; and that he reserve cabinet posts for them in his government. Diem resisted such extensive concessions while adroitly undermining the solidarity of the front that the sect leaders formed to deal with him. By selectively dispersing the funds provided by the United States, Diem bribed enough of the sects' key leaders to fragment their opposition.* According to one estimate, "The total amount of American dollars spent on bribes during March and April, 1955, by Diem may well have gone beyond $12 million." [8] Although seriously crippled by these political maneuvers, the sects still maintained a formidable resistance against Diem for several months, until his military forces ultimately defeated their remaining armies and subjugated most of their territories. Even so, a few Cao Dai and Hoa Hao districts successfully warded off Saigon's rule throughout the Diem regime.

---

* With the united front of the sects and the Binh Xuyen broken, Diem first turned his attention to the latter, expelling them from Saigon on April 28, 1955, and overcoming their residual forces a few days later. Almost immediately thereafter Diem's troops moved against those elements of the Cao Dai and Hoa Hao that still refused to accept his terms.

In April 1955, Bao Dai, still residing in France, tried to check Diem's consolidation of power. He appointed a new chief of armed forces and summoned Diem to France for "consultations." Most observers then anticipated that these consultations would result in Diem's dismissal. But Washington's earlier hesitation about backing Diem had been largely dissipated by his success in dealing with the sects and the Binh Xuyen. The Eisenhower Administration no longer doubted that Diem was the man, and the only one, to build up a new state, and it resolved that his achievement of this goal should not be impeded by Bao Dai. Leading Democrats shared this partiality for Diem. In the Senate, Hubert Humphrey joined Senator Mansfield in voicing strong Democratic support, stating:

> Premier Diem is the best hope that we have in South Vietnam. He is the leader of his people. He deserves and must have the wholehearted support of the American Government and our foreign policy. This is no time for uncertainty or half-hearted measures. . . . He is the only man on the political horizon of Vietnam who can rally a substantial degree of support of his people. . . . If we have any comments to make about the leadership in Vietnam let it be directed against Bao Dai. It is time we broke our ties with him and not with Diem. If the Government of South Vietnam has not room for both of these men, it is Bao Dai who must go.[9]

With the U.S. now so fully behind him, Diem defied the orders of Bao Dai and with American encouragement took steps to remove him from his position as Chief of State. In October, Diem organized a referendum wherein the people were asked to choose between him and Bao Dai. Although he probably would have defeated the ex-Emperor in any honest contest, Diem ignored the counsel of his American advisors (who felt that a reasonable margin was sufficient and would make a better appearance) and conducted a grossly unfair election in which he claimed a total of 98.2 per cent of the vote. Bao

Dai, still absent in France at the time, remained there and never returned. Three days after the referendum, on October 26, 1955, Diem proclaimed the establishment of a Republic of Vietnam, with himself as its President.

By the beginning of 1956, then, eighteen months after first coming to office, political power in South Vietnam had shifted decisively in Diem's favor. The army, police, and capital city were firmly in his hands. He had largely deprived the sects of their territorial bases and military forces, successfully ousted Bao Dai, and secured from France control over Vietnam's currency and exchange. Saigon now took command over Vietnamese nationals in the French Union army and obtained French agreement to evacuate the remainder of their Expeditionary Corps. The United States had assumed France's financial and training responsibility for Saigon's army and embarked upon a massive program of economic aid to Diem's government. The scale of this program can be readily seen from Table 1 opposite. In place of a relatively passive French political and military presence, Diem could now rely upon America's energetic support and lavish aid.

Diem's consolidation of power did not involve a complete break with the regime of Bao Dai.[10] Except for the removal of French officials and the enhanced role of Catholics in senior positions, the composition of the bureaucracy remained very much as it had under Bao Dai. As with the officer corps of Diem's new army, his civil service was largely staffed by Vietnamese who had collaborated with the French. Most of the top positions in the Saigon government previously held by colonial officials were now filled by refugees from the North. These were generally Catholics who had fled Tonkin with the French evacuation. Consequently, friction soon developed in Diem's bureaucracy . between Southerners and the corps of newcomers, with their different dialect and frequent manifestations of superiority.

Many of these Northerners must have realized that with a Catholic assuming the office of Prime Minister in the South

TABLE 1

Cumulative Assistance
(Aid and Public Law 480)
1954 to Present to Vietnamese Government
(IN MILLIONS OF DOLLARS)

U.S. FISCAL YEAR	ECONOMIC AID [2]	PUBLIC LAW 480 [4]	TOTAL ECONOMIC AID
1954	—	0.1	0.1
1955	323.6	2.2	325.8
1956	202.0	14.3	216.3
1957	258.3	22.8	281.1
1958	[3]182.4	9.7	192.1
1959	200.6	6.5	207.1
1960	169.0	11.5	180.5
1961	132.6	12.0	144.6
1962	110.7	32.5	143.2
1963	133.2	64.3	197.5
1964	159.2	71.0	230.3
1965 [1]	224.9	53.6	278.5
TOTAL	2,096.6	300.5	2,397.1

1. Public Law 480 excludes U.S. uses.
2. Includes loans and grants on obligations basis.
3. Includes a loan funded from regional funds.
4. Total of Title I sales (less U.S. uses portion) plus Title II and III grants.

SOURCE: U.S. House of Representatives, *Supplemental Foreign Assistance Authorization Fiscal Year 1966,* 89th Congress, 2nd Session (Washington: U.S. Government Printing Office, 1966).

their own fortunes would be better assured there than under the Vietminh. Ho Chi Minh's government, though formally guaranteeing religious freedom, would not easily forget that many of these Catholics had collaborated with the French and provided their most reliable Vietnamese backing.* Quite apart from the issue of collaboration, "the leaders of the Catholic Church and the priests felt that they could not preach their religion freely in the North and had persuaded as many believers as possible to leave for the South." [11] There seems to be no basis for the allegation that the overwhelmingly Catholic exodus was instigated by the Vatican, but little doubt exists that "the movement [of Catholics from the North] had been officially encouraged by the Prime Minister, by the Vietnamese Catholic hierarchy, and by the local authorities." [12] Moreover, the American government appears to have been actively involved in promoting this exodus. Bernard Fall states:

> . . . the mass flight was admittedly the result of an extremely intensive, well-conducted, and, in terms of its objective, very successful American psychological warfare operation. Propaganda slogans and leaflets appealed to the devout Catholics with such themes as "Christ has gone to the South" and the "Virgin Mary has departed from the North." [13]

However effective its psychological campaign may have been, the United States played a major role in the physical resettlement of these Northern refugees. It assigned units of the U.S. Seventh Fleet to transport them south and provided a sum of $93 million for the overall relocation program.[14]

Possibly an additional factor may have been "a vague fear of atomic attack," which, according to the Indian Deputy Secretary General of the ICC, caused a large number of people to leave. "The International Commission's Teams came

---

* The bishoprics of Phat Diem and Bui Chu were foremost among these, their pastors having organized an autonomous Vietnamese militia against the Vietminh. The precipitate flight of the Apostolic Vicar of Phat Diem, Mgr. Le Huu Tu, from his bishopric probably reflected the fact that he had already been sentenced to death on five separate occasions by the Vietminh for collaboration with the French. See Donald Lancaster, *The Emancipation of French Indochina* (London: Oxford University Press, 1961), p. 330. See also Jean Lacouture, *Vietnam: Between Two Truces* (New York: Random House, 1966), pp. 104–106.

across a great number of people who really believed that if they remained in the North the Americans would drop atom bombs." [15]

Out of a total of almost 900,000 Vietnamese who came south * the vast majority—between 80 per cent and 85 per cent—were Catholics, representing about two-thirds of the Catholic population of the North. Their arrival in the South more than tripled that area's Catholic population, bringing it to slightly over a million, or about 7 per cent of the total.[16] The other refugees comprised Vietnamese soldiers of the French Union forces (approximately 110,000) and officials of the French-controlled administration in the North, along with their dependents.

Many of the Northern Catholics with higher education and administrative experience were appointed to important political positions in Saigon, and many were sent to fill senior administrative posts in the provinces. Refugee Catholic peasants were generally settled *en bloc* with their parish priests, some in Montagnard areas of the highlands, some just south of the 17th parallel, and others in a cluster of villages around Saigon.

This large increment of Northern Catholics provided Diem with the most reliable and effective element in his power base. At the same time it introduced an unsettling and potentially disruptive political factor, which in the years to come was to eventuate in serious political friction at all levels of society. Thus Bernard Fall observes:

> . . . the arrival of that tightly knit community in a South Viet-Nam that is largely Taoist, spiritualist, and Buddhist created new political tensions there—the more so as the government of President Ngo Dinh Diem immediately used the Northern Catholics as its major base of political power. . . .[17]

---

* Approximately 150,000 Vietminh troops with their families were transported north on Polish and Russian vessels. R. P. Stebbins and the Research Staff of the Council on Foreign Relations, *The United States in World Affairs 1954* (New York: Harper and Bros., 1956), p. 285.

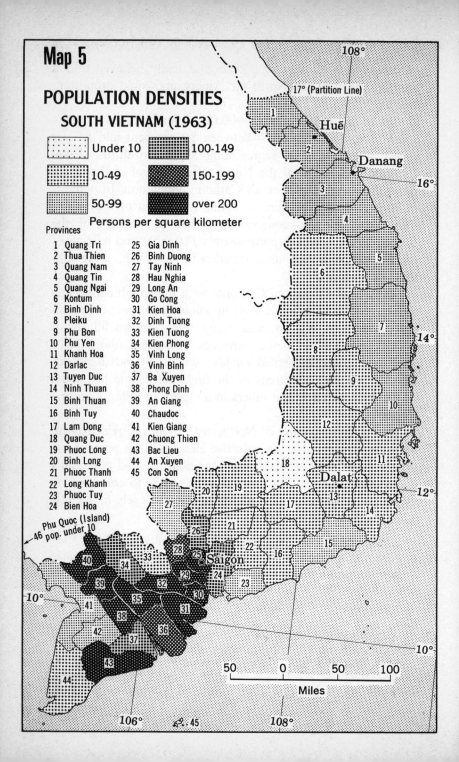

Map 5

POPULATION DENSITIES
SOUTH VIETNAM (1963)

Under 10
10-49
50-99
100-149
150-199
over 200

Persons per square kilometer

Provinces

1	Quang Tri	25	Gia Dinh
2	Thua Thien	26	Binh Duong
3	Quang Nam	27	Tay Ninh
4	Quang Tin	28	Hau Nghia
5	Quang Ngai	29	Long An
6	Kontum	30	Go Cong
7	Binh Dinh	31	Kien Hoa
8	Pleiku	32	Dinh Tuong
9	Phu Bon	33	Kien Tuong
10	Phu Yen	34	Kien Phong
11	Khanh Hoa	35	Vinh Long
12	Darlac	36	Vinh Binh
13	Tuyen Duc	37	Ba Xuyen
14	Ninh Thuan	38	Phong Dinh
15	Binh Thuan	39	An Giang
16	Binh Tuy	40	Chaudoc
17	Lam Dong	41	Kien Giang
18	Quang Duc	42	Chuong Thien
19	Phuoc Long	43	Bac Lieu
20	Binh Long	44	An Xuyen
21	Phuoc Thanh	45	Con Son
22	Long Khanh		
23	Phuoc Tuy		
24	Bien Hoa		

Phu Quoc (Island)
46 pop. under 10

108°
17° (Partition Line)
Hué
Danang
16°
14°
Dalat
12°
Saigon
10°
Miles
50 0 50 100
106°
108°
10°
45

2 : **The United States had begun,** meanwhile, to build up the Vietnamese military establishment, its bureaucracy, its economy, and the public image of its leaders. After the departure of the last French troops in April 1956, it was the only foreign military presence in all Vietnam. Without initially increasing the numbers of the Military Assistance Advisory Group (MAAG), which had existed before Geneva and hence could legitimately be maintained thereafter, the U.S. organized it under a new American command in the spring of 1956. Its mission was to streamline the Vietnamese army of 250,000 men into a smaller force of 150,000, organized to meet any possible thrust from the North.[18] Under MAAG guidance the U.S. equipped and began training this new army, while shouldering its entire payroll as well as most of the wages of the 40,000 men in the newly established local milita, the Self-Defense Corps.[19] The U.S. dispensed its funds for the South Vietnamese armed forces directly through Diem, thereby strengthening his control over the military.

The U.S. had already undertaken to train and equip a 50,000 man Civil Guard,[20] most of whose officers were regular army personnel. Responsibility for this task was, somewhat surprisingly, assigned to a Michigan State University advisory group, presumably because of that institution's unique School of Police Administration and possibly because its president, a former Assistant Secretary of Defense, had close ties within the Republican Administration. Michigan State's contract with the U.S. Government also charged it with helping Diem strengthen his administrative services—a task rather more appropriate for a university.[21]

This task was but one in the massive U.S. program of economic aid that in effect paid almost all governmental salaries as well as Diem's other operating expenses—a total of $320 million allocated for fiscal 1955 alone [22] and almost $2 billion during the fiscal years 1955 to 1960. In addition to this economic aid the United States provided military equipment that averaged $85 million a year prior to the major increase that commenced early in 1962.[23]

Of the total American economic aid during this period, approximately three-quarters paid South Vietnam's military budget. With respect to the nonmilitary side of the budget, approximately 30 per cent went to transportation projects, with only very minor amounts set aside for education, health and sanitation, community development, social welfare, and housing.*

For supplying its economic aid to Vietnam, the U.S. consciously chose a method designed to reduce inflationary pressures. This had the additional effect, however, of disproportionately benefiting part of the urban middle class. Approximately 80 per cent of American aid was injected through an import-subsidization program whereby the United States paid for commodities imported into the South. These goods were sold to Vietnamese importers for local currency that was then deposited in a counterpart fund. The fund so accumulated

---

* The following table shows the various components of American economic-aid allotments during 1955–60 in U.S. dollars:

PROGRAM	AMOUNT
Transportation	126,373,000
PL 480 (Surplus Food)	57,234,000
Food and Agriculture	53,837,000
Refugee Program	45,803,000
Public Administration and Safety	33,036,000
Development Loan Fund	29,200,000
Industry and Mining	24,783,000
Education	18,588,000
Health and Sanitation	18,043,000
Community Development, Social Welfare, and Housing	10,513,000
Labor	395,000
TOTAL	417,825,000

These statistics are compiled from the following sources: USOM, *Annual Statistical Bulletin,* 1960, p. 117; 1961, p. 119; and 1962, p. 120; and John D. Montgomery, *The Politics of Foreign Aid* (New York: Praeger, 1962), pp. 284, 289, 294.

served as the major American subsidy to the Saigon government and was utilized by it in accordance with agreements reached with American officials. It was from the Vietnamese currency so generated that the entire payroll of the armed forces was met and a large part of the civilian officials paid.

Additional benefit accrued to the Vietnamese government through its taxation of these American-financed imports, and, in fact, this provided the major portion of the government's tax revenue. An American tax specialist assigned to Saigon observed that because the counterpart funds were actually provided at a rate faster than they could be spent by the Vietnamese government, it was able to build up its foreign-exchange reserves from $125 million to $216.4 million between 1955 and 1960. "In other words," he concluded, "during this period Viet-Nam used part of the proceeds from its own exports to build up a financial hoard while using American aid 'for living expenses.' " [24] As John Osborne described it: "The aid program in 1955 and 1956 was designed almost entirely to put and keep Diem's government on its feet. It was a jumble of military hardware delivered directly to the armed forces of Vietnam; economic assistance (labeled 'defense support') intended to pay primarily the costs of internal security; and assistance intended to benefit the economy as such." [25]

Despite its magnitude, the U.S. program of aid only seldom touched the lives of South Vietnam's preponderantly rural populace. Further, the bulk of the benefits, both direct and indirect, were concentrated in the urban middle classes, whose stake in the status quo grew disproportionately as a result. Because the American subvention freed him of the normal fiscal worries of governing an economically underdeveloped nation, Diem lacked the incentive to bring about changes for either the disadvantaged classes in the cities or the bulk of the peasantry or to create reliable links to the countryside as a measure for insuring the flow of tax funds. Relieved of the demands for a domestic income tax, Saigon could much more easily insulate itself from the troublesome realities beyond its outskirts. U.S. aid thus provided Diem with a degree of financial independence that isolated him from basic economic and political realities and reduced his need to appreciate or respond to his people's wants and expectations.

America's political sponsorship of Diem was graphically illustrated by the all-out effort of the United States Information Service to help build up Diem's prestige among the Vietnamese population.[26] This campaign in South Vietnam was soon paralleled by a publicity effort in the United States. Diem's government engaged an American public-relations firm to project a favorable image of him to the American public. The fact that he had emerged as the only anticommunist symbol in Vietnam made it easier for his American friends to complement the work of his hired public-relations agents. There being so few Vietnam specialists in the U.S., Diem's advocates had an almost open field and exerted a disproportionate influence on American opinion.[27] Moreover, with increasing American involvement in Vietnam, a high proportion of writing on that country was by individuals sent there directly or indirectly under the auspices of the United States Government. Perhaps it is not surprising that the views expressed by a considerable number of them reflected this sponsorship.

3 : Despite Diem's unexpectedly firm hold on the Saigon government and his attraction of large-scale American economic support, at the conclusion of his first year of rule he still dared not risk the internationally supervised elections that the Geneva Agreements had stipulated. When, in mid-1955, Ho Chi Minh's government sought to begin consultations on the elections in accordance with the conference's provisions, Diem refused to cooperate. In a statement on July 16, 1955, he declared: "We have not signed the Geneva Agreements. We are not bound in any way by these agreements, signed against the will of the Viet-Namese people." [28] The United States clearly supported Diem in this stand. However, while making this clear to him, the Department of State indicated that it would have preferred his paying at least lip-service to the Geneva Accords by going "through the motions of trying to organize free elections in cooperation with the Communist North." [29] The Saigon government was unwilling to go even this far, adamantly refusing to participate in preelection consultations under any circumstances. It spelled out its position further on August 12 stating:

> Serving the cause of true democracy the Viet-Nam Government considers the principle of really free elections to be a peaceful and democratic institution, but the conditions of freedom of life and of the vote must first be satisfied. Nothing constructive from this point of view will be achieved so long as the Communist regime of the North does not allow each Viet-Namese citizen to exercise democratic liberties and the fundamental rights of man.[30]

The South Vietnamese government's policy statement thus echoed an argument already put forward as early as June 28 by Secretary Dulles [31] that, without the appropriate preconditions, elections could not be held. The governing clauses of the Geneva Agreements, it will be recalled, stipulated that it was the supervision by an international body that was to insure that "the necessary conditions obtain for free expression of the national will." These national elections themselves were to pave the way for the democratic institutions that were certainly quite as absent in the South as in the North.

In retrospect, Diem's refusal even to participate in the discussions for working out election arrangements signified his estimates of his true political strength. Such discussions were scheduled by the Geneva Agreements to begin after July 20, 1955, between "the competent representative authorities of the two Zones." In these discussions he could have freely argued for whatever safeguards he felt were necessary, in addition to the stipulated supervision by a commission composed of representatives from Canada, India, and Poland. Diem could not help realizing that under free electoral conditions his chances would be diminished drastically and that elections supervised by the International Commission might well have established conditions that were sufficiently free to insure that even in the South he would suffer defeat.

The legal and political bases for even a temporary preelection administration south of the 17th parallel was the Franco-Vietnamese Armistice Agreement. Without its sheltering military truce Diem and the United States would have had no opportunity to build up a separate government in the South between 1954 and 1956. As legal successor to the French, Diem was either bound by the terms of this armistice, politically as well as militarily, or obliged to turn authority in the South back to France until the elections were held. By choosing instead a third course, the disavowal of key political terms of the armistice, he rendered the military truce null and void and could hardly expect the peace that the armistice had secured to be maintained. The Eisenhower Administration was advised of this logical conclusion at the SEATO meeting in February 1955. There the United States was cautioned by its allies that SEATO would not function if a South Vietnamese refusal to hold the required elections resulted in an attack from the North. The British and French, nearly a decade before full-scale escalation began in Vietnam, unequivocally declared that in this case Saigon could expect no aid whatever from them.[32]

Nevertheless, backed by Washington, Diem declared on September 21 that ". . . there can be no question of a conference, even less of negotiations" with the Hanoi Government.[33] Diem adamantly held to his position. The election date of July 1956 passed with Diem still refusing even to discuss the possibility of sitting down with Vietminh representatives to discuss the modalities of such elections. In this stand he continued to receive warm American encouragement and the fullest American diplomatic backing. Without these discussions even being attempted, there is no way of knowing whether agreement on such modalities was possible and whether the elections could have been genuinely free or not.

4: **Meanwhile, north of the 17th parallel,** after regrouping its forces, the Hanoi government concentrated on two main tasks: preparations for the expected reunification elections and economic rehabilitation of the Northern zone. Almost all the Vietminh who withdrew to the North were members of the armed forces, since its civilian adherents were asked to remain in the South.

The Vietminh's unwavering commitment to elections was initially expressed by Premier Pham Van Dong at the final meeting of the Geneva Conference on July 22, 1954:

> A big step has been made. It remains to take other steps. We will have to reestablish lasting and durable peace in Indochina by a settlement of political issues, first among which is the accomplishment of the national unity of our people through elections. . . .
>
> The conference has set up the date for our unity. We shall achieve it just as we have won the war. No force in the world, internal or external, can make us deviate from our path to unity through peace and democracy. This will be the consummation of our national independence. . . .[34]

Thereafter public statements by Ho Chi Minh and other leaders repeatedly reiterated this commitment.[35] It was emphasized that peaceful political struggle was now to supersede the nine years of fighting. Broadcasts to the South stressed that violence should be avoided: "It [the political struggle] . . . demands that our people avoid every provocation and use peaceful measures to win democracy, freedom . . . [and to bring about] general elections to unify our country." [36]

Initially Ho ordered an electoral effort to be conducted throughout the whole of the country aimed at "winning support in all levels of the population with a view to winning the general elections for a united Vietnam." [37] In September 1955, with Hanoi's establishment of the Vietnam Fatherland Front, a program was spelled out in considerable detail for consultations and elections that would lead to a reunification of Vietnam and provide for considerable autonomy of the two regroupment zones.*

Activities of Vietminh political workers in the South confirmed Hanoi's commitment to reunification through elections. The Vietminh was reported to be "working hard in the South to consolidate its influence," [38] and political workers "intensified their activity" as Vietminh military forces withdrew, with the Vietminh "plainly preparing to win the national elections scheduled . . . for 1956." [39] In March 1955, *New York Times* correspondent C. L. Sulzberger reported that Vietminh campaigners were active in the South "lining up votes." [40] Active interest in elections came also from groups in the South with no manifest connection with the Vietminh. One such organization, called the "Movement for the Defense of Peace and the Geneva Accords," organized demonstrations in favor of the Geneva Accords as early as August 1954. †

On June 6, 1955, Premier Pham Van Dong announced

---

* The platform of the Fatherland Front provided that, following extensive consultations among all social and political groups, "free general elections, organized on the principal of universal, equal and secret ballot," were to be held for a National Assembly. There was to be no attempt "by either side to annex or incorporate the other," and the two regroupment zones were to retain considerable autonomy. Allowances were to be made for differences between the two zones: "Taking into account the different situation in the two zones, there will be set up in each zone a People's Council and an administrative body provided with wide powers. These organs have the right to promulgate local laws consistent with the characteristics of the zone concerned and not at variance with common national laws." The platform called for the immediate restoration of normal economic, cultural, and social relations between the two zones and for negotiations for the gradual integration of the armed forces. *Viet-Nam Fatherland Front and the Struggle for National Unity* (Hanoi: Foreign Languages Publishing House, 1956), pp. 16–26.

† Many leaders of this organization were promptly arrested by

that, as provided by Geneva, Hanoi stood ready to join pre-liminary discussions on the preparations for national elections with "the competent representative authorities" from the South. His government, the Premier said, wanted "free general elections throughout the whole territory of Vietnam" with guarantees of "freedom" of electioneering "for all political parties, organizations and individuals." [41] On July 19 he wrote to Diem pointing out that the preliminary discussions were supposed to begin in accordance with the Geneva Agreements' provisions on the elections.[42]

The Vietminh also sought international support for the elections. In his mission to India in April 1955, Pham Van Dong solicited Prime Minister Nehru's backing in enlisting support from the neutral nations at the forthcoming Afro-Asian Conference at Bandung. In the first paragraph of their joint communiqué Nehru and Pham Van Dong declared "their firm resolve to respect and seek to implement [the Geneva Agreements] both in their terms and spirit," and they "agreed on the importance of free elections and the achievement of unity of Vietnam as provided for by the Geneva Agreements." [43]

In addition to persevering in its efforts to bring Saigon into a preelection conference, Hanoi throughout 1955 appealed to the Co-Chairmen of the Geneva Conference.[44] Concurrently Ho's government prodded France to uphold her paramount responsibility under the armistice agreement. As early as January 1, 1955, when France assigned its political and economic powers to Diem, Premier Pham Van Dong declared, ". . . it was with you, the French, that we signed the Geneva Agreements, and it is up to you to see that they are respected." [45] Some French political leaders acknowledged with no little embarrassment this responsibility [46] but blamed their predicament on American pressure, which had obliged France

---

Diem. Nguyen Huu Tho, its Vice-Chairman, who was later to become the President of the National Liberation Front, spent the next six years under arrest.

to renege on her solemn Geneva commitment. The French Minister of Foreign Affairs stated, on February 23, 1956:

> We are not entirely masters of the situation. The Geneva Accords on the one hand and the pressure of our allies on the other creates a very complex juridical situation. . . . You ask me what will be our position after the reckoning [*l'écheance*] of July 1956 provided by the Geneva Accords. The position in principle is clear: France is the guarantor of the Geneva Accords. . . . But we do not have the means alone of making them respected.[47]

In April 1956, ten days after France had served official notice to the Co-Chairmen of the Geneva Conference of her decision to disengage from South Vietnam,[48] an editorial in *Le Monde,* Paris' most influential newspaper, asked: "But who will assume in our place the obligations undertaken at Geneva. . . . People will long discuss this French withdrawal, abandoning responsibilities which it no longer has the means of honoring."[49]

On May 8, 1956, the Co-Chairmen of the Geneva Conference invited both South and North Vietnam to transmit "their views about the time required for the opening of consultations on the organization of nation-wide elections in Viet-Nam and the time required for the holding of elections as a means of achieving the unification of Viet-Nam."[50] The Hanoi government promptly responded three days later by sending a letter to Diem in which it requested the immediate commencement of consultations.[51] On June 4 it replied directly to the Co-Chairmen indicating that its letter to the Saigon government had remained unanswered and asking the Co-Chairmen to take whatever steps were necessary to bring about a consultative conference between the North and South. It further declared that if the South continued to reject the holding of consultations and general elections it would request the Co-Chairmen to convene a new Geneva Conference. In early August, Premier Pham Van Dong again wrote to the Co-Chairmen, repeating

North Vietnam's request that they convene a new Geneva Conference.[52] In view of this, it is difficult to understand why, almost a decade later, the Assistant Secretary of State for Far Eastern Affairs should state to the American public that, ". . . when the issue arose concretely in 1956, the regime in Hanoi . . . made no effort to respond to the call of the Soviet Union and Great Britain." [53]

During the second half of 1956, the Hanoi government persisted in its attempts to arrange for the conference on elections with Diem. But these efforts were to no avail, and they elicited little effective backing from Britain, China, or the Soviet Union,[54] and none, of course, from Saigon. Despite continuing rebuffs, in June 1957 Pham Van Dong wrote again to the Geneva Conference Co-Chairmen, calling on them to take steps to facilitate the holdings of elections. And, in July 1957, March and December 1958, July 1959, and July 1960, he sent notes to Diem urging the convening of a consultative conference to discuss reunification elections.[55] Diem remained steadfastly opposed, and Moscow and Peking confined their backing to little more than moral platitudes.

5 : **The North's desperate need** to restore her devastated economy made the resumption of trading relations with the South of paramount importance to Hanoi. The two halves of Vietnam had always been closely integrated economically, with the overpopulated North heavily dependent on the South's surplus rice. In return for coal and light manufactures the North had in previous years imported some 250,000 tons of southern rice. The South's population of less than 14 million produced 60 per cent of the country's rice, while the Northerners had to feed an estimated population of nearly 16 million from less than 5 million acres of arable land.

Thus, while trying to arrange for the preelection consultations, Hanoi also attempted to resume normal relations with the South, at least on a basis similar to that of relations between East and West Germany.[56] It declared its willingness to ease restrictions on the sending of mail and the conduct of business enterprises and other exchange activities, as well as to help "the population in the two zones in all economic, cultural, and social exchanges advantageous for the restoration of the normal life of the people." [57] However, as with elections, Saigon refused even to discuss the matter.

Hanoi was thereby forced into greater dependence on external trade and economic aid for survival. Destruction from the years of war had hit the North harder than the South. Faced with an immediate and severe food shortage, the North was in critical need of economic assistance. As a stop-gap relief measure the Soviet Union promptly dispatched 150,000 tons of rice, which it had obtained from Burma, while Communist China provided other temporary economic relief. In the summer of 1955, Ho Chi Minh on a visit to Peking and Moscow secured additional and more substantial economic aid from both powers. He negotiated an aid and friendship treaty with China that promised his government about $200 million for factories and for technicians and equipment to restore railroads, air fields, and roads.[58] From the U.S.S.R. he obtained about $150 million in grants and credits for economic development, including equipping of the Hanoi engineering plant.

While of generous proportions this economic and technical assistance from the other communist states could not compensate for the reconstruction of war damage and the loss of Southern rice imports. The socialist state envisaged by Ho and his lieutenants had to be established in a predominantly agricultural country whose domestic capital for rehabilitation and industrialization could only be derived from forced savings in the agrarian sphere. To achieve such savings, Ho relied primarily on agrarian reorganization. He initially borrowed from Chinese experience in this regard and precipitously inaugurated a radical system of farming and ownership that was quite unsuited to Vietnamese conditions. In several provinces agrarian reorganization sparked widespread discontent, since it often called for dispossession and repression of landlords whose plots were often scarcely sufficient to provide a living for themselves and their families. Hastily trained political cadres were put in command of this "reform" and were over-zealous in their interpretation of the agrarian laws. In the resultant confusion, "middle" and "rich" peasants frequently were classified erroneously as landlords and indiscriminately brought to trial and condemned.[59] Many of them were killed. Peasant resentment erupted into full-fledged uprisings in the fall of 1956, and the repression of the rebellion in at least one province required the use of the armed forces. These uprisings discredited the agrarian policies that had been adapted from Chinese models and promoted by Truong Chinh, the Party Secretary-General. As a consequence, both he and the Minister of Agriculture were forced to resign. Ho Chi Minh assumed the position of Secretary-General until 1961 [60] and personally took charge of the agricultural program.[61] A more moderate system of agrarian reorganization that accorded better with Vietnamese conditions was then introduced, and at the same time it helped win back the peasants' allegiance to the central government.[62]

Hanoi received another grave setback in late 1956, when it granted almost unfettered freedom of the press. As with the highly-publicized "Hundred Flowers Movement" in China, this liberalization resulted in more criticism of the regime than Vietminh leaders felt could be tolerated, and, as in China, the period of press freedom gave way again to one of tight censorship such as normally prevails under communist governments.

In general, however, and with increasing regularity after these two experiences, Ho's leadership evidenced a pragmatic eclecticism in its borrowing from the experience of other communist countries. The government cautiously adapted features from communist systems abroad, evidencing a nondoctrinaire selectivity in its policies that gave them a distinctively Vietnamese cast.[63]

From mid-1956, when Ho could no longer hope for reunification elections in the near future, Hanoi turned inward, more and more preoccupied with completion of the North's economic rehabilitation and the long struggle to establish a viable socialist state. Though not abandoned, efforts to arrange consultations with Diem concerning elections now inevitably took second priority. While buckling down to solving its internal problems, Hanoi began to emphasize that the struggle for peaceful reunification would be far longer and more arduous than anticipated at Geneva. In view of this, Ho in a letter of June 19, 1956, to Southern cadres regrouped in the North, undertook to explain the shift in priorities that this situation dictated:

> Our policy is: to consolidate the North and to keep in mind the South. To build a good house we must build a good foundation. . . . The North is the foundation, the root of the struggle for complete national liberation and the reunification of the country. That is why everything we are doing in the North is aimed at strengthening both the North and the South. Therefore, to work here is the same as struggling in the South, to struggle for the South and the whole of Vietnam.[64]

Later events were to indicate that this changed order of priorities was not altogether welcome either to those regrouped Southern cadres or to political adherents of the Vietminh in the South.

In April of 1958 the Hanoi government launched a modest Three-Year Plan (1958–60),[65] which singled out "agricultural production, with a view to solving the food problem" for special concern.[66] Concurrently the Plan would lay the foundation for a future program of rapid industrialization. Since foreign aid was considered essential in that program Ho actively solicited funds from his communist allies. As a result, during this period the Soviet Union and communist states in Eastern Europe provided grants and credits totaling the equivalent of $159 million, and Communist China gave a total of $100 million.[67]

According to Premier Pham Van Dong, "the Three-Year

Plan must take fully into account the political tasks and ensure, in two to three years' time, the basic completion of socialist transformation of the individual economic sector and of the private capitalist sector." [68] The emphasis given to the plan reinforced the necessity of postponing active pursuit of plans for reunification—particularly any that might risk involvement in war. Perhaps to placate restive Southern Vietminh who felt abandoned by the failure to hold elections, the plan was described as taking the North "a step further forward in the transition period, making of the North a still firmer base for the struggle to reunify the country." [69] But in fact, of course, this announcement must have conveyed to these Southern Vietminh veterans the cheerless message that the Diem regime had been given a further reprieve before Hanoi would be willing to pursue policies involving a more militant approach to the goal of reunification.

The Three-Year Plan was implemented slowly and cautiously in the years up to 1960. One probable reason for this caution was that the Democratic Republic of Vietnam (DRV) had profited from mistakes made in China during the abortive "great leap forward" there, as well as from Hanoi's own blunders in its earlier agrarian programs. Despite the official commitment to the collectivization of agriculture, progress towards this goal was slow. Not until April 1963 could the government report that as many as 87.7 per cent of the peasant households had joined even "elementary-level" collectives, and only 36.8 per cent were by then organized into advanced, "fully socialized" collectives. [70] Nationalization of industries proceeded more briskly, but was not yet fully completed by 1960. Hanoi Radio reported that the proportion of the state-owned sector in the total industrial output of the North had then reached 90 per cent.

The pattern of communism emerging in North Vietnam in the five years after the Geneva Conference had, after many false starts, come to reflect Vietnamese realities fairly well. The government, while highly authoritarian and sometimes harsh, had become reasonably effective. Even in the awkward setting of the Sino-Soviet dispute in which Peking and Moscow vied for its allegiance, Hanoi maintained an essentially independent course. Standing sometimes closer to Moscow, sometimes to Peking it avoided irrevocable commitments to either. Despite a great need for Soviet and Chinese assistance, the DRV, Bernard Fall observes, appeared determined not to become overly dependent on foreign aid. He notes that her "desire to avoid a new 'colonialism' (particularly by the ever-present Chinese 'Big Brother')" was illustrated by the diminishing share that foreign aid represented in her budget—a drop that he reports to have been from 65.3 per cent in 1955 and 60.8 per cent in 1957 to 21 per cent by 1960.[71]

Although partition had left the North with a weaker economic base than the South, by 1960 the Northern government had become far less dependent upon outside economic assistance than had Saigon. American assistance remained as vital for South Vietnam's survival in 1960 as it had been in 1955 (and as it was to be in 1966). A withdrawal of American economic assistance would have removed the essential foundation of the state, and it would have collapsed. Loss of Soviet and Chinese aid would have crippled Hanoi's industrialization program and necessitated a more severe austerity, but the North Vietnamese state could still have stood.

Notes to Chapter IV

1. See Appendix 4 for full text of Eisenhower's letter. It was delivered to Diem on October 23, 1954.

2. Senator Mike Mansfield, Senate Committee on Foreign Relations, Report in Congress, *Congressional Record*, Vol. 100, Pt. 12 (Washington: U.S. Government Printing Office, December 1, 1954), p. 16252.

3. *New York Times*, November 18, 1954.

4. *Ibid.*, November 17, 1954.

5. Brian Crozier, "The Diem Regime in Southern Vietnam," *Far Eastern Survey*, Vol. 24, No. 4, April 1955, p. 51.

6. Peter Schmidt, "Free Indo-China Fights Against Time," *Commentary*, January 1955, pp. 18–29.

7. In April 1955, the strength of these groups was estimated at: Cao Dai, 15,000–20,000; Hoa Hao, 10,000–15,000; Binh Xuyen, 2,000–2,500. *New York Times,* April 21, 1955.

8. Bernard B. Fall, *The Two Viet-Nams* (New York: Praeger, 1964), p. 246. Of this amount Fall estimates that $2 million went to Cao Dai General Trinh Minh Thé; $3.6 million, plus monthly payment for his troops to another Cao Dai, "general" Nguyen Thanh Phuong; and $3 million to the Hoa Hao military leader, Tran Van Soai. John Osborne concurs as to the figure of $3.6 million to General Nguyen Thanh Phuong and adds the "promise of further monthly payments for his troops and a sinecure command in the national army." Osborne, "The Tough Miracle Man of Vietnam," *Life,* May 13, 1957. Joseph Alsop, reporting on the same phenomena, estimates a lesser amount for General Trinh Minh Thé of about 20 million piasters, or about $570,000 at the official rate of exchange. *New York Herald Tribune,* April 1, 1955.

9. U.S. Congress, *Congressional Record,* Vol. 101 (Washington: U.S. Government Printing Office, May 2, 1955), p. 5290.

10. Diem attempted to disassociate the new Republic of Vietnam from the French-sponsored Associate State of Vietnam by producing a new national flag and a new national anthem. His National Assembly was unable to think of any replacements for these, so both the anthem and the flag of South Vietnam remained the same as for the earlier French-controlled state, although a new hymn was introduced praising the leadership of Ngo Dinh Diem. Colonial law underwent only minor modifications and "Nationalists still carry legal disabilities for having been convicted during the colonial period for political crimes." Robert Scigliano, *South*

Vietnam: Nation Under Stress (Boston: Houghton Mifflin, 1963), p. 63.

11. B. S. N. Murti, *Vietnam Divided* (New York: Asia Publishing House, 1964), p. 87.

12. Donald Lancaster, *The Emancipation of French Indochina* (London: Oxford University Press, 1961), pp. 343–344.

13. Fall, *op. cit.,* pp. 153–154.

14. For a detailed treatment by an on-the-spot observer, see Murti, *op. cit.,* pp. 70–92. The fullest coverage of the refugee program is in the *First and Second Interim Reports of the International Commission for Supervision and Control in Vietnam,* Vietnam No. 1 (1955), Command 9461, and the *Third Interim Report of the International Commisison for Supervision and Control in Vietnam,* Vietnam No. 2 (1955), Command 9499 (both published by Her Majesty's Stationery Office, London, in May and June 1955 respectively).

15. Murti, *op. cit.,* p. 83.

16. Robert Scigliano notes that in 1960 Catholic authorities estimated "the Catholic population of North and South Vietnam at 1,807,784, with 793,000 members of the faith living above the 17th parallel." Scigliano, *op. cit.,* p. 53.

17. Fall, *op. cit.,* p. 154. Jean Lacouture reports that "some villages filled with refugees from the North formed a sort of belt surrounding Saigon; it was as though the beleaguered regime wanted to fortify its capital with an iron guard composed of those people most hostile to communism and most violently attached to militant Catholicism." Jean Lacouture, *Vietnam: Between Two Truces* (New York: Random House, 1966), p. 105.

18. Robert Shaplen, *The Lost Revolution* (New York: Harper and Row, 1965), p. 138.

19. Scigliano, *op. cit.,* pp. 162–164.

20. The Michigan State University advisory group's view of the Civil Guard as "a rural police organization" was opposed by Diem, who wished it to serve as a "supplement to the army." The issue was not resolved until 1959, when Washington agreed to Diem's terms. Responsibility for training the organization was then initially transferred to the U.S. economic-aid mission, and in December 1960 to the U.S. military mission. See Scigliano, *op. cit.,* pp. 164–165. For the fullest and most balanced account of Michigan State's role, see Robert Scigliano and Guy H. Fox, *Technical Assistance in Vietnam: The Michigan State University Experience* (New York: Praeger, 1965).

21. It was later revealed that the CIA had used the MSU advisory group as "cover for several of its agents." For a lively discussion of some of MSU's extracurricular activities in Vietnam, see Robert Scheer, *How the United States Got Involved in Viet-*

nam (Santa Barbara, Cal.: Center for the Study of Democratic Institutions, 1965), pp. 34–38; Warren Hinkle, Sol Stern, and Robert Scheer, "MSU—The University on the Make," *Ramparts,* Vol. 4, No. 12, April 1966, pp. 11–22.

22. Hollis W. Barber and the Research Staff of the Council on Foreign Relations, *The United States in World Affairs, 1955* (New York: Harper and Bros., 1957), p. 114.

23. Scigliano, *op. cit.,* p. 114, citing AID, *U.S. Foreign Assistance and Assistance from International Organizations, July 1, 1945–June 30, 1962,* revised (Washington, April 23, 1963), pp. 61, 69.

24. Milton C. Taylor, "South Viet-Nam: Lavish Aid, Limited Progress," *Pacific Affairs,* Vol. 34, No. 3, Fall 1961, p. 248.

25. John Osborne, "The Tough Miracle Man of Vietnam," *Life,* May 13, 1957.

26. Scigliano, *op. cit.,* p. 207.

27. Particularly active in this effort was Diem's close friend Wesley Fishel, a Michigan State professor who had become an advisor to Diem and who was a leader of the MSU advisory group in Vietnam. During this period the Luce publications, *Time* and *Life,* also took a generally highly partisan view in favor of Diem.

28. *Documents Relating to British Involvement in the Indo-China Conflict 1945–1965,* Command 2834 (London: Her Majesty's Stationery Office, 1965), p. 107.

29. *New York Times,* August 9, 1955.

30. *Documents Relating to British Involvement,* pp. 109–110.

31. *Department of State Bulletin* (Washington, July 11, 1955), p. 50. (Press release dated June 28, 1955.)

32. Brian Crozier, *op. cit.,* p. 56.

33. *The Times* (London), September 22, 1955.

34. Radio Moscow, July 22, 1954. See also Ho Chi Minh's statement of the same day in *New York Times,* July 26, 1954.

35. See Vietnam News Agency, July 25, 1954; November 1, 1954. See also Radio Hanoi, September 28, 1954; March 28, 1955; and April 29, 1956. For the fullest discussion of Hanoi's attitude towards elections, see Franklin B. Weinstein, *Vietnam's Unheld Elections* (Ithaca, N.Y.: Cornell Southeast Asia Program, 1966).

36. Vietnam News Agency, September 28, 1954.

37. *New York Times,* January 13, 1955.

38. *Ibid.,* September 29, 1954.

39. *Ibid.*

40. *Ibid.,* March 13, 1955. See also *ibid.,* June 2 and June 8, 1955.

41. *Ibid.,* June 7, 1955.

42. *Ibid.,* July 21, 1955.

43. *Times of India,* April 11, 1955.

44. See in particular "Message to the Co-Chairmen of the Geneva Conference on Indo-China from Premier Pham Van Dong, Hanoi, 17 August, 1955," *Documents Relating to British Involvement,* pp. 110–113; and his letter of February 14, 1956, in *ibid.,* pp. 115–117.

45. Philippe Devillers, "The Struggle for the Unification of Vietnam," in *North Vietnam Today,* ed. by P. J. Honey (New York: Praeger, 1962), p. 31.

46. See, for instance, statements of Cabinet ministers before the French Chamber of Deputies, as noted by Roger Pinto (legal consultant to the United Nations, 1949–56), in "La France et les Etats d'Indochine devant les Accords de Genève," *Revue Française de Science Politique,* Vol. 1, January-March, 1955.

47. *Le Monde,* February 25, 1956; *Journal Officiel de la République Française, Débats Parlementaires, Conseil de la République,* February 24, 1956 (Paris: 1956), p. 197. See also *The Times* (London), February 24, 1956, which reports Pineau as stating France's belief in the desirability of elections for the whole of Vietnam but noting that while France was supposed to guarantee these elections it could not enforce its desire. See also Crozier, *op. cit.,* p. 54.

48. *New York Times,* April 24, 1956.

49. *Le Monde,* April 12, 1956.

50. *Documents Relating to British Involvement,* p. 97.

51. Vietnam News Agency, May 12, 1956; *New York Times,* May 13, 1956.

52. Vietnam News Agency, June 8, 1956; *New York Times,* August 15, 1956.

53. Statement by William P. Bundy, May 13, 1965. *Department of State Bulletin* (Washington, June 7, 1965), p. 893.

54. In the cases of China and the Soviet Union, their policies toward North Vietnam continued to reflect the basic objectives which led them to support the compromise at the Geneva Conference. For a discussion see Chapter 3, pp. 45–46. For a comprehensive discussion of China's motivations during this period, see Chapter 11.

55. See *Economist,* June 29, 1957; *New York Times,* July 21, 1957; Vietnam News Agency, March 9, 1958; Vietnam Peace Committee, *Five Years of the Implementation of the Geneva Agreements in Vietnam,* (Hanoi: Foreign Languages Publishing House, 1959), p. 8; Devillers, *op. cit.,* p. 33.

56. As Jean Lacouture observes, Ho would like "to establish commercial relations permitting the North to buy rice from the South at a reasonable price." "Uncle Ho Defies Uncle Sam," *New York Times Magazine,* March 28, 1965.

57. Vietnam News Agency, February 7, 1955.

58. Roy Jumper and Marjory Normand, "Vietnam," in *Governments and Politics of Southeast Asia,* 2nd ed., ed. by George McT. Kahin (Ithaca, N.Y.: Cornell University Press, 1964), pp. 463–464.

59. *Ibid.*

60. Fall, *op. cit.,* p. 157.

61. "Report to the Seventh Session of the National Assembly on September 10, 1957," on Hanoi Radio, September 11, 1957. In assuming this responsibility in late 1956, Ho stated with regard to the uprisings: "As for the Catholic compatriots, the mistakes committed during the land reform have also infringed upon their religious freedom. The Party, Government and the Front clearly realize these mistakes and are determined to correct them." Hanoi Radio, November 20, 1956.

62. From September 1956 to November 1957 rural cadres embarked on a "mistakes correction" campaign that resulted in "the reinforcement of the organizations of the party administrations and mass organizations from the provincial down to the village levels." Vietnam News Agency, September 11, 1957. See also the article by V. P. Karamyshev in *Zemledeliye ("Agriculture"),* No. 10, 1957, pp. 78–86; Ho Chi Minh "Thirty Years of Activity of the Viet-Nam Workers' Party," *Selected Works* (Hanoi: Foreign Languages Publishing House, 1960–62), Vol. 4, pp. 430–445.

63. See Nguyen Ngoc Bich, "Vietnam—An Independent Viewpoint," in *North Vietnam Today,* ed. by P. J. Honey (New York: Praeger, 1962), pp. 128–134.

64. Ho, *Selected Works,* Vol. 4, p. 158.

65. For documents see *The Three-Year Plan to Develop and Transform Economy and to Develop Culture (1958–1960)* (Hanoi: Foreign Languages Publishing House, 1959).

66. Statement by Nguyen Duy Trinh in *ibid.,* p. 37. Despite this emphasis the overall proportion of agricultural output in the national production of North Vietnam fell during these years. Using 1955 as a base of 100, agricultural production rose from 141 in 1958 to only 147 in 1961. *World Marxist Review,* Vol. 6, No. 8, Supplement, August 1963.

67. William Kaye, "A Bowl of Rice Divided," *The China Quarterly,* No. 9, January–March 1962, p. 92.

68. *World Marxist Review,* Vol. 3, No. 11, November 1960, p. 29.

69. *Ibid.,* pp. 30–31. The Vietminh would, of course, deny that the struggle had ever been interrupted and thus needed to be "resumed." According to Pham Van Dong on September 2, 1960, "Rivers may run dry, mountains wear away, but our entire people's will for reunification will never falter." Quoted in Quang Loi,

Growing Oppression, Growing Violence (Hanoi: Foreign Languages Publishing House, 1961), p. 132.

70. See Normand and Jumper, *op. cit.,* p. 502. The first stage consists of organizing low-level or elementary agricultural-producers' cooperatives into which peasants sink their land as well as animals but technically keep title to their property and are paid dividends commensurate with the amount of land contributed to the cooperative. When they are functioning effectively, small-scale cooperatives are then enlarged but remain "semisocialist" in status. They are finally incorporated into higher or advanced cooperatives that own all property directly and pay their members on the basis of work units performed.

71. Fall, *op. cit.,* p. 177. He gives a figure of 19.9 per cent for 1961.

CHAPTER V

The Origins of the Civil War

1: **Despite Diem's unexpected initial success** in establishing his rule in the South, he soon alienated important elements of the South Vietnamese population through the repressive measures he introduced. Beginning as early as mid-1955, but particularly after the French had left, Diem moved to suppress the Vietminh. Directly contrary to the Geneva provisions against political reprisal,* he carried out acts of retaliation on a wholesale basis, not only against actual communist and non-communist members of the Vietminh, but also against most of its known followers. This meant that nearly all Vietnamese who had actively opposed French rule were now declared enemies of Diem's State of Vietnam.

In mid-1955 Diem launched an Anti-Communist Denunciation Campaign, in which his government's Department of Information and Youth organized mass meetings of the population to inform against Vietminh members and sympathizers.[1] By May 1956 the head of this campaign announced that in the previous ten months more than 94,000 former communist cadres had "rallied to the government" and that an additional 5,613 other cadres had surrendered.[2] There is no telling how many of these were communists or members of the Vietminh

---

* The Geneva-created International Control Commission proved unable to overcome the obstacles set in its path by Diem, causing it to declare in September 1956: "While the Commission has experienced difficulty in North Vietnam, the major part of its difficulties has arisen in South Vietnam." *Sixth Interim Report of the International Commission for Supervision and Control in Vietnam,* Vietnam No. 6 (1957), Command 31 (London: Her Majesty's Stationery Office, 1957), p. 30.

and how many were simply considered politically unreliable by Diem's government.

Nor is it possible to estimate the numbers jailed, executed, or sent to so-called "reeducation camps." As usual Saigon's "statistics" tell only part of the story, but even so it is a grim one. Around May of 1956, for example, the Secretary of State for Information admitted that between 15,000 and 20,000 communists and active sympathizers had been detained in political-reeducation centers since 1954.[3] According to a document published by the Ministry of Information at the end of 1960 a total of 48,250 had been jailed between 1954 and 1960.[4] There is reason to believe that these official figures are low;[5] Philippe Devillers, for example, has estimated that about 50,000 were in jail at the end of 1956.[6] Diem used this anticommunist purge as a pretext to strike at foes all across the political spectrum and, as P. J. Honey observed on the basis of talks with former inmates of the reeducation camps, ". . . the consensus of the opinions expressed by these people is that . . . the majority of detainees are neither Communist nor pro-Communists."[7] By the end of 1956, an analyst writing in *Foreign Affairs* concluded:

> South Viet Nam is today a quasi-police state characterized by arbitrary arrests and imprisonment, strict censorship of the press and the absence of an effective political opposition. . . . All the techniques of political and psychological warfare, as well as pacification campaigns involving extensive military operations, have been brought to bear against the underground.[8]

Under Diem's Ordinance No. 6 of January 1956 the Saigon government was given virtually a free hand to eliminate all opposition. Until order and security were fully restored, anyone considered as a danger "to the defense of the state and public order" was to be placed under house arrest or imprisoned. The resulting situation was well described in the May 13, 1957, issue of *Life,* which, while expressing considerable enthusiasm for Diem, stated:

Behind a facade of photographs, flags and slogans there is a grim structure of decrees, political prisons, concentration camps, milder "re-education centers," secret police. Presidential "Ordinance No. 6" signed and issued by Diem in January, 1956, provides that "individuals considered dangerous to national defense and common security" may be confined by executive order in "a concentration camp." . . . Only known or suspected Communists who have threatened or violated public security since July, 1954, are supposed to be arrested and "re-educated" under these decrees. But many non-Communists have also been detained. The whole machinery of security has been used to discourage active opposition of any kind from any source.

These measures were continued through 1958, and at the beginning of 1959 Diem intensified and expanded the scope of his repression. Indicative of the scale of this was the report at the end of February of the Information Chief of the province of An Xuyen. A five-week campaign in that one province, he stated, had resulted in the surrender of 8,125 communist agents and the "denunciation" of 9,806 other agents, and 29,978 "sympathizers." [9]

The culmination of this campaign came with Law 10/59 of May 6, 1959, which served to legalize the long-established patterns of suppression. This law also initiated a system of special military courts that, within three days of a charge, were to sentence to death "whoever commits or attempts to commit . . . crimes with the aim of sabotage, or of infringing upon the security of the State" (Article 1) as well as "whoever belongs to an organization designed to help to prepare or to perpetrate [these] crimes" (Article 3).[10] Even more comprehensive was the provision of Article 11 that gave these new courts jurisdiction over crimes of espionage and treason determined by Ordinance No. 47 of August 21, 1956, and "crimes of speculation and sabotage of the economy and finances of the States," as defined by Ordinance No. 61 dated October 3, 1955. Ordinance No. 47 had made it a capital offense to work with any organization designated as "Communist." Ordinance No. 61 prescribed death for anyone "who intentionally proclaims or spreads by any means unauthorized news about prices, or rumors contrary to the truth, or distorts the truth concerning the present or future situation of markets in the country or abroad, susceptible of provoking economic or financial perturbations in the country." Thus, the special military courts were granted almost unlimited latitude, and the defendants brought before them had no right of appeal against their decisions.[11]

The agrarian programs that Diem introduced between 1956 and 1958 did nothing to counter the resentment engendered by his dictatorial acts and were anything but effective in attracting peasant allegiance. Their impact can be appreciated only by recalling that the new "land reform" was carried out largely in areas that the Vietminh had administered for many years. Prior to Geneva, the Vietminh, according to French experts, had ruled between 60 and 90 per cent of all southern villages apart from those where the Cao Dai and Hoa Hao were dominant.[12] The strength of the Vietminh's following derived in significant degree from the popularity of their agrarian policies under which lands abandoned by absentee French and Vietnamese landlords were simply turned over gratis to the cultivators. After visiting a Vietminh-administered area in December 1954, shortly before the withdrawal of their military forces, an influential American columnist reported:

It was difficult for me, as it is for any Westerner, to conceive of a Communist government's genuinely "serving the people." I could hardly imagine a Communist government that was also a popular government and almost a democratic government. But this was just the sort of government the palm-hut state actually was while the struggle with the French continued. The Viet Minh could not possibly have carried on the resistance for one year, let alone nine years, without the people's strong, united support.[13]

Southerners did not forget that it was this Vietminh regime that had driven out the French and had also divided up the estates of landlords for the peasants' benefit.

Diem's approach to the peasantry stood in striking contrast to that of the Vietminh and later provided insurgent groups with a major issue by which to advance their cause. Several aspects of the agrarian program introduced by Saigon were certain to antagonize that large part of the peasantry that had benefited from the Vietminh's land policies; other aspects, though looking moderately attractive on paper, were carried through in a way that inevitably alienated most of the peasantry.

Large numbers of peasant tenants were suddenly obliged to pay rent to landlords who, during the nine years of the colonial war, had sat safely in Saigon under French protection. Having come to regard the lands they were tilling as their own, these peasants were hardly overjoyed when Diem's officials not only collected taxes from them but also demanded rent in behalf of these landlords. Saigon's decree that rents be reduced to 25 per cent of crop value held little attraction for peasants who had paid no rent at all under the Vietminh. Landlords, in fact, frequently did charge more than the prescribed 25 per cent,[14] and "agrarian" courts established to settle landlord-tenant disputes soon came under the domination of landlords and officials friendly to them, to the obvious disadvantage of the ordinary peasants.[15] As John Montgomery has observed:

> . . . the Vietnamese government, not wishing to disturb the strong landowning classes, resisted the proposed transfers of land and the sharper rent controls.[16]

Referring to the report of J. Price Gittinger, a principal American agricultural advisor, he continued:

> "Government officials, beginning with the Minister for Agrarian Reform, have divided loyalties, being themselves landholders." The Minister of Agrarian Reform was reported as not having "signed leases with his tenants as provided for by land reform decrees and he is most certainly not interested in land distribution which would divest him of much of his property."[17]

Furthermore, by decrees in June and August 1956, Diem abolished the elected village councils, replacing them with officials appointed by his provincial governors upon approval by the Ministry of Interior in Saigon. At one stroke the autonomy that South Vietnam's 2,560 villages had enjoyed even under the French rule was swept away, and a centralized administration, usually out of touch with their problems,[18] was substituted.

Moreover, this direct impingement of Saigon's authority appeared the more oppressive because so many of the new provincial heads and local officials were outsiders, a large proportion being recently-arrived Northern Catholics. Without roots in the South, such men were rendered sufficiently dependent upon Diem for him to be reasonably assured of their personal loyalty to him as well as of their anticommunism. However, the lack of Southern experience among the new officials left them with little understanding of the particular social and economic problems of the heavily Buddhist rural South. Most of the government's information and civic-action agents were also Northerners, "strangers who spoke a different dialect and practiced a different religion." [19] Thus throughout much of the South, the Diem regime "assumed the aspect of a carpetbag government in its disproportion of Northerners and Centralists, in the ease of access to high positions granted officials from the Hué area, and in its Catholicism." [20]

Frequently Diem's government ousted able and popular district and village officials with strong local ties from their positions in the rural areas because they had served the Vietminh administration. They were replaced by outsiders who, in addition to lacking legitimacy in terms of customary local criteria, were all too often both oppressive and corrupt. Charged with the responsibility for carrying out Diem's agrarian policies, they also presided over denunciation campaigns [21] and answered for these to the Saigon government rather than to the old village councils. It was inevitable that these newly appointed village chiefs would soon become the focal point for peasant resentment. As a consequence, even prior to any resumption of militant tactics by the Southern Vietminh a considerable number of them were murdered. And, in later years when the resurrected Vietminh forces did become active, they recognized that a campaign of assassination of unpopular village chiefs could provide a means of building peasant support.[22] Thus, Diem's policies divided his officials from the people and created explosive issues that his adversaries could easily exploit.

When, at American urging, Diem finally introduced a program of land redistribution, this was both in scope and actual practice far less than U.S. officials had proposed. The funds allocated for it were grossly inadequate, and a considerable part was diverted for the financing of security programs.[23] In its implementation, the program was so emasculated and rigged in favor of the landlords that it tended to inflame rather than diminish the peasant's hostility. Diem never appreciated that a pacification and security program could not simply be imposed from the top down and that its success depended upon the loyalty and active participation of the peasantry.

Under continued American prodding, Saigon's "agrarian-reform" program finally got underway in 1958. It was restricted to rice-growing lands, but even here landlords were allowed to retain up to 284 acres—a tremendous area for land so fertile and remunerative. Even absentee owners, despite American advice, were permitted to keep rice lands up to this maximum.[24] Where "excess" properties were actually relinquished, the peasant did not receive the redistributed land as a grant. The state insisted that the land be paid for in full, and the peasant actually got title to it only after paying the final installment. Since the Vietminh had simply given them ownership of plots belonging to absentee landlords, the peasants naturally resented having to purchase what they already regarded as their own.[25]

As late as 1962 only about a quarter of the land classified as suitable for expropriation and purchase had reached the landless peasants.[26] Slightly more than a million acres were actually transferred, but of this amount approximately 65 per cent had been French owned, with the French government itself lending Diem's administration the money required for purchase. Despite the persistence with which the U.S. urged agrarian reform on Diem, between 1955 and 1960 it spent on agriculture only 1.4 per cent ($15 million) of its total aid to Saigon.

2: While failing to build popular support in the South among the ethnic Vietnamese, Diem's officials also pursued measures that soon antagonized a large part of the Montagnard population of the interior. In contrast to Hanoi's policy of allowing the Montagnards in its territory a significant degree of administrative and cultural autonomy, Diem sought to impose Vietnamese culture on these groups * and denied them even the measure of independence they had possessed under French rule. In March of 1955, the central highland areas, which the French had administered separately, lost their autonomy and were incorporated into the South Vietnamese state. This paved the way for a program of population transfer whereby, beginning in 1957, approximately 210,000 ethnic Vietnamese from the coast were regrouped in fortified villages on lands that the Montagnards had always regarded as their

---

* The Vietminh has long been seriously concerned about the loyalty of the ethnic minorities, living as they do in the strategically and economically important regions bordering on Laos and China. Autonomous zones for the Montagnards were established in 1955 and 1956 in 35,500 square miles of North Vietnam (well over half of the country's total territory). These include the Thai-Meo area, containing 330,000 people and the Viet Bac area with 800,000 inhabitants. Although under central control, these areas have run much of their local affairs and have significant scope to develop culturally and economically in conformity with local conditions. The government has helped standardize scripts for their national languages and has established a secondary school in Hanoi with courses in the various tribal languages. See Roy Jumper and Marjorie Weiner Normand, "Vietnam," in *Governments and Politics of Southeast Asia,* 2nd ed., ed. by George McT. Kahin (Ithaca, N.Y.: Cornell University Press, 1964), pp. 499–501.

own and as necessary to their support.* Two years later this was followed by a program of regrouping and consolidating various Montagnard tribal communities.[27]

Diem's policy of annexing Montagnard lands sharply contrasted with the policy the Vietminh had previously pursued in the South, wherein they had turned back to the tribal groups French-owned estates. Moreover, Saigon officials continued to reflect the traditional Vietnamese air of superiority toward the Montagnards, referring to them as "savage" ("*moi*") and attempting to assimilate these "inferior" peoples into Vietnamese culture. The Montagnard peoples in the South, unlike those in the North, were not permitted to attend schools using their own languages. Where schools were available to them they were obliged to follow curricula taught in Vietnamese. Saigon's policies, coupled with the arrogance of its agents, antagonized the Montagnards to such an extent that their widespread intransigence against Saigon's authority ultimately erupted in rebellion, early flickers of which were already visible in 1959.

3: **In the face of Diem's coercive actions** and unpopular policies, it is remarkable that a guerrilla-type insurrection by the Southern adherents of the Vietminh did not break out earlier. Two important factors contributed to their continuing

---

* The impingement of these Vietnamese settlements on traditional tribal lands became one of the major grievances of the Montagnards against the Saigon government. In 1964, at the time of their rebellion, the five-point demand of FULRO (a Montagnard autonomy movement) stated: "Solutions must be found for the resettlement villages which have infringed upon the land of the highland people, and for the highland villages which are surrounded by military camps and consequently do not have enough land to make a living." It is interesting that one of the other five points dealt with education, stating: "Education must be in the highland languages at the primary level and in Vietnamese from high school on up." Brigadier General Vinh-Loc, *The Thing Called "Autonomy Movement" FULRO* (Pleiku-Banmethuot, 1965), pp. 57–58. (Translation from the Vietnamese.)

quiescence for so long after Saigon's 1956 repudiation of the armistice.

The first of these was the thoroughness and stringency of Diem's widespread repression, specifically his abrupt removal of a large proportion of the Southern Vietminh leaders to jail, to concentration camps, or to be shot. With startling rapidity, that major part of the rural population that the Vietminh had administered during the long struggle against France was bereft of those leaders who could have channeled and directed its mounting grievances. Thus, for several years militant reactions remained inchoate and sporadic, without effective guidance and coordination. Because Diem had so shattered the Vietminh's organization in the South and so successfully blocked its reintegration, considerable time was to elapse before its former followers could thrust up new leaders capable of responding sensitively and effectively to the smouldering rural discontent.

The other major factor that helped prolong the lull in the fighting was Hanoi's continuing unwillingness to encourage armed resistance to Diem's regime. By September 1960, when the Northern government at last publicly sanctioned the insurrection in the South, the strength and potential of that insurgency had become so manifest that if Hanoi had not proclaimed its approval it might well have lost any influence over the future course of events below the 17th parallel. But for long after the date stipulated for the reunification elections, the Hanoi government had consistently cautioned Southern supporters of the Vietminh against the use of violence and urged them to employ peaceful methods in working towards unification.

From the outset Ho Chi Minh appeared confident that the attempt to build a separate state in the South would fail. Even after it became clear that the U.S. had decided to underwrite Diem indefinitely, North Vietnamese leaders still apparently believed Diem's efforts would ultimately prove futile because of his progressive alienation of the population. Furthermore, they seemed to expect that his fall would open the way for a new regime in Saigon with a different outlook, one prepared to enter into negotiations with the North for a resumption of economic relations and an ultimate peaceful reunification.[28]

Moreover, by 1958 economic development of the North had temporarily superseded national reunification as Hanoi's most immediate goal. Its disposition to avoid any effort at reunification that might risk the outbreak of war was undoubtedly reinforced by its dependence upon the Soviet Union for the technological and economic assistance and machinery imports so essential to its development plans. With the Soviet Union embarked upon a policy of peaceful coexistence with the United States, Hanoi would have jeopardized her relations with Moscow by pursuing policies in the South likely to precipitate armed conflict with Saigon that might in turn lead to American involvement. When the deadline for the promised elections passed in July 1956, Hanoi Radio continued to counsel moderation and peaceful tactics to its Southern-based supporters.

For the next two years revolts against Diem emanated primarily from non-Vietminh quarters. There was persistent opposition from some Hoa Hao and Cao Dai groups. Bribes or threats had silenced most of the sects' leaders, and many of their troops had been merged into the Vietnamese army; but significant numbers of Cao Dai forces remained independent, and some four Hoa Hao battalions retained their autonomy until at least 1962 before finally being subdued.[29]

Another anti-Diemist force was the anticommunist Dai Viet party,[30] whose armed units remained in the field, particularly in Quang Tri province, for several years before being overcome. Its anti-Diem radio broadcasts (Voice of the Dai Viet National Liberation Troops)[31] lasted until at least mid-March of 1956, while some of its adherents engaged in clandestine political activity throughout the Diem period.*

---

* The Dai-Viet Dan-Chinh Dang was formed in the early 1940's and initially drew its strength from graduates of Hanoi University, who organized branches in Tonkin, Annam, and Cochin China. They were supported by some groups connected with the imperial court at Hué and by a number of young, Western-educated Viet-

In June 1957 another political group, calling itself the National Salvation Movement and vigorously opposed to Diem, was organized by anticommunist Vietnamese leaders in Paris. By October the movement had installed its own clandestine radio station in South Vietnam, and its broadcasts indicated that it spoke for armed insurgents then suffering pressure from Diem's military campaigns against them.[32] As was the case with the Dai Viet, their views combined strong anticommunism with unreserved antagonism for Diem.

Hanoi, however, persisted in its refusal to encourage its former adherents in the South to embark upon such militant action. Its attitude was underscored by its reaction during 1958 to the broadcasts of a clandestine radio in the South. Using the theme song of the former Vietminh resistance radio, the Voice of Nambo (Voice of the South), this new station identified itself as the Voice of the South Vietnam Liberation Front, employing the name in mid-1958, well over two years before Hanoi accorded official recognition to such an organization.* Although the consistent theme of these clandestine

---

namese, and in some areas the party was able to build up rural cadres. In Tonkin the party developed close connections with the Japanese in 1945, and in 1947 supported the French. Although some of the group supported Bao Dai, many refused to participate in his regime. The party firmly opposed Diem and went into underground opposition against his government. Following Diem's overthrow, its three regional leaders assumed positions of prominence in Saigon: Dang Van Sung is now editor of *Chinh-Luan;* Ha Thuc Ky was Minister of Interior in the first Khanh government; and Nguyen Ton Hoan was for a time Deputy Premier in Khanh's first government. In addition, a close adviser (though not actual member) of the party, Dr. Phan Huy Quat, served as Prime Minister during the spring of 1965.

* There are some other indications of the prior establishment of the Liberation Front. In speaking of a village in the South that he had studied intensively, the Yale anthropologist Gerald Hickey wrote that by 1958 it had "for the first time experienced the activities of a relatively new political movement—the Mat Tran Dan Toc Giai Phong Mien Nam Viet Nam (National Front for the Liberation of Vietnam), referred to by the South Vietnamese government as the

broadcasts was "struggle against oppression by the dictatorial American Diemists," [33] they were denounced by Hanoi as provocations by Saigon and American agents.* Whether or not this charge was correct, the North Vietnamese government felt obliged to answer the points raised by the broadcasts in detail, clearly regarding their line as a challenge to its established policies toward the South.

Every one of the numerous recorded Hanoi broadcasts dealing with the Front attacked it violently. As early as June 28, 1958, the Front was accused of "using their broadcasts to distort Marxist-Leninist theories. They have . . . falsified the policies of the Vietnam Lao Dong [communist] party and DRVN [Hanoi] government." [34] Such Front statements as "the working class considers the bourgeois and petty bourgeois class as enemies" and "classes must soon be eliminated" were denounced as an unjust representation of Hanoi's views and as "vilest slander and distortion of the truth." [35] Hanoi also sharply opposed the Front's advocacy of a radical, communist-

---

Viet Cong or Vietnamese Communists . . . and invariably called the Viet Minh by the villagers. In the vicinity of Khanh Hau the initial efforts of the Viet Cong were largely confined to anti-government propaganda." *Village in Vietnam* (New Haven: Yale University Press, 1964), p. 10.

General Nguyen Chanh Thi states that in March 1959 he was in command of an operation in Zone D against Hoa Hao, Cao Dai, and Binh Xuyen remnants that were working together with communist elements. His troops captured several flags which, he states, were exactly the same as those later used by the National Liberation Front. (Interview with one of the authors, Washington, October 5, 1966.)

* It is, of course, possible that Hanoi's claim that these broadcasts originated from an American or Diemist intelligence source was correct. During this period provocative intelligence operations relying upon clandestine radios seem to have been fairly widespread in Indochina, as apparently they still are. See, for instance, Radio Hué's allegation that Marshall Ky's government had set up a "fake revolutionary broadcasting station" for the purpose of making it appear that the Buddhists were sympathetic to communism. Hué Radio, May 20, 1966.

oriented program, including the Front's insistence that socialism in the South be striven for concurrently with the struggle
for national unification.[36] Its hostile reaction may well have
reflected its appreciation that a radical program would frighten
the urban middle class in the South and cause many of these
Southerners to oppose reunification with the North.*

Hanoi Radio also attacked the Voice of the South Vietnamese Liberation Front for not supporting "the urgent problems presented to our people," such as the convocation of a
consultative conference on elections as prescribed by Geneva,†
the establishment of commercial and postal relations between
North and South, and the reduction of military forces.[37] It
accused the Front's broadcasts of divisiveness and provocation—"maneuvers to divide the revolutionary forces and push
them prematurely into action." The tenor of Hanoi's statements revealed sharp anxiety that its overall strategy for reunification was being jeopardized by the militant tactics and
socially radical policies advocated by the Liberation Front
radio. §

---

* Thus a Hanoi broadcast on July 10, 1958 stated: " . . . the 'voice
of the South Vietnam liberation front' gives its listeners the impression that the revolutionaries of South Vietnam are trying to
wipe out the peasant class, the petit bourgeois, and the national
bourgeois, as well as the other forces of individual production
which form the classes that the enemies are to beat, and not the
American imperialists and the Ngo Dinh Diem clique. These words
seem to be revolutionary, but in reality they are not aimed at the
principal enemies of the revolution. That is why this radio causes
a listener who is not vigilant to be frightened, terrified about the
revolution, about socialism."

† The Front broadcast on September 2, 1958, did in fact state:
"We have also decided to intensify our demand that they [the
Saigon government] correctly apply the Geneva accords by opening a consultative conference with the northern government to
discuss national unification."

§ Possibly it was because of this danger that Hanoi reportedly sent
Le Duan, a prominent leader of the ruling Communist (Lao
Dong) Party, to make an extended trip to the South late in 1958.
George A. Carver, Jr., "The Faceless Viet Cong," *Foreign Affairs,*

The intensification of Diem's repression in 1959 and the excess of his wide-ranging military courts established under law 10/59 of May 6,* resulted in a commensurate reaction from the rural population. It was still difficult to ascertain which of the fitful and as yet small-scale insurgent actions in the rural South represented the continuing resistance of non-Vietminh rebels and which were indicative of the beginnings of a new insurgency. † Elements of both existed. Scattered forces of the Cao Dai, Hoa Hao, and the Dai Viet were active throughout this period. But apparently they were being joined by some former Southern Vietminh adherents, who had become too restive to abide any longer by Hanoi's injunctions against armed rebellion. During the second half of 1959 a marked upsurge in guerrilla action indicated that the ranks of the insurgents were swelling. While it is impossible to say how much of this increase was accounted for by former Vietminh adherents, they were now probably responsible for a growing proportion of the activity.

The insistence of former Southern Vietminh upon a program of armed struggle culminated in March 1960 with their "Declaration of the Resistance Veterans." [38] This landmark statement, though studiously ignored in official American accounts of the development of insurgency in the South, registered the

---

Vol. 44, No. 3, April 1966, p. 359. There is no evidence to support Mr. Carver's inference that Le Duan was sent south to speed up the pace of the revolt. All evidence points to the exact opposite. Himself a Southerner, Le Duan's mission may well have been calculated to counteract the effect of these broadcasts, which continued until at least mid-February 1959. Hanoi Radio, February 11, 1959, reported in *Vietnam Presse Bulletin d'Informations Confidentielles.*

* See above, p. 101.

† Thus, as late as April 1959, *New York Times* staff correspondent Tillman Durdin reported on the continuing existence of "fugitive remnants of the Binh Xuyen, Cao Dai, and Hoa Hao groups that rebelled against President Ngo Dinh Diem in 1955," and stated that it was "difficult to differentiate between actions of Communist and non-Communist agents," *New York Times,* April 13, 1959.

climax of these Southerners' frustrations and impatience with
Hanoi's long insistence upon a demonstrably fruitless struggle
on the political level alone.

In their declaration, these ex-Vietminh veterans demanded
a new approach. They justified their departure from Hanoi's
policy of peaceful struggle in the South as the inevitable result
of Diem's oppression. His actions had "forced the people into
legitimate self-defense," for, "if the people take up arms to
struggle against terror or to punish blood-thirsty traitors, no-
torious criminals, faithful valets of the American-Diemists, it
is only to defend themselves." [39] Reviewing their previous six
years of patient suffering, they called for "the rigorous and
integral application of the Geneva Accords, the fruit of immense sacrifice in human lives of all our people." Appealing to
"all classes, all social strata, all milieu to struggle" against
repression by the South Vietnamese authorities, the declaration
called upon the "Former Resistance Fighters and all of the
people of South Vietnam" to replace the Diem regime with a
broad coalition government and liberate South Vietnam "from
submission to America, eliminate all U.S. bases in South Vietnam, expel the American military advisers and not accept any
form of American interference in South Vietnam."

The bitter and militant frame of mind of the Southern veterans and their impatience with Hanoi's insistence on non-
violent policies must have been readily evident to Ho Chi
Minh's government. Jean Lacouture states that a Hanoi agent
attended the meeting of Resistance Veterans and reported
back that they represented a popular movement that sooner
or later would develop into a major armed struggle Hanoi
could not ignore. Emissaries sent south to test public opinion
after the Declaration were badly received, called cowards, and
asked "what are you waiting for to help us? If you don't do
anything, you Communists, we will rise up against you too." [40]

Even so, not until six months after the Southern Veterans
had taken matters into their own hands did Hanoi publicly
endorse their stand. Only at the Third Congress of the Vietnamese Lao Dong Party held in Hanoi from September 5–10,

1960, did the Northern leadership make it clear that it sanctioned formation of a United Front and approved a program for the violent overthrow of the Diem government.* The Congress resolved that the first of the two "strategic tasks" of the present stage of the Vietnamese revolution was still "to carry out the socialist revolution in the North." "Closely related" to it now, however, was the second task: "to liberate the South from the rule of the American imperialists and their henchmen [and] achieve national reunification and complete independence and freedom throughout the country." The socialist revolution in the North was to be regarded as "the most decisive task for the development of the whole Vietnamese revolution for the cause of national reunification," but the Southerners were now encouraged to take direct and militant action. The Resolution stated:

> In the completion of the national people's democratic revolution throughout the country, and the achievement of national reunification, our compatriots in the South have the task of directly overthrowing the rule of the American imperialists and their agents in order to liberate south Viet Nam. . . . The im-

---

* In none of the official statements of the Hanoi Government or the Lao Dong Party is it possible to find earlier evidence for Hanoi's encouragement of militant tactics by the Southerners until this meeting of September 1960. Even in 1959 in Northern press comment on this matter there appears to have been nothing approaching unequivocal support for such action. Probably the strongest appeared in the Hanoi newspaper *Nhan Dan* of May 15, 1959, when it stated: "Our people are determined to struggle with their traditional heroism and by all necessary forms and measures so as to achieve the goal of the revolution." At the same time, however, it defined this goal as compelling "the other side to carry out correctly the Geneva Agreements, to reestablish normal North-South relations and to hold consultations on general elections to reunify the country." The official communiqué of the Lao Dong Party Central Committee issued the previous day, did not even go so far as this. It gave the main task in achieving reunification as endeavoring "to consolidate the north and actively take it step by step towards socialism," their Southern compatriots being offered no more than "its heartfelt salute" for their suffering.

mediate task of the revolution in the South is to achieve the unity of the whole people, to fight resolutely against the aggressive and war-mongering U.S. imperialists, to overthrow the dictatorial ruling Ngo Dinh Diem clique, lackeys of the U.S. imperialists, to form a national democratic coalition government in south Viet Nam, to win national independence and . . . to achieve national reunification.[41]

To reach this objective in the South, Southerners were called upon

. . . to bring into being a broad National United Front directed against the U.S. and Diem and based on the worker-peasant alliance. This Front must rally all the patriotic classes and sections of the people, the majority and minority nationalities, all patriotic parties and religious groupings, together with all individuals inclined to oppose the U.S. and Diem.[42]

Only with the emergence of a successor to Diem's government would arrangements for reunification be worked out. The importance of building the North into a strong economic base antecedent to any reunification received added emphasis at this Third Party Congress by the launching of Hanoi's first five-year plan for economic development,[43] and the announcement of a major cutback in the country's defense budget in order to finance that development.*

---

* Hanoi's Minister of Defense, Vo Nguyen Giap, stated to the Congress: "Today, the economic construction in the North has become the central task of the Party. Therefore it is necessary to cut down defence budget, adequately reduce our army contingent so as to concentrate manpower and material in economic construction." *Third National Congress of the Viet Nam Workers' Party: Documents* (Hanoi: Foreign Languages Publishing House, n.d.), Vol. 3, p. 62. In commenting on Giap's statement, P. J. Honey observed: "This is a policy which is certainly based upon the Russian contention that war is not inevitable." With regard to the Congress as a whole, he stated: "Vietnam will follow the Russian policy of peaceful co-existence based on the possibility of avoiding war." P. J. Honey, "North Vietnam's Party Congress," *The China Quarterly,* No. 4, October–December 1960, pp. 69, 74.

4 : **In the meantime,** Southern reaction to Diem's dictatorship and repression spread beyond the confines of the countryside. In Saigon strong dissatisfaction was now being voiced in political and army circles. On April 26, 1960, a group of eighteen notables—ten of them former ministers [44]—took their fates in their hands and issued a public manifesto to Diem.[45] Their statement referred to "anti-democratic elections" and to "continuous arrests [that] fill the jails and prisons to the rafters," and it charged that "effective power" had been "concentrated in fact in the hands of an irresponsible member of the 'family' [Ngo Dinh Nhu, Diem's brother] from whom emanates all orders." All who signed the manifesto were subsequently arrested.

The army's discontent came to a head on November 11. Paratroop units, acting for other elements of the armed forces as well, encircled Diem's palace and called on him to rid himself of his family advisors and follow a political course more sensitive to the country's needs. After adroit stalling, Diem summoned loyal units, who overpowered the paratroops. Fearing Diem's reaction to this abortive revolt, a considerable number of civilian and military leaders went underground or fled the country. Opposition to Diem's government had spread widely through the country and penetrated Saigon itself. The force and momentum that it was gathering were so great that any organization wishing to channel it would need to act quickly. At the time it even seemed possible that opposition Saigon elements, either in the army or outside, might be able to capitalize on the widespread dissidence. Diem's fall appeared daily more imminent. Neither the Southern insurgents nor Hanoi could anticipate that in the face of the mounting opposition ranged against Diem the United States would react by bolstering him so unstintingly that he would be able to maintain himself in power for another three years.

5 : **On December 20, 1960,** a meeting of Southern dissidents was held somewhere in the South at which, according to subsequent reports, a National Liberation Front of South Vietnam was established.* Six weeks later Hanoi publicly announced this and indicated its endorsement of the organization.[46] At this meeting, the Front elaborated a ten-point program,[47] calling for the overthrow of the Saigon government and its replacement by "a broad national democratic coalition administration," and the election of "a new National Assembly through universal suffrage." Among its other points were the granting of "general amnesty to all political detainees," a wide range of social and economic reforms, including land reform and autonomy for minorities, and the ousting of U.S. military advisors.

The phraseology of the program suggested a considerable period of separate governance for the South before its reunification with the North. Reunification was to be "gradual" and by "peaceful means" through "negotiations and discussions." Prior to this, "the governments of the two zones" were to "negotiate and undertake not to spread propaganda to divide the peoples or in favor of war, not to use military force against each other." They would "carry out economic and cultural exchanges between the two zones" so as to "ensure for the people of both zones freedom of movement and trade, and the right of mutual visits and correspondence." Moreover, the program called for a foreign policy of "peace and neutrality" wherein South Vietnam would "refrain from joining any bloc or mili-

---

* It is not certain whether December 20, 1960, was the actual date of the organization's establishment or simply whether as of then it was accorded official recognition by Hanoi. It is somewhat puzzling that Hanoi took almost six weeks after the December 20 meeting to make public announcement of the Front's formation, references to its establishment having appeared somewhat earlier in Saigon and Phnom Penh. See *La Dépêche du Cambodge,* January 25, 1961, *Ngon Luan* (Saigon), January 20, 1961, and Saigon Radio, January 22, 1961.

tary alliance . . . with any country," and "establish diplomatic relations with all countries irrespective of political regime." This emphasis on gradualness of reunification and a separate and neutral foreign policy pending its consummation was not momentary and, as will be seen, was to become even stronger in the 1962 Program of the First Congress of the South Vietnam Liberation Front.[48]

In sum, the insurrection is Southern rooted; it arose at Southern initiative in response to Southern demands. The Liberation Front gave political articulation and leadership to the widespread reaction against the harshness and heavy-handedness of Diem's government. It gained drive under the stimulus of Southern Vietminh veterans who felt betrayed by the Geneva Conference and abandoned by Hanoi. After the withdrawal of their troops to the North these Southern Vietminh were left with no effective means for enforcing the political terms of the armistice—either the conducting of the elections or protection against reprisal. They were denied the promised opportunity to reassert their political ascendancy through elections and then savagely persecuted for their past political affiliations. Not surprisingly, they lost patience with the communist North and finally took matters into their own hands. Hanoi, despite its reluctance, was then obliged to sanction the Southerners' actions or risk forfeiting all chance of influence over the course of events in South Vietnam.

Contrary to U.S. policy assumptions, all available evidence shows that the revival of the civil war in the South in 1958 was undertaken by Southerners at their own—not Hanoi's—initiative. There is no evidence to assert, as does the U.S. "White Paper" of 1965, that "the Liberation Front for South Viet-Nam . . . was formed at Hanoi's order."[49] This assertion is merely a convenient assumption and is quite as devoid of actual foundation as is Secretary Rusk's dependent assumption that the civil war "could end literally in 24 hours . . . if these people in Hanoi should come to the conclusion that they are not going to try to seize Vietnam and Laos by force."[50]

The most knowledgeable noncommunist French specialists have long known all this,[51] but their views have been studiously ignored in Washington. And one does not have to rely on their writings to reach the inescapable conclusion that the Liberation Front is not "Hanoi's creation"; it has manifested independence and it is Southern.* Insurrectionary activity against the Saigon government began in the South under Southern leadership not as a consequence of any dictate from Hanoi, but contrary to Hanoi's injunctions. Abundant data have been available to Washington † to invalidate any argument that revival of the war in the South was precipitated by "aggression from the North." The Administration's admission of this would, however, undercut the very cornerstone of its justification of American military involvement in the South and escalation of the war against the North.

---

* The U.S. White Paper of 1965 states: "The Liberation Front is Hanoi's creation; it is neither independent nor southern, and what it seeks is not liberation but subjugation of the South." U.S. Department of State, *Aggression from the North: The Record of North Viet-Nam's Campaign to Conquer South Viet-Nam* (Washington: U.S. Government Printing Office, 1965), p. 20.

† There is a great deal of this data that spokesmen for the Administration's policies have chosen to ignore. An apparent disregard of much pertinent information has accompanied efforts to justify current Administration policy and previous mistakes. Distortions of the record are not confined to public addresses of government officials but are also to be found in the published writings of officials in the employ of government, who disguise the fact that they have any governmental connections.[52]

Notes to Chapter V

1. The Saigon government insisted that the words "Vietminh" and "Communist" be regarded as "synonyms." See its official pamphlet, *The Fight Against the Subversive Communist Activities in Vietnam,* (n.p, n.d.), p. 14. In mid-1957 Ellen J. Hammer observed: "To strip the D.R.V.N. [the Hanoi government] of its nationalistic associations in the public mind, the term 'Viet Minh' is no longer used officially in the south to describe the northern enemy; instead, the D.R.V.N. is publicly designated and denounced as Viet Cong or Communist Party." "Progress Report on Southern Viet Nam," *Pacific Affairs,* Vol. 30, No. 3, September 1957, p. 225.

2. Robert Scigliano, *South Vietnam: Nation Under Stress* (Boston: Houghton Mifflin, 1963), p. 168, quoting U.S. Operations Mission to Vietnam, *Saigon Daily News Round-Up,* May 14, 1956, p. 3.

3. See John Osborne, "The Tough Miracle Man of Vietnam," *Life,* May 13, 1957.

4. Georges Chaffard, *Indochine: dix ans d'indépendance* (Paris: Calmann-Lévy, 1964), pp. 168, 169.

5. See Scigliano, *op. cit.,* p. 171.

6. Philippe Devillers in lectures to Cornell seminar in "International Politics of Southeast Asia," August 1965. M. Devillers is one of the leading French social scientists working on Vietnam and is editor of the scholarly journal, *France-Asia.*

7. P. J. Honey, "The Problem of Democracy in Vietnam," *The World Today,* Vol. 16, No. 2, February 1960, p. 73. See also Philippe Devillers, "The Struggle for the Unification of Vietnam," *The China Quarterly,* No. 9, January–March 1962, p. 12, where he states: "This repression was in theory aimed at the Communists. In fact it affected all those, and they were many—democrats, socialists, liberals, adherents of the sects—who were bold enough to express their disagreement with the line of policy adopted by the ruling oligarchy."

8. William Henderson, "South Viet Nam Finds Itself," *Foreign Affairs,* Vol. 35, No. 2, January 1957, pp. 285, 288.

9. USOM, *Saigon Daily News Round-Up,* February 28, 1959, pp. 4–5, as quoted in Scigliano, *op. cit.,* p. 169.

10. The full text of the law may be found in Marvin E. Gettleman, ed., *Vietnam: History, Documents, and Opinions on a Major World Crisis* (New York: Fawcett, 1965), pp. 256–260. For a

discussion of these laws, see Jean Lacouture, *Vietnam: Between Two Truces* (New York: Random House, 1966), pp. 29–30; Bernard B. Fall, *The Two Viet-Nams* (New York: Praeger, 1964), p. 272.

11. Article 17 of the law states: "The decisions of the special military court are not subject to appeal, and no appeal is allowed to the High Court."

12. Hammer, *op. cit.,* p. 36, citing *New York Herald Tribune,* March 1, 1955. Americans in Saigon then gave an estimate of 50 to 70 per cent.

13. Joseph Alsop, "A Reporter at Large," *The New Yorker,* June 25, 1955, p. 48.

14. "Tenants generally appear to pay somewhat more than the legal 25 per cent maximum rent, often up to about a third of the crop." J. Price Gittinger, "Progress in South Vietnam's Agrarian Reform (I)," *Far Eastern Survey,* Vol. 29, No. 1, January 1960, p. 2.

15. Robert Shaplen, *The Lost Revolution* (New York: Harper and Row, 1965), p. 144.

16. John D. Montgomery, *The Politics of Foreign Aid* (New York: Praeger, 1962), p. 124.

17. J. Price Gittinger, *Agrarian Reform Status Report* (m.s., n.d.), quoted in Montgomery, *op. cit.,* p. 126.

18. Scigliano, *op. cit.,* p. 32.

19. Montgomery, *op. cit.,* p. 71.

20. Scigliano, *op. cit.,* p. 54.

21. See Devillers, "The Struggle for the Unification of Vietnam," *op. cit.,* p. 13.

22. Denis Warner, in *The Last Confucian* (New York: Macmillan, 1963), p. 89, observes: "Summary Viet Cong justice for a village chief guilty of corruption or brutality did not offend the peasants. On the contrary, it tended to endow the Viet Cong with some of the characteristics of Robin Hood and his band of merry men."

23. According to U.S. Congress, Senate, *Situation in Vietnam,* 86th Congress, 1st Session (Washington: U.S. Government Printing Office, 1959), pp. 203–204, the vast proportion of U.S. aid, exclusive of military assistance, went for defense support. Of these "nonmilitary" funds, spent between 1955 and 1959, only about $16 million out of more than $1.1 billion went for technical cooperation. In 1959, Diem put virtually all of his emphasis on a plan for large-scale rural resettlement in "agrovilles." According to one study of these: "There is no doubt that the agroville program was primarily a measure of counterinsurgency." Joseph J. Zasloff, "Rural Resettlement in South Viet Nam: The Agroville Program," *Pacific Affairs,* Vol. 35, No. 4,

Winter 1962–63, pp. 327–340. With respect to the diversion of funds, see William A. Nighswonger, *Rural Pacification in Viet Nam: 1962–1965* (Washington: Advanced Research Project Agency, 1966).

24. David Wurfel, "Agrarian Reform in the Republic of Vietnam," *Far Eastern Survey,* Vol. 26, No. 6, June 1957, p. 89.

25. Scigliano, *op. cit.,* pp. 122–123.

26. Fall, *op. cit.,* p. 312.

27. Scigliano, *op. cit.,* pp. 31, 44, 181–182; Roy Jumper and Marjory Weiner Normand, "Vietnam," in *Governments and Politics of Southeast Asia,* 2nd ed., ed. by George McT. Kahin (Ithaca, N.Y., Cornell University Press, 1964), p. 411.

28. See for example, Hanoi Radio, July 29, 1958. See also Le Duan's statement reported in *Vietnam Presse Bulletin d'Informations Confidentielles,* July 21, 1958, where he states: "the movement against U.S. imperialism will expand . . . among the upper classes of the South Vietnam administration and army. . . . Only two alternatives face them: either to remain in tow to the U.S. interventionists against the nation, or to comply with the desire of the people and seek together with the D.R.V.N. [Hanoi] government measures to bring about national reunification." This limited and restricted edition of *Vietnam Presse,* largely devoted to a monitoring of Hanoi broadcasts, was circulated to only a few top officials in the Saigon (Diem) government.

29. Bernard B. Fall, "Vietcong—The Unseen Enemy in Viet-Nam," *New Society,* No. 134, April 22, 1965, p. 10.

30. Considerable confusion has arisen concerning the name Dai Viet, because during the last twenty-five years there have been several Dai Viet parties, each separate and quite different from the others. The one whose strength endured and which is referred to here is the Dai-Viet Dan-Chinh Dang, established in Hanoi in the early 1940's by Truong Tu Anh.

31. During early 1956 its anti-Diem radio broadcasts singled out particularly for their attacks Diem's organization of elections for the National Assembly which they described as "a farce." Dai Viet Radio (Clandestine), March 3, 5, 7, 1956.

32. See "Voice of National Salvation Movement," *Vietnam Presse Bulletin d'Informations Confidentielles,* October 16, November 21, November 25, 1957.

33. Voice of the South Vietnam Liberation Front, July 8, 1958. Indicative of the Front's attitude towards Diem and the United States is their broadcast of August 4, 1958, which was captioned "The Seven Cardinal Sins of the Americans." It read:

> Not only are the Americans enemies of the world, they also are our implacable foes. During the past few years, they have

caused such destruction and such suffering to our people. Their crimes are innumerable, but we can point out seven cardinal sins:

1. They have interfered in the Indochinese war, encouraged the French colonialists to invade Vietnam, and supplied the French with ammunition. With American arms, the French killed our people.

2. They plotted to develop the Indochinese war, planned to bring their troops and those of their satellites into the Indochinese war, introduced atomic weapons into Vietnam, subverted the carrying out of the Geneva agreement, and have impeded the unification of Vietnam.

3. They established a dictatorship in South Vietnam, took the wealth of South Vietnam, ordered the southern authorities to force the people to enroll in the army, brought South Vietnam under the protection of SEATO, turned South Vietnam into an American colony and military base, and prepared for a new war in Vietnam.

4. They ordered Ngo Dinh Diem to force more than 500,000 people in the north to leave their villages, families, and relatives and move south in order to live in misery.

5. They encouraged the southern authorities to launch anti-communist campaigns; thus thousands of former cadres of the resistance were arrested and killed, and democracy and freedom in the south were stifled. The south has become a big prison.

6. They introduced a reactionary and debauched culture into South Vietnam to poison the southern minds and throw the south into a state of disorder fraught with murder and retaliation, and to oppress the struggle of the southern people.

7. They organized a spy system in the north in order to subvert peace and impede the north on its way to socialism. They are preparing to conquer the north and enslave our people.

34. *Nhan Dan* (*"The People"*), editorial of June 28, 1958, reported in *Vietnam Presse Bulletin d'Informations Confidentielles*, June 29, 1958.

35. Hanoi Radio, July 29, 1958.

36. Voice of the South Vietnam Liberation Front, September 2, 1958.

37. Hanoi Radio, July 10, 1958.

38. For text see Appendix 5.

39. This portion of the declaration has not been quoted in the excerpt found in Appendix 5.

40. *Le Monde,* April 15, 1965.

41. "Resolution of the Third National Congress of the Viet Nam Workers' Party on the tasks and line of the Party in the new stage," in *Third National Congress of the Viet Nam Workers' Party: Documents,* Vol. 1 (Hanoi: Foreign Languages Publishing House, n.d.), pp. 221–222, 224–225.

42. *Ibid.,* pp. 225–226.

43. *Ibid.,* Vol. 2, is devoted to "a report of the tasks and direction of the First Five Year Plan for the development of national economy."

44. See Georges Chaffard, *op. cit.,* p. 176.

45. For the full text of the manifesto, see Bernard Fall, *The Two Viet-Nams,* pp. 442–447.

46. Hanoi Radio, January 29, 1961, announced the formation of the Front and described its program. On January 30, 1961, Hanoi Radio quoted the official newspaper *Nhan Dan* as stating that "the people in North Vietnam . . . greatly rejoice at and warmly welcome the news on the founding of the National Liberation Front of South Vietnam."

47. See Appendix 6-B.

48. See below, pp. 134–136.

49. U.S. Department of State, *Aggression from the North: The Record of North Viet-Nam's Campaign to Conquer South Viet-Nam* (Washington: U.S. Government Printing Office, 1965), p. 2.

50. U.S. Senate, *Supplemental Foreign Assistance Fiscal Year 1966—Vietnam,* 89th Congress, 2nd Session (Washington: U.S. Government Printing Office, 1966), p. 15.

51. These views have been available for a number of years in various French journals, particularly in *Le Monde,* and are easily accessible in the following more recently published monographs: Philippe Devillers, "The Struggle for the Unification of Vietnam," *The China Quarterly,* No. 9, January–March 1962, pp. 2–23; Jean Lacouture, *Le Vietnam entre deux paix* (Paris: Editions du Seuil, 1965) and its translation, *Vietnam: Between Two Truces* (New York: Random House, 1966); and Georges Chaffard, *Indochine: dix ans d'indépendance* (Paris: Calmann-Lévy, 1964).

52. A notable example is George A. Carver, Jr., whose writing the Assistant Secretary of State for Far Eastern Affairs, William Bundy, singled out for commendation to Americans desirous of understanding the situation in Vietnam. Neither Bundy nor the editors of *Foreign Affairs,* for whom Carver wrote two lead articles, disclosed the fact that he is a CIA official. In addition to commending Carver's "excellent article," Assistant Secretary Bundy found it possible to tell the American public, "There should be no doubt of the true nature of the Viet Cong and its National Liberation Front. They are a completely different movement from the political opposition to Diem." Mr. Bundy made this statement in a

speech in Dallas on May 13, 1965, which was printed in the *Department of State Bulletin* (Washington, June 7, 1965), and published in revised form a month later under the title "South Viet-Nam: Reality and Myth" in the Department's *Foreign Affairs Outline*. Mr. Carver's two lead articles in *Foreign Affairs* appeared in its issues of April 1965 and April 1966. In both cases the editors of *Foreign Affairs* provided their readers with no other information concerning Mr. Carver than "student of political theory and Asian affairs, with degrees from Yale and Oxford; former officer in the U.S. aid mission in Saigon; author of "Aesthetics and the Problem of Meaning.' "

Noting that Carver's second article in *Foreign Affairs* ("The Faceless Vietcong") was "a compilation of the evidence for the Administration's contention that the National Liberation Front of South Vietnam is a 'contrived political mechanism' of the Communist party of North Vietnam," the *New York Times* reported that Senator William Fulbright had asked the CIA to take a look at the propriety of letting its analysts present official statements and conclusions to American readers in the guise of independent scholarship. *New York Times,* April 30, 1966.

CHAPTER VI

Limited Involvement

1: **Throughout most of the Kennedy Administration** Vietnam remained an area of secondary importance to the United States. It was a problem that worried President Kennedy, but one to which he never devoted his full attention.[1] His Administration, like Eisenhower's, based its policy upon the maintenance of a separate state in South Vietnam, and he too remained sensitive to the possible domestic repercussions that might result were the area to pass under communist dominion.

By postulating that the land south of the 17th parallel constituted a separate state, any Northern support of the insurgency in the South could be viewed as external aggression, an opinion endorsed by those who considered the conflict simply as an example of communist expansion. While the President and a number of his advisors saw the insurgency primarily as a civil war, his Secretary of State, Dean Rusk, tended to ignore the highly complex causes and history of the insurgency [2] and developed the theme of "aggression from the North," which was to become increasingly prominent as the American-supported efforts of the Saigon regime proved ineffective against the rebellion. As early as 1961 Rusk was speaking of "the determined and ruthless campaign of propaganda, infiltration, and subversion by the Communist regime in north Viet-Nam to destroy the Republic of Viet-Nam." [3] President Kennedy, appreciating the internal aspects of the conflict, was always alert to the danger of turning it into a "white man's war" [4] and eventually recognized the failure of an American policy that had been tied so exclusively to military measures and unquestioning support of Diem. His concern that the United States might be following the disastrous path of the French was reflected in his assignment to Maxwell Taylor and Walt Rostow in October 1961. The President then "charged them to find out whether we were better off now than the French had been" when he had visited Indochina in 1951 and "whether Vietnamese nationalism had turned irrevocably against us or still might serve as a basis for the fight against communism." [5]

During the course of 1961, the Kennedy Administration moved cautiously in responding to the erosion of Saigon's authority and the expansion of territory under Vietcong rule. Vice-President Lyndon B. Johnson was sent to Saigon in May while on a general tour of East Asia. After publicly hailing Diem as the Winston Churchill of Southeast Asia, Johnson reported to President Kennedy that he found Diem a man of "admirable qualities" but "remote from the people" and "surrounded by persons less admirable than he." He concluded, nevertheless, that South Vietnam could be saved from communism by prompt American action and called for an increase in the size of the Vietnamese army, coupled with programs of political and economic reform. [6]

Johnson's trip was soon followed by two fact-finding missions, one headed by Professor Eugene Staley from May to July [7] and the other the Taylor-Rostow mission in early October. The Staley Plan, as it came to be known, advocated among other measures the establishment of "strategic hamlets" as part of a general strategy emphasizing local militia defense. The recommendations of this and the later mission were to guide U.S. policy during the next two years. General Maxwell Taylor and White House aide Walt Rostow led a delegation that, in its very composition, "expressed a conscious decision by the Secretary of State to turn the Vietnam problem over to the Secretary of Defense." [8] The major theme of the Taylor-Rostow report was that the Vietnam problem was primarily a military one, which could be solved by a larger commitment of American power including, if necessary, American fighting men. Minimally, U.S. troops would fulfill highly skilled functions, such as helicopter airlifts and air reconnaissance, and would act as advisors to Vietnamese officers and technicians. The report proposed sending a 10,000-man task force, which, though serving chiefly for self-defense and perimeter security, could on occasion provide an emergency reserve. The report predicated such plans on the continuing absence of major infiltration from the North.

While accepting most of the recommendations in the Taylor-Rostow report, President Kennedy declined to make explicit or final any direct American military commitment.[9] In refusing to do so, he stressed that the Vietnamese war could only be won so long as it was their war. In an exchange of letters between Diem and Kennedy in December, the U.S. officially described the limited and somewhat ambiguous extent of its commitment.[10] Kennedy told Diem:

> The United States, like the Republic of Viet-Nam, remains devoted to the cause of peace and our primary purpose is to help your people maintain their independence. If the Communist authorities in North Viet-Nam will stop their campaign to destroy the Republic of Viet-Nam, the measures we are taking to assist your defense efforts will no longer be necessary. We shall seek to persuade the Communists to give up their attempts of force and subversion. In any case, we are confident that the Vietnamese people will preserve their independence and gain the peace and prosperity for which they have sought so hard and so long.

The growth of the insurgency in South Vietnam during 1961 was rapid, and by the middle of the year Saigon had lost control over large areas of rural South Vietnam. As the pace of the war quickened, the former adherents of the Vietminh assumed a larger role in the uprisings. Although non-Vietminh armed groups still engaged Diem's forces, during 1961 they became completely overshadowed by the resurrected Vietminh. Until 1960 infiltration had remained minimal, but in 1961 the Southerners regrouped in the North began to return in significant numbers. Even by official reckoning, however, they totaled only 6,200 by the end of 1961.[11] Aside from the infiltration of these men, Hanoi provided very little tangible aid to the insurrection during this period.* The White Paper

---

* On the issue of infiltration in this period, U.S. government sources invariably quote the International Control Commission's report of June 2, 1962, which, in its first half, concluded that "there is evidence to show that armed and unarmed personnel, arms, munitions and other supplies have been sent from the Zone in the North to the Zone in the South with the object of supporting, organizing and carrying out hostile activities, including armed attacks, directed against the Armed Forces and Administration of the Zone in the South. . . . there is evidence to show that the PAVN [People's Army of Viet-Nam] has allowed the Zone in the North to be used for inciting, encouraging and supporting hostile activities in the Zone in the South, aimed at the overthrow of the Administration in the South." International Commission for Supervision and Control in Vietnam, *Special Report to the Co-Chairmen of the Geneva Conference on Indo-China,* Command Paper 1755 (London: Her Majesty's Stationery Office, 1962), p. 7. For typical uses of these ICC statements, see *Department of State Bulletin* (Washington, July 16, 1962), pp. 109–110; and U.S. Department of State, *Aggression from the North: The Record of North Viet-Nam's Campaign to Conquer South Viet-Nam* (Washington: U.S. Government Printing Office, 1965), p. 2 and Appendix A.

The Department of State has never seen fit to quote the second half of the ICC report, which deals with violations by South Vietnam. The commission concluded that "the Republic of Viet-Nam has violated Articles 16 and 17 of the Geneva Agreement in receiving the increased military aid from the United States of America. . . . The Commission is also of the view that, though there may not be any formal military alliance between the Governments of the United States of America and the Republic of Viet-Nam, the establishment of a U.S. Military Assistance Command in South Viet-Nam, as well as the introduction of a large number of U.S. military personnel beyond the stated strength of the MAAG (Military Assistance Advisory Group), amounts to a factual military alliance, which is prohibited under Article 19 of the Geneva Agreement." On balance, the ICC finally concluded, "Fundamental provisions of the Geneva Agreement have been violated by both Parties, resulting in ever-increasing tension and threat of resumption of open hostilities." *Special Report, op. cit.,* p. 10.

of 1961 could point to no evidence that a significant proportion of the insurgents' arms had come from the North, the vast majority of them being either captured American weapons or relics of the war with France.[12]

Despite the mounting threat it posed to his regime, Diem was quite unable to appreciate the extent to which the insurgency was a response to his continuing repression. Authoritarian measures, he insisted, were rendered all the more necessary by the uprisings, which in his book were simply the result of communist subversion. Indeed, by February 1962 Diem's government was so agitated by American and Western representations of the insurgency as a civil war that it called on foreign correspondents to cease labeling the Vietcong "rebels" and "insurgents" and urged them instead to "use the following terms: Viet Cong, Communists, Hanoi's agents and aggressors from the North." [13] Wedded to the idea that social and political reform should await the prior establishment of full security, Diem, like Washington, did not perceive that the war was first of all a political problem and could only be solved through primarily political means.[14]

Following the abortive coup of November 1960, the effective operation of Saigon's armed forces was further handicapped by Diem's overzealous interference in military matters. He sought to preclude any repetition of the coup by making appointments in the officer corps even more contingent upon personal fidelity to him than upon combat experience and ability. He often jeopardized military campaigns by ordering changes spasmodically in the disposition of troops in the field from his palace in Saigon. Also, after November 1960 Diem began to delegate increasing authority to his ambitious brother, Ngo Dinh Nhu, a trend that became even more pronounced after two air force planes strafed his palace in February 1962. Thereupon Diem imposed even stricter curbs on the independent judgment of his generals and transferred additional powers to Nhu and his secret police.

2: **The expanding military strength of the Vietcong** was accompanied by the political growth of the National Liberation Front. Although welcoming support from all quarters, from its inception the organization seems to have been dominated by communists. Its core, militarily and politically, was the resurrected Southern Vietminh. On January 1, 1962,* a component of the NLF known as the People's Revolutionary Party (PRP) was established.[15] The reason for the emergence of this unconcealed communist element within the Front is unclear, for at the time the NLF was obviously striving to develop a program that would win as wide a Southern audience as possible. Several analysts have stated that Hanoi created the PRP to ensure a permanent core of communist militants in the NLF, in the event that a détente between Saigon and the Front should later develop.[16] Yet, the 1962 elaboration of the NLF declaration of December 20, 1960, demonstrated a continuing sensitivity to the strong regional sentiment in the South and the special conditions existing there, an emphasis symbolized in the Front's adoption of a different flag from that of the North.[17]

At its first formal congress, of February 16–March 3, 1962, the Front revealed for the first time its constituent political components † as well as its top leaders. As president the dele-

---

* According to *Hoc Tap* (*"Study"*), No. 1, 1966, the first congress of communist representatives was held in the South in late December 1961. At this congress, the representatives "decided to establish the Vietnam People's Revolutionary Party and passed the party's platform and statutes. The Peoples' Revolutionary Party was officially established on January 1, 1962."

† The organizations represented were listed as: the Peoples' Revolutionary Party, the Democratic Party, the Radical Socialist Party, the Association of Workers for Liberation, the Women's Union for Liberation, the Union of Revolutionary People's Youth, the Association of Patriotic and Democratic Journalists, the Association of Writers and Artists for Liberation, the Movement for the Autonomy of Tay Nguyen (High Plateau), and the self-defense forces. (There is no way of ascertaining the extent of actual mem-

gates selected Nguyen Huu Tho, formerly a prominent and politically active Saigon lawyer, who had been arrested by Diem in 1954 but had escaped with the help of NLF agents in December 1961.* A number of other central leaders in the NLF hierarchy do not appear to have joined the underground resistance movement until 1960 or thereafter. One of its vice-presidents, Superior Bonze Son Vong, a Buddhist from Vietnam's Cambodian minority, reportedly did not join until July 1961, after Saigon military forces had conducted a destructive

---

bership in these component organizations.) *Declaration of the First Congress of the South Viet Nam National Front for Liberation* (Hanoi: Foreign Languages Publishing House, 1962), pp. 5–6.

* According to Tran Van Huu, who as Bao Dai's Prime Minister in the period 1950–53 had ordered Tho's arrest, he was "very well known in Saigon as a person who was very active in opposing the French during the colonial period." (From an interview with one of the authors, Paris, September 15, 1965.) Georges Chaffard writes that Nguyen Huu Tho studied law at the School of Law in Aix-en-Provence and that from 1940 to 1945 he collaborated with the outstanding French legal specialist Roger Pinto, then professor at the University of Hanoi (and currently at the University of Paris). In 1947, shortly after having been admitted to the bar in Saigon, he was arrested by the Vietminh. During the brief period of detention, he was favorably impressed by the ideals and patriotic spirit of the Vietminh and upon returning to Saigon participated in the activities of groups of intellectuals who sought peace through negotiations. Then, after being placed under arrest for two years on orders of Tran Van Huu, he resumed his place at the Saigon bar, serving as counsel for imprisoned members of the Vietminh. Georges Chaffard, *Indochine: dix ans d'indépendance,* (Paris: Calmann-Lévy, 1964), pp. 190–191. According to a Hanoi publication (untitled and undated) available to the writers, Tho was born in Cholon, Saigon's sister city, in 1910 and became active in the anti-French underground in 1949. This source states that on March 19, 1950, he was arrested by the French and interned in North Vietnam for two years for having led demonstrations in Saigon against American intervention in Indochina. It credits him with founding and becoming vice-president of the Saigon-Cholon Steering Committee in 1954. This account is consistent with the somewhat brief one found in Tran Van Giau and Le Van Chat, *The South Vietnam Liberation Front* (Hanoi: Foreign Languages Publishing House, 1962), pp. 62–63.

sweeping operation through his province during which pagodas were shelled and monks imprisoned. After an apparently unsuccessful effort to petition the province chief for the release of the Buddhist monks caught in this operation, the monk joined the NLF. Another vice-president, Phung Van Cung, fled Saigon in 1960. The three other vice-presidents, again all Southerners, were Vo Chi Cong, Huynh Tan Phat, and Ydut Ramago (apparently later replaced by Ybih Aleo).[18]

The Front's program of January 17, 1962, endorsed by its congress the following month, once more called for the "correct implementation of the 1954 Geneva Agreements." [19] It viewed reunification as a step for the distant future and one that would have to reflect the interests of the South Vietnamese as well as those of Hanoi. The program of the congress stated: "The reunification of the Fatherland will be solved step by step on the basis of the aspirations and interests of all sections of the people of South Viet Nam as well as the people of North Viet Nam, on the principles of freedom and democracy, negotiations and agreement between the two sides." [20] The congress warned that if the "aspirations of the people in South Viet Nam are not heeded" and "if the U.S. imperialists and their agents obdurately go further and further into a bloody military adventure of aggression in South Viet Nam," then:

> In case of necessity, the people of South Viet Nam and the South Viet Nam National Front for Liberation will use their legitimate and effective right to appeal to the people and Government of North Viet Nam, to peace- and democracy-loving peoples and governments the world over, irrespective of political system, requesting that active support, including material and manpower support, be afforded to the just struggle of the people of South Viet Nam.[21]

The Front's 1962 program also underscored the previous emphasis on a neutralist foreign policy for the South. In addition to endorsing its ten points of 1960 (see Appendix 6) this new program read:

The Congress solemnly asserts that after recovering its independence, South Viet Nam will establish diplomatic relations with all countries without distinction of political system, in conformity with the principles of the Bandung Conference. It will not enter into military alliance with any country whatever, and will accept aid, economic and otherwise, from any country willing to provide such assistance without political conditions attached. . . . with a foreign policy of peace and neutrality, South Viet Nam will be able to get unconditional aid,—economic, technical, cultural and social—, from many countries with different political systems, in order to build up a prosperous and advanced South Viet Nam. The experiences of peaceful and neutral Cambodia, which borders on our country, and of several other countries in Southeast Asia have testified to this possibility.[22]

The congress affirmed "that it is the intention of the South Viet Nam National Front for Liberation to struggle for the formation of a peace and neutrality zone comprising Cambodia, Laos and South Viet Nam" and that it "warmly welcomes the positive initiative of Prince Norodom Sihanouk concerning the formation of such a peace and neutrality zone." [23]

Commenting on this program, two important Hanoi leaders of Southern origin, Tran Van Giau and Le Van Chat, wrote in an official Hanoi publication shortly afterwards that:

As citizens of the Democratic Republic of Viet Nam and natives of the South, we admit that, at the first reading, the program of the South Viet Nam Liberation National Front is not likely to get our full approval. The neutrality of the South means for Viet Nam a divergence of political character each side of the 17th parallel, while our country has always constituted a single entity.[24]

However, they continued:

Neutrality is the solution acceptable to all patriots and would constitute an important step forward compared with the present disguised colonial regime. To speak of the necessity of uniting all national and democratic forces, is to recognize their necessity to make concessions to one another, each group drawing nearer to its allies to actively contribute to the defence of national interests.[25]

The neutralization of Laos by the major powers in the summer of 1962 seems to have strengthened the NLF's interest in a similar settlement for South Vietnam, one that presumably would provide, as in Laos, for a coalition government as well as for neutralization. The NLF's advocacy of such a solution was publicized on July 20, 1962, the eighth anniversary of the signing of the Geneva Agreements of 1954.

On that day the Front issued "four proposals for national salvation." [26] The first two of these four proposals demanded: (1) an end to American "acts of armed aggression" and a withdrawal of all American troops and military personnel and (2) a cessation of hostilities and restoration of peace in South Vietnam through a "settlement of internal affairs by the South Vietnamese themselves." Its third point called for the establishment of a government made up of representatives of "parties, sects and groups belonging to all political tendencies, social strata and classes, religions and nationalities existing in South Viet Nam." The coalition government that was being set up in Laos was regarded as a model for this.[27] The new South Vietnamese coalition government would be responsible for "organizing free general elections in order to endow South Viet Nam with a democratic National Assembly" and for securing "democratic freedoms for all political parties and groups." [28]

The fourth point in the NLF's declaration of July 20, 1962, here quoted in full, provided:

South Viet Nam will follow a foreign policy of peace and neutrality, establish good relations with all States, first of all with the neighbouring countries, refrain from joining any military bloc, refuse to all countries the right to set up military bases on its territory, receive economic aid from any country without political conditions attached. A badly-needed international agreement will be quickly concluded to enable the powers from different camps to guarantee respect for the sovereignty, independence, territorial integrity and neutrality of South Viet Nam which is ready to form a neutral zone together with Cambodia and Laos, three States enjoying full sovereign rights.[29]

In commenting on these proposals the *New York Times* stated that although such an idea apparently ran counter to U.S. interests, it "has considerable support among Communists and their partisans, in Asian neutral nations and sections of opinion in this country." [30] But whatever appeal a program for a coalition government and neutralization might have had for the people of South Vietnam, Diem would not countenance either proposal. The United States backed him in this stand and gave no encouragement to the peace efforts of Prince Sihanouk of Cambodia, who was then working to elicit international support for the guarantee of a neutralized zone of his country, South Vietnam, and Laos.

3: During 1962, the United States undertook a major buildup in Vietnam in accordance with the Taylor-Rostow recommendations. The emphasis here was heavily on the military side of the program, the Saigon government proving quite unwilling to implement its economic provisions. Beginning in January, greatly augmented material aid began to arrive in Vietnam along with larger numbers of American military advisors and helicopter pilots. The advisors, including a high proportion of officers and noncoms, worked directly with Vietnamese army "counterparts" both in Saigon and in the field. In addition to giving technical advice, they also helped plan military actions. Meanwhile, the role of those Americans who manned the helicopters was to acquire extreme importance in providing great tactical mobility to the Vietnamese. By mid-October 1962 the helicopter crews had begun to take the initiative in firing at insurgents, and less than a year later armed helicopters were often assigned to fly strafing missions.[31]

One of the most disturbing developments in this period was

the drastic rise in the incidence of terrorism directed against the civilian population. The Vietnamese war had long been stamped by an unusual degree of cruelty from both sides, but the Vietcong's acts of violence as such had until late 1961 usually been directed against specific government agents (particularly village chiefs) and local defense forces.[32] Though Vietcong casualty rates were reportedly far higher than those of the government, the Vietcong usually restricted its terrorism to the achievement of political ends and endeavored to restrain its followers from resorting to mere acts of vengeance. But when the heavy influx of new weapons, especially the armed helicopters, caused communist deaths to soar in 1962, the Vietcong loosed a wave of assassinations and kidnappings of Saigon supporters, presumably to offset the drastic effects of its staggering losses. According to official U.S. statistics there was a major increase in this calculated terrorism between 1960 and 1962 (see Table 2).

TABLE 2

Estimated Vietcong Assassinations and Kidnapping of Civilians, 1960-65

	ASSASSINATIONS	KIDNAPPING
1960	1,400	700
1962	1,719	9,688
1963	2,073	7,262
1964	1,795 (436 officials)	9,554 (1,131 officials)
1965	1,895 (230 officials)	12,778 (329 officials)

SOURCES: Figures in this table are taken from U.S. Senate, *Supplemental Foreign Assistance Fiscal Year 1966—Vietnam,* 89th Congress, 2nd Session (Washington: U.S. Government Printing Office, 1966), p. 128; and U.S. Department of State, *A Threat to the Peace* (Washington: U.S. Government Printing Office, 1961), p. 13.

Regardless of its causes, the Vietcong's campaign of terror, which grew so quickly in the fall of 1961, appears to have had a profound effect on President Kennedy's view of the war. As he wrote President Diem on December 14, 1961: "We have been deeply disturbed by the assault on your country. Our indignation has mounted as the deliberate savagery of the Communist program of assassination, kidnapping and wanton violence became clear." [33]

The substantial infusion of American advisors and new equipment, particularly the American-piloted helicopters with which the Vietcong were unfamiliar, appeared to stabilize the military situation in early 1962. As the communists themselves acknowledged, "In terms of territory and population, Diem made a considerable comeback in 1962," and at one point the NLF almost decided to evacuate the Delta and retreat into the mountains. [34] But during the course of the year the Vietcong learned to cope better with the helicopters and compensated for the superior firepower of the other American equipment by capturing a considerable part of it for their own use. The tide of battle once more began to turn against Saigon.

Ngo Dinh Diem's powerful brother, Ngo Dinh Nhu, and Nhu's wife were no less opposed than Diem to the reform measures urged by the United States and considerably more adroit than he in dealing with American officials. They had apparently sensed that the United States could find no one other than Diem to support, and indeed this was the steadfast view of Ambassador Frederick Nolting and General Paul Harkins, who in 1962 was appointed U.S. military commander in Saigon. Both believed that Diem was the only available instrument of American policy, and "both were convinced that attempts to bring pressure on him would be self-defeating." [35] As reporter David Halberstam described it, the government of Diem and his brother "became more convinced than ever that it had its ally in a corner, that it could do anything it wanted, that continued support would be guaranteed because of the Communist threat and that after the commitment was made, the United States could not suddenly admit it had made a vast mistake." [36] In this frame of mind, Ngo Dinh Nhu launched a vitriolic anti-American campaign in the government-controlled press,[37] which he hoped would force the U.S. to abandon its insistence upon reforms. Washington soon after instructed the American Mission in Saigon "to get along with President Ngo Dinh Diem's regime come hell or high water and forget about political reforms." [38] Consequently, the military aspects of the American effort became even more prominent, with the major emphasis falling on the "strategic hamlets" program, a project to which Ngo Dinh Nhu was unusually partial.[39]

Under this program, peasants were to be resettled in semi-fortified communities, where they were to be provided with comprehensive social services and where, while being politically insulated from the Vietcong, they would also have better protection against its armed attacks. Since in practice most of the peasantry involved were dragooned into compliance, they bitterly resented the sacrifice of their ancestral homes and fields. Widespread corruption attended the enterprise, so most of the peasants could not discover the promised social services and usually were not even adequately compensated for the land they had been forced to abandon. They often received harsh treatment and in most cases were no better protected than previously from the fighting.* Thus, what began as a

---

* American advisors in Vietnam were initially highly enthusiastic over prospects of the "strategic hamlets" because of the success of the British a decade earlier in the resettlement program in Malaya. Having little knowledge of the very different social and political conditions governing the Malayan experience, they jumped to the quite mistaken conclusion that what had worked in Malaya ought to work in Vietnam. But, whereas the British, with full support from the Malays, had undertaken to move recently settled alien Chinese squatters (not Malayan peasants), in South Vietnam those who were forced to resettle were *indigenous* peasants, with strong local roots, living in socially cohesive communities, where family ties with the land went back as much as two centuries. For an ex-

highly promising project to attain local security ended in bitterness and recrimination on the part of the peasantry.

4: **Even though the Taylor-Rostow program** had proved ineffective militarily as well as politically by the end of 1962, a calculated optimism pervaded almost all official American pronouncements on the situation in Vietnam. The idea seemed to be that, "if the Americans expressed enough optimism, Diem would come to trust them and be more receptive to their suggestions" and that "a sensitive Administration back home wanted to hear that it was winning the war." [40] The tone of the statements made by Defense Secretary Robert McNamara on his first visit to Vietnam in 1962—"Every quantitative measurement we have shows we're winning this war"—was echoed by General Maxwell Taylor when he visited the country later in the year.[41] Although there were those in Washington who realized that such optimism was unwarranted,* the official line prevailed. On March 8, 1963, Secretary Rusk described the struggle against the Vietcong as "turning an important corner" and concluded that Saigon's forces "clearly have the initiative in most areas of the country." [42] Even more distantly related to the facts of the situation was his speech of

---

cellent comparison of the two experiences, see Milton Osborne's study, *Strategic Hamlets in South Viet-Nam,* Data Paper 55 (Ithaca, N.Y.: Cornell Southeast Asia Program, 1965).

* Foremost among these were Chester Bowles, Deputy Under Secretary of State; Averell Harriman, Assistant Secretary of State for Far Eastern Affairs; and Roger Hilsman, head of the State Department's Bureau of Intelligence and Research. Hilsman argued that there was a danger of "over-militarization" and "over-Americanization" of the war and that, in the circumstances, an effective policy required "as much political and civic action" as it did military effort. Arthur M. Schlesinger, Jr., *A Thousand Days: John F. Kennedy in the White House* (Boston: Houghton Mifflin, 1965), p. 985. However, their views were so overshadowed by those of McNamara, Rusk, Harkins, and Ambassador Nolting that they apparently had no appreciable effect upon the President's understanding of the situation.

April 22, wherein he spoke of a "steady movement [in South Vietnam] toward a constitutional system resting upon popular consent." The strategic hamlet program, he said, was producing "excellent results . . . morale in the countryside has begun to rise," so to the Vietnamese peasant the Vietcong looked "less and less like winners." [43] In fact, after the brief military improvement in Saigon's position in mid-1962, the tide of battle began to run decisively against its forces—very heavily so during the first half of 1963. *New York Times* correspondent David Halberstam summed up the situation of mid-1963 in the following words: "A year after the American build-up of weaponry and personnel had reached its peak, it was clear that the Government had lost the initiative, that the enemy had benefited more from the weapons than we had. . . ." [44] According to "private figures" of the Vietnamese Joint General Staff for this period, "Government weapons losses had risen about 20 per cent and Vietcong weapons losses had dropped about 25 per cent." [45]

It was only with the Buddhist rising against Diem's government in May 1963 that the veil of official optimism was torn aside and something of the real character of the Diem regime was disclosed to the American public. Administration spokesmen could no longer gainsay the reporting of American correspondents, whose earlier reports gained added credence in the light of Buddhist suppression. Clear for all to see was the fact that a deep-felt resentment had long been smoldering among the Buddhist majority in South Vietnam as a consequence of Diem's autocratic methods and his discrimination in favor of the Catholic minority.* When their essentially

---

* As against a Catholic population in South Vietnam of about 1 million in 1960, one estimate calculated that about 6 million South Vietnamese could "be considered practicing Buddhists," but that "perhaps another 5 million, many of them members of the Cao Dai and Hoa Hao religious sects accepted basic Buddhist tenets." Robert Scigliano, *Epilogue: The Coup,* Supplement to

religious protest was met by brutally repressive measures from the government, the Buddhists' reaction acquired political overtones, so they became "a spearhead for other discontented elements." [46] Social tensions mounted toward an explosion.

The spark for that explosion came on May 8 in the city of Hué, when government troops fired into a crowd protesting Saigon's order against displaying the Buddhist flag. Instead of making the modest concessions needed to placate the Buddhists, Diem, at the urging of his brother and Madame Nhu, stubbornly refused to compromise. The demonstrations spread to Saigon, with younger and more militant Buddhists assuming a crucial role in the leadership of the movement. In order to dramatize the Buddhist protest, on June 11 in Saigon a monk committed suicide by setting himself afire. For Vietnamese Buddhists, human self-immolation can give a movement special credibility and urgency, and during the next six months, as the monk's example was followed by six others, these suicides became a powerful symbol of political opposition.

The culminating act of government repression came on August 21, when, on orders of Ngo Dinh Nhu, Diem's own elite Special Forces attacked pagodas in Saigon, Hué, and other cities and arrested a large number of Buddhists. This move served as a catalyst to bring previously wavering anti-Diem forces into the open. Thousands of students joined the swelling Buddhist ranks in demonstrations lasting well into September. The government retaliated by closing the universities in Saigon and Hué and all secondary schools in Saigon, arresting some 4,000 students. Since most of these students

---

South Vietnam: Nation Under Stress (Boston: Houghton Mifflin, 1963), p. 2. The French correspondent Max Clos calculates that, out of a 1966 South Vietnam population of about 16 million, not more than 2 million seriously practice Buddhism but that "fully 13 million people are intimately bound to Buddhism and to the bonzes who control it." *New York Times Magazine,* August 21, 1966, p. 28.

were the children of military officers and civil servants, the very core of Diem's already slender power base was drastically eroded.* Ngo Dinh Nhu had meantime gained the antagonism of top Vietnamese army officers by making it appear that it was the army that had desecrated the pagodas.†

President Kennedy voiced his concern in a CBS television interview on September 2, stating that in the previous two months Diem's government had "gotten out of touch with the people" and that he believed it could regain that support only if there were "changes in policy and perhaps with personnel." [47] In the middle of this crisis the President sent Secretary McNamara to Saigon to assess the situation. The Defense Secretary agreed with the newly appointed American Ambassador, Henry Cabot Lodge, that political pressure on Diem must be exerted, and McNamara expressed doubt that Diem could at this late hour survive even by taking corrective action.[48] The United States then suspended its subsidies for Vietnamese imports and for Diem's 2,000-man Special Forces. Future payment to these troops was to be contingent on their departure from Saigon and resumption of combat duty against the Vietcong. Though intrinsically of no immediate consequence to Diem and Nhu, these actions had great political significance. They communicated symbolically to opponents of the regime that the United States disapproved of its policies and of the anti-Buddhist acts of President Diem's Special Forces.

---

* The extent of public opposition was underscored by the resignation of Diem's Foreign Secretary, Vu Van Mau, himself a Buddhist, in protest against the attack on the pagodas. Almost immediately afterwards, the Vietnamese Ambassador to the United States (Mme. Nhu's father) and most of his staff also resigned.

† Nhu had also aroused the concern of some officers because of reports that he had begun to approach Hanoi with a view to a settlement. There were, indeed, reports that Nhu, whether to put pressure on the U.S. or for other reasons, was at this time indicating an interest in talks with Hanoi. See David Halberstam, *The Making of a Quagmire* (New York: Random House, 1965), p. 278; and Joseph Alsop, in the *Washington Post,* September 18, 1963. See also Schlesinger, *op. cit.,* p. 990.

5 : During October the signs abounded that President Kennedy for the first time contemplated abandoning America's eight years of unstinting and unqualified support for the Diem regime.* A number of army officers concluded that the United States would stand aside if they moved to unseat Diem and would work with them after his overthrow.[49] On November 1, the generals struck. Both Diem and Nhu were murdered, and a military junta led by General Duong Van Minh seized the reins of government.

When Minh's Military Revolutionary Council took power, considerably less than half of the territory of South Vietnam was under firm Saigon rule. During the previous three years, Diem's government had surrendered control over ever larger areas to the National Liberation Front. The Front in this period had established an alternative *de facto* government in rural Vietnam with the degree of its administrative authority varying from province to province.† In many places, its governance was firm and uncontested by Saigon. In others, Saigon exerted its will during the daytime, while the NLF ruled at night. In many areas claimed by Saigon, its authority was actually confined to those daylight hours when its patrols

---

* Max Frankel, in the *New York Times,* November 2, 1963, succinctly summed up the Administration's attitude towards Diem's overthrow: "The Administration welcomes the coup d'état in South Vietnam, assumes that its policies helped to bring it about and is confident of greater progress now in the war against the Communist guerrillas. . . . It is conceded here, however, that the United States Government had created the atmosphere that made the coup possible."

† One measure of the extent of its control was a report by the United States Operations Mission in Saigon that by June 1963 the NLF was levying taxes in all but three of South Vietnam's forty-four provinces. Cited in Bernard B. Fall, "The Agonizing Reappraisal," *Current History,* February 1965, p. 98. This did not mean that it controlled forty-one provinces, but it did mean that it carried out some functions of government in parts of that many provinces.

were active, and when they returned to their bases the Viet-cong would take over.

President Kennedy's assassination came too soon after the fall of Diem for his reaction to the new situation to have become clear. Perhaps the best clue is to be found in his statement of September 2, 1963:

> In the final analysis, it is their war. They are the ones who have to win it or lose it. We can help them, we can give them equipment, we can send our men out there as advisers, but they have to win it—the people of Viet-Nam—against the Communists. . . . All we can do is help, and we are making it very clear. But I don't agree with those who say we should withdraw. That would be a great mistake.[50]

Haunted by the memory of the French debacle of 1954, Kennedy had tried to draw a line of distinction between tactful assistance that could strengthen the Saigon government's self-reliance and direct American military and political intervention that would ultimately prove self-defeating. But preoccupied by other problems and bombarded by contradictory advice, until only shortly before his death he largely delegated actual formation of Vietnam policy to others less able to appreciate this distinction. In the crisis surrounding Diem's downfall the President had come to realize the gravity of the situation and was beginning to devote more of his attention to it. Given the ambiguities of his view, it is quite impossible to predict what he might have done.

Notes to Chapter VI

1. Arthur M. Schlesinger, *A Thousand Days: John F. Kennedy in the White House* (Boston: Houghton Mifflin, 1965), p. 997.

2. When later asked for his views on the emergence of the insurrection, Secretary Rusk, in answer to a question put to him by Senator Fulbright on January 28, 1966, replied: "Senator, I regret that I did not, in the words of the House of Commons, have notice of this particular questioning on this particular period [1954–60]. I would need to review the record and be much more briefed and detailed on it." U.S. Senate, *Supplemental Foreign Assistance Fiscal Year 1966—Vietnam,* 89th Congress, 2nd Session (Washington: U.S. Government Printing Office, 1966), p. 50.

3. Secretary Rusk's News Conference of November 17, 1961. Reported in U.S. Senate, Committee on Foreign Relations, *Background Information Relating to Southeast Asia and Vietnam,* 2nd rev. ed., 89th Congress, 2nd Session (Washington: U.S. Government Printing Office, 1966), p. 87.

4. Schlesinger, *op. cit.,* p. 547.

5. *Ibid.,* p. 545; Theodore C. Sorensen, *Kennedy* (New York: Harper & Row, 1965), p. 654.

6. Schlesinger, *op. cit.,* pp. 541–543. See also David Halberstam, *The Making of a Quagmire* (New York: Random House, 1965), p. 69.

7. Jean Lacouture, *Vietnam: Between Two Truces* (New York: Random House, 1966), pp. 64–65; *Time,* August 4, 1961.

8. Schlesinger, *op. cit.,* p. 545. According to Sorensen, *op. cit.,* p. 655, Kennedy's "effort to keep our own military role in Vietnam from overshadowing our political objectives was handicapped by the State Department's inability to compete with the Pentagon." For a significant glimpse of Rostow's views on insurgency at the time of his mission with General Taylor, see his "Guerrilla Warfare in Underdeveloped Areas," in *The Viet-Nam Reader,* ed. by Marcus G. Raskin and Bernard B. Fall (New York: Vintage, 1965), pp. 108–116.

9. As Theodore Sorensen puts it: "Formally, Kennedy never made a final negative decision on troops. In typical Kennedy fashion, he made it difficult for any of the pro-intervention advocates to charge him privately with weakness." *Op. cit.,* p. 654.

10. For texts of the Diem letter of December 7 and Kennedy's letter of December 14, see *Department of State Bulletin* (Washington, January 1, 1962), pp. 13–14.

11. See below Table 3, p. 185. For an official description of the infiltration see U.S. White Paper, *A Threat to the Peace* (Washington: U.S. Government Printing Office, 1961), pp. 23–38. The report summed up the arms situation as follows: "No one seriously contends that the Viet Cong are getting all their supplies, equipment, food, and weapons from outside South Viet-Nam. We know, in fact, that they are able to get much of what they need from the areas in which their military units operate. Most of the methods used to get their supplies involve force, fear, or fabrication, but they are nonetheless effective." *Ibid.,* p. 38.

12. As late as December 1962 the *New York Times* reported: "Up to now the Vietcong have operated with a collection of handmade and homemade weapons and arms taken from Government troops." *New York Times,* December 6, 1962. See also Halberstam, *op. cit.,* pp. 189–190. For a discussion of the situation in June 1964 that shows the vast proportion (reported to be as much as 90 percent) of weapons to have been captured, see U.S. Senate, *Foreign Assistance 1964,* 88th Congress, 2nd Session (Washington: U.S. Government Printing Office, 1964), pp. 293–294.

13. *New York Times,* February 15, 1962.

14. Interview with one of the authors, Saigon, January 1961. This perception of Diem's viewpoint was shared by most of those who discussed the matter with him. According to Secretary of State Dean Rusk in 1963: "Part of the problem [in creating a broad political base in the South] has been that those who have collaborated in the war days and immediate postwar days with Ho Chi Minh were pretty much ruled out of consideration in Vietnam, and properly so. . . ." U.S. Senate, *Foreign Assistance Act of 1963,* 88th Congress, 1st Session (Washington: U.S. Government Printing Office, 1963), p. 250. Rusk never faced the implication of the lack of wisdom, let alone the propriety, of "ruling out" of the body politic virtually every authentic nationalist in the South.

15. *New York Times,* January 20, 1962, gives a date of late December 1961. See also Robert Scigliano, *South Vietnam: Nation Under Stress* (Boston: Houghton Mifflin, 1963), p. 147.

16. Philippe Devillers, "The Struggle for Unification," *The China Quarterly,* No. 9, January–March 1962, p. 23, and Lacouture, *op. cit.,* pp. 57–58.

17. Devillers, *op. cit.,* p. 19; and Lacouture, *op. cit.,* pp. 57–58.

18. See Raskin and Fall, *op. cit.,* pp. 255, 258–259; Denis Warner, *The Last Confucian* (New York: Macmillan, 1963), p. 129; *New York Times,* July 9, 1962; and Tran Van Giau and Le Van Chat, *The South Viet Nam Liberation National Front* (Hanoi: Foreign Languages Publishing House, 1962), pp. 62–64.

19. Restated in *Declaration of the First Congress of the South Viet Nam National Front for Liberation* (Hanoi: Foreign Languages Publishing House, 1962), p. 26.

20. *Ibid.,* p. 21.

21. *Ibid.,* pp. 30–31.

22. *Ibid.,* pp. 20–21, 23–24.

23. *Ibid.,* p. 25.

24. Giau and Chat, *op. cit.,* p. 31.

25. *Ibid.*

26. For the full text of the four proposals see *ibid.,* pp. 37–38. See also *New York Times,* July 21, 1962.

27. With respect to this, Tran Van Giau and Le Van Chat concluded: "All obstacles are thus removed on the side of the South Viet Nam Liberation National Front to bring the South Vietnamese people to accept a solution similar to that which triumphed in Laos. . . ." They then quoted what was apparently official NLF commentary in this vein shortly afterwards: "The recent brilliant success of the Laotian people shows that where the U.S. imperialists are forced to give up their intervention in the internal affairs of other peoples, it is then possible to find a reasonable solution conforming to the interests of the nation, of each social stratum, and of all national groups, for all internal disputes, however acute they may be. If in Laos the opponent parties can find a reasonable solution to their dispute, there is no reason why the South Viet Nam people cannot do likewise." Giau and Chat, *op. cit.,* p. 39.

These two North Vietnamese spokesmen concluded their discussion of the NLF's advocacy of neutralization for the South by observing that (as in Laos) a guarantee by the Western as well as communist powers was being requested: "The writing of this point into the Front's program as presented in July 1962 is concrete proof of the Front leaders' sincerity, that the future neutrality of South Viet Nam must be guaranteed by the powers belonging to the different camps." *Ibid.,* pp. 42–43.

28. *Ibid.,* pp. 37–38.

29. *Ibid.,* p. 38.

30. *New York Times,* July 21, 1962.

31. *Ibid.,* October 16 and 18, 1962. Halberstam, *op. cit.,* p. 81.

32. Robert Shaplen, *The Lost Revolution* (New York: Harper & Row, 1965), pp. 15, 138; Lacouture, *op. cit.,* p. 178; Bernard B. Fall, *The Two Viet-Nams* (New York: Praeger, 1964), pp. 326–328, 342–343, 359–362; and Wilfred G. Burchett, *Vietnam: Inside Story of the Guerrilla War* (New York: International Publishers, 1965), pp. 96–98.

33. *Department of State Bulletin* (Washington, January 1, 1962), p. 13. ·

34. Burchett, *op. cit.,* p. 193.

35. Schlesinger, *op. cit.,* p. 548.

36. Halberstam, *op. cit.,* p. 68.

37. *Ibid.,* p. 69.

38. Homer Bigart in the *New York Times,* June 3, 1962.

39. For a critical assessment of the program see the monograph by Milton E. Osborne, *Strategic Hamlets in South Viet-Nam,* Data Paper 55 (Ithaca, N.Y.: Cornell Southeast Asia Program, April 1965).

40. Halberstam, *op. cit.,* p. 71.

41. Schlesinger, *op. cit.,* pp. 549–550.

42. *Department of State Bulletin* (Washington, March 25, 1963), pp. 435–436. See also *ibid.* (March 11, 1963), pp. 364–365; and *Foreign Assistance Act of 1963,* pp. 228–229.

43. *Department of State Bulletin* (Washington, May 11, 1963), pp. 729–730.

44. Halberstam, *op. cit.,* p. 189.

45. *Ibid.,* p. 190.

46. *Ibid.,* p. 207.

47. *New York Times,* September 3, 1963.

48. Schlesinger, *op. cit.,* p. 996.

49. For the fullest account of Diem's overthrow, see Halberstam, *op. cit.,* pp. 277–299. See also *New York Times* for the period.

50. *Department of State Bulletin* (Washington, September 30, 1963), pp. 498–499.

CHAPTER VII

Americanization of the War

1: **Diem's death** initially appeared to open up possibilities for a peaceful settlement of the Vietnam question. Public feeling against the war began to be expressed more openly in Saigon and other cities, and both the politically active Buddhists and student elements advocated pursuit of a neutralist solution to the conflict.

A fortnight after coming to power the Military Revolutionary Council of General Duong Van Minh received a manifesto (dated November 8) from the NLF that called on

> the parties concerned in South Vietnam [to] negotiate with one another to reach a cease-fire and solve important problems of the nation, to stabilize the basic internal and external policies, with a view to reaching free general elections to elect state organs and to form a national coalition government composed of representatives of all forces, parties, tendencies, and strata of the South Vietnamese people.[1]

The manifesto further advocated a policy of neutrality and the establishment of friendly relations with all countries and suggested that the reunification of the whole of Vietnam be "realized step by step on a voluntary basis."

The removal of Diem also affected the international scene. President de Gaulle's offer of August 29, 1963, to cooperate with the people of Vietnam in an effort to unify their country in peace, free of outside influences, now seemed much more plausible.[2] The *New York Times* editorialized on November 10 that "a negotiated settlement and 'neutralization' of Vietnam are not to be ruled out" and that the time had come to try to restore the Geneva settlement by negotiations. Subsequently, it was disclosed that Secretary General U Thant suggested that the United States promote a coalition government in Saigon to include noncommunist Vietnamese political exiles, especially those who had taken refuge in Paris.[3] Shortly after John Kennedy's assassination, U Thant met with President Johnson and was reported to have conveyed a message to the President from Ho Chi Minh proposing talks on a settlement.[4] In December, renewed support for a neutralization of South Vietnam also came from Cambodian Chief of State Norodom Sihanouk, who again invited South Vietnam to join his country in a neutral confederation.[5]

The Administration in Washington quickly made clear its opposition to a neutralist solution. In mid-December Defense Secretary Robert S. McNamara told Saigon's military leaders that Washington did not envisage neutralism for the country and that President Kennedy's plan for withdrawing American forces by the end of 1965 had been revised.[6] Any lingering doubts regarding the U.S. rejection of compromise and its determination to prosecute the war were resolved by President Johnson's New Year's message to General Duong Van Minh, which stated:

Neutralization of South Vietnam would only be another name for a Communist take-over. . . . The United States will continue to furnish you and your people with the fullest measure of support in this bitter fight. . . . We shall maintain in Vietnam American personnel and material as needed to assist you in achieving victory.[7]

The Minh junta took stern measures against advocates of neutralism, issuing strong statements against them, suppressing several proneutralist newspapers, and organizing anti-French, antineutralism demonstrations.[8] Nevertheless, General Minh came under criticism from both the United States and from some of his own generals for failing to stem the tide of neutralist feeling.[9] When General Nguyen Khanh overthrew the Minh junta in a coup of January 30, 1964, he justified this as a necessary step to halt the movement toward neutralism that General Minh had been unable to control.* He accused the Minh regime of "paving the way for neutralism and thus selling out the country." [10]

The week after Khanh's accession to power, the NLF again called for negotiations to end the war,[11] but by then Saigon's course toward continuing the conflict had become more decided. The Khanh junta repudiated both neutralism and negotiations and squarely aligned itself with Washington. The United States immediately declared its willingness to work with the new regime.

During the first six months of General Khanh's rule, the ground previously lost to the Vietcong was not regained, and the areas it controlled even expanded.[12] In accounting for the growth of the Vietcong, Secretary of Defense McNamara, on March 26, 1964, referred to its "large indigenous support" and the "bonds of loyalty" underlying its organization.[13] A U.S. official report released on April 1, 1964, stated that only 34 per cent of Vietnam's villages were government controlled; 24 per cent were "neutral"; and 42 per cent were outright Vietcong. In January 1964, *The Observer* (U.S. Army newspaper in Saigon) wrote that "some four to five million people support the NLF (National Liberation Front) in varying degrees." [14] On the offensive, the communist troops fought to destroy the reserves of the Saigon army and fragment the territory held by the Republic into small enclaves.† The lack of success of

---

* At its second congress on January 25, 1964, the NLF apparently felt there was sufficient sympathy in favor of negotiation among the officers of the South Vietnamese army for it to direct an appeal for unity to them. Liberation Radio, February 5, 1964.

† The most important NLF military campaign during these months aimed to annihilate Saigon's strategic reserves. The Vietcong would strike at isolated posts in an effort to lure the reserves from their bases and ambush them en route. Most unofficial observers believe that by late 1964, Saigon's reserves had been substantially destroyed. A typical result of a Vietcong operation is described in the *New York Times,* February 7, 1964. For figures on size of forces in this period, see below, Table 3, p. 185.

General Khanh's armies kindled a mounting frustration among American officials. The rise in the level of U.S. military and economic aid and the modest influx of American forces were clearly proving ineffective.[15] The Pentagon had long argued in favor of extending military activity into North Vietnam,[16] and this argument probably gained added force as a result of Senator Barry Goldwater's advocacy of such a course during his campaign for the Presidential nomination.[17] The outgoing ambassador, Henry Cabot Lodge, typified the growing militancy of the Administration's position when he declared at the end of June that he was recommending to the Administration not merely "more of the same" policy, but additional measures about which he declined to be specific on the grounds of security.[18]

In Saigon, Prime Minister Khanh who had already publicly urged extension of the war to the North was reportedly encouraged in this by Senator Goldwater's nomination as the Republican Party's Presidential candidate. "He [Khanh] interpreted it as a sign there was support in the United States for a more aggressive war policy including attacks outside South Vietnam's frontiers, and, he points out, attacks on North Vietnam were American ideas in the first place." [19] On July 19, General Khanh delivered a major address, the keynote of which was *bac tien* ("to the North").[20] Two days later Nguyen Cao Ky, the commander of the Vietnamese Air Force, announced that it was prepared to bomb North Vietnam at any time. He further disclosed that his pilots were being trained to fly jets on bombing attacks and stated: "We are ready. We could go this afternoon. I cannot assure that all of North Vietnam would be destroyed, but Hanoi would certainly be destroyed." [21] The new U.S. Ambassador, General Maxwell D. Taylor, reportedly reprimanded the Air Commander and even criticized General Khanh for permitting him to make this provocative statement. General Khanh said in response, however, that, so far as he understood the situation, there were no basic policy differences—only differences about timing and about what to announce publicly.[22]

Concerned over this imminent threat of major escalation of the war, Secretary General U Thant had at the beginning of July 1964 again attempted to arrange a peaceful settlement in Vietnam. Military methods, he stated on July 8, could not bring about peace; ". . . the only sensible alternative is the political and diplomatic method of negotiations which, even at this late hour, may offer some chance of a solution." The first steps toward this, he suggested, could be taken at a reconvened Geneva Conference.[23]

This initiative received immediate backing from France. Noting that "some people" imagined that a military solution in South Vietnam could be secured by extending the war to the North, French President de Gaulle warned on July 23 against the "tremendous risk" of a generalized conflict. The impossibility of achieving a military decision meant, he said, "returning to what was agreed upon ten years ago and, this time, complying with it."[24]

Moscow and Hanoi as well as Paris sent communications to the fourteen nations that had participated in the 1961–62 Geneva Conference on Laos, urging that it be reconvened in order to deal with the renewal of fighting there.[25] Prompt support for this was indicated by China, the NLF, and Cambodia. In view of the mounting intensity of the Sino-Soviet dispute, China's endorsement of the Soviet proposal was unusually prompt and positive. Peking appealed for a reconvening of the conference to "stop the U.S. imperialist aggression and intervention in the Indochinese states, safeguard the Geneva agreements, and defend the peace of Indochina."[26]

Neither the Secretary General of the United Nations, the French President, nor the Soviet government received any encouragement from the United States. Indeed the Johnson Administration's rejection of their efforts was brusque and uncompromising. There was no hint of a willingness to explore even tentatively the possibilities that seemed to be opening up for a peaceful settlement of the conflict.* "We do not believe in conferences called to ratify terror," [27] the President stated, and the following day the United States announced that its military mission in South Vietnam would be increased by 30 per cent, from 16,000 to 21,000.[28]

With the 1964 Presidential campaign now warming up, Johnson wished to forestall a Republican attack on the issue of a compromise with communism. To accept negotiation proposals might well have left him vulnerable to such a charge, since the political balance in South Vietnam made it virtually certain that the NLF would play a significant role both in any serious negotiations and in any viable South Vietnamese government that issued from them. Thus, President Johnson reassured the public during the campaign that American boys would not be sent to fight in Vietnam, but at the same time he asserted that he would never permit communist expansion there.

Across the Pacific, the war was moving into a new phase. Air Vice-Marshal Ky had stated publicly in his news conference of July 23 that South Vietnamese commando teams had already been engaged in sabotage missions inside North Vietnam "by air, sea and land." † Two days later Hanoi Radio charged that the Americans and their "lackeys" had fired on North

---

* Washington's rationale for opposing negotiations was that any such course would damage the morale of Khanh's shaky regime. Public dissatisfaction had become widespread, and even Khanh's own deputy premier, Nguyen Ton Hoan, was openly calling on him to step down in favor of a civilian government. Saigon's repudiation of all peace initiatives was every bit as uncompromising as Washington's. Khanh termed such proposals "prejudicial to the fight that Vietnam leads in the vanguard of the free world against aggression imposed upon it by the Communist international." *New York Times,* July 25 and 26, 1964.

† See *New York Times,* July 23, 1964. South Vietnamese commandos had been conducting such operations against the North since 1957 and particularly since 1961. See *New York Times,* January 1, 1962, and July 26, 1964; and *Le Monde,* August 7, 1964.

Vietnamese fishing craft, and the Hanoi government lodged a formal protest with the International Control Commission. On July 30 it accused the South Vietnamese naval vessels of again raiding its fishing boats in Tonkin Gulf and, with the protective cover by an American destroyer, bombarding two North Vietnamese islands.* This alleged bombardment occasioned another Hanoi protest to the ICC on July 31.[29]

The official U.S. version of developments thereafter was that on the night of August 2, North Vietnamese torpedo boats launched an unprovoked attack upon the U.S. destroyer *Maddox,* while it was engaged in a "routine patrol." Hanoi admitted the attack but said it was in reprisal for the bombardment of nearby North Vietnamese islands.† Hanoi and Washington thus agreed that North Vietnamese PT boats had deliberately engaged the *Maddox* on August 2, though they differed as to where the engagement took place, the reason for the attack, and its outcome.

According to the United States, on August 4, North Vietnamese torpedo boats launched a second attack, this time against both the *Maddox* and another destroyer, the *Turner*

---

* American destroyer patrols in the Gulf of Tonkin had long been assumed to be "covering" South Vietnamese naval attacks on the North Vietnamese coast; the South Vietnamese were reported to have had increasing success with raids by their coastal force. *New York Times,* August 10, 1964.

† Although Senator Richard B. Russell suggested that the North Vietnamese might have been "confused" because there had been some South Vietnamese naval activity in the Gulf of Tonkin, State Department officials rejected the explanation. See *New York Times,* August 4, 1964. Referring to Hanoi's charge that an attack by South Vietnamese naval forces against nearby islands had provoked North Vietnamese retaliation against the *Maddox,* Assistant Secretary William P. Bundy stated that the *Maddox* "was attacked approximately 2 days after this alleged South Vietnamese attack and at a time when she was well off the coast of North Viet-Nam, and the *Maddox* . . . had no connection whatever with whatever may have been going on in connection with these islands." See *Department of State Bulletin* (Washington, September 7, 1964), p. 335.

Joy, at a time when they were sixty-five miles from shore. Neither of the destroyers suffered any casualties or damage, and they were reported to have repulsed the attacking boats, possibly destroying two of them. Hanoi insisted that this second attack never, in fact, occurred. As Senator Fulbright later observed:

> But this Gulf of Tonkin incident, if I may say so, was a very vague one. We were briefed on it, but we have no way of knowing, even to this day, what actually happened. I don't know whether we provoked that attack in connection with supervising or helping a raid by South Vietnamese or not. Our evidence was sketchy as to whether those PT boats, or some kind of boats, that were approaching were coming to investigate or whether they actually attacked. I have been *told* there was no physical damage. They weren't hit by anything. I heard one man say there was one bullet hole in one of those ships. One bullet hole! [30]

Damage and doubt aside, the American response was prompt. President Johnson went on television at 11:30 P.M. on the evening of August 4, thirteen hours after the attack. He informed the American public that retaliatory action was already under way: "Air action is now in execution against gunboats and certain supporting facilities in North Vietnam which have been used in these hostile operations." His decisions on the domestic front came with equal swiftness. Prior to his broadcast he had met with leaders of both parties in the Congress and informed them that "I shall immediately request the Congress to pass a resolution making it clear that our Government is united in its determination to take all necessary measures in support of freedom and in defense of peace in Southeast Asia." They had, he said, given him "encouraging assurance" that "such a resolution will be promptly introduced, freely and expeditiously debated, and passed with overwhelming support." [31]

The next day the President addressed a message to Congress asking it to "join in affirming the national determination that all such attacks will be met," and to approve "all necessary action to protect our Armed Forces and to assist nations covered by the SEATO treaty." He requested speed in passing the resolution, not merely because of the events of Tonkin Gulf, but also because "we are entering on 3 months of political campaigning. Hostile nations must understand that in such a period the United States will continue to protect its national interests, and that in these matters there is no division among us." The resolution was promptly passed 466–0 in the House, 88–2 in the Senate (with only Senators Gruening and Morse opposing). It authorized the President to "take all necessary measures to repel any armed attack against the forces of the United States and to prevent further aggression." The measure further stated that the United States was prepared "as the President determines to take all necessary steps, including the use of armed force, to assist any member or protocol state of the Southeast Asia Collective Defense Treaty requesting assistance in defense of its freedom." [32]

President Johnson had with solid congressional endorsement now embarked on a major commitment. He had taken a giant step beyond anything President Kennedy had ever felt appropriate. As columnist James Reston observed just afterwards in the *New York Times*:

> This is a little different from merely sending arms and "advisers" to South Vietnam. It would approve any military action "as the President determines" in any part of Southeast Asia, including military action in support of any nation in the Southeast Asia treaty . . . provided our military action were sought and the President approved. [33]

2: With evident American encouragement, on August 16 General Khanh assumed the position of Chief of State taking over broad emergency powers that gave him an almost dictatorial position. He indicated that in the new situation American military representatives would be allowed greater participation in decisions on the pursuit of the war. The unpopularity of his move and Vietnamese resentment at the increasing American interference in their political life led to protests from Buddhist monks and students in Saigon, Hué, and other cities. To combat the mounting criticism, Washington warned that "it would take an extremely serious and negative view of any move to oust the regime of President Nguyen Khanh." [34] Antigovernment riots nonetheless increased in intensity, and, to rescue his position, Khanh was obliged to reach a provisional agreement on August 27, whereby a triumvirate under his leadership would hold power. Two days later a civilian, Nguyen Xuan Oanh, was appointed acting premier. Opposed to Khanh's concessions, the United States informed South Vietnamese leaders that it would have to reappraise its role in the fight against the communists if Khanh's former position were not restored. [35]

By this time the Buddhists had emerged as the strongest political faction in the country, [36] and even with solid American backing behind him a leader could remain in power only if he accommodated to the Buddhist demands. Khanh was thereby caught between conflicting pressures. Washington believed that the politically ascendant Buddhist leadership might help install a government intent on ending the war and negotiating with the NLF to achieve a settlement,* and it pressed Khanh to stand firm against the rising pressure. Khanh's compromise of August 27 had not satisfied the Buddhist leaders, and they maintained their pressure until on September 4 General Khanh capitulated.

He accepted "in general and in detail an immediate Bud-

---

* This possibility was being seriously considered in Washington at least as early as June, when a study prepared by the CIA concluded that there was "serious doubt that a victory can be won" and that at best "a prolonged stalemate" could be achieved and recognized that "There is also a chance that political evolution within the country and developments upon the world scene could lead to some kind of a negotiated settlement based on neutralization." Reported in the *New York Times,* August 23, 1964. (This study, which had been prepared in June by a member of the Board of National Estimates of the Central Intelligence Agency, had been given general approval by the board as a whole. It was leaked to an American newspaper on August 22.)

dhist formula for reforming his Government along new civilian lines." This called for his promise to transfer power to civilian hands within two months. Despite countermoves from the Catholics and some generals, culminating in an abortive coup on September 13, the power of the Buddhists remained substantially unchallenged, and General Khanh appeared resigned to fulfilling his pledge and stepping down in favor of a civilian cabinet at the end of October. Although Washington was reported to be seeking "desperately . . . to help keep Major General Nguyen Khanh in power in South Vietnam at least as a symbol of governmental authority," he could no longer be regarded as an effective instrument of American policy.[37]

During the second week in September, Ambassador Taylor flew to Washington for a quick review of the Vietnam crisis with top Administration officials. He reported to the President that Saigon controlled no more than 30 per cent of the country's territory, that at least 20 per cent of the land was in Vietcong hands, with the balance contested, and that the guerrillas had expanded their hard core of 20,000 men in 1961 to about 50,000.* It was his conclusion that the Vietcong insurgency could not be ended in the foreseeable future unless the war

---

* This figure later turned out to be exaggerated. See Table 3, p. 185. According to Peter Grose in the *New York Times Magazine,* January 24, 1965, by the end of 1964 the Vietcong had developed "a stable and orderly political machine across the country, their cadres paralleling the Saigon administrative structure at every level. Only a final political shift at the top is awaited before the entire Communist-led apparatus surfaces and exercises its control in the open. Under the Vietcong provincial commissars and their central committees come district commissars, then the village or township cadres and finally the hamlet committees. Where Vietcong control is firm, the administration functions with scarcely any interruption. . . . By conservative estimate 8,000 to 10,000 political administrators govern the areas of South Vietnam controlled by the Vietcong." Immediately after Taylor's return, the areas controlled by the government shrank further with a major uprising of Montagnard tribes in the Central Highlands areas. See *New York Times,* September 29, 1964, and October 2 and 4, 1964. So serious was this that it was reported that the authority of the Saigon government had all but disappeared in much of this area.

was made so costly for the communists, and particularly for North Vietnam, that rather than risk further heavy losses they would discontinue the struggle. The Administration reportedly agreed to maintain and increase, as needed, its assistance to Saigon, but it felt a great anxiety over the degree of popular opposition to the Saigon government. At the end of the conference, in the words of a Washington correspondent of the *New York Times,* "The Administration was left with the fundamental question. . . . Would there be, and how much longer, a South Vietnamese structure for the United States to go on supporting." [38]

By now a debate was developing within Administration circles on the conduct of the war in Vietnam. While President Johnson, in the last weeks of the Presidential campaign, continued to reassure the electorate that "we don't want our American boys to do the fighting for Asian boys" or to "get tied down in a land war in Asia," [39] his Assistant Secretary of State for Far Eastern Affairs, William P. Bundy, was suggesting a far different course. At the end of September, Mr. Bundy stated in Tokyo: "Expansion of the war outside South Vietnam, while not a course we want or seek, could be forced upon us by the increased pressure of the Communists including a rising scale of infiltration." He appeared to be threatening air action against the North and was quoted as saying that the guerrillas could thereby be reduced to manageable proportions "in a matter of months." [40]

Columnist James Reston viewed the division of opinion in official Washington as "between those Johnson aides who want to expand the war into Communist North Vietnam with the direct participation of U.S. troops and those who believe that the risks of such a policy outweigh the advantages." He found it "difficult to understand why some prominent officials, a few weeks before a national election, should be talking so openly about expanding the war, and not only advocating but almost lobbying for such a course of action," and he observed that "the nation is entitled to a clearer definition of our war aims there and specifically to an assurance that our ships are in the Gulf of Tonkin to end the war and not to 'provoke an incident' that might expand the war." [41]

After the Presidential election, powerful voices within the Administration actively pressed for an expansion of the war. The entire membership of the Joint Chiefs of Staff reportedly argued for broadening the conflict, and Ambassador Maxwell Taylor, the former head of that body, publicly advocated bombing both Vietcong infiltration routes through Laos and the "training and staging areas in North Vietnam itself." [42] This insistence on decisive American military steps was also reflected by Senator Richard B. Russell, Chairman of the Senate's Armed Services Committee. After talking with President Johnson on November 25, he stated: "We either have to get out or take some action to help the Vietnamese. They won't help themselves. We made a big mistake in going there, but I can't figure out any way to get out without scaring the rest of the world." [43] The next day Ambassador Taylor flew home for high-level strategy sessions. In his discussions with the President and cabinet members on December 1, Taylor painted so gloomy a picture of the overall situation in Vietnam that at the end of the meeting, as newspapermen filed in for a briefing, Defense Secretary McNamara was overheard remarking to President Johnson: "It would be impossible for Max [General Taylor] to talk to these people without leaving the impression the situation is going to hell." The press conference scheduled to follow the briefing was abruptly canceled. [44]

3 : **UN Secretary General U Thant**, against the background of these deliberations in Washington, made yet another plea to bring about negotiations between the U.S. and North Vietnam. Shortly before the Presidential election (apparently in late September) he proposed that Hanoi and Washington secretly send emissaries to Rangoon to discuss the Vietnam crisis. Hanoi accepted the proposal while the Administration insisted on the postponement of any discussion until after the elections.[45] Mr. Thant complied with this American request and waited until after Johnson's sweeping reelection before resurrecting the matter. Hanoi declared its continuing willingness to cooperate, but the U.S. Secretary of Defense "flatly opposed the attempt." McNamara stated that the Saigon government would have to be informed and that negotiations would certainly have a demoralizing effect on it.* [46]

At the end of October 1964, a civilian government was installed in Saigon with Tran Van Huong as Premier and Phan Khac Suu as Chief of State. General Khanh, now out of American favor, still wielded significant political power as commander of the army, but it appeared that a number of other senior army officers could be counted upon to stand behind the new government. Washington approved the new cabinet and prepared to back it. Huong's cabinet did not, however, find favor among the Buddhists, who soon organized street demonstrations against it. The government had to employ paratroops in suppressing them and was obliged to declare martial law. During December, the Buddhists intensified their oppositionist campaign and threatened to take an anti-American position if the United States persisted in its endorsement of Premier Huong.[47]

The test of strength between the American-supported

---

* The American public was not informed of Secretary General Thant's initiative until this was disclosed by the *New York Times* on March 9, 1965. Eight months later, the State Department spokesman Robert McCloskey confirmed that the United States had in fact rejected U Thant's proposal for the Rangoon meeting, thereby reversing previous denials of such a rejection. Mr. McCloskey stated that Secretary of State Rusk's "antennae is sensitive" and that if Hanoi was "prepared for serious talks . . . the Secretary of State said he would recognize it when it came." Concerning this, the *New York Times* editorialized: "This comment reminds one of the ancient Roman practice of drawing auspices from the flight or the entrails of birds. It would be a shuddering thought that the fate of nations and of thousands of young Americans depended on Dean Rusk's antenna. Yet this is what Mr. McCloskey indicated." See *New York Times,* November 17, 1965.

Huong government and its Buddhist opponents altered the balance of power within the military leadership. The rise of the Buddhists gave an advantage to some of the "young Turk" officers, including Air Vice-Marshal Nguyen Cao Ky and General Nguyen Chanh Thi, Commander of the I Corps area. The latter had particularly close ties with the Buddhist leadership. Whether or not the initiative for an attempted coup on December 19 came from these two subordinates or from Khanh himself, the three promptly joined forces in a move to topple Huong. As a result, a newly formed Armed Forces Council with Khanh at its head emerged as the locus of power in the Saigon government,[48] although Chief of State Suu and Premier Huong were permitted to remain as little more than figureheads. The Buddhists, however, balked at the limited change and demanded the removal of Suu and Huong. For several weeks, nevertheless, they bided their time, muting their protest as they awaited the resolution of the power struggle between the Armed Forces Council and the rump civilian government.

Complicating the picture, U.S. Ambassador Taylor almost immediately denounced the military coup and warned that unless the "fabric of legal government" were restored, Washington might have to reconsider its close alliance with Saigon.[49] He privately urged Premier Huong to resist the military's demands even to the point of resigning rather than functioning without the legal basis of his now dissolved civilian High National Council. The domestic pressures proved dominant, however, and both Premier Huong and Chief of State Suu agreed to cooperate with the military commanders.[50]

In the face of American opposition, General Khanh remained intransigent. Despite Washington's prompt endorsement of Ambassador Taylor's policies, Khanh forbade the restoration of the civilian provisional assembly and publicly reproved Ambassador Taylor for interfering in internal Vietnamese politics. Washington signaled its dissatisfaction with General Khanh and the "young Turks" by official hints that

U.S. aid might be curtailed if a full civilian government were not reestablished. General Khanh replied with a public declaration of independence from what he charged to be foreign manipulation, cautioning the United States, and particularly General Taylor, against imposing unwanted leaders on the people and army of South Vietnam.[51] In this polemic, General Khanh's stand was buttressed by active encouragement from the Buddhist monks whose formidable influence he had come to appreciate and whose backing would be essential to him in any sustained challenge to the United States or to American-backed politicians. The Buddhists shared his resentment at the interference of the United States in Saigon's politics and charged that only support of "foreigners" was keeping the Premier in power.[52] The strained relations between Taylor and Khanh produced what the *New York Times* described as "the most direct clash with Vietnamese leaders since the veiled threats leveled against the regime of Ngo Dinh Diem before it was overthrown last year." [53]

The intensity of this political struggle also threw into bold relief the alignment of the power centers operating on the Saigon scene. Three major elements overshadowed all others: the American political and military presence, the Buddhist political leadership, and the Vietnamese army—the pivotal and most variable factor, since the political orientation of many of its officers remained unpredictable. A few army leaders, such as General Nguyen Chanh Thi, stood close to the Buddhists, while others, especially such Catholic officers as General Nguyen Van Thieu, tended to align closely with U.S. military commanders. Apart from these two extremes, the majority of the military elite had made no obvious commitment by which their moves could be anticipated. Personal ambition and opportunistic considerations probably weighed with many of them, and all senior officers realized fully the military establishment's absolute financial dependence upon the United States.

The situation was further beclouded by the fact that certain high officers, notably General Khanh, had lost favor with the United States, so they had to look elsewhere for support in advancing their own careers. Such men sought backing from the only major alternative political force—the Buddhists. Apparently, it was primarily among those who enlisted Buddhist endorsement that there was some disposition to consider the possibilities of a negotiated peace and a neutralist solution for South Vietnam. Most of their fellow officers, in contrast, had long ago concluded that—in General Taylor's words—they had burned their bridges vis-à-vis the communists.[54] Any peaceful solution would, they knew, leave them in a position of diminished stature, if not actual danger.* Somewhat ironically, General Khanh now emerged as the symbol and spokesman for those officers opposed to the U.S. political presence in Saigon and most inclined to seek a peaceful settlement to the war. As such, he became the target of American criticism and a major effort to oust him. Whatever affinity of purpose may have originally existed between Khanh and the Buddhist leadership, American policies now brought them into closer harmony.

On January 20, 1965, Premier Huong broadened the character of his cabinet by granting portfolios to four generals, including Major General Nguyen Van Thieu, commander of the IV Corps area, and Air Vice-Marshal Nguyen Cao Ky. This provoked a sharp Buddhist reaction, with increasingly bitter anti-American overtones. The USIS library in Saigon was sacked, and in Hué a mob of 5,000 overran the USIS building and clamored for the withdrawal of Ambassador Taylor.[55] Five leading Buddhist monks, including Thich ("Venerable") Tri Quang and Thich Tam Chau publicly

---

* A year before, a group of French-trained and French-oriented officers, among whom General Duong Van Minh was the principal figure, had comprised an important bloc within the military establishment, but by this time their power had declined markedly. Several of their leaders had been arrested on December 20 on orders from General Khanh.

began a fast aimed at unseating Premier Huong and as a protest against the Americanization of the government. On January 27, military leaders led by General Khanh staged a successful coup against Huong.

Intense political in-fighting in Saigon prevailed during the next three weeks. The *New York Times* reported American pressure for a cabinet headed either by the caretaker premier, Nguyen Xuan Oanh, regarded as "strongly pro-American," or by Dr. Nguyen Luu Vien, who had been closely associated with the late President Diem.[56] With the coup on January 27, however, the Buddhists—in particular Tri Quang, the Secretary General of the Buddhist Institute for Religious Affairs (*"Vien Hoa Dao"*)—had apparently achieved a prominent position of power. Tri Quang was reportedly not frightened by talk of neutralism, and some observers believed that General Khanh also "might examine closely a neutralist solution" if he were frustrated by the United States.[57] Western correspondents in Saigon somberly predicted "the emergence within six months of a government that will present an ultimatum-invitation to the United States to get out of Vietnam." * [58]

4: On January 31, 1965, Moscow announced that Soviet Premier Alexei Kosygin would head a delegation to Hanoi. There was speculation in Washington that the trip was meant to underline Moscow's previous warnings against any Ameri-

---

* The *New York Times* commented on January 31: "In view of this deteriorating political situation, Washington was faced with two questions. Was it possible that a government might soon come to power which might demand that the U.S. get out of South Vietnam? Even without such a development, should the U.S. either expand its war effort or voluntarily withdraw?"

On February 3, reports from Paris stated that "unofficial representatives" of South Vietnam and from Hanoi were holding discussions in both Paris and Saigon. American sources expressed doubt that "any important element in the present Government in Saigon" was represented in these talks. See *ibid.,* February 4, 1965. However, given the confusion as to the actual political balance in Saigon, this report must have created additional apprehension in Washington.

can extension of the fighting into North Vietnam and also to gain Hanoi's support for Moscow in the latter's dispute with Peking. Moscow was considered fearful that an escalation of the war to North Vietnam might eventually lead to direct Russian involvement. There was a "developing speculation in the Administration and among informed diplomats that Mr. Kosygin's trip might be the opening move in a broad Soviet attempt to mediate between the United States and the Hanoi regime for a settlement of the Vietnamese war," and Washington expected that after his visit Moscow "would start a campaign to reconvene the Geneva Conference on Vietnam." [59]

In retrospect it seems certain that President Johnson had by this time decided in favor of bombing the North and was waiting only for an appropriate pretext before ordering the initial raids. On February 5 he responded affirmatively to a Soviet invitation issued the previous month for a meeting between him and Kosygin, a reply undoubtedly calculated to reassure the Russians that Washington hoped to maintain friendly relations with Moscow despite the impending American actions against the Soviet's North Vietnamese ally.[60] While Premier Kosygin was flying to Hanoi, the President's Special Assistant for National Security Affairs, McGeorge Bundy, was en route to Saigon. Arriving there on February 4, Bundy learned that the overthrow of Premier Huong had immeasurably bolstered the influence of the Buddhists and that they were then toying with the idea of neutralism and negotiations with the communists.[61] The next day President Johnson declared that the Administration was determined to pursue its policy of "helping the people of South Vietnam resist aggression and preserve their freedom" and that it aimed to make its assistance "more efficient and more effective." He refused to discuss the possibility of a negotiated settlement.[62]

On February 7, the Vietcong provided the awaited act of provocation. The guerrillas staged a night raid against American barracks at Pleiku, killing 8 Americans and wounding 126.[63] Only twelve hours later, while Premier Kosygin and his party were conferring with North Vietnamese leaders in Hanoi, the war escalated. American jets attacked North Vietnam in what was officially described as a reprisal for the Vietcong raid at Pleiku.[64] The Administration also referred to its response as a "test of will," where inaction would have been interpreted as defeatist,[65] and later provided the additional rationalization that the air strikes would stiffen the resistance spirit of the South Vietnamese. Following the announcement of the first raid, President Johnson declared that the United States sought "no wider war," [66] but in the course of the next five days two other raids were carried out as "retaliation" against specific Vietcong attacks. In each case Administration officials insisted on the distinction between the retaliatory strikes and outright war.

Nonetheless, a major escalation had in fact been launched. In response, Secretary General U Thant, Soviet Russia, and President de Gaulle each sought to divert the United States away from this course and onto one of negotiation and compromise. On February 12, U Thant appealed to all the parties in the crisis to move "from the field of battle to the conference table," either inside or outside the United Nations, and called for the revival of the Geneva Conference.[67] The Soviet government, after warning the United States on February 8 that the American bombings would require it "to take further measures to safeguard the security and strengthen the defense capability" of the Hanoi government,[68] quickly followed U Thant's lead. On February 16, just after his return to Moscow, Kosygin proposed to both Hanoi and Peking that a new international conference on Indochina be called.[69] The Hanoi government had reportedly asked France to intensify her efforts in behalf of a negotiated settlement of the war,[70] and on February 10 de Gaulle expressed French interest in reconvening the 1954 Geneva Conference.[71] U Thant was informed by Hanoi that it accepted his suggestion for informal negotiations,[72] and on February 23 the Soviet government disclosed its support for de Gaulle's January appeal concerning a negotiated peace and agreed to a reconvening of the 1954 Geneva Conference.[73]

Thereupon, on February 24 U Thant again called for a

resort to "diplomatic and political methods of negotiation and discussion" that, if sincerely tried, might lead to political stability in Vietnam. When this had been achieved the United States would be able to "withdraw its troops with dignity." He revealed that he had earlier presented "concrete ideas and proposals" to the principal parties directly involved in the Vietnam dispute and urged that diplomatic and political methods be tried. He also intimated that the American public had not been given the relevant information on the possibilities for a negotiated peaceful settlement and previous attempts to reach such a solution. He stated: "I am sure the great American people, if only they know the true facts and the background to the developments in South Viet-Nam, will agree with me that further bloodshed is unnecessary. . . . As you know, in times of war and of hostilities the first casualty is truth." [74]

The White House's response to U Thant's proposals was sharp and negative. It stated that President Johnson had not authorized negotiations for a peaceful settlement and was not contemplating them. Furthermore, it denied that any proposals had been placed before the President by U Thant or anyone else.[75] Secretary of State Rusk reiterated that no one had been authorized to speak for the United States and that no one would be allowed to negotiate until North Vietnam agreed to respect the independence and national security of South Vietnam.[76] The Administration, as before, insisted on the permanent division of Vietnam and its own right to protect the South Vietnamese state it had built up, repudiating in advance any settlement that failed to recognize a separate and sovereign South.* It was now also assuming the right to retaliate against any "aggression" from the Northern half of the country.

---

* The Assistant Secretary for Far Eastern Affairs, William P. Bundy, stated on February 5: "Negotiation will in the end certainly be an answer if it produces an independent and secure South Viet-Nam. But, on the other hand, there's no sign that Hanoi would really go for that at the present time. And negotiation that admitted communism to South Viet-Nam or legalized it, that didn't

Meanwhile, the gravity of the political situation in Saigon caused deepening apprehension in Washington. Although the bombing attacks against the North may have stiffened the spine of some military leaders, the army desertion rate remained very high,[77] and there was no discernible increase in enthusiasm for the war among the civilian population. In fact, neutralist feeling and the desire for peace still gripped the war-weary populace, and the political base of the Buddhists continued to grow. During the three-week period following the January 27 coup against Premier Huong,* Buddhist influence strongly conditioned Khanh's deliberations with military and political leaders. As a result, the premier finally selected, Dr. Phan Huy Quat,† was known to be acceptable to the Buddhists, and it was remarked that the two political leaders who had been in close touch with Maxwell D. Taylor, the U.S. Ambassador, were not in the new cabinet.[78] Installed on February 16, 1965, with the backing of the Buddhists, General Khanh, and a number of other important officers, the new cabinet reflected Quat's attempt to enlist broadly based civilian representation.[79]

---

get Hanoi and the North Vietnamese out, or that set up some structure under nebulous, not very clear guarantees, simply would not provide the independent and secure South Viet-Nam that nation is entitled to and that we're after." *Department of State Bulletin* (Washington, March 1, 1965), p. 293.

* A caretaker government under Dr. Nguyen Xuan Oanh officially governed during this period. Dr. Oanh was a Harvard-trained economist who had served as third deputy premier in the Huong cabinet.

† Phan Huy Quat originated from Ha Tinh, about eighty-five miles north of the 17th parallel, and was regarded as having considerable influence in the northern part of South Vietnam. He had received his medical degree from the University of Hué where he had helped found and was president of the Vietnamese Students Association. From 1949 to 1953 he had served under Emperor Bao Dai, first as Education Minister and then as Defense Minister. During the early period of the Geneva negotiations (while Prince Buu Loc was in Geneva) he had served briefly as acting premier. Opposed to Diem, Dr. Quat did not resume a government position until after Diem's fall. Though not a member, he was an influential advisor to the Dai Viet party.

Within three days of Dr. Quat's installation as premier, another coup was attempted, conducted this time against the army's commander-in-chief, General Khanh, who was regarded as the new government's principal military guarantor. Three influential Catholic officers instigated this move—Colonel Pham Ngoc Thao, Brigadier General Lam Van Phat, and Lieutenant General Tran Thien Khiem. The *New York Times* remarked: "The available evidence suggests that the abortive coup was hatched in the South Vietnamese Embassy in Washington, where Colonel Thao was press attaché until recently and where Lieutenant General Khiem is currently Ambassador." [80] Whether or not they acted independently in their attempt, the three leaders obviously adhered more closely to Washington's policy aims than did General Khanh and Dr. Quat.

In the aftermath of this coup attempt General Khanh was deposed as the commander of the army and sent into exile, thus seriously weakening Premier Quat's position with the army leadership. Upon hearing in Washington of Khanh's overthrow, Lieutenant General Khiem was jubilant and stated: "For me I am very happy. I think my objective has been realized." [81] Khiem failed to mobilize sufficient backing in Saigon to displace Dr. Quat as premier, but the coup did succeed in altering the balance of power within the army. Khanh's removal had also been a major objective of Washington for a considerable time, and American officials in Saigon reportedly welcomed his departure. [82]

Nevertheless, the surge of neutralist sentiment continued to mount as Buddhist leaders launched a peace movement throughout the South. They demanded the withdrawal of all foreign troops from North and South Vietnam * and advocated the establishment of a "reconciliation committee" to

---

* The groundwork for this peace movement had been laid painstakingly for several weeks. One of the top Buddhist leaders, Tam Chau, had toured much of South Vietnam calling on his followers to pray "for an early end of the fratricidal war." See *New York Times,* February 28, 1966.

negotiate with the leaders of North and South Vietnam for reunification of the nation.[83] The Buddhists gave articulation and active leadership to the widespread popular desire for peace and neutralism, tending to offset the opposition within the army to such a course. Thus, although the coup had detached some pro-Quat elements within the army, his other major source of strength, the Buddhists, gained increasing power, and some of his statements initially appeared to reflect their influence. On February 25 he stated: "Vietnam is suffering too much. We want to end the war with honor." [84]

Premier Quat remained caught in the middle between a dominantly antineutralist army leadership and the Buddhists. American influence was also being exerted against any disposition of the government to accept a policy of negotiations and neutralism. The United States was poised to embark upon a planned air action against the North, on a sustained rather than retaliatory basis, involving increased "intensity, frequency, importance of targets and proximity to the [North Vietnamese] capital." The objective of this "peace through pressure" plan was reportedly not to bomb North Vietnam into submission "but to do something we could stop doing to them, in return for equivalent concessions." [85] As the *New York Times* staff correspondent in Saigon observed: "A guarantee by the Quat Government that the war would continue was considered here to be a necessity for a United States decision to proceed with further air strikes against the north." [86]

It was in this unstable situation that the Premier met with Nguyen Van Thieu and other members of his cabinet to decide upon the official line to be taken toward the neutralist trends of the Buddhists and others.[87] These intensive deliberations in the last few days of February finally resulted in a decisive victory for those who advocated expansion of the war. With Quat's Vice-Premier, Major General Thieu, replacing General Khanh as chairman of the Armed Forces Council, that body reasserted its political dominance. Air Vice-Marshal Ky, as its spokesman, declared that the council controlled the direction of South Vietnamese politics and would replace any government "that threatened to betray the country." [88] As a result of the political reshuffling in late February the effective governmental power was in the hands of the Armed Forces Council, and it unequivocally opposed any negotiated settlement.

Though "talk of peace through negotiations was increasing in Saigon," [89] on March 1 Premier Quat made the public announcement American officials had sought for three weeks. He declared that the war in South Vietnam was "obviously a case of self-defense" and that there could be no peace until "the Communists end the war they have provoked and stop their infiltration." [90] The following day American bombers attacked North Vietnam in the first nonretaliatory raid.

Notes to Chapter VII

1. A partial text of this manifesto is in Appendix 8.
2. *New York Times,* August 30, 1963.
3. *Ibid.,* March 9, 1965.
4. *Ibid.,* February 23, 1965.
5. Prince Sihanouk stated that he regarded unification of North and South Vietnam as "premature if not impossible" but that neutralization of South Vietnam "would have as its principal advantage the ending of the bloody war there. . . . Then if South Vietnam lives up to a statute of neutrality," he said, "Cambodia would agree to the creation of a confederation of associated states, on equal footing." *Ibid.,* December 4, 1963. See also *ibid.,* December 8, 1963.
6. *Ibid.,* December 21, 1963. Concerning the reversal of the policy of troop withdrawal, Max Frankel noted in the *New York Times:* "The purpose of setting the deadline at that time was never explained. Some officials below Cabinet level criticized the statement as a move intended primarily to appease a restive Congress and to keep the issue of Vietnam out of the 1964 election campaign." *Ibid.,* December 22, 1963. The original pledge was made on October 2, 1963.
7. *Ibid.,* January 1 and 2, 1964.
8. *Ibid.,* January 14, 1964. According to Jean Lacouture, General Minh and his junta "quickly provoked the disappointment of the Americans, particularly of the officers on General Harkins' staff, who soon began to look for candidates and to sound out the malcontents." Jean Lacouture, *Vietnam: Between Two Truces* (New York: Random House, 1966), p. 131.
9. According to *Le Monde* they saw "a proof of their [Minh and his junta's] balance—or their hesitation—in the fact that on many occasions anti-French demonstrations were followed by counter-demonstrations favorable to neutralization without the police having received orders to intervene." *Le Monde,* February 1, 1964.
10. Saigon, Vietnam Press Agency, February 1, 1964. Khanh reportedly told U.S. officials that he "had seized power to foil a threatening French plot to steer Vietnam toward neutralism." *New York Times,* January 31, 1964.
11. Proposal of February 3, 1964, as broadcast by Hanoi Radio, February 10, 1964.

12. *New York Times,* June 18, 1964, stated that a ranking U.S. military adviser had reported that the communist guerrilla threat to South Vietnam was far more serious than when he first came to Vietnam nearly three years before. The Vietcong, who control much of the countryside, are "much better armed and professionally more competent" than they were then.

13. *New York Times,* March 27, 1964.

14. Both of these sources are cited in Bernard B. Fall, *The Two Viet-Nams* (New York: Praeger, 1964), p. 396.

15. On May 18, 1964, President Johnson asked Congress for an additional $70 million for economic assistance and $55 million for military assistance to South Vietnam.

16. See Hanson Baldwin's report in the *New York Times,* July 1, 1964.

17. *New York Times,* March 14, 1964. In the same month, Senator Goldwater "advocated 'carrying the war to North Vietnam—ten years ago we should have bombed North Vietnam, destroyed the only access they had to North Vietnam, with no risk to our lives' (the previous day he had mused aloud to the students how ten years ago we might have dropped a low-yield atom bomb on North Vietnam to defoliate the trees)." Quoted in Theodore H. White, *The Making of the President 1964* (New York: Atheneum, 1965), p. 106.

18. *New York Times,* July 1, 1964.

19. Peter Grose in *ibid.,* July 26, 1964.

20. *Ibid.,* July 20, 1964.

21. *Ibid.,* July 23, 1964.

22. Peter Grose in *ibid.,* July 24, 1964. See also *ibid.,* July 26, 1964.

23. *Ibid.,* July 9, 1964.

24. "President de Gaulle Holds Tenth Press Conference," *Ambassade de France, Service de Presse et d'Information,* New York, No. 208, July 23, 1964, p. 11.

25. Hanoi Radio, July 24, 28, and 29, 1964; Moscow Radio, July 26, 1964, as quoted in *Documents Relating to British Involvement in the Indo-China Conflict 1945–1965,* Command 2834 (London: Her Majesty's Stationery Office, 1965), p. 239.

26. Peking Radio, August 2, 1964. See *Peking Review,* Vol. VII, No. 32, August 7, 1964, p. 22.

27. *New York Times,* July 25, 1964.

28. *Ibid.,* July 28, 1964.

29. *New York Times* of July 29, 1964, reported a North Vietnamese protest to the International Control Commission for intrusion by United States and South Vietnamese warships into its territorial waters. On August 3, 1964, it reported: "Yesterday the Vietnamese protested what they called an attack by United States

and South Vietnamese warships on North Vietnamese islands last Thursday."

30. "Why Our Foreign Policy Is Failing," an interview with Senator Fulbright by Eric Sevareid, in *Look,* May 3, 1966, pp. 25–26.

31. *New York Times,* August 5, 1964.

32. See Appendix 9 for full text of the resolution.

33. *New York Times,* August 7, 1964.

34. *Ibid.,* August 25, 1964. See also *ibid.,* August 17, 22, and 24, 1964.

35. *Ibid.,* September 2, 1964.

36. *Ibid.,* September 4, 1964.

37. *Ibid.,* September 13 and 14, 1964.

38. *Ibid.,* September 11 and 13, 1964.

39. *Ibid.,* October 2, 1964.

40. *Ibid.,* October 2, 1964.

41. *Ibid.,* October 2, 1964.

42. *Ibid.,* November 25, 1964.

43. *Ibid.,* November 27, 1964.

44. *Ibid.,* December 2 and 6, 1964.

45. Eric Sevareid, "The Final Troubled Hours of Adlai Stevenson," *Look,* November 30, 1965, p. 84.

46. *Ibid.,* p. 84.

47. *New York Times,* December 11, 1964.

48. *Ibid.,* December 20, 1964.

49. *Ibid.,* December 21, 1964.

50. *Ibid.,* December 23, 1964.

51. *Ibid.,* December 23, 24, and 28, 1964.

52. *Ibid.,* January 3, 1965.

53. *Ibid.,* December 24, 1964. James Reston later described General Taylor's role in this situation and his alienation of Saigon leaders as his "barracks-room diplomacy in the last Saigon crisis." *New York Times,* February 3, 1965.

54. Statement by General Taylor on CBS News Special Report, *Vietnam Perspective: Part II: How We Can Win,* broadcast on August 16, 1965.

55. *New York Times,* January 23 and 24, 1965.

56. *Ibid.,* February 10 and 16, 1965. See also *ibid.,* January 29, 1965.

57. *Ibid.,* January 31, 1965.

58. *Economist,* January 30, 1965.

59. *New York Times,* February 2, 1965. See also *ibid.,* January 31 and February 1, 1965.

60. *Ibid.,* February 4, 1965.

61. Seymour Topping's report in *New York Times,* February 5, 1965.

62. *Ibid.*

63. *Ibid.,* February 9, 1965, gives this as a casualty figure.

64. *Department of State Bulletin* (Washington, February 22, 1965), p. 238.

65. *New York Times,* February 8, 1965.

66. *Department of State Bulletin* (Washington, February 22, 1965), p. 239.

67. *New York Times,* February 13, 1965.

68. *Ibid.,* February 9, 1965.

69. Bernard B. Fall, "The Year of the Hawks," *New York Times Magazine,* December 12, 1965.

70. *New York Times,* February 23, 1965.

71. *Ibid.,* February 11, 1965.

72. *Ibid.,* February 26, 1965.

73. *Ibid.,* February 24, 1965.

74. See Appendix 11 for further excerpts of Secretary General Thant's press conference.

75. *New York Times,* February 25, 1965, *The Times* (London), February 26, 1965.

76. *New York Times,* February 26, 1965.

77. *The Times* (London), March 6, 1965, reported that during February 1965 alone, 1,450 men had deserted.

78. These were Dr. Oanh and Dr. Nguyen Luu Vien, who had been First Deputy Premier in the caretaker administration. See *New York Times,* February 16, 1965.

79. The overall character of Quat's cabinet was a broad coalition of anti-Diemist political elements. An unusually high number of Ministers (thirteen out of twenty-one) were local Southerners rather than political emigrés from the North. The number of Catholics was limited to four, while the Cao Dai and Hoa Hao sects each obtained one seat. Only one Minister from the previous Huong regime reappeared—Lu Van Vi, a Catholic who became Minister of Justice. The military component of the government was also limited to three members, though the Deputy Premier–Defense Minister, Major General Nguyen Van Thieu, a strongly antineutralist Roman Catholic, represented a powerful veto power within the new government.

80. *New York Times,* February 20, 1965.

81. *Ibid.,* February 22, 1965.

82. *Ibid.,* February 22 and 23, 1965. According to a well-informed general of the South Vietnamese army, one reason that he and other top officers found it necessary to remove Khanh was because "our army was dependent on the Americans and we could not get along without them." (Interview with this general by one of the authors.)

83. *New York Times,* February 28, 1965.
84. *Ibid.,* February 25, 1965.
85. *Ibid.,* March 1, 1965.
86. *Ibid.,* March 2, 1965.
87. *Ibid.,* February 28, 1965.
88. *Ibid.,* March 4, 1965.
89. *Ibid.,* March 3, 1965.
90. *Ibid.,* March 2 and 3, 1965.

CHAPTER VIII

Escalation

1: **When the term "escalation"** was first popularized in the early 1960's it referred to a process of increasing violence set in train by miscalculation and reflected a fundamental concern with the problems relating to the use of force in the nuclear age. "Escalation" was defined as "the unpremeditated increase or spread of a limited operation," [1] in which any military response was considered escalatory if it led to the expansion of a conflict. It was recognized that each side would tend to meet the actions of the other with a somewhat stronger response of its own, thereby leading the two adversaries onto an "escalation ladder," the last rung of which is all-out nuclear war. [2]

Strategists argued that, to inhibit escalation, recognizable limits must be imposed on all specific operations and a general ceiling placed on a nation's goals. To this end, President Kennedy in several addresses stressed the common—and circumscribed—purposes that united the peoples of the world and urged the avoidance of unrealistic objectives that could be regarded as threatening other nations. [3] He viewed the definition of clear and limited goals as a method of relieving the pressures toward escalation, and he invited the Soviet leadership to restrict its national objectives and unambiguously indicate the perimeters of those areas of conflict where a common view was as yet unattainable. Kennedy appreciated the dangerous potential inherent in any step-by-step escalation of violence whereby a nation's objectives are gradually broadened as it becomes more committed to a favorable outcome.

But, where Kennedy tried to clarify and enforce those limits that restrict escalation, the Johnson Administration has been following a policy in Vietnam of escalation that is graduated, but open ended. It has neither set any upper limit to the amount of force it may employ nor been able to describe with any realism the ultimate political aims in Vietnam that this application of force is meant to secure. In large measure, of course, this is because the rationale for projecting this military power now bears little relation to the target area against which it is physically focused. The use of force has, in fact, become ever more concerned with a global image and the wish to demonstrate to an international audience (and to voters in the United States) that the Administration is resolute and that America's allies can rely upon its power for their protection. More and more the weight of American power in Vietnam has been increased because of considerations transcending that country and even Southeast Asia as a whole. Thus, insofar as escalation involves a relationship between ends and means, in its involvement in Vietnam the United States is concerned with ends that go far beyond that country itself.

The first attacks on the North, the Tonkin Gulf incident, and the February 1965 bombings, were justified by Washington as merely *ad hoc* acts of retaliation in response to unprovoked attacks on American ships and bases. When these were superseded in March 1965 by sustained aerial raids against the North, the original rationale for this new phase was the interdiction of supply lines from the North to the South, an operation that for several months the Administration described as successful.[4] Yet by June 1966, when the latest step in escalation was taken with the bombing of the Hanoi and Haiphong oil depots, Secretary McNamara was obliged to state that, in fact, "the North Vietnamese units in South Vietnam are estimated to have increased by more than 100 percent since the end of 1965."[5] President Johnson announced in his speech of June 30, 1966, that the North Vietnamese had undertaken a "transformation of jungle trails into all weather roads" with trucks from the Soviet Union and China replacing coolie back as the mode of transportation.[6] Thus, by mid-1966 a still further escalation of the war was considered necessary to counter the North's response to the previous U.S. escalation.*

When marines were first introduced into Vietnam in March 1965, their mission was defined as the defense of American bases. It was stated that this would not involve any pacification operations. Until June of that year, other U.S. military personnel were still theoretically acting in advisory capacities. Both the base-defense and advisory roles of these Americans, which had long ceased to be more than a convenient fiction, were then dropped, while American troops gradually assumed the major brunt of the offensive fighting. By mid-1966 U.S. units were frequently suffering a higher weekly casualty rate than their South Vietnamese allies.[7] A change was also manifest at the tactical level. For example, the use of nonlethal-gas warfare was initially presented as a humanitarian measure to save innocent lives.[8] By May 1966 it was explained that gas was being used to drive the Vietcong from tunnels, so that they could be killed more easily by high-explosive bursts above ground.[9] As with all other stages of escalation, each of these changes has further extended the conflict and lessened the possibility of a compromise settlement.

This process of American military escalation in Vietnam is rationalized by the concept of "strategic persuasion." By this reasoning, increasingly forceful threats and actions serve a dual purpose. The continuing escalation is calculated to dispose the enemy toward negotiations and a peaceful settlement. At the same time it underscores the uncompromising determination of the United States to defeat the Vietcong or so

---

* The commentary of air officers on this new phase of bombing is instructive. They had long held that the raids on communications had not stopped infiltration, despite the Administration's claims. It was their view that "in the recent past Washington officials argued that air strikes had significantly slowed infiltration, but that they adopted a different argument to meet different needs today." *New York Times,* June 30, 1966.

weaken the communist position as to insure that any eventual negotiated peace will be on Washington's terms. Thus, the bombing attacks on fuel depots in Hanoi and Haiphong were described by the then Under Secretary of State George Ball as "designed to speed the day when there can be a political settlement." This objective would be achieved by "raising the cost" of North Vietnamese aggression against South Vietnam, and by persuading the communists that the United States is "very determined and intends to stay on course." [10] Yet as the *New York Times* observed editorially on the same day, this escalatory step, like those preceding it, was "not likely to force Hanoi to sue for peace and negotiations . . . " but did involve a major escalation, "suggesting that the United States now believes it must achieve its political aims in Vietnam through military 'victory'." [11] With this new step the United States was advancing from the limited object of securing a favorable negotiating position toward the next level of defeating its adversaries militarily.

2 : **The course of escalation thus far** in the Johnson Administration's effort at "strategic persuasion" is portrayed in the accompanying table of figures on the military buildup in Vietnam since 1954. Until 1962 they show a relatively moderate but steady increase of ground troops. Begun long before the United States had accepted any formal obligation to defend South Vietnam by arms, the growth of the American force was not then seen as constituting an irrevocable or unilateral American commitment. It was not until early 1965 that U.S. troop strength attained significant proportions, when it numbered 23,000 men. By mid-June, 1966, this number had multiplied eleven times over, and it was authoritatively reported that American personnel in the South would total over 375,000 by the end of 1966.[12] At the same time, the South Vietnamese army, numbering almost 380,000 (200,000 regulars) in January 1965, expanded by approximately 70 per cent to over 614,000, while Australian and New Zealand and South

TABLE 3   Troop Buildup in South Vietnam

(DATE AT MIDYEAR)	U.S. Ground Forces	Allies	South Vietnamese Regular	South Vietnamese Irregular	Vietcong Regular	Vietcong Irregular	Total No. Infiltrated from the North During Year	Average Monthly Rate of Infiltration §	Number of Peoples' Army of Vietnam Units Located in the South
1954	685	0	242,000		3,000	unknown	—	—	—
1961	2,000	0	157,000	50,000	12,000	unknown	6,200*	515	0
1962	10,000	0	183,000	68,000	15,000–20,000	unknown	12,800*	1,100	0
1963	14,000	0	200,000	100,000	22,000–25,000	unknown	7,900*	660	0
1964	16,500	285	200,000	156,000	28,000–34,000	60,000–80,000	12,400*	1,000	4,500 (3 regiments)
1965	53,500	2,285	246,000	250,000	65,000	80,000–100,000	46,000*	4,500	7,500 (5 regiments)
1966	267,000	29,150	275,000	339,000	101,000	170,000	35,000†	5,000	30,000**

SOURCES: These figures have been compiled from all available data in official testimony given by Defense Department personnel before the U.S. Congress. They have been reported in published hearings of the Congress and in the *New York Times*. Where discrepancies have occurred, the most recent estimates have been used. Until official figures have been compiled, the statistics given here must be considered tentative. For a comment on these and other statistics of the Vietnam war, see Bernard B. Fall, *Viet-Nam Witness, 1953–66* (New York: Praeger, 1966), pp. 307–312.

* These figures represent the estimated total of infiltrators for the entire year rather than figures as of the month of June.
† This represents the number of infiltrators for the period January–July 1966 only.
§ During 1965 and 1966, an increasing proportion of the total infiltrators was assigned to PAVN units rather than infiltrated into Vietcong units.
** From the available statistics it is not clear what part of this total, if any, is subsumed under the total of 101,000 regular Vietcong.

Korean troops increased in the same period from about 2,300 to 29,150. Total allied strength had thus, by mid-1966, reached about 910,000 men, of which 614,000 were South Vietnamese regular-army men or paramilitary forces. This constituted about a 3-to-1 ratio against the known Vietcong and North Vietnamese in the South.

The escalation of the air war also proceeded steadily and rapidly. In August 1964, carrier planes first struck at Northern targets, bombing in particular the bases of the torpedo boats involved in the Tonkin Gulf incident. Six months later, planes were sent against the facilities in the North from which armed units were infiltrated into South Vietnam. These three attacks in February 1965 were also labeled as retaliatory. From the third week of that month, jet bombers commenced attacks against Southern targets on a daily basis; and, on March 2, without citing specific acts of provocation, raids against Northern logistical centers were begun on a sustained basis. On the following December 15, U.S. bombers destroyed the thermal power plant at Uongbi, marking the first American air raid on a major North Vietnamese industrial plant. B-52 strategic bombers were employed against area targets in South Vietnam by June 1965 and against the North from April 1966. By March 1966, the United States was dropping two-and-a-half times the bomb load per month that it had dropped in Korea [13] and was flying almost as many missions into Laos as against North Vietnam. By August 1966 it was dropping each week a tonnage of bombs larger than the amount dropped on Germany at the peak of World War II.[14] Raids had shifted from strikes against selective targets to attacks on extensive areas. The risk of killing civilians (the earlier argument against any bombing of the oil depots on the fringes of Hanoi and Haiphong) became so inconsequential a consideration by June 1966 that it no longer stood in the way of such air raids. On July 30, 1966, the United States began deliberate bombing of the demilitarized zone between North and South Vietnam. On the three previous occasions, all in 1965, when the zone was bombed, this had been "unintentional," but in July it was designated as a "warning" against the North's use of the zone for the infiltration of troops.[15]

Accidental killing of civilians during American ground and bombing operations in the South was at first stated to be slight.[16] In 1966, statistics given in a congressional report indicated that a ratio of two civilian casualties for each Vietcong casualty was likely.[17] Only in August 1966, after considerable adverse publicity, did the U.S. issue firm orders "to minimize casualties to civilians to the maximum extent possible." [18]

In response to this American ground and air escalation, the number of enemy troops, both regular and irregular, expanded from approximately 116,000 in early 1965 to an estimated 282,000 in August 1966.* Less than half this increase (81,000 out of 166,000) had reportedly been infiltrated from the North. However, it was reported that Vietcong losses during this same period exceeded 73,000 men.† Since Vietcong strength grew by 166,000 in 1965–66, it follows that the loss replacements, as well as most of the new units, must have been drawn from the local population in the South. Official reports in August revealed that 15 new Vietcong battalions (6,000 men) were being recruited in the South each month.[19] In August, 96 (54 per cent) of the total of 177 enemy battalions in the South were manned by South Vietnamese.

In the same month, American officials estimated that about

---

* This August 1966 figure breaks down as follows: 112,000 combat soldiers, 18,000 men in combat support, 113,000 militiamen and local guerrillas, and 39,000 political cadres. *New York Times,* August 10, 1966.

† With regard to the then official figure of over 56,000 Vietcong killed in action on the battlefield since January 1965, Charles Mohr stated in June 1966 that "Some American officials in Vietnam have grave doubts about the validity of this figure." He noted pressure from U.S. Army headquarters in Saigon for body counts, even when these cannot be carried out, and the disposition at times to exaggerate in order to measure up to headquarters' expectations. *New York Times,* June 27 and August 10, 1966.

TABLE 4

United States and Vietcong
Casualties in South Vietnam

U.S. PERSONNEL KILLED IN ACTION		VIETCONG KILLED IN ACTION	
1960	0	1960	5,669
1961	1	1961	12,133
1962	31	1962	21,158
1963	77	1963	20,575
1964	146	1964	16,285
1965	1,363	1965	35,436
1966 (through September)	3,523	1966 (through September)	40,149
TOTAL	5,141	TOTAL	151,405

NOTE: There is widespread agreement that these official figures on Vietcong casualties are exaggerated. In the first place, it is often impossible to differentiate between a dead peasant and a dead Vietcong soldier, and a significant number of what have been reported as Vietcong killed in action have been civilians. In addition, the means for determining the number of killed, even on the basis of a body count, are often highly unreliable, tending to exaggerations rather than underestimates. With regard to this matter, see the instructive article by *New York Times* correspondent Charles Mohr (June 27, 1966), who concluded: "Statistically the war has been won several times already."

SOURCE: U.S. House of Representatives, *Foreign Assistance Act of 1966,* 89th Congress, 2nd Session, Vol. II (Washington: U.S. Government Printing Office, 1966), p. 252; and *New York Times*, October 7, 1966.

35,000 (81 battalions) regular North Vietnamese troops had entered the South. This meant that Hanoi could easily offset the projected American buildup of 400,000 by mid-1967 for these infiltrators represent only about 7 per cent of its highly trained and well-equipped regular army of approximately 500,000. Any projection, then, of the likely consequence of a more drastic American escalation must recognize that Hanoi still retains the overwhelming bulk of its regular army for deployment at the moment it regards as the most propitious. The United States and its allies, outnumbering the Vietcong by 3-to-1 and employing massively superior firepower, are currently managing to maintain hardly more than a state of military equilibrium in the South. To muster the "victory" ratio of between 5- and 10-to-1 often used by military officers now appears out of the question.[20] Even if the 3-to-1 ratio is to be sustained, each enemy soldier recruited or infiltrated will need to be matched by an additional three allied soldiers. Quite apart from the alarmingly high desertion rate in the South Vietnamese army,* the population under Saigon's authority is insufficient to provide any significant proportion of these forces. Thus, the men needed to offset any substantial influx of Northern troops or to change the ratio in the South's favor would have to be drawn primarily from the United States, as none of the allies in Europe or elsewhere are likely to commit much more than token forces. It was presumably this calculation that led Hanson Baldwin, military analyst of the *New York Times,* to project even a year ago a total requirement of one million Americans in Vietnam rather than the Administration's present estimate of 400,000 American combat troops.[21] This is the number required merely to cope with enemy Vietnamese forces. Should China become militarily involved, the figure would, of course, be grossly inadequate, even in the unlikely event that the fighting were restricted to Vietnam itself and did not spread into other parts of Southeast Asia and China.

During the period since February 1965, both Russia and China have supplied Hanoi with economic assistance and military equipment. Although prior to that date most of the aid delivered to the North Vietnamese for transshipment to the Vietcong reportedly came from Red China,[22] some evidence indicates that Russian weapons—mortars, light machine

---

* This rate averaged between 10,000 and 12,000 per month in May 1966. See footnote, pp. 331–332.

guns, and recoilless-rifle ammunition—are now being sent to the Vietcong.[23] The Soviet Union has always been the North's principal supplier and in 1965 alone delivered ground-to-air missiles and jet aircraft as well as other military equipment amounting to more than $550 million.[24] China has provided small arms and work brigades. Chinese engineering troops, now numbering approximately 50,000 men,[25] are repairing roads, railroads, and bridges and engaging in unidentified types of construction work in the North. In 1965, both China and Russia threatened to send "volunteers" to Vietnam if requested.[26]

3: **In the past** where internal wars have been contained and prevented from exploding into wider conflicts this has been achieved through the imposition of strict limits on them by the interested major powers. These limits include the conscious decision on the part of these outside states not to intervene against one another, the confinement of the military operations to the country involved, and the acceptance of certain external areas as "sanctuaries." These three "limits" have, of course, benefited both sides, for in virtually every internal conflict in the past both the insurgents and the government forces have received outside assistance. From the Spanish Civil War to the communist uprising in Greece and the insurrection in Algeria, external sanctuaries have been tolerated in order to prevent military actions within a single country from spilling over into a broader geographic arena. The antagonists have usually placed a higher premium on limiting the war than on wreaking vengeance on the other governments who, contrary to international law, have intervened.[27]

In the escalation of its military intervention in Vietnam the United States has already erased those limits. The military theater has gradually been expanded to include adjacent countries of Southeast Asia. On July 11, 1965, the U.S. Secretary of State asserted that the "idea of the sanctuary is dead" and stated that this held for the Chinese and "everybody who elects to get into this war." [28] In December 1965, the U.S., after months of systematic bombardment of the Laotian "Ho Chi Minh trail" and North Vietnam from airfields in Thailand, authorized pursuit of retreating enemy troops into Cambodia.[29] On August 5, 1966, Secretary Rusk hinted that the escalation of the air war beyond the boundaries of South Vietnam could well be followed by land operations [30] and did not rule out the physical invasion of the demilitarized zone or North Vietnam itself. Thus, in principle, geographical escalation already encompasses all of Indochina and Thailand.

The crucial step in the escalation may well have been the initial decision in 1965 to send bombers across the demarcation line into North Vietnam. This geographic escalation, carrying the war into what was regarded as the base area of the Southern insurgency, was made "for sound military reasons" and believed to involve only modest risks. The Administration justified its action in part on the grounds that the enemy enjoyed an unfair advantage in retaining a sanctuary immune from attack. This is an appealing argument for those many Americans who, through their own unique historical conditioning, have developed the notion that in those wars in which they are engaged a "sanctuary" is somehow right and proper for them but wrong for their adversary.*

---

* The popular concept of sanctuary has also been affected by what has become the widely accepted view of the Korean War. This view holds that the United States granted the Chinese a safe base for prosecuting the war without any reciprocal advantages accruing to the United States. However, General Matthew Ridgway has written that "Not one of our major allies would have approved this adventure [the bombing of China] and the coalition formed to stop Communist aggression would have dissolved. Furthermore, our 'shoestring' Air Force (this was Gen. Hoyt Vandenberg's own description) would have dwindled through combat losses and natural attrition to a shadow." Ridgway, "Pull-out, All-out, or Stand Fast in Vietnam?" Look, April 5, 1966. In addition, as General Curtis E. LeMay has written, Chinese Migs (then a much closer match for American fighter planes) in Manchuria could have attacked our front lines, and "any energetic [Chinese] com-

In mounting its air action against North Vietnam, the U.S. has not only enjoyed the advantage of a home-base sanctuary invulnerable to any North Vietnamese response; it has also utilized what might be called auxiliary sanctuaries in such places as Guam, Okinawa, Taiwan, and the Philippines. In addition, it has developed bases for attack against North Vietnam that have thus far had sanctuary status, although in contrast to island bases they are potentially vulnerable to ripostes of communist power.

It cannot be assumed that these mainland bases will retain "sanctuary status" indefinitely, particularly if American bombardment of the North increases to a point where Hanoi has little more to lose to such assaults or if the United States should undertake a seaborne landing on the coast of North Vietnam.* It would be unrealistic to presume that the Vietnamese communists themselves would not then take action toward removing the limits of the conflict. They too have the

---

mander could have cleaned out all the airfields we had in Korea and mighty soon." LeMay, *Mission with LeMay* (New York: Doubleday, 1965), p. 462. Although General LeMay's prose may be slightly exaggerated, an American air assault on China would have triggered a strong Chinese riposte, which, given the circumstances then existing, could have done great damage to the American position in South Korea and possibly to facilities in Japan.

* Premier Ky, in explaining a story in a U.S. news magazine on his views of the war, said: "The present struggle of the Republic of Vietnam is only a self-defense struggle. Nevertheless, the Republic of Vietnam cannot accept, and especially the leaders of the Republic of Vietnam today cannot accept, that slaughter and destruction in South Vietnam will continue for 10 or 20 years or longer. Therefore, the bandits must be punished. With respect to the bandits [i.e., the Vietcong], punishment cannot be restricted within any boundary. Therefore, if the Communists of the North do not actually stop their aggressive intentions, then we should adopt firm measures to quickly end the war by destroying them right in their most secure place, in the very place from which they feel it is safe to send men and materials to invade us. This is also a concept of peace and of war in Vietnam." Saigon Radio, July 27, 1966.

capacity to escalate the war geographically and could thrust into the American sanctuaries in western Laos and Thailand.*

If indeed the idea of sanctuary is "dead" it is surely unwarranted to assume that Hanoi would continue to limit its intervention in Laos to the present level. It is certainly capable of doing much more than keeping open the "Ho Chi Minh trail" in the east and carrying out operations in Laos largely restricted to providing the procommunist dissidents (the Pathet Lao) with technicians and advisors. The sanctuary in western Laos, from which an American-supported Laotian air force has launched major operations against North Vietnamese supply routes to South Vietnam could quickly find most of its bases under attack. Of more importance to the American military effort, the American airfields in Thailand might be threatened. The North Vietnamese have for several months been painfully conscious that at least half the U.S. bombing runs against their territory originate from the mammoth complex of American air bases that has been established in eastern Thailand.† Hanoi has the capability to do a great deal more towards creating unrest in these areas than training and arm-

---

* Moreover, should the United States bomb the cities of Hanoi and/or Haiphong, the privileged American sanctuary in the city of Saigon might well lose that status. See U.S. Senate, *The Vietnam Conflict: The Substance and the Shadow,* 89th Congress, 2nd Session (Washington: U.S. Government Printing Office, 1966), p. 4. If so disposed the Vietcong could launch a major terrorist campaign against the thousands of Americans in that city. It is because of this recognized capacity that it has often been said that Hanoi and Saigon are interdependent hostages. Americans who urge bombardment of the city of Hanoi should be prepared to assume a heavy burden of responsibility not only for the lives of Vietnamese in that city but for the lives of many Americans in Saigon.

† The *New York Times* of August 11, 1966, reported that the sixth major American air base has just been opened near Sattahip on the coast of Southeast Thailand. It has a 11,500-foot runway, large enough to accommodate B-52 bombers. It was noted that of the 25,000 U.S. servicemen in Thailand, two-thirds were at these six air bases. See also *New York Times,* July 7, 1966.

ing a handful of Thai dissidents. Just as the North Vietnamese troops could cut through Laos to the Mekong River, so too it would be possible for them to cross the Mekong and penetrate Thai territory in an effort to destroy those bases.

The number of additional American troops required to cope with such potentially powerful thrusts would be considerable and, if timely enough to be effective, would seriously reduce the American military manpower needed in Vietnam.* There has been a disposition on the part of our military and civilian leaders to congratulate themselves at having "gotten away" with the mounting aerial assault on the communist North without the cost of an equal retaliatory reaction while the United States itself has built up an additional sanctuary in Thailand. It is more than possible that this judgment will prove premature.

In order to appreciate the broader implications of American incursions into former sanctuaries in North Vietnam and Laos, one need only recall that the United States in 1956 rejected the right of the Israelis to use force against adjacent areas in the Arab states, then being used as sanctuaries for *feydayeen* raids against Israel. Speaking to the nation on October 31, 1956, President Dwight D. Eisenhower said that he was fully aware of the anxieties of Israel (and also Britain and France) after being subjected to great and repeated provocations.[31] However, he said, the Israeli invasion of Egypt could scarcely be reconciled with the principles and purposes of the United Nations to which all had subscribed. "We believe these actions to have been taken in error," the President stated. "For we do not accept the use of force as a wise or proper instrument for the settlement of international disputes." It was then the dedicated purpose of the United States to do

---

* Whatever the outcome, the fact that Thailand had been made such an important adjunct in the devastating American air war against North Vietnam is sowing seeds of bitterness among the Vietnamese that are bound to plague relationships between the Vietnamese and Thai for years to come.

all in its power to localize the fighting and to end the conflict by collective means.[32] Though recognizing that wrongs had been committed against Israel, the President stated: "I do not believe that another instrument of injustice—war—is the remedy for these wrongs." The following day Secretary of State John Foster Dulles added:

> . . . if we were to agree that the existence of injustices in the world, which this organization [the UN] so far has been unable to cure, means that the principle of renunciation of force is no longer respected and that there still exists the right wherever a nation feels itself subject to injustice to resort to force to try to correct that injustice, then . . . we would have, I fear, torn this [UN] charter into shreds and the world would again be a world of anarchy.[33]

The present Administration has departed from the stand usually taken by all previous postwar U.S. administrations on the necessity to localize wars.[34] President Johnson, as Bill Moyers has paraphrased his speech of July 12, 1966,[35] has stated that the United States is trying to "prove to others that the use of force is a losing game. . . ."[36] As this suggests, the United States has by force set out to demonstrate for a global audience that it is proper for stronger powers to bombard sanctuaries while operating from safe havens of their own. But by what legal or moral arguments will we in the future restrain others from allowing their conflicts to erupt into major conflagrations? After twenty years of adhering to the principle that force should not be met by unilateral force, has the United States not taken a step backward toward "a world of anarchy" by not allowing itself to be subject to the laws that should govern all other members of the international community? Instead of supporting the idea that the use of force in international relations is no longer justifiable, are we not demonstrating that the nation with the strongest arms enjoys privileges denied to others until they can match that nation's strength?

4 : **When escalation has once begun,** pressures build up to continue it. Each move is countered by the other side and only further escalation seemingly offers a way out of the resulting stalemate. With the failure of one level of escalation the arguments mount for yet another step that might succeed where the earlier level failed. The reactions and counter-reactions are by no means primarily rational. For both sides, the fact that the rising toll of human life still leads to no resolution of the conflict inevitably begets a sense of frustration. This produces a wide sentiment for the government to "do something" to break through the impasse. The sacrifices already made appear to justify an even greater escalation.* As the sense of frustration engendered by continuing casualties increases, the public's mind becomes more receptive to methods of warfare previously regarded as uncivilized.† People are less prepared to accept a compromise settlement, which would only highlight the uselessness of the past fighting and the loss of life. Any de-escalation comes to be regarded as a unilateral

---

* Illustrative of this was the statement of Congressman Wayne L. Hays of Ohio on his return from Vietnam: ". . . there are additional steps we must take to hasten the end of the war," Hays declared. "Attempts to keep the conflict within certain limitations could indefinitely prolong the struggle and encourage the aggressors by misleading them about our intentions. Our forbearance has been misunderstood by the calculating leaders in Hanoi." Hays suggested that "we should discard our inhibitions about increasing the number of military targets for bombing." U.S. House of Representatives, *Report of Hon. Wayne L. Hays,* 89th Congress, 2nd Session (Washington: U.S. Government Printing Office, 1966), pp. 9–10.

† For example, there was little public response when, on March 9, 1966, the Department of State revealed that "about 20,000 acres of South Vietnamese crops had been destroyed by herbicides to deny food to the guerrillas." This figure does not include the extensive acreage affected by defoliants used to deny cover to the guerrilla forces. *New York Times,* March 10, 1966. On September 10, 1966, the *Times* reported that the military is taking steps to triple its efforts at chemical defoliation and crop destruction.

"concession." Escalation can be unilaterally initiated, but the process can never be reversed except at a price.[37] And the rationale of the military approach is such that the failure of a previous level of violence will lead to an insistence that it was too restrained, rather than excessive.

Once the President has chosen to escalate, he places his own prestige on the line. He may fervently believe that this course is likely to strengthen the resolve of anticommunist governments elsewhere, but he is also sure to bear in mind the exigencies of domestic politics, where he would be open to attack from his political opponents by any appearance of being "soft on communism." His own prestige is involved even more than that of the nation, and it is difficult for him to resist public demands for a broader commitment to unconditional victory.

In our democracy, particularly in an election year, an act of military intervention abroad tends to polarize public opinion, and normally the two-party system channels controversial decisions into a for-and-against division. It is in order to counter this tendency that the pressures are great for the party of the Administration to close its ranks over an issue potentially advantageous to the opposition party. Thus during the Presidential elections in 1964 the Congress, according to Chairman Fulbright of the Senate Foreign Relations Committee, abdicated its Constitutional "responsibility of careful examination of a Presidential request." [38] It endorsed the Tonkin Gulf Resolution (August 7, 1964) [39] "in an atmosphere of urgency that seemed at the time to preclude debate." [40] Later, the President was able to translate what the Congress then regarded as authority limited to "the problem of further aggression against our ships and our Naval facilities" [41] into a blank check and to alter radically Southeast Asian policy and, in the process, his own power as well.*

---

* Fulbright led the floor debate in the Senate on the bill that brought about its rapid and overwhelming adoption. He states: "I did so because I was confident that President Johnson would use

A policy commitment such as that in Vietnam not only has a momentum of its own but also receives continuing impetus from the ongoing domestic debate. The opposition party is bound to exploit any indications of weakness, real or imagined, and will hold the President personally responsible for failures that may, in fact, be beyond his power to control. Politicians usually assume that the President and his party will secure advantage at the polls if his actions have been bold and decisive. His instincts may caution restraint, but his supporters may later desert him if cautious policies fail to attain their stated objectives. Moreover, more aggressive acts are presumed to carry less onerous political liabilities in their wake because they generate a feeling of patriotic excitement and shared danger. A decisive, well-publicized action by the President in nearly any direction constitutes an act of leadership, and, as such, it is likely to gain the support of a large part of the public that would otherwise be uncommitted.

The President's inclination to take bold action is likely to be reinforced if his earlier moves have led to a painful impasse that begets a public mood of impatience and frustration. The fact that the personal interests of countless citizens have been

---

our endorsement with wisdom and restraint. I was also influenced by partisanship: an election campaign was in progress and I had no wish to make any difficulties for the President in his race against a Republican candidate whose election I thought would be a disaster for the country." Fulbright personally helped persuade the Senate to defeat an amendment by Senator Gaylord Nelson that explicitly limited the President's Vietnam commitment to "the provision of aid, training assistance, and military advice" and stated that "except when provoked to a greater response, we should continue to attempt to avoid a direct military involvement in the Southeast Asian conflict." J. William Fulbright, "The Fatal Arrogance of Power," *New York Times Magazine,* May 15, 1966; and Department of State, *The Legality of U.S. Participation in the Defense of Vietnam* (Washington: U.S. Government Printing Office, 1966), p. 13. See also, U.S. Senate, *Supplemental Foreign Assistance Fiscal Year 1966—Vietnam,* 89th Congress, 2nd Session (Washington: U.S. Government Printing Office, 1966), pp. 52–62.

engaged through such measures as the draft and combat casualties will sharpen their sense of uneasiness or hostility. As this mood grows more widespread the President may fear untoward domestic political repercussions and may find it easier to respond by commanding the application of greater force even though there is no real likelihood that this will bring a political settlement any closer.

5: **As escalation continues,** the original aim of the conflict tends to be forgotten, and it is no longer considered appropriate to question the assumptions on which the policy is based or to ask whether gross miscalculation in the first instance may not cast doubt on the whole policy of increased violence.* The very assumptions that underlay the Administration's decision to follow a policy of controlled escalation supposedly justify, without further reappraisal, a continual extension of the limits to the war. If these assumptions are false, the risk of an ever broader war becomes greater without any compensating improvement in the ultimate prospect of an outcome congenial to U.S. interests. With the Johnson Administration refusing to question the assumptions on which its policies are based, the United States has proceeded blindly, without any assurance that it is moving toward its stated goals or whether the war has simply acquired direction and a momentum of its own.

One of the major assumptions underlying the Administration's policy in Vietnam has been that the Vietcong is controlled by Hanoi, which, in turn, is decisively influenced by Peking.[42] Nevertheless, the evidence has become increasingly great that there is no neat chain of command from Peking to Hanoi and thence to the Vietcong and that the interests of

---

* Vice-President Humphrey on April 25, 1966, said: "Many people feel today, they say, we should not be there in Vietnam. Well, whether we should or not, we are. And we have been there a long time. So I am not going to argue about whether we should have been there. That is ancient history and it cannot be repealed; it is a fact." *New York Times,* April 26, 1966.

these parties differ on major points with severe limits, both practical and in principle, on their interdependence.

In its actions the Administration has recently come to accept that there are differences between Hanoi and Peking, but it still regards the Vietcong as nearly totally dependent on Hanoi. Thus, Washington professed mystification when the January 1966 bombing pause against the North did not cause the "number of incidents" in the South to diminish. Though contact in the South with Northern troops practically ceased, engagements with Vietcong forces did not diminish.[43]

The Vietcong has for years suffered casualties in its rebellion against Saigon, and it is unrealistic to expect it to abandon the fight just because the North has also been subject to direct assault. A call for negotiations following a bombing pause against the North alone might well serve to aggravate the suspicion of the Southern communists that Hanoi would once again make peace at their expense. In 1954, the Vietminh could induce its numerous supporters in the South to accept an armistice because Vietnam's partition was regarded as a temporary measure to last only until elections. But we cannot at this late date assume that procommunist elements in the South will surrender without any promise of future returns from what they have won through long and arduous struggle. If over the last six years the doctrine of uncompromising resistance and the real expectation of victory have been so assiduously nurtured among the Southern-rooted Vietcong cadres, it is scarcely sensible to assume that Hanoi can abruptly call off their opposition or enforce compliance with a settlement they do not regard as being in their own interests.

There is equally no supportable basis for assuming that greater application of American power against North Vietnam, even the complete destruction of all its cities and industries, will persuade its leaders to enter into negotiations or exert whatever influence they may have with the Vietcong to persuade the Southerners to come to a compromise. There is nothing in the Vietnamese character to suggest that North

Vietnam will react any differently to such efforts at "strategic persuasion" than have other nations, despite unparalleled destruction that the United States has the capacity to inflict. They are every bit as likely to respond with courage and tenacity as did the British or Russians in World War II. Surely this is a human reaction Americans can understand. There is nothing exclusively American in the moral anger of President Johnson in the spring of 1965, when, after the American Embassy in Saigon was bombed, he said that such an "outrage" would "only reinforce the determination of the American people and Government." [44] The North Vietnamese response to increased American violence is likely to be the same, especially since it is their country that is under attack. They are no more likely than Americans would be to sit down at a conference table and make the concessions necessary to placate an enemy operating on their own soil.

Another assumption directly undermining the possibility of a peaceful solution has been the Administration's continuing pursuit of that will-o'-the-wisp of negotiating "from a position of strength." Although a political settlement has been the declared goal of the escalation, Washington has ruled out the possibility of negotiating from any position reflecting a diminution of the status of U.S. power in Vietnam. The introduction of American armies into the country is regarded as contributing to the creation of the requisite position of strength. In answer to a question before the U.S. Senate, the former Ambassador to South Vietnam, General Maxwell D. Taylor, said: "Well, all conferences or all settlements of course simply record the assumed balance of power at the moment, so obviously no one should go to a conference table from a weak position unless he is ready to come out with a weak solution." [45] General Taylor remarked further that the Vietcong and the North Vietnamese have not "been convinced yet that they are bound to lose" and that "we are going to stay on until they mend their ways." But, of course, the Vietcong and Hanoi also have every intention of going to a negotiating table with a strong hand to play. And they are unlikely to be willing to enter negotiations if they know that the United States will only do so when its forces command such superior strength as to insure U.S. dominance at the conference table.

6: **Without any clear warning signs** in the current stage of the conflict, an explosion in the Vietnam war could occur quite suddenly. Once the "distinct and obvious" limits have been removed, far fewer guideposts exist by which the risks in applying "graduated" violence can be judged. The use of escalation as a way to achieve negotiations leads to an ever broader arena of danger and uncertainty. When negotiations on favorable terms are the expected consequence of escalation, failure to achieve such negotiations is seen as the result of having applied an inadequate amount of coercive pressure. As long as a major explosion is avoided, advocates of greater escalation may belittle those who are wary of its possible consequences. They can argue that the limits of the enemy's endurance have yet to be reached and that payoffs will not be forthcoming until they are. Brinkmanship may have merit as long as one does not fall over the edge. In Vietnam, we may no longer know where this edge lies.

Notes to Chapter VIII

1. Herman Kahn, *On Thermonuclear War,* 2nd ed. (Princeton, N.J.: Princeton University Press, 1961), p. 229.

2. Herman Kahn, *Thinking About the Unthinkable* (New York: Horizon, 1962), p. 185.

3. See the speech delivered at the American University, June 10, 1963. Published by the United States Arms Control and Disarmament Agency as Publication 17, June 1963.

4. General Taylor in his congressional testimony had made this a central reason for the bombing of the North. See *Department of State Bulletin* (Washington, March 7, 1966).

5. *New York Times,* June 30, 1966.

6. President Johnson's statement on Hanoi-Haiphong bombings of June 30, in *ibid.,* July 1, 1966. For additional evidence on the growth of the Ho Chi Minh trail, see *ibid.,* August 21, 1966.

7. *Ibid.,* April 16, and October 6 and 13, 1966.

8. On March 24, 1965, Secretary Rusk said: "The decision was made to employ tear gas to try to deal with that situation [where the Vietcong held villagers in hostage] as a riot-control type of problem in order to avoid the problem of whether to use artillery or aerial bombs that would inflict great damage upon innocent people." *Department of State Bulletin* (Washington, April 12, 1965), p. 529.

9. *New York Times,* February 22 and May 10, 1966. For an earlier discussion of the implications, see "Gas and Guerrillas, A Word of Caution," *The New Republic,* March 19, 1966, pp. 13–14.

10. *New York Times,* July 1, 1966.

11. *Ibid.,* June 30, 1966.

12. *Ibid.,* June 8 and 12, 1966.

13. Statement by Secretary of Defense McNamara on March 30, 1966, in U.S. House of Representatives, *Foreign Assistance Act of 1966,* 89th Congress, 2nd Session (Washington: U.S. Government Printing Office, 1966), p. 315.

14. *New York Times,* August 21, 1966.

15. *Ibid.,* July 31, 1966.

16. U.S. Senate, *U.S. Policy with Respect to Mainland China,* 89th Congress, 2nd Session (Washington: U.S. Government Printing Office, 1966), p. 315.

17. *Ibid.,* p. 349.

18. *New York Times,* August 17, 1966. Although a similar order was issued on September 7, 1965, it was generally dis-

regarded. As one American put it: "I never saw a place where so many military orders are disobeyed as in Vietnam." *Ibid.* The *New York Times* said editorially on August 21, 1966: ". . . what is really needed is a major investigation of the whole bombing policy and its effects on South Vietnam. To besmirch the good name of the United States in a program that challenges all moral principles—and may even be defeating its asserted purposes—is to compound horror with folly." For typical reports on destruction of villages, see *ibid.,* November 30, 1965, and August 11, 1966.

19. *New York Times,* August 10, 1966.

20. Maxwell Taylor, for example, has said that "history has shown that the Government forces successfully opposing a guerrilla insurgency in the past have required a much greater preponderance of strength, 10-to-1 or 12-to-1 for example. . . ." U.S. Senate, *Supplemental Foreign Assistance Fiscal Year 1966—Vietnam,* 89th Congress, 2nd Session (Washington: U.S. Government Printing Office, 1966), p. 435. For a discussion of this point see also *ibid.,* pp. 270 and 271.

21. See Hanson W. Baldwin, "Vietnam: New Policy in the Making," *The Reporter,* August 12, 1965, pp. 16–20; and Baldwin, "The Case for Escalation," *New York Times Magazine,* February 27, 1966, pp. 22 and 79–82; and Baldwin, "The Case for Mobilization," *The Reporter,* May 19, 1966, pp. 20–23.

22. *Department of State Bulletin* (Washington, March 15, 1965), p. 367. According to the Department of State White Paper of February 27, 1965, "Communist China and other Communist states have been the prime suppliers of these weapons and ammunition, and they have been channeled primarily through North Viet-Nam." (See Appendix 10, below.)

23. *New York Times,* August 10, 1966.

24. *Time,* April 4, 1966, p. 28.

25. *New York Times,* August 12, 1966.

26. See *Jen-min Jih-pao ("People's Daily"),* March 25, 1966; and *New York Times,* March 24, 1965.

27. Maxwell D. Taylor has asked, "Can we admit the establishment of the common law that the party attacked and his friends are denied the right to strike the source of the aggression after the fact that external aggression is clearly established?" *Supplemental Foreign Assistance,* p. 435. The right to strike at the source of aggression has long been established in international law, which prohibits intervention in civil war; but parties, in order to restrict the conflict, have chosen in the past not to exercise this right. For a discussion of the legal principles involved, see Erik Castrén, *Civil War* (Helsinki: Suomalainen Tiedeakatemia, 1966).

28. *New York Times,* July 12, 1965; and *Department of State Bulletin* (Washington, August 2, 1965), p. 185.

29. *New York Times,* December 21, 1965.

30. *Ibid.,* August 6, 1966.

31. *Department of State Bulletin* (Washington, November 12, 1956), pp. 743–745. See also speech by Secretary Dulles, November 1, 1956, in *ibid.,* pp. 751–755.

32. U.S. Department of State, *U.S. Participation in the UN 1956* (Washington: U.S. Government Printing Office, 1957), pp. 49–50.

33. *Department of State Bulletin* (Washington, November 12, 1956), p. 752.

34. It is not being suggested that the Eisenhower Administration was completely consistent in its adherence to this principle. As Anthony Eden points out, the United States, in order to preserve the principle that the Israelis and their allies did not have the right to attack sanctuaries used against them, was not acting entirely consistently. Eden remarks bitterly, "We could not help contrasting the American attitude now with our own attitude at the time of the Guatemala campaign [in 1954]. In that country the United States had encouraged the overthrow of a communist-influenced Government, which it considered a menace to the peace of central America. We had understood their action there and done what we could not to hamper them in the Security Council. They were now behaving in a precisely contrary manner towards us. When this point was put to the United States officials, they had no answer." *Full Circle* (London: Cassell, 1960), p. 566.

35. *New York Times,* July 13, 1966.

36. *Ibid.*

37. For a discussion of the military approach to negotiations see *Supplemental Foreign Assistance,* pp. 255–256. In early 1966, General Earle G. Wheeler, Chairman of the Joint Chiefs of Staff, argued this viewpoint as follows: "Now, we have, from the military point of view, three blue chips when it comes to negotiations. One of them is the bombing of North Vietnam; the second is the deployment of United States and third-country forces into South Vietnam; and the third is the prospective withdrawal, under appropriate circumstances, of our forces and third-country forces. If you stop bombing North Vietnam, in effect you throw one of your blue chips for negotiations over your shoulder." *Ibid.,* p. 256.

38. J. William Fulbright, "The Fatal Arrogance of Power," *New York Times Magazine,* May 15, 1966.

39. For full text of this joint resolution, see Appendix 9.

40. Fulbright, *op. cit.*

41. *Supplemental Foreign Assistance,* p. 54.

42. In 1965, President Johnson said: "Over this war—and all Asia—is another reality: the deepening shadow of Communist China. The rulers in Hanoi are urged on by Peiping. . . . It is a

nation which is helping the forces of violence in almost every continent. The contest in Viet Nam is part of a wider pattern of aggressive purposes." (See Appendix 13.) Since Peking's behavior towards Vietnam contradicts this flat assertion by the President, Secretary of State Dean Rusk in 1966 modified the official assessment of China's role in Vietnam. He said: "We have tried to make it clear over and over again that, although Hanoi is the prime actor in this situation, it is the policy of Peiping that has greatly stimulated Hanoi and has apparently blocked the path toward a conference." *Supplemental Foreign Assistance,* p. 24.

43. *New York Times,* January 31 and February 1, 1966. U.S. casualties in the South were "appreciably higher" in January than in December. During the four-week period, January 2 to 29, a total of 176 Americans were killed and 1,049 wounded. *Ibid.,* February 3, 1966.

44. *Ibid.,* March 30, 1965.

45. *Supplemental Foreign Assistance,* p. 451.

CHAPTER IX

The Response

1: **Hanoi's initial response** to the American bombing attacks above the 17th parallel may have been influenced by the schedule of the raids. It will be remembered that at first they were conducted on a sporadic basis. Three major attacks took place on February 7, 8, and 11, 1965, and no further air strikes were launched against the North until March 2 (although in the interval missions were flown against targets in South Vietnam and Laos). Moreover, Washington described its first raids as a "retaliatory" measure, differentiating between such attacks and outright war.[1] During the three-week lull the North Vietnamese government responded positively to the peace initiatives of U Thant, Kosygin, and President de Gaulle, apparently assuming that during this lull the possibilities for negotiations could be explored.

The United States, however, at this time rebuffed all efforts to arrange for a conference. It resumed the bombings on a systematic scale on March 2, and American marines landed in the South a few days later. The North Vietnamese leaders were therefore led to conclude that Washington opposed an early settlement of the dispute on a compromise basis. Accordingly, at the Indochinese People's Conference in Phnom Penh, Cambodia (March 1–9, 1965), and in reply to the appeal of the conference of the seventeen nonaligned nations in Belgrade (March 3–17), Hanoi manifested no interest in the call for negotiations "without preconditions." [2] From its point of view these had already been rejected by the United States.

By March, the Administration had also announced its position that any negotiated settlement would be conditional upon

Hanoi's acceptance of South Vietnam as a separate and independent state and its agreement to pull its forces out of the South.[3] Washington sought to justify this stand in the Department of State's White Paper on February 27.[4] In effect, Washington was demanding the surrender of the Vietcong and withdrawal of all infiltrators to the North before peace talks could be held.* It would not in any case be inclined to consider negotiations until after it had built up a position of superior military strength in Vietnam.[5]

The Liberation Front responded to this turn of events with its harsh five-point manifesto of March 22, 1965.[6] This statement recognized that the United States would not be disposed to compromise with it and expressed the Front's refusal to enter into negotiations until after U.S. troops had been withdrawn.[7] There is reason to believe, however, that Hanoi's approach to negotiations was somewhat less stringent than that of the Vietcong. In rebroadcasting and publishing the NLF's five-point statement, the North effected a number of moderating changes in it. Probably the most significant difference in the Hanoi text was a wording that implied that withdrawal of foreign troops need not precede negotiations so long as it was pledged beforehand.† Peking's translation of the five-point

---

* On February 25, 1965, Mr. Rusk stated: "Political channels have been and are open, and a considerable number of governments are actively interested in keeping them open to explore the possibilities of a peaceful solution. But a negotiation aimed at the acceptance or the confirmation of aggression is not possible. And a negotiation which simply ends in bitterness and hostility merely adds to the danger." *Department of State Bulletin* (Washington, March 15, 1965), pp. 363–364.

† The Hanoi version of the five points read: "All negotiations with the U.S. imperialists at this moment are entirely useless if they *still refuse to* withdraw from South Vietnam. . . ." The original NLF broadcast, according to U.S. interception of it, stated: "All negotiations with the U.S. imperialists at this moment are entirely useless if they *do not* withdraw from South Vietnam. . . ." (Emphasis added in both quotations.) It was apparently never established by Washington whether its radio-intercept version constituted

statement accorded with this Hanoi version. Three lead editorials in the *People's Daily* (Peking) gave prominence to the North's wording on an agreement to withdraw.[8]

The inference that Hanoi's approach was somewhat more moderate than the Front's appeared to be confirmed by the North's own "four points" published three weeks later.[9] This statement was Hanoi's deliberate response to American escalation and constituted a specific declaration of willingness to enter into negotiations. In explaining the four points on April 8, 1965, Premier Pham Van Dong said that they were to be regarded as a basis for a settlement. "If *this basis is recognized*," * he stated, "favorable conditions will be created for the peaceful settlement of the Vietnam problem, and it will be possible to consider the reconvening of an international conference along the pattern of the 1954 Geneva conference on Vietnam." While the first point read: "According to the Geneva Agreements, the U.S. Government must withdraw from South Vietnam U.S. troops, military personnel, and weapons of all kinds," it insisted, not on withdrawal prior to negotiations, but only on agreement in principle to a later withdrawal. (The United States, unlike Saigon, later gave such an assurance in its well-publicized "fourteen points" of January 1966.)[10] The second and fourth of Pham Van Dong's points, referring back to the 1954 Geneva Agreements, stipulated that their provisions on military neutralization must be

---

the real view of the Liberation Front, that is, that withdrawal must precede negotiations (which would have indicated a significant disagreement between Hanoi and the NLF), or whether the official Hanoi translation really represented the Front's position. Washington has consistently held that the five points and Hanoi's "four points" demanded that the United States pull out before a peace conference could be considered.

* (Emphasis added.) On the first anniversary of this speech, in 1966, the Lao Dong Party journal *Hoc Tap ("Study")*, No. 4, April 1966, pp. 1–6, devoted its lead article to the "four points" and reiterated with special force this qualification made by Premier Pham Van Dong.

strictly respected and that the peaceful reunification of Vietnam must be settled without foreign interference.

The Administration objected most strongly, however, to the third of these points, which stated: "The internal affairs of South Vietnam must be settled by the South Vietnamese people themselves, in accordance with the program of the NFLSV, without any foreign interference." Washington from the outset utilized the broadcast version, which did not of course record the commas. It thus interpreted point three as a rigid stipulation that the Liberation Front could be the only representative of the South in negotiations [11] and consequently would dominate any future Saigon government.* Until the United States actually entered into discussions with Hanoi, however, it would remain difficult to ascertain how far this third point was only an initial bargaining position or intended as a reassurance to the NLF that the North would back its hand in negotiations.†

---

* The original printed Vietnamese text of the third point includes the modifying commas, but even so its translation into English is susceptible to considerable ambiguity. *Nhan Dan ("The People")*, April 13, 1965. In translating this third point into Chinese, Peking gave an official interpretation that is not ambiguous and that translates literally into English as follows: "According to the program of the Southern National Liberation Front, the affairs of the South must be settled by the Southern people themselves without foreign interference." See *Jen-min Jih-pao ("People's Daily")*, April 14, 1965. Ironically, Peking's formulation would make the third point acceptable to the United States. Washington, however, has always assumed that the correct version was the broadcast version, which contained no commas and which assigned the greatest role to the NLF.

† Initially Hanoi did not adopt this phrase, incorporated in the second of the Front's five points, that the NLF was "the only genuine representative of the fourteen million South Vietnamese people." However, after a year of bombing Hanoi's attitude had apparently hardened, and Ho Chi Minh asserted unequivocally on January 24, 1966: "If the United States really wants peace it must recognize the NLFSV as the sole genuine representative of the people of South Vietnam and engage in negotiations with it." Hanoi Radio, January 28, 1966.

Hanoi's viewpoint on this third point was amplified in a Foreign

President Lyndon Johnson's speech of April 7, 1965,[12] was delivered about the same time as that of the North Vietnamese premier, and presumably neither was aware of the other's statement when he made his own. In this major policy address, the President stated that the United States was prepared for "unconditional discussions." Yet, his phrase "discussion or negotiation with the governments concerned" was interpreted generally as an exclusion of the Front from any talks. In addition, he insisted that the "path of peaceful settlement . . . demands an independent South Viet-Nam—securely guaranteed." Finally the President seemed to close all avenues to a compromise with his ringing words: "We will not be defeated. We will not grow tired. We will not withdraw, either openly or under the cloak of a meaningless agreement." Given the political situation obtaining in the South, Hanoi's relations with the NLF, and the course of Vietnamese history

---

Ministry memorandum on "the so-called U.S. campaign in search of peace," broadcast over Hanoi Radio on February 3, 1966. Concerning the third of the four points, this stated: "The United States alleges that the four-point stand of the DRV could be accepted with the exception of point three. This point says the affairs of South Vietnam will be solved by the South Vietnamese themselves according to the program of the NFLSV without foreign interference. Everybody knows that . . . this program is to unite the entire people to struggle for South Vietnam's independence, democracy, peace, and neutrality, [accomplish] the peaceful reunification of the fatherland, and establish in the south a national coalition and democratic government comprising representatives of all strata, nationalities, political parties, religions, and patriotic personalities. This program fully conforms to the 1954 Geneva agreements on Vietnam and the entire Vietnamese people's aspirations. This is a very important point in the four-point stand of the DRV Government, which forms with the other points a single whole. The United States rejects this point because it wants the South Vietnamese people to decide their own affairs under the U.S. troops' occupation and after they have surrendered to the United States and accepted the domination of the U.S. puppet regime. To reject the program of the NFLSV is to oppose the South Vietnamese people's right to self-determination and the Vietnamese people's basic national rights."

during the previous two decades, the conditions that the President was in fact stipulating effectively precluded a positive response by Hanoi.

Any doubts by Hanoi as to whether preconditions were attached to the "unconditional" American approach were quickly dispelled by Saigon. On April 11, the South Vietnamese government published a leaflet [13] that was scattered by planes over North Vietnam. The preamble to the statement said that, since President Johnson's address had "divergent interpretations," the Saigon government deemed it necessary to emphasize that negotiations could not begin until "preconditions" that were "laid out by" the Saigon government "will have been accepted and carried out." Notable among these was an insistence on "previous withdrawal of the Viet Cong armed units and political cadres. . . ." It added that "Even if the preconditions set by the Republic of Viet Nam are fulfilled, the government of the Republic of Viet Nam can only negotiate with recognized representatives of the opponent," and that Saigon "does not, recognize the so-called 'South Viet Nam Liberation Front.'"

If Hanoi and the NLF were undecided as to the measure of agreement between the United States and Saigon over these preconditions, Washington's position was clarified in mid-May. From May 12 to 17, 1965, the United States undertook a pause in its bombing of the North.* At the beginning of the pause Secretary Dean Rusk secretly sent Hanoi a message, which it interpreted as an ultimatum demanding that the Viet-

---

* Coming as it did at a time of major public criticism of the Administration's apparent unwillingness to negotiate, there were, as noted in the *New York Times,* "strong indications" that one "motive for the pause was the Administration's desire to convince its critics at home and abroad that North Vietnam and China were preventing negotiations, not the United States. . . . Sometime before the bombings were suspended, sources familiar with President Johnson's views said he believed the main result of a pause would be to demonstrate that the Communist governments were not interested in negotiations while military victory in South Vietnam was possible." *New York Times,* May 19, 1965.

cong lay down its arms as the price for a permanent cessation of American bombing of the North.[14] Since the Rusk message and prompt resumption of the bombings so soon after its delivery confirmed Hanoi's mistrust of Washington's intentions with regard to negotiations, it is of great importance in understanding all subsequent responses from the Hanoi government to U.S. peace overtures. An awareness of the content of this message is also of importance in dispelling confusion concerning U.S. policies. Not until Hanoi Radio broadcast Rusk's message on December 10, 1965, did a few American newspapers publish it and the American public learn what the Hanoi government had known for the previous six months. (Washington acknowledged the veracity of the report but stated it had no plans for releasing the text of the message.)[15] Rusk's message stated:

> The highest authority in this Government has asked me to inform Hanoi that there will be no air attacks on North Vietnam for a period beginning at noon, Washington time, Wednesday the 12th of May, and running into next week.
> In this decision, the United States Government has taken account of repeated suggestions from various quarters, including public statements by Hanoi representatives, that there can be no progress toward peace while there are air attacks on North Vietnam.
> The United States Government remains convinced that the underlying cause of trouble in Southeast Asia is armed action against the people and Government of South Vietnam by forces whose action can be decisively affected from North Vietnam. The United States will be very watchful to see whether in this period of pause there are significant reductions in such armed actions by such forces.
> The United States must emphasize that the road toward the end of armed attacks against the people and Government of Vietnam is the only road which will permit the Government of Vietnam and the Government of the United States to bring a permanent end to their air attacks on North Vietnam.
> In taking this action, the United States is well aware of the risk that a temporary suspension of these air attacks may be

understood as an indication of weakness, and it is therefore necessary for me to point out that if this pause should be misunderstood in this fashion by any party, it would be necessary to demonstrate more clearly than ever, after the pause has ended, that the United States is determined not to accept aggression without reply in Vietnam.

Moreover, the United States must point out that the decision to end air attacks for this limited trial period is one which it must be free to reverse, if at any time in coming days, there should be actions by the other side in Vietnam which required immediate reply.

But my Government is very hopeful that there will be no such misunderstanding and that this first pause in air attacks may meet with a response which will permit further and more extended suspension of this form of military action in expectation of equal constructive actions by the other side in the future.[16]

The pause lasted five days. This was much too short a time to expect consultations between Hanoi and the Vietcong and resultant "significant reductions" in armed actions that could be spotted and reported by intelligence sources. The U.S. statement, it will be noted, contained no reference to negotiations or even discussions and ignored Hanoi's four points. Even so, the North Vietnamese did make a preliminary move in response to the pause, although for seven months this fact was denied by the Administration.*

---

* Shortly before the bombings were resumed, a North Vietnamese diplomatic official, Mai Van Bo, contacted the French Foreign Office and reportedly reiterated Premier Pham Van Dong's four points for transmittal to Washington. *New York Times,* November 18 and 19, 1965. According to a well-informed and reliable Washington correspondent, Joseph Kraft, on May 18, Mai Van Bo, in talks at the Quai d'Orsay, "called particular attention to a phrase that indicated that if the four points were recognized as a basis, 'favorable conditions will be created for a peaceful settlement of the Vietnam problem.' He then said that if the four points, including withdrawal of American troops and self-determination for South Vietnam, were accepted in principle, the application of the principle might be delayed over a very long time." *Washington Post,* January 5, 1966.

On July 13 President Johnson solemnly assured the American people: "I must say that candor compels me to tell you that there has not been the slightest indication that the other side is interested in negotiation or in unconditional discussions, although the United States has made some dozen separate attempts to bring that about." [17] By withholding the facts of Hanoi's response, this statement undoubtedly further persuaded its leaders of the President's opposition to compromise. This statement also must have seemed incredible and disheartening to UN Secretary General U Thant and to others who had attempted to find an honorable means for the United States to disengage peacefully from Vietnam.

In an address on July 28, 1965, President Johnson once again restricted his offer of "unconditional discussions" to "any government," thereby ruling out negotiations with the immediate adversary, the Vietcong.[18] He stated that the United States did "not seek the destruction of any government, nor . . . covet a foot of any territory." * The President also took this occasion to announce an increase in U.S. troops in Vietnam from 75,000 to 125,000 men and a rise in the draft call from 17,000 to 35,000 per month.[19]

It was at the press conference following this address that Mr. Johnson indicated for the first time that in negotiations the Vietcong "would have no difficulty being represented and

---

* Hanoi and the NLF alleged that the scale and apparent permanence of the new facilities then being built by the United States at Camranh Bay and other places along the Vietnamese coast contradicted Washington's disavowal of any desire to retain bases in Vietnam. That their allegation may not be entirely irrational is suggested by the report from Saigon of James Reston in the *New York Times* on August 27, 1965: "In fact, the United States base at Camranh, which has one of the best natural ports in Asia, is being developed into another Okinawa, not merely for the purposes of this war, but as a major power complex from which American officials hope a wider alliance of Asian nations, with the help of the United States, will eventually be able to contain the expansion of China."

having their views represented." [20] The ambiguity of this remark made it the subject of varying interpretations over the following months. That ambiguity was, however, effectively dissipated by Secretary Rusk on December 7 when he asserted that the United States would not compromise by giving the Liberation Front any political status or influence in South Vietnam. [21] There was, therefore, a note of incongruity in President Johnson's statement two days later in which he expressed his determination to exhaust every prospect for peace in Vietnam before "other hard steps are taken" and said that he had given Secretary Rusk "special instructions" to ensure this. [22] As the *New York Times* editorialized: "The Secretary of State, while continuing to express readiness for negotiations on American terms, gives the impression of placing more faith in military measures than in diplomacy. He has virtually ruled out compromise with the Communists in South Vietnam." Rusk's statement, "Hanoi either leaves South Vietnam alone or does not," the editorial commented, "is a phrase that implies unconditional surrender rather than the unconditional negotiations President Johnson has been urging." [23] It further noted that Rusk's continued insistence that the Vietcong could come to a conference, if at all, only as members of a Hanoi delegation meant that they could come only as "self-admitted puppets" of Hanoi. [24]

This was the period in December when Secretary Rusk was, to use his own words, requesting "clarification" * of reported

---

* In the letter to President Johnson of November 20, Mr. Fanfani conveyed the contents of a conversation that two prominent Italian citizens stated they had had with Ho Chi Minh and Premier Pham Van Dong. The President of the UN Assembly believed that the views expressed were important enough to justify President Johnson's consideration of Mr. Fanfani's statement in efforts at finding a negotiated solution for the Vietnamese conflict. According to the two Italians, the view of the North Vietnamese leaders could be described in the following words: ". . . in order for the peace negotiations to come about, there will be necessary (a) a cease-

peace feelers from Hanoi that had been relayed to Washington by the President of the UN General Assembly, Foreign Minister Amintore Fanfani of Italy. The Administration appeared dubious as to the authenticity of the reported peace feelers, but instead of awaiting the clarification it had asked Signore Fanfani to obtain, chose this moment to launch the first U.S. air strike on a major industrial target in the Hanoi-Haiphong area. On December 15, 1965, American bombers destroyed the large power plant at Uongbi, only fourteen miles from Haiphong, knocking out 15 per cent of North Vietnam's total power output,[25] and the next day Secretary McNamara said that the United States expected to continue with such attacks. There was widespread belief [26] that this raid eliminated whatever negotiation possibilities might have been opened by the peace feelers.* If they had not done so, publication two

---

fire . . . in the entire territory of Vietnam (North and South); the cessation . . . of all belligerent operations (including . . . cessation of debarkation of further American troops); (b) a declaration according to which the Geneva agreements of 1954 will be taken as the basis for the negotiations—a declaration made up of the four points formulated by Hanoi, points that are in reality the explanation of the Geneva text and which, therefore, can be reduced to a single point: application, in other words, of the Geneva accords." Fanfani added that the communication he had received from the two Italians stated that "the Government in Hanoi is prepared to initiate negotiations without first requiring actual withdrawal of the American troops." Secretary Rusk took two weeks even to acknowledge and reply to Fanfani's letter and took issue with the claim that Hanoi's four points "constitute an authentic interpretation of the Geneva Agreements of 1954." In his letter to Fanfani of December 4, Rusk encouraged Fanfani to secure clarification of Hanoi's views. See *New York Times,* December 18, 1965, and *Department of State Bulletin* (Washington, January 3, 1966), pp. 10–13, for the texts of Rusk's and Fanfani's notes.
* Hanoi's response, just after the bombings of the power plant, was a bitter one: "This act of the United States is part of its peace hoax. It is known to everybody that each time the U.S. imperialists jabbered about peaceful negotiations, they intensified and expanded the war in Vietnam." Hanoi Radio, December 18, 1965.

days later of the Fanfani-Rusk correspondence insured this.*

2 : **From December 24, 1965, to January 31, 1966,** a second pause in the bombing of North Vietnam highlighted a widely publicized U.S. peace offensive. But by this time, almost eleven months after the February escalation, the patterns of response were substantially set.

During January, American diplomats toured the world with a fourteen-point statement [27] that described the "elements which the U.S. believes can go into peace in Southeast Asia." [28] The first of these points stated that the Geneva Agreement of 1954 (along with the 1962 agreement on Laos) constituted "an adequate basis for peace." The Administration thus appeared genuinely willing to accept these agreements as a basis for negotiation. The two sides, however, interpreted the common referent of a return to the Geneva Agreements in fundamentally different ways. In its covering statement on the fourteen points, the U.S. said: "In other words, we have put everything into the basket of peace except the surrender of South Viet Nam." [29] General Taylor told the Senate a few weeks later: "How do you compromise the freedom of 15 million South Vietnamese. . . . That is the issue at stake. How do you compromise the issue? They are either free or not free." [30]

The continuing and well-advertised U.S. troop buildup † and the intensified American artillery and air bombardment

---

* The *St. Louis Post-Dispatch*—the newspaper to which the story had been leaked—published the account only after the Department of State had indicated to it that the matter was not being taken seriously. The fact that the Fanfani-Rusk correspondence was made public because of the leak of the memorandum of the two Italians "made certain Hanoi's retreat from any relaxation of the war it might, just might, have been disposed to make." Arthur Krock in the *New York Times,* December 21, 1965.

† On January 21, Senator Russell stated that he expected the U.S. buildup to reach 400,000–500,000 men. *New York Times,* January 22, 1966. It was reported on January 28 that there had been an

against Vietcong positions that occurred throughout the January pause added to Hanoi's skepticism of the motives behind Washington's peace offensive. Moreover, the American peace mission was unaccompanied by any indication that the Saigon government was at all willing to accept negotiations. So long as Washington's partner disassociated itself from the position of the Johnson Administration and so long as the United States would not compromise on the role of the NLF and was continuing to extend its military involvement in the South, it is perhaps understandable that Hanoi and the Vietcong found it difficult to believe that the United States would make any concessions that would permit a compromise settlement.

Had Hanoi agreed during the bombing pause to negotiate over the heads of the Vietcong while the North alone was spared from the punishment, it would have alienated much of its Southern support. Thus it continued to demand that representatives of the Front be seated at the conference table as full and equal participants. In the middle of the January pause, however, Saigon's foreign minister, Tran Van Do, stated that he had received "firm assurances" from the United States that it would never recognize the NLF.[31] This was confirmed by Secretary Rusk when, before the House Foreign Affairs Committee on January 26, 1966, he stated that the NLF could be represented at the negotiating table only as a part of a North Vietnamese delegation. "If they [the Vietcong] come to the table as an equal partner of some sort," he said, "there won't be any agreement unless they succeed wholly or in large part in achieving that purpose ['of taking over South Vietnam by force'], and it is to prevent this that we and others have joined with the South Vietnamese in this strug-

---

increase of 6,000 in U.S. troops in the previous ten days. *Ibid.,* January 29, 1966. Officials announced on January 23, 1966, that U.S. bombs had struck supply routes in Laos. Also in the course of the pause, President Johnson requested an additional $12.76 billion in supplemental funds primarily for Vietnam expenses and on January 24 submitted a budget for fiscal 1967, which requested $9.1 billion of new obligational authority for Vietnam expenses.

gle." [32] What one columnist later called the "indispensable condition of a negotiated peace—that there be negotiation with the enemy in the field" [33] was being rejected outright.*

In a letter of January 24 to various communist leaders, Ho Chi Minh gave his response to the January peace offensive.[34] He did not call for an American troop withdrawal prior to negotiations, but he questioned whether the United States would ever willingly depart and insisted that the United States had to accept Hanoi's four points. This acceptance must be demonstrated "by actual deeds," he said, and Washington must also "end unconditionally and for good all bombing raids and other acts of war against the Democratic Republic of Vietnam." He went on to say that:

> The United States talks about respecting the Geneva agreements. But one of the main provisions of the said agreements bans the introduction of foreign troops into Vietnam. If the United States really respects the agreements, it must withdraw all U.S. and satellite troops from South Vietnam. . . . If the United States really wants peace it must recognize the NLFSV as the sole genuine representative of the people of South Vietnam and engage in negotiations with it. . . .

---

* One alternative recommendation has been to accord belligerent status to the NLF: "The National Liberation Front must be recognized as a principal belligerent in the war, and as a necessary party to any peace conference and settlement." U.S. House, *Ad Hoc Congressional Conference on Vietnam,* 89th Congress, 2nd Session (Washington: U.S. Government Printing Office, 1966), p. 2. Under international law, this could be achieved by the formal recognition of insurgency in South Vietnam. According to Erik Castrén, the Finnish member of the International Law Commission and a distinguished authority on international law, "Recognition of insurgency means acknowledgement of the existence of an armed revolt of grave character and the incapacity, at least temporarily, of the lawful Government to maintain public order and exercise authority over all parts of the national territory." *Civil War* (Helsinki: Suomalainen Tiedeakatemia, 1966), p. 211. By conferring specific belligerent rights on the NLF, the Vietcong would be considered no longer traitors and criminals but rather belligerents with legitimate interests and status.

Although Ho's letter indicated a less compromising position and reiterated Hanoi's refusal to accept American terms for a peace conference, it did not reject the idea of a conference. As the *New York Times* observed, "The really serious point at issue seems to be that Hanoi wants the Vietcong accepted at the conference as 'full partners' in Secretary Rusk's phrase, while Mr. Rusk's view is that they represent 'only a fraction' of the South Vietnamese people and Saigon refuses to recognize the Vietcong at all. But are these differences irreconcilable? More important, do they warrant breaking off diplomatic discussions through the bombing of North Vietnam before further efforts are made to achieve agreement?" [35]

In addition to restating its negotiating position in terms of the four points, there is some indication that Hanoi may also have responded to the pause by reducing its military activity in the South. On January 13, President Johnson said: "The number of incidents have dropped off some. I don't say there is any connection with that and our peace moves, but that is a fact." [36] For about a month there was virtually no contact with Northern forces in the South despite the intensification of American search-and-destroy operations. (As distinct from the apparent suspension of forward actions by North Vietnamese forces operating in the South, no reduction occurred in the overall activity of the Vietcong.) [37] Indications were that North Vietnamese troops called a halt to any aggressive acts during this period. The only report of fighting in which they were involved came at the very end of the pause, when the United States launched a major offensive aimed at crushing a concentration of North Vietnamese troops. Undertaken by the U.S. First Cavalry Division and supporting Americans, South Vietnamese, and South Koreans, this involved more than 20,000 troops in the largest operations of the war—"Masher" and "Double Eagle"—and the biggest amphibious landing since the Inchon operation in the Korean War. [38] The apparent suspension of all offensive military activity by North Vietnamese troops during the pause was not regarded by the Administration as signaling an adequate response to the peace offensive.[39]

Toward the end of the pause there were indications, of which Washington was aware, that a debate was developing in Hanoi over the position it should adopt in response to the call for negotiations. The strict government control of the press made these revelations particularly significant. They indicated that the pause may have influenced the stand of some of Hanoi's leadership concerning negotiations * and that a strong enough minority favored concessions to warrant publicized denunciation.[40]

During this same period debate was also mounting in Washington on whether and how soon the bombing pause should be ended. On January 30, 1966, former Vice-President Richard Nixon served notice that Republicans would make a political issue of what he termed "the soft line, the appeasement line." [41] Although not individually identifying the proponents of this view, he referred to congressional advocates of an indefinite suspension of air attacks against North Vietnam. At least

---

* In referring to the division within North Vietnam's Communist Party, Max Frankel noted in the *New York Times* on February 13, 1966: "This opposition, of unspecified rank, has been accused of favoring negotiations with the United States, or at least of taking seriously the offers of negotiation from Washington." In the most important article that appeared in the February 1966 edition of *Hoc Tap,* the official journal of the Lao Dong Party Central Committee, the following statement appeared: "Concerning the combat task, they have made an incorrect assessment of the balance of power between the enemy and us and of the enemy ruses. Now, they entertain subjectivism and pacifism, slacken their vigilance, and fail to get ideologically ready for combat. Now, they see only difficulties and do not see opportunities; display pessimism, perplexity, and a reluctance to protracted resistance; *fail to realize clearly the deceptive peace negotiation plot of the enemy;* and rely on outside aid." (Emphasis added.) Broadcast on Hanoi Radio, February 6, 1966. For the full text of the article, see *Hoc Tap,* No. 2, February 1966, pp. 8–24. The January issue of *Hoc Tap* had said that "It is necessary to educate the masses comprehensively as to the vicious schemes of the U.S. imperialists and the reactionary clique of their lackeys; to expose in time all of their psychological warfare arguments and tricks. . . ."

twenty-nine members of the U.S. Senate, believing that possibilities still existed for reaching agreement on negotiations, had urged the Administration to continue the suspension in the bombing while these possibilities were explored.* Important ambiguities still existed in the positions of Hanoi and the NLF that could only be clarified at a conference table. A mountain of mutual distrust had grown up between the parties to the dispute, and if there were no such effort at clarification each side would tend to translate the ambiguities in the other's position in a way that would maximize rather than minimize the actual range of differences. Until they sat down together, neither could know the extent to which the other's statements were merely a bargaining position or, instead, a rock-bottom minimum.†

---

* A letter to President Johnson stating this view was signed by E. L. Bartlett of Alaska, Quentin N. Burdick of North Dakota, Frank Church of Idaho, Joseph S. Clark of Pennsylvania, Ernest Gruening of Alaska, Vance Hartke of Indiana, Eugene J. McCarthy of Minnesota, George McGovern of South Dakota, Lee Metcalf of Montana, Wayne Morse of Oregon, Gaylord Nelson of Wisconsin, Maurine B. Neuberger of Oregon, William Proxmire of Wisconsin, Harrison Williams of New Jersey, and Stephen M. Young of Ohio. (They cited support from fourteen other members who did not actually sign the letter, including Senators J. William Fulbright of Arkansas, Albert Gore of Tennessee, Philip A. Hart of Michigan, Mike Mansfield of Montana, Frank E. Moss of Utah, Claiborne Pell of Rhode Island, and Jennings Randolph of West Virginia.) *New York Times,* January 28, 1966.

† Certainly in the history of negotiation there has rarely if ever been a case when either party has gone to the table having described its minimum position at the outset. Negotiations, after all, presuppose initially different stands by parties who hope to discover through discussions some minimally acceptable area of common ground. As the *New York Times* observed on the earlier Fanfani-Rusk correspondence: "The wheels of diplomacy—which often turn on the grease of ambiguity—may well remain frozen if Washington insists, as suggested in the Fanfani-Rusk correspondence, that Hanoi clarify everything in advance of a negotiation. For this very ambiguity, it may be surmised, is what papers over Hanoi's differences with Peking and the Vietcong and, most likely, divergencies within Hanoi itself." *New York Times,* December 30, 1965.

On January 31, 1966, President Johnson ordered a resumption of the bombing raids against the North. On the same day he responded to an appeal from Pope Paul VI * that he place the Vietnam issue before the United Nations. While the United Nations might possibly have been able to take constructive action during the bombing pause, it had virtually no scope for exerting influence once the bombings were resumed. Understandably, representatives of countries friendly to the United States were bitter at the President's timing, and Hanoi reiterated its theme that whenever the United States talked of peace it was in fact preparing to accelerate the war.[42]

North Vietnam also had long-standing reservations concerning the United Nations, not only because of its own exclusion and the fact that Communist China was refused admission, but also because it regarded the UN as largely dominated by the U.S. Thus, Hanoi immediately repudiated any UN jurisdiction in the Vietnamese crisis. Internationally, Hanoi Radio stated, "the consideration of the U.S. war acts in Vietnam falls within the competence of the 1954 Geneva conference on Indochina and not the UN Security Council. Any resolution of the UN Security Council intervening in the Vietnam question will be null and void." [43] It suggested that "If the United Nations wants to act in favor of peace, it must compel its member country, the United States, to stop the aggressive war in Vietnam, strictly implement the 1954 Geneva agreements on Vietnam which the United States undertook to respect." [44]

3: **If the bombing pause** of December 24, 1965, to January 31, 1966, accomplished nothing else, it did elicit responses from Hanoi that showed more clearly than ever that the prin-

---

* As it became evident that the advocates for resumption of the bombing were in the ascendant in Washington, Pope Paul VI made a major plea on January 29 for a peaceful resolution of the conflict "by way of reasonable and honorable negotiations" and urged that neutral nations undertake an arbitration of the conflict under the auspices of the United Nations.

cipal roadblock to negotiations was the difference in views concerning the National Liberation Front. Hanoi would not and could not—without dangerously alienating the Southerners—come to a negotiating table with the NLF in a satellite role. The United States, however, insisted upon by-passing its main adversary on the battlefield and negotiating only with Hanoi. Hanoi insisted that in any settlement the Front's interests would have to be protected, while the United States refused to give any assurances of this. While Washington supported the idea of elections in South Vietnam, it continued to insist that any "free elections" could never bring the Liberation Front or any procommunists to power, because Administration spokesmen knew a priori that the people of South Vietnam would never elect communists in a free election.* The communists were convinced that the United States would never countenance elections in South Vietnam that would permit the NLF to be accorded representation reflecting its actual political strength.† They in turn could never accept elections run by the Saigon military government, yet the United States never unequivocally stated that it would accept an impartial outside supervision of elections in South Vietnam (whether restricted to Saigon-controlled areas or in South Vietnam as a whole).

---

* Secretary Dean Rusk on December 7, 1965, said: "If the South Vietnamese people have a chance in free elections to make their own choices, they will not elect a Communist to power in Saigon." *New York Times,* December 8, 1965.

† Thus the memorandum of North Vietnam's Ministry of Foreign Affairs of February 3, 1966, stated: "The United States says that it supports free elections in South Vietnam to give the South Vietnamese a government of their own choice but on a condition: viz., after the Vietcong has laid down their arms and accepted amnesty [it ascribed this statement to Secretary of State Rusk]. . . . It is clear that the United States wants to force the people of South Vietnam to surrender and to recognize the U.S.-fostered puppet administration." Hanoi Radio, February 3, 1966. On December 30, 1965, Rusk said: ". . . if the Viet Cong would lay down their arms, accept amnesty, engage in free elections, these questions can be answered." *Department of State Bulletin* (Washington, January 17, 1966), p. 88.

On the issue of NLF representation, Senator Robert Kennedy, with backing from Senator J. William Fulbright, Senator Eugene McCarthy, and several other senators, in mid-February unsuccessfully attempted to induce the Administration to change its approach. Senator Kennedy said: "To admit them to a share of power and responsibility is at the heart of the hope for a negotiated settlement." [45] Realizing that the NLF would not accept the results of elections run under the aegis of a South Vietnamese political authority from which it was excluded, he called for its participation in a Saigon coalition government pending the elections. In this statement and his clarification of it three days later, Senator Kennedy suggested placing the country under "the rigorous supervision of a trusted international body" pending elections and asked for international guarantees to back up whatever agreements were reached. [46]

In the week that followed, Vice-President Humphrey, among other Administration spokesmen, took sharp issue with the Senator and argued against any NLF participation in a South Vietnamese government, declaring that the communists were quite unfit to share in any such government. On the key issue of NLF participation in a preelection coalition such as Senator Kennedy had advocated, the Vice-President reiterated views long advanced by Secretary Rusk.* In language strikingly

---

* The example of Poland is frequently advanced by critics of the proposal to have communists participate in a coalition government. Assistant Secretary William Bundy has described this proposal as one "which is that the liberation front moves into a coalition government in Saigon, which I call the Polish route, which simply means that you get in short order a Communist takeover." U.S. Congress, Senate Committee on Foreign Relations, *Background Information Relating to Southeast Asia and Vietnam,* 89th Congress, 2nd Session (Washington: U.S. Government Printing Office, 1966), p. 252. Such statements, however, completely ignore the fact that the presence of the Russian army and Russian machinations were crucial to the communist takeover in Poland. With regard to this argument it is also worth noting that communists participated in the Italian, French, and Belgian cabinets after the war and failed completely in their efforts to gain power.

similar to that of the Secretary of State, he said: "I am not going to be any part, sir, of suggesting to the people of South Vietnam or any other government that you should reward the kind of banditry and murder which has characterized the Vietcong by giving it legitimacy in a government." [47]

But the leaders of the Liberation Front obviously would not agree to negotiations if they could expect nothing more than a demand for their unconditional surrender. As the escalation of the war continued, the interest of both sides in any compromise settlement became steadily more remote, and Washington's unwillingness to compromise was matched by an equal intransigence on the part of the NLF and Hanoi.

4 : **In March 1964,** Ho Chi Minh had firmly predicted that decisive aid would flow from the communist nations and "other forces for peace" if North Vietnam were attacked. The magnitude of assistance it received to offset the American escalation, however, was slight in comparison with the staggering increase in U.S. war matériel and firepower. Since February 1965 both China and the Soviet Union have supplied Hanoi with economic aid and military equipment; * but both

---

* See above, pp. 189–90. Sino-Soviet military assistance has been accompanied by the acid exchanges between Peking and Moscow on alleged Chinese obstruction of the transit of Soviet military equipment to Vietnam via China. Typical of these was the Soviet letter in mid-March 1966, which complained "of impediments imposed by Peking on the movement of goods by rail from Manchouli on the Siberian border to the North Vietnamese frontier." *New York Times,* March 20, 1966. Peking had long vilified Moscow for "assiduously spreading this lie" and later commented: "We have invariably held that it is the bounden proletarian-internationalist duty of all countries in the socialist camp to aid the fraternal Vietnamese people. The Vietnamese people who are standing in the forefront of the struggle against U.S. imperialism have every right and reason to demand and receive aid from every socialist country. China is helping the Vietnamese people to the best of its ability. . . . But what have the new leaders of the C.P.S.U. done? Whether in quantity or quality their aid to Vietnam is far from commensurate with the strength of the Soviet Union." *Jen-min Jih-pao,* November 11, 1965.

have also spoken of the need for North Vietnam's self-reliance and even, in the case of the Soviet Union, of a settlement.

The need for outside economic and military support limits the degree to which North Vietnam can follow a self-chosen path, but at the same time this need has enabled Hanoi to retain greater neutrality in the Sino-Soviet dispute. Hanoi's leaders can point out to both Peking and Moscow that such assistance is so crucial to North Vietnam that it cannot afford to antagonize either side in the dispute since much of the contribution that each can make is unique. (Moscow can, for instance, supply sophisticated antiaircraft defense systems unavailable from China, while Peking can give food and road and railroad-repair gangs on a scale difficult for Moscow.)

The Vietnamese have with no little finesse joined statements of gratitude and comradely solidarity with brashly independent acts. Moreover, on occasion Hanoi has been able to hew a Chinese line in print, while responding to Soviet political pressure in practice. During the bombing pause in January 1966, the Russians sent a first-rank delegation to North Vietnam led by A. N. Shelepin, Secretary of the Soviet Party's Central Committee. They discussed measures for consolidating Soviet-Vietnamese relations and "studied concrete questions concerning the continued Soviet aid to develop the economy and strengthen the defense potential of the DRV." [48] Soviet Premier Alexei N. Kosygin's visit to North Vietnam a year earlier had apparently induced Hanoi to maintain a relatively neutral position in the Russo-Chinese feud, and, as a consequence of the 1966 visit by Shelepin, this stand appeared to be reinforced.

The 1966 Soviet visit rendered more difficult China's relations with the Vietnamese leaders. The Vietnamese, for example, agreed to attend the March 1966 Twenty-third Congress of the Soviet Communist Party. This congress was being boycotted and publicly attacked by the Chinese who had announced that "on all fundamental issues of the present epoch the relation [of China and Russia] is one of sharp opposition;

there are things that divide us and nothing that unites us." [49] In February and March, Peking went so far as to "call on Hanoi to end Soviet cooperation" [50] and to revile the Russian leadership for wanting "by hook or by crook" to lead the Vietnamese communists to the conference table so as "to bring about another 'Munich.' " [51] The Vietnamese listened, made threatening remarks about "revisionism," but sent a high-level delegation to the Moscow congress. [52]

A significant inconsistency has marked the positions of Hanoi's two major allies. The Russians, while actually giving important military aid, have sought to avoid unduly provocative threats that might seriously damage their relations with Washington. [53] In contrast, loud threats and temperate actions came to symbolize the Chinese posture in the Vietnam conflict. If in Hanoi's view there were still any "paper tigers" around, the Chinese probably appeared to fit this description best.

5 : **Although it is impossible** to make an accurate assessment of the effect of the bombings on North Vietnam, some information can be assembled from Vietnamese and Western accounts. First, the physical damage in the North has been severe. Transportation facilities have been disrupted and industries and power plants have been destroyed. The cities have been partially evacuated, and the whole tenor of the peoples' lives has been changed.

The bombardment, while creating hardship and a "bleak austerity," does not appear, however, to have led to any spirit of defeatism. [54] Concerning this, one Westerner, a noncommunist correspondent, stated after a four-week visit to the North in October and November 1965:

> So far from terrorising and disrupting the people the bombings seemed to me to have stimulated and consolidated them. By the nature of the attacks so far, civilian casualties had not been very great, but they had been great enough to provide the government of the Vietnam Republic with the most totally unchallengeable propaganda they could ever have dreamed of. A nation of

peasants and manual workers who might have felt restive or dissatisfied under the stress of totalitarian conditions had been obliged to forget all their differences in the common sense of resistance and self-defence. From the moment the United States dropped its first bomb on the North of Vietnam, she welded the nation together unshakably.[55]

"One thing is sure," this reporter wrote, "if the bombing of North Vietnam is designed either to terrorize the people into submission or to crush their economy into ruin, its effect on both counts is precisely the reverse." When the bombings were extended to the outskirts of Hanoi and Haiphong in June 1966, the timing was explained in terms of capitalizing on the North's weakened morale. If morale was, in fact, sagging there,[56] nothing would have counteracted this more surely than the bombing assault.

To the extent that, as General Maxwell D. Taylor put it, "In a very real sense, the objective of our air campaign is to change the will of the enemy leadership," American raids have failed.[57] Since the resumption of the bombings in January 1966, the rate of infiltration has quadrupled, Northern influence over the struggle in the South has increased, and Hanoi's prestige with the Vietcong and NLF has grown. In the last year, the communist component within the NLF has become more powerful, the membership of the People's Revolutionary Party (the communist organization in the South) having reportedly tripled,[58] and the NLF has had to rely more heavily on support from the North.*

---

* The nature of American military operations in the South has helped insure this. The mounting scale of the warfare—both in intensity and number of forces involved—has made it necessary for the Vietcong to impose greater burdens on the populace for food, recruits, and supplies. Thus, although the Vietcong have been able to maintain a high level of local recruitment, their forces have not been able to settle into base areas to the extent possible previously. Obliged to keep more on the move, they have been less

The air attacks on North Vietnam have also helped the Hanoi government strengthen its internal political control. North Vietnamese sources present a composite picture of efforts to blend patriotism, fear, and ideology into a single program of political action and indoctrination. In the various ideological and political movements now under way, the activities of all sections of the population have come under systematic review,[59] and patriotism has provided the Communist (Lao Dong) Party with a formidable weapon for regimentation. Much of their defense program is organized on the neighborhood level by "self-defense units," which hold patriotic discussions and prepare for the war that they are assured will eventually be fought on the ground in North Vietnam.[60]

With the intensification of the air war against them, the North Vietnamese have concluded that the United States was "plotting a widening of the war of aggression." [61] This expectation increased in mid-1966 as B-52 strategic bombers were used for the first time against the North [62] and as air raids inched closer to the large population centers of Hanoi and Haiphong.

Hanoi's leaders are bracing themselves for an eventual land invasion of the North and have concluded that priority must be given to its long-run defensive capabilities. With this pros-

---

able to use forces native to the immediate locality. Of equal if not greater importance in depriving the Vietcong of their formerly largely benign peasant environment has been the scale of American air strikes against areas suspected of harboring Vietcong. Since these attacks are likely to have caused twice as many civilian as Vietcong casualties (U.S. Senate, *U.S. Policy with Respect to Mainland China,* 89th Congress, 2nd Session [Washington: U.S. Government Printing Office, 1966], p. 349), it is understandable why in many areas the peasantry refuses to cooperate with the Vietcong for fear of attracting air or artillery bombardment. With their local base less secure and the weight of the enemy greater, the Southern communists were becoming more dependent on the support of Northern troops. The U.S. escalation of the air and ground action has therefore been engendering in the Vietcong the very dependency Washington had claimed existed long before.

pect in view, Defense Minister Vo Nguyen Giap stated: "We must make sure that each citizen is a soldier, each village is a fortress, each party echelon or each party chapter committee is a combat staff." [63] The North Vietnamese have stressed the importance of "self-defense" and the mobilization of a large militia, and their statements contain constant reminders that men, not weapons, determine the outcome of any war. [64] For the past eighteen months, they have prepared as a last bastion of defense the wide mountainous arch that surrounds the irrigated plains and merges into the highlands of Laos and South China. These extensive areas, constituting over half the territory of the North, could defy easy penetration and would constitute the major base for a protracted war. An American invasion of the North would face an unremitting assault by both regular troops and a nation of guerrillas. It is Hanoi's defiant and confident prediction that, with its forces operating from their jungle-clad mountain bases, a long war of attrition would ensue from which ultimately the United States would be obliged to withdraw. [65]

Notes to Chapter IX

1. *New York Times,* March 2, 1965.

2. The speech of Hanoi's chief delegate to the Phnom Penh Conference, Hoang Quoc Viet, is reproduced in *Nhan Dan ("The People"),* March 7, 1965. For the text of the appeal of March 15, 1965, of the seventeen nonaligned nations, see *Department of State Bulletin* (Washington, April 26, 1965), pp. 611–612; and *New York Times,* April 2, 1965.

3. See Secretary Rusk's statement, February 25, 1965, in *Department of State Bulletin* (Washington, March 15, 1965), pp. 362–371. Mr. Rusk said: "But let me come back again with great emphasis—because I do think that it is central to this question of negotiation. And that is that the missing piece—the missing piece is any indication that Hanoi is prepared to stop doing what it is doing against its neighbors." *Ibid.,* p. 364.

4. See Appendix 10.

5. In commenting on the President's attitude toward negotiation at this time, Senator Albert Gore of Tennessee said: "We know that at one time President Johnson opposed negotiation. He was very much opposed to negotiation or a negotiated settlement at the time I suggested more than a year ago. . . . Fortunately at his speech at Johns Hopkins [in April 1965], he changed his strategy and came to what I think was a far more realistic defensible, feasible position." U.S. Senate, *Supplemental Foreign Assistance Fiscal Year 1966—Vietnam,* 89th Congress, 2nd Session (Washington: U.S. Government Printing Office, 1966), pp. 303–304.

6. Text in Appendix 12. This text in the appendix is based on the Hanoi version of the five points.

7. For the full text of the radio intercept see Liberation Radio, March 23, 1965. See also *The Viet-Nam Reader,* ed. by Marcus G. Raskin and Bernard B. Fall (New York: Vintage, 1965), pp. 232–239. Appended in the Raskin-Fall text are the discrepancies between the Hanoi and radio-intercept versions. *Ibid.,* pp. 249–252. The latter version also shows a number of points where reception was garbled.

8. *Jen-min Jih-pao ("People's Daily"),* March 25, 29 and April 11, 1965.

9. For the full text of the "four points," see Appendix 14.

10. See Appendix 16.

11. On the first anniversary of its announcement of the "four points," Hanoi stated: "Legally speaking . . . , under the terms of the 1954 Geneva Agreements on Vietnam, the puppet administration in South Vietnam is illegal *because it has never recognized the Geneva Agreements* and has always sabotaged the provisions of these Agreements. Only the NLFSV, *which has recognized the Geneva Agreements* and has striven for implementation of those Agreements in South Vietnam, is the sole and legal representative of the South Vietnamese people." (Emphasis added.) *Hoc Tap* (*"Study"*), No. 4, April 1966, pp. 1–6.

12. See Appendix 13.

13. Text published in Appendix 13B.

14. Hanoi Radio, December 10, 1965. Hanoi regarded Secretary of State Rusk's message as "an ultimatum to the Vietnamese people, urging the South Vietnamese to abandon their patriotic struggle as a condition for a halt in the bombing of the DRV," demonstrating that "the unconditional discussion offer of Johnson is only a bid to make the Vietnamese people lay down their arms and submit to the brute force of aggression."

15. *New York Times,* December 12, 1965.

16. Hanoi Radio, December 10, 1965, *New York Times,* December 12, 1965.

17. *New York Times,* July 14, 1965.

18. *Department of State Bulletin* (Washington, August 16, 1965), p. 264.

19. *Ibid.,* p. 263.

20. *New York Times,* July 29, 1965. This later became the thirteenth of the fourteen points. See Appendix 16.

21. *Ibid.,* December 8, 1965.

22. *Ibid.,* December 10, 1965.

23. *Ibid.,* December 12, 1965.

24. *Ibid.,* December 12, 1965.

25. The Fanfani letter was dated November 20, 1965; Rusk replied on December 4, 1965; the U.S. bombing raids were launched on December 15, two days before the disclosure of the letter. *New York Times,* December 8, 16, and 18, 1965.

26. See *The Times* (London), December 18, 1965, for an example of this view.

27. See Appendix 16.

28. *Department of State Bulletin* (Washington, January 24, 1966), p. 116.

29. *Ibid.*

30. *Supplemental Foreign Assistance, op. cit.,* p. 545.

31. *New York Times,* January 30, 1966.

32. U.S. House, *Supplemental Foreign Assistance Authorization Fiscal Year 1966,* 89th Congress, 2nd Session (Washington: U.S. Government Printing Office, 1966), p. 18.

33. Walter Lippman in *Washington Post,* February 10, 1966. Any peace plan that attempted to get around this rejection was in their view unworkable and could be repudiated by the Administration as unrealistic.

34. Hanoi Radio, January 28, 1966.

35. *New York Times,* January 30, 1966.

36. *Ibid.,* January 14, 1966.

37. *Ibid.,* February 3, 1966.

38. *Ibid.,* January 31 and February 2, 1966.

39. *Ibid.,* January 17, 1966. Secretary Rusk confirmed the lack of direct, large-scale contact with North Vietnamese troops until the end of January. See *Department of State Bulletin* (Washington, February 14, 1966), p. 227.

40. *New York Times,* February 13, 1966.

41. *Ibid.,* January 31, 1966.

42. Hanoi Radio, February 1, 1966. See also the Hanoi reaction in response to the Secretary of State's first intimation that a second bombing pause might soon commence, Hanoi Radio, December 10, 1965.

43. *Ibid.,* February 1, 1966.

44. *Ibid.,* February 2, 1966.

45. *New York Times,* February 20, 1966.

46. *Ibid.,* February 20, 1966. See also *ibid.,* February 23, 1966.

47. *Ibid.,* February 28, 1966.

48. Hanoi Radio, January 15, 1966. The quotation is from the Soviet-Vietnamese joint communiqué of January 14, 1966. For a discussion of the communiqué, see *New York Times,* January 15, 1966.

49. *Jen-min Jih-pao,* November 11, 1965.

50. *New York Times,* February 11, 1966.

51. *Jen-min Jih-pao,* March 7, 1966.

52. For the text of the fairly moderate speech delivered by Le Duan at the Soviet Party Congress, see TASS, March 30, 1966.

53. See the statement by Leonid I. Brezhnev at the March Congress, Moscow Radio, March 30, 1966. A partial text of this appears in *New York Times,* March 30, 1966.

54. Unless otherwise cited, statements of fact in this paragraph are based on the eyewitness account by James Cameron in the *New York Times,* December 7–11, 1965. In its editorial of De-

cember 11, 1965, on these articles the *New York Times* added: "Mr. Cameron further challenges the theory that failure can be converted into success now by bombing the industry in the Red River Valley, including the port of Haiphong and, perhaps, the capital, Hanoi. He points out that North Vietnam is 'a peasant, agrarian society, immensely resilient.' Bombing can only be 'troublesome, infuriating . . . not disabling.' "

55. From James Cameron, *Here Is Your Enemy* (New York: Holt, Rinehart, and Winston, 1966), p. 66. For the uses that the Hanoi government has made of the bombings, see the articles on maintaining public order in *Hoc Tap,* No. 3, March 1966, pp. 51–59; *Tuyen Huan ("Propaganda Training"),* No. 3, March 1966, pp. 19–21; and on the Tinh Gia District in *Hoc Tap,* No. 5, May 1966, pp. 66–70.

56. See the statement by George W. Ball, *New York Times,* July 1, 1966.

57. U.S. Senate, *Supplemental Foreign Assistance, op. cit.,* p. 437.

58. Jean Lacouture, "Vietnam: The Turning Point," *New York Review of Books,* May 12, 1966.

59. The party has paid particular attention to the activities of the militia, newsmen, scientific cadres, students, women, and, above all, Lao Dong Party members. For example, on women, see *Nhan Dan,* October 2 and November 8, 1965; *Phu Nu Viet Nam ("Vietnamese Women"),* October 20, 1965, p. 6, and December 1, 1965, p. 1; *Hoc Tap,* No. 3, March 1966, pp. 13–21. On the Party, see *Thu Do Hanoi ("Hanoi Capital"),* October 9, 1965, p. 4; *Nhan Dan,* October 7, 11, 28, and 31, 1965, February 4, 1966, March 1 and 6, 1966, and April 19 and 20, 1966; *Quan Doi Nhan Dan ("People's Army"),* April 19, 1966; and *Hoc Tap,* No. 4, April 1966, pp. 60–64; No. 5, May 1966, pp. 33–41; and No. 6, June 1966, pp. 1–9.

60. *Quan Doi Nhan Dan,* April 19 and 21, 1966.

61. Article by Vo Nguyen Giap in *Hoc Tap,* No. 7, July 1965, pp. 7–16.

62. For North Vietnam's reaction to these raids, see Hanoi Radio, April 13, 1966; and *Nhan Dan,* April 11, 12, 19, 20, and 23, 1966.

63. Article by Vo Nguyen Giap, *Hoc Tap, op. cit.*

64. See the articles on the militia in *Quan Doi Nhan Dan,* October 8, 1965, and March 26, 1966; and *Nhan Dan,* December 7 and 10, 1965, and May 27 and 28, 1966. On the "resistance hamlets" see *ibid.,* June 6, 1966.

65. The Party Central Secretariat's Instruction No. 114/CT-TU of December 6, 1965, is entitled: "Strengthen the Leadership of

the Cultural Work in the Mountain Region During the Present Stage of Resisting America and Saving the Nation." For other articles on the mountain regions, see *Nhan Dan,* October 7, 1965; *Tap Chi Van Hoc ("Literary Journal"),* September 1965, pp. 101–106; Peking Radio, February 5, 1966; *Hoc Tap,* No. 3, March 1966, pp. 60–72; and No. 4, April 1966, pp. 35–47; and *Tuyen Huan,* No. 3, March 1966, pp. 22–28, 47.

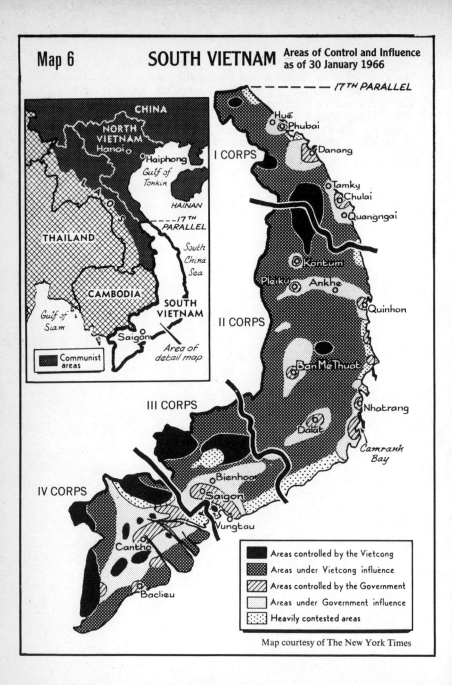

Map 6 **SOUTH VIETNAM** Areas of Control and Influence as of 30 January 1966

17ᵀᴴ PARALLEL

I CORPS

II CORPS

III CORPS

IV CORPS

Hué
Phubai
Danang
Tamky
Chulai
Quangngai
Kontum
Pleiku
Ankhe
Quinhon
Ban Me Thuot
Nhatrang
Dalat
Camranh Bay
Bienhoa
Saigon
Vungtau
Cantho
Baclieu

Inset map:
CHINA
NORTH VIETNAM
Hanoi
Haiphong
Gulf of Tonkin
HAINAN
17ᵀᴴ PARALLEL
LAOS
THAILAND
CAMBODIA
Gulf of Siam
Saigon
South China Sea
SOUTH VIETNAM
Area of detail map
■ Communist areas

Legend:
■ Areas controlled by the Vietcong
▓ Areas under Vietcong influence
▨ Areas controlled by the Government
□ Areas under Government influence
⠿ Heavily contested areas

Map courtesy of The New York Times

CHAPTER X

The Unstable South

1: **The systematic bombing of North Vietnam** that began on March 2, 1965, apparently provided temporary encouragement to the groups in Saigon opposed to any compromise settlement. This effect did not last. The bombardment of the South Vietnamese countryside, which intensified almost concurrently, accelerated the disintegration of the rural society. Terror from aerial bombing and artillery shelling became the major factor in pushing a vast flow of refugees into the Saigon-controlled cities, which provided the only sure sanctuaries from napalm and fragmentation bombs.* Their abandoned fields produced no crops, and the formerly rice-rich South became heavily dependent for its food on imports from the United States.[1] The country's fragile economy sagged further from the strains imposed by these migrant hordes, despite the additional aid provided by the United States for their care. The rapid and massive buildup of American troops made the war seem identified more with American than with Vietnamese interests,[2] and the full measure of Saigon's dependence on Washington be-

---

* This exodus, which had totaled over 700,000 by the end of 1965 (5 per cent of the total population), had reached more than a million by mid-1966. With the United States dropping more than one ton of bombs, napalm, and rockets during 1965 for each of the Vietcong fighting in South Vietnam and with the ratio of civilian to Vietcong casualties reported as high as 2 to 1, it is understandable why such aerial bombardment (not to mention artillery shelling) did lead to such an exodus of peasants from the rural areas. U.S. Senate, *U.S. Policy with Respect to Mainland China*, 89th Congress, 2nd Session (Washington: U.S. Government Printing Office, 1966), p. 349; *Washington Post*, February 7, 1966; and *New York Times*, November 17, 1965.

came more apparent. Among great numbers of South Vietnamese the feeling grew that they had lost command of their own destiny and were fated to suffer just so long as the United States chose to continue the war.[3]

In this situation little concern attended the easing from power of Dr. Phan Huy Quat's cabinet four months after its inauguration.* The movement to unseat him initially came from powerful and conservative Catholics who alleged that his cabinet was soft on communism and was preparing the country for a neutralist settlement.[4] Then on May 20, 1965, extremist factions associated with Colonel Pham Ngoc Thao attempted to seize and possibly assassinate Premier Quat.[5] As in the case of Colonel Thao's previous coups against General Khanh, the ensuing crisis served the ends of certain army elements not directly involved in the coup attempt. While hostile on personal grounds to the ambitious Thao, these officers were nonetheless keen to exploit the chaos in order to augment their

---

* Elections for provincial and city councils held on May 30, 1965, in the last days of Quat's rule demonstrated how decisively ultimate power in Vietnam lay in military rather than in cabinet hands. The Quat government had originally intended these to be the trial run for subsequent national elections to create a broad-based assembly. If carried out they could have provided for the genuine expression of a wide range of political opinions and have given the Saigon government for the first time some significant attributes of legitimacy. The May elections, however, fell far short of their potential promise. Those elected were to perform only advisory functions and have no real power, so that few widely known individuals were interested in running for such empty offices. The local councillors elected were often denied even the advisory roles assigned to them and certainly contributed little, if anything, to providing a political foundation for the regime. Since both the military leadership and the United States opposed the inclusion in the government of any "neutralist" or "pro-communist" elements (in short, men who might favor talks with Hanoi or the NLF), the campaign discussions centered on municipal affairs and were so sterile that even the Vietcong treated them with indifference. For a good account of the staging of these elections see the article by Ward Just in the *Washington Post,* April 24, 1966. See also *New York Times,* May 31, 1965.

own power. This was notably the case with Air Vice-Marshal Nguyen Cao Ky,* who at the end of May and in early June emerged as Quat's most probable successor.

The hostility of the conservative Catholic groups to Dr. Quat's regime thus facilitated his removal by the military officers, and on June 19, 1965, Ky was installed as premier.[6] By this time it was evident that only a military junta—not the cautious, relatively representative civilian grouping that Quat had led—was tailored to the new tempo and directions of the war. Ky's seventeen-man cabinet, although containing only three military men besides himself, was subordinated to a ten-man military National Leadership Committee ("Directorate") headed by General Nguyen Van Thieu, Quat's former defense minister and an architect of his fall.

Ky's first actions sufficiently revealed the differences between him and the previous government. He announced that he would rule with an "iron hand" and promised to mete out the death penalty to hostile or corrupt elements. He issued a program for his government that included plans for a full-scale mobilization of all able-bodied men into military service and

---

* Nguyen Cao Ky was born on September 8, 1930, in Son Tay, just west of Hanoi. He received his early flight training in France and then served with the French against the Vietminh. During the Diem regime he was given minor commands; in 1960 and 1961 he ferried agents into North Vietnam on sabotage missions. Although he played no large part in the anti-Diem coup of 1963, almost immediately thereafter Ky was promoted to a two-star rank for which he devised the title "air vice-marshal." Based near Saigon, the new air commander rallied a loyal following among his pilots and used this position to become one of the leading "young Turks" of the Khanh regime. In September 1964 he ordered his planes to help crush an attempted coup against General Nguyen Khanh and from then to his inauguration as premier in June 1965 worked his way into a key political position in the junta. Because of his once close alliance with General Khanh and the fact that he was nominally a Buddhist, Ky was not regarded by Catholics as especially friendly to their interests, although his well-known opposition to negotiations and his aggressive attitude toward the North were second to none.

the declaration that South Vietnam was in a state of war. The new premier then proceeded to cut civil-service salaries, while doubling the pay of the army.[7] Reflecting, in part, his adamant opposition to any sort of neutralist settlement for South Vietnam, Ky a few days after his inauguration severed diplomatic relations with France, accusing de Gaulle of aiding Saigon's enemies.[8] With regard to the possibility of peace talks in the South, Premier Ky stated that he would never sit down at the negotiating table with the Vietcong, "those lackeys of the Chinese Communists."[9] Some embarrassment for American officials was created when, shortly after his assumption of office, Ky reportedly stated that to meet its problems South Vietnam needed a leadership like Adolf Hitler's. Apparently informed of the unfortunate effects of this comment in the United States, Ky in July issued an official "explanation" of his statement.[10]

Reluctantly, and with some misgivings, Washington had been obliged to concede that it could not secure a popularly backed civilian government in Saigon disposed to carry out a policy concomitant with American war aims. Only a military government such as that led by Marshal Ky could be counted upon to meet these requirements. It was, however, difficult to make Marshal Ky's regime seem attractive to the American public. Since civilian backing for him was so lacking and his actions so dictatorial, considerable effort was expended to make him appear popular and democratic.

To this end, the premier was persuaded to deliver a series of speeches in which he voiced a new-found concern with social justice, the needs of the peasantry, and unification of the conflicting religious interests of his country. In September 1965, when a special U.S. team headed by General Edward G. Lansdale began to advise the Vietnamese Central Rural Construction Council, headed by Ky, the Air Vice-Marshal made more frequent references to reforms for correcting social and economic injustices.[11] By November, one correspondent could report that the remarks of both Ambassador Lodge and Premier Ky on the need for a social revolution "are virtually interchangeable—a statement by one sounds like a statement by the other." [12] This campaign to reshape Ky's image culminated in his State of the Union address of January 15, 1966, wherein he went so far as to claim: "Our third goal is to build democracy. . . . In pure theory, democracy is the basic factor for victory over communism. If there is no democracy, we lose even the reason for our struggle, let alone the means of victory." [13]

It attested to the skill of the public-relations effort that such statements were often fed by the news media to the American people without critical comment. For Ky's new credo was, to say the least, incongruous when juxtaposed against his own harsh and autocratic actions.[14] The timing and the content of his speeches seemed intended more for an American audience than for his own.

A final step in the furbishing of Marshal Ky's public image was taken at the Honolulu Conference with President Johnson in early February 1966. This was fully consistent with what was probably the principal objective of the conference—vindication of the President's conduct of the war. Called just after the resumption of U.S. bombing of the North, the prominence accorded this meeting by President Johnson appeared to reflect his sensitivity to domestic criticism of his Vietnam policy and his desire to overshadow Senator J. W. Fulbright's televised hearings on America's China policy. Considerations of domestic U.S. politics evidently outweighed those of diplomatic courtesy and respect for South Vietnamese sensibilities, as Ky and General Thieu, Saigon's Chief of State, were summoned to this meeting with the President—on U.S. soil—a scant two days before the opening of the conference.[15]

The two major documents produced by the Honolulu Conference were a declaration and a joint communiqué of February 8, 1966. The declaration bound Washington and Saigon to a common struggle against communism and against the economic poverty of South Vietnam.[16] The South Vietnamese section of the declaration stated that: "We must defeat the Viet Cong and those illegally fighting with them on our soil. We are the victims of an aggression directed and supported from Hanoi. That aggression—that so-called 'War of National Liberation'—is part of the communist plan for the conquest of all Southeast Asia." The joint communiqué fully endorsed these objectives, in effect committing President Johnson to Premier Ky's mirroring of American Southeast Asia policies as previously expressed by the U.S. President.

2 : The Honolulu Conference had serious and largely un-anticipated consequences in Saigon. On the one hand, the prestige of the Ky government plummeted within South Vietnam as the story of the Premier's summons to Honolulu and his embrace by the American President circulated freely in Saigon.[17] On the other hand, the conference encouraged Ky to believe that the United States was now so committed to him that he could act more freely against his rivals within the military junta. Ky obviously concluded that so soon after the Honolulu Conference Washington simply could not afford to withhold its backing from him.

Accordingly, he moved to consolidate his own power within the National Leadership Committee and, on March 10, announced that General Nguyen Chanh Thi was being relieved of his position as commander of the I Corps area (see Map 6) and ousted from the junta. General Thi, highly regarded by his American counterparts as one of the ablest anti-Vietcong commanders, had succeeded in building his own base of power in the region around Hué. The exigencies of his rivalry with Premier Ky had for some time prompted him to look for sources of backing in addition to his own military subordinates, and it was from the Buddhists that he received the widest support. Yet the compatibility of immediate interests between General Thi and Buddhist-nationalist circles in opposing Ky did not disguise the fact that their long-term interests were divergent. Thi remained basically a regional warlord, but the Buddhist-nationalist forces found in him a convenient ally in their own struggle against Ky.

On March 12, Buddhist monks in the cities of Danang and Hué mounted demonstrations—ostensibly in support of General Thi—and began an extended campaign against the Ky-Thieu government which developed substantial support from non-Buddhists as well as from Buddhists.[18] Coincident with the serious split within the armed forces' National Leadership Committee in the wake of Thi's dismissal, Buddhist pressure led to the further weakening of Ky's authority. The Buddhists thereby gained an unusual opportunity for elaborating an alternative to the policies followed by Saigon since Ky's advent to power in June 1965, and indeed since Quat's declaration of the previous March.

The Buddhist-nationalist position fundamentally contradicted that of Ky on almost every point. The basic line of the Ky government had consistently been: the war in South Vietnam is an externally directed military aggression resisted by a vast proportion of the Vietnamese people; it must therefore be ruthlessly crushed by military means; the leadership group best qualified to accomplish this is the patriotic officer corps; the problem is military and not political, and opposition to the war is, *ipso facto*, treason. The general thrust of the Buddhist view—to the extent that one can describe a common denominator among their politically active elements—ran very much the reverse. From their viewpoint, the conflict is a cruel civil war, in which vast numbers of the Vietnamese people are the suffering, innocent, and desperate victims; military suppression cannot eliminate its causes; therefore peace can only be achieved through other means; since American-backed military governments will follow only the path of war, their rule must be ended; the essential problem is thus political, and the only genuinely patriotic course is one that permits the South Vietnamese to decide their own fate, free from American as well as other outside interference.

The fundamental premises of the Ky-Thieu-Johnson position have been repeated so often in this country that ultimately they may be taken for granted as the truth. At the same time, the position of the dominant elements within the diverse Buddhist-nationalist groups has often been distorted and generally inadequately presented to the American public. This arises in part as a consequence of Saigon's penchant for branding all political criticism as subversive. Because of this, Buddhist leaders who wish to remain politically active are obliged to obfuscate and camouflage their views in public to an extent that is confusing to outsiders. It would seem warranted therefore to devote additional space to a discussion of the Buddhists' views.[19] *

The basic aims of the Buddhists have been summed up as: "defense of Buddhism, anti-Communism, independence, peace and social revolution through revival of authentic Vietnamese values and the reestablishment of national dignity."[20] The fundamental political convictions of most Buddhist-nationalists are twofold. First, they believe that the present war can only end in the destruction of Vietnam as a viable society. They appreciate better than most, certainly better than President Johnson or Premier Ky, that American interests diverge in many respects from Vietnam's and that the partial destruction of Vietnam could become a logical, if unwelcome, part of America's wider operations in Asia. The Buddhists therefore hold that their overriding goal must be the end of the devastation before the interests of the Great Powers, especially the United States, demand even further sacrifice from the people of Vietnam. Secondly, given this perspective there is an apparent consensus among the Buddhists that the struggle in Vietnam must be removed from a purely military plane— where the only effective participants are the Saigon officer

---

* The discussion that follows describes their views in the present tense—as they were discernible in the spring of 1966. It is impossible to ascertain the extent to which there have been changes in their views as a result of the tremendous pressure subsequently applied against the Buddhist leaders.

elite and the Vietcong military cadres—to the political level, where the whole range of South Vietnam's complex political interests can be voiced and represented.

The Buddhists assert that communal ties and religious beliefs—Catholic, Hoa Hao, and Cao Dai, as well as Buddhist—have a far stronger popular appeal than any communist doctrines. Indeed, the Buddhists have faith that if all the religious predispositions of the people could be politically channeled, the communists would rapidly lose ground in the crucial struggle for the allegiance of the people. The Buddhists agree, naturally for quite different reasons, with Washington's own assessment that the NLF claims of political strength have been exaggerated.[21] Whereas Washington feels that fear of the Vietcong is the primary reason for its hold on the countryside, the Buddhists state that the Front's support springs from many causes: fear of Saigon and its rulers, a spirit of revenge among those hurt by actions of Saigon or the United States, communist coercion, and a belief by some in communist promises or principles.

Most Buddhists apparently agree that the political strength of South Vietnam's religious communities remains largely an unrealized potential, not only because of the restrictions on organizational activity imposed by the Saigon government, but also because of the practical difficulties attending any period of unrestricted military operations. They believe that the various religious groups will be able to develop strong and unhindered ties within their communities only after Saigon and the United States have halted all *offensive* ground campaigns as well as the bombings within the South. The Buddhists are convinced that under such circumstances their monks could move unmolested through most rural areas. They insist that Vietcong cadres have seldom troubled those monks already living in communist-controlled hamlets for fear that local villagers might turn against the communists on religious grounds.

In those extensive areas where their own religion is dominant, the Buddhists believe themselves capable of developing effective ties between the villages and cities of South Vietnam. Where the "multiplicity of small interests has made it easy for outsiders to divide and rule" in the past,[22] the Buddhists believe that these divergent interests can be turned into an asset. To this end, though pitifully short of funds, they have already started to set up training classes—a School of Youth for Social Service was opened in August 1965—for the army of monks and welfare workers who would ultimately move into the countryside as a permanent "peace corps." Some of these trainees, along with other Buddhists, have already begun forming close relationships with the peasants, but on occasions their work comes to nothing when the villages where they have been operating have automatically come under attack as designated targets within the shifting battle areas. Moreover, the Buddhists say, the Vietcong has sometimes succeeded in directing American bombers or artillery against the very villages where the monks' progress has initially been most promising. Often the communists have simply fed false intelligence to the Saigon military authorities, indicating that these villages are in the hands of the NLF; the villages are then destroyed.[23] Consequently, in broad sections of the countryside it has been impossible to maintain a continuous presence of religious personnel.

Most important to the Buddhist-nationalist program is the political attraction of their call for peace. To a rural population sickened and bone-weary of the tension and travail of the fighting that continues to sweep around and over them, this is a factor of enormous political importance. Saigon's announcement of its desire and willingness to work for an armistice and a peaceful settlement would, many Buddhists predict, revitalize the sagging morale and spirit of the army as well as of the vast majority of the populace. With such a goal, the Buddhist leaders argue, the men in the army would have something worth fighting for. Their commitment to Saigon would be all the greater if the prospect of a peace settlement were coupled with the promise of substantial autonomy and freedom for their ancestral villages from the central government's heavy-handed control. By the transfer to the local sphere of a wide range of governmental responsibility, the Buddhists anticipate that the Vietcong would be deprived of a crucial propaganda issue. They believe that if Saigon were regarded as seriously interested in a peaceful settlement and if the argument concerning Saigon's dictatorial control were spiked, many of the Front's noncommunist adherents would fall away from the organization.

The Buddhists have for several years advocated the holding of free elections in the South to select delegates for a representative national assembly, which would, it was confidently expected, make their programs more attainable.* Elections to the assembly, if carried out by a government sincere in its efforts to ensure that they were fully representative, would not, they believe, need to be limited to those areas actually controlled by Saigon. Conducted under international supervision, they could be held in contested areas as well.[24] Said one Buddhist leader: "The goal of the Buddhist struggle movement is to ask for the election of a constituent assembly; and if we want to win over the communists we must have a strong government elected by the people." [25] The main function of such a representative national assembly would initially be to authorize the local autonomy necessary for Saigon to develop stronger ties with the peasantry. In the course of grappling with those responsibilities left to it, the assembly could provide the various communal, religious, and political groups with an arena for the exchange of views. In this way it could perhaps

* The Buddhists recognized that to hold such elections it would first be necessary to establish an interim civilian government reflecting as wide as possible a range of interests. Their demonstrations for a change in the composition of the Ky cabinet in the spring of 1966 and for truly representative elections for a national assembly reflected their conclusion that a military government such as Ky's would never allow authority to devolve onto a peace-oriented civilian legislature.

establish a wider consensus that could contribute to a rebuilding of the Vietnamese nation.

With Saigon having developed a stronger political base, it could then better undertake political discussions with the NLF and in the more distant future could explore the problem of South Vietnam's reunification with the North. It would be up to the elected assembly to decide whether and when peace negotiations should be opened with the NLF.[26] (Preliminary talks with the Front and efforts to arrange for a cease-fire would not have to be deferred and could be undertaken immediately by the assembly's representatives.) The Buddhists belittle the pessimistic and defeatist view of the government that "any peace talks will only give the Viet Cong a chance to intensify the war." [27] According to one knowledgeable reporter, the Buddhists see themselves becoming "the nucleus for a popular majority in South Vietnam that might, in time, serve as a means of bringing an honorable peace to their country. . . . Once this majority is attained, I think they believe that they could talk to the other side and arrange a peace that would be neither victory nor defeat for either party." [28]

Clearly the Buddhist perspective briefly outlined above poses several major problems, among them: 1) What is and will be the attitude of the other religious communities in South Vietnam? 2) What is and could be the attitude of the United States?

The Catholic community in South Vietnam has long been politically divided. The emigration of hundreds of thousands of Tonkinese Catholics to South Vietnam in 1954–55, under the leadership of bitterly anti-Vietminh and powerful Northern bishops,[29] created a strong, politically vocal bloc, which undergirds Saigon's rigidly hostile and doctrinaire policies toward the communists. This group provided the most reliable civilian support of the Diem regime and has been described as continuing to "form the popular backbone of recent military regimes, and to serve as the death weapon against more moderate regimes." [30]

There is, however, a large group of Southern Catholics whose attitudes on the war and toward Hanoi differ from those of the Northerners. The main political instrument of these Southern Catholics (far less privileged in the Diemist political and administrative organizations than their more "reliable" Northern confrères) has been the Liaison Office of the Archbishopric of Saigon, which on January 5, 1966, lined up many Catholics with the Buddhist-nationalists in advocating a negotiated settlement of the war. The Vatican, which has for some years been exerting sustained pressure for the acceptance of negotiations, provided powerful backing to this Catholic group. As early as February 13, 1965, Pope Paul VI sent a letter to Vietnam's bishops telling of his efforts to achieve peace in their country and warning of "the horrors of a prolonged and extensive commitment of arms." [31] In spite of the clear division of Catholic opinion in Vietnam,* the exigencies of the present United States position have required ignoring the "Southern" current and giving publicity only to emigré opinion as if it were representative of Catholic opinion as a whole. This will probably continue so long as the course of American policy remains unchanged.

Persistent opposition to the Buddhist alternative has not been confined to the senior officer corps and influential prelates in the emigré hierarchy. It also comes from small groups of businessmen and intellectuals in the big cities, who have built their careers by acting as intermediaries, advisors, and suppliers, first for the French and now for the Americans. These latter Vietnamese are the ones who profit most from the protracted prosecution of the war. While those who oppose the Buddhists' objectives are powerful and strategically situ-

---

* There have been indications that even the flamboyant Father Hoang Quynh, leader of the emigré militant Catholics, has begun to move closer to the Buddhist-nationalist position. See his insistence on democratic elections and his visits to Tri Quang. *Song,* April 15, 1966; and Joseph Kraft, "Politics in Vietnam," *The New York Review of Books,* June 23, 1966, p. 6.

ated in the South Vietnamese social structure, they remain a small minority of the total population. Should Washington decide to alter the course of its policy, a wide and active base of support for a "peace line" exists not only among the Buddhists but among the non-Buddhist religious communities as well.

The relationship between Washington and the Buddhist-nationalists has been an ambiguous one since the time in 1963 when Ambassador Lodge gave the monk Tri Quang sanctuary from persecution by Diem's secret police. After the disastrous Diem years, when political power was so narrowly confined to the Northern Catholics, the United States has acknowledged the need to extend the popular backing of the Saigon government and has recognized the potential of the Buddhist community to form this mass base. In the hope of rallying substantial Buddhist backing for the military regimes in Saigon, American officials have tried to foster friendly contacts within the Buddhist political community. But, while attempting to cultivate leading Buddhist figures, Washington has made no serious effort to meet the demands and aspirations they represent. This has frequently served to destroy the reputations of those Buddhists concerned (the best example to date being the once highly respected Tam Chau, who was ousted in August 1966 from the directorship of the Buddhist Institute) and to antagonize deeply the Buddhist community as a whole. Most Buddhists now believe that, whereas the United States will do a great deal to court individual leaders, it will do practically nothing to satisfy the aspirations of the Buddhist community as a whole.

The ambiguous relationship of the Buddhist activists and the United States has made any dialogue between them increasingly confused and easy to misrepresent. Washington's overall objective has been to buttress any government that would effectively prosecute the war. While lauding the idea of a democratic government for South Vietnam, the United States has been prepared to back such a government only if it geared its policies to sustaining the war effort and enlisting popular support for fighting the communists. Thus, Washington has had to ally itself closely with the only type of government that could share its objective—the military junta of Marshal Ky. The Administration, however, has continued to pay homage to the ideal of democracy for South Vietnam and welcomed civilian political groupings, on the unstated assumption that they too must share Washington's aims. The Buddhists who adamantly oppose this assumption have been put in an exceedingly difficult position by the Washington-Saigon alliance. They fully realize that if Ky is unreservedly backed by the United States, he will prove too strong for them. Yet they also recognize that only American influence can restrain Ky from drastic repressions against their leaders.

The long-run Buddhist-nationalist objectives contradict American policies in Vietnam. But the exigencies of their short-run survival often lead them calculatedly to obscure this contradiction in order to appease Washington and the military leaders in Saigon. The Buddhists' public declarations have therefore tended to be ambiguous and exposed to the most invidious interpretations that could be put upon them by elements bitterly opposed to any peace through compromise. Yet, once the assumptions and perspectives of the Buddhists have been set forth within the actual political context operating in Vietnam, naive and simplistic equations of Buddhist and communist goals can no longer be excused. Then the Buddhist perspective can be seen as a possible "third way" for the United States out of the present impasse, requiring neither escalation and devastation nor capitulation and humiliation.

3: **The post-Honolulu crisis** in South Vietnam, when Premier Ky sought to capitalize on Johnson's unqualified pledge of support by dismissing General Thi from the I Corps area command, opened the way for a far more explicit statement of the Buddhist-nationalist alternative than had previously been practicable. Under the pressure of the civil disobedience in Danang and Hué led by Buddhist monks and students, Marshal Ky announced on March 25, 1966, that South Vietnam would get a constitution within two months and that elections would possibly be advanced from some time in 1967 to a date in late 1966.[32] Ky took pains to insist, however, that the government would have to be "very careful not to allow Vietcong or corrupt elements to sit in the next national assembly." [33] Since the Marshal had always been liberal in applying these epithets to any opposition groups, his assurances on elections did little to halt the growing tide of disaffection with his regime. His government's overall control in the country diminished when, with the obvious complicity of local army officers, the radio stations in Danang and Hué passed into anti-Saigon hands. On March 29 powerful elements in the Catholic community, including Father Hoang Quynh, issued statements strongly critical of Ky's government and demanding a return to civilian rule.[34]

The situation in Saigon became so critical that one reporter was able to write that Washington now faced a crucial dilemma: could "it afford to let the present military government fall or should it move openly to keep it in power if that becomes necessary." [35] Open moves on Ky's behalf would exacerbate congressional criticism of the Administration's Vietnam policies, heighten anti-Americanism in South Vietnam, and make Ky appear more like an American puppet. Yet Ky's fall, so soon after the Honolulu embrace and in the wake of popular demonstrations, would be an intolerable embarrassment to President Johnson.

With the northern provinces completely independent of Saigon's control, many Catholics as well as the Buddhists issued ever stronger criticism of the military junta, demanding a return to a civilian cabinet and calling for national elections. This popular call for representative government could have demonstrated to the Johnson Administration that it now had a meaningful alternative to further militarization of the struggle in the South. It evidently rejected this, for on April 5, at the order of Ambassador Henry Cabot Lodge,[36] American planes and pilots flew a regiment of Vietnamese marines into Danang—a critically important move, which began the process of subduing that city to Saigon's will.[37] The scale was being tipped in favor of Ky.

As the crisis deepened, the United States became more concerned that the whole structure of military control in South Vietnam would disintegrate in the face of the Buddhist opposition,[38] and for the first time U.S. officials publicly censured the Buddhists' most forceful leader, Tri Quang.[39] However, the pressure mounted by the Buddhists remained so strong that, in order for his government to survive, Premier Ky was obliged to promise his political opponents major concessions. Reluctantly, on April 14, 1966, the junta agreed officially to the holding of elections for a constituent assembly within three to five months.[40] The Buddhist-nationalist group, then at the zenith of its influence, demanded that this constituent assembly eventually be transformed into a national legislature as well [41] and that the government "guarantee" that "those who had taken part in the anti-Government agitation would not be punished." [42] On the next day, the members of a National Political Congress, appointed by the military leadership as a counterforce to the Buddhists, came out with a program of demands, which, to the junta's dismay, was "virtually identical" with that of the Buddhists.[43]

The Buddhists then called off anti-Ky demonstrations on condition that the premier would honor his promises.[44] They still hoped to induce the United States to permit a changeover to a representative civilian government by making this alternative appear feasible and reasonably in accord with Washington's policies. The diminishing volume of demands for Ky's dismissal after the April 14 "guarantees" testified less to any growing confidence in Ky than to the Buddhists' deep concern not to panic the United States into backing punitive measures against them.[45] By early May 1966 a *modus vivendi* appeared to have been achieved between the Buddhists and Washington, with the latter pledging its official endorsement of elections.

It was soon to become evident, however, that the Buddhist victory had been a hollow one, for in the meantime the government had prepared its counterattack. On May 4, Ky made the first move in reasserting his power when he stated that "we will try to hold the elections by October" (they had earlier, in spite of Lodge's public disagreement, been scheduled for August 15) and a few days later added that he expected to remain in office for yet another year.[46] On May 15, again with the direct assistance of the United States—its planes, gasoline, and airbases—Ky's troops began the forcible occupation of one of the Buddhist strongholds, the city of Danang, and not long afterwards, with similar U.S. assistance, subdued the Buddhist-controlled center of Hué.[47]

Having completed the seizure of Danang by force, the junta began a steady whittling down and reinterpretation of the promises of April. On the day of that city's reoccupation, an army communiqué stated that the "struggle movements" (Buddhist groups in Hué and Danang) had "exerted a harmful influence on the combat potential and the anticommunist spirit of the armed forces" and that the "just and free character" of the forthcoming elections would depend on the firm establishment of "security" throughout the country.[48] Over the previous month, activist Catholic groups among the refugees had accused the Buddhists of harboring communist sympathies. They criticized Buddhist leaders for being neutralists who would open negotiations with the Liberation Front if they gained power, and in mid-May they called upon the government to put down the Buddhist demonstrations.[49]

On May 21, 1966, Premier Ky publicly denounced the principal leader of the Buddhist militants, Thich Tri Quang, as a "communist" [50] (an allegation that Vietnamese would hardly believe but Americans might) and warned: "We must eliminate all disturbances, division, and rebellion because they constitute important obstacles to the building of democracy." [51] On May 24, Ky added that the election could only be held if the government could first create "security and order." [52] On the same day the Chief of State, General Thieu, emphasized that the holding of the elections would be conditional upon the government's establishment of full security and "social discipline." Otherwise, he said, the assembly would be "full of communists," and democracy would be lost.[53] There was an increasing emphasis on the barring of "neutralists" as well as communists from the forthcoming elections.[54] "Neutralist" was a term that military spokesmen had come to apply to all advocates of a peaceful settlement of the civil war and to anyone willing to explore the possibility of negotiations with the Vietcong. Since the government had taken to calling the Buddhist insurgents in Danang and Hué "communists" as well as "neutralists" [55] and had proscribed neutralists and communists from participating in the elections to which it had committed itself, an attempt was clearly underway to bar these and other Buddhist activists from effective participation.

The full extent of Ky's commitment to the destruction of the Buddhists as a political force in the South was revealed in his forcible suppression of their struggle committees in Danang and Hué and the wave of arrests and repressions that followed. Equally revealing were his reactions to the recommendations of the body he had himself appointed to draw up an elections law.* This civilian Electoral Law Commission, though boycotted by the Buddhists, presented a draft electoral law to Ky's government on June 5. It recommended that the elections create a national assembly that, aside from its power to draft a constitution, could exercise legislative powers as a full-fledged national assembly.[56] Moreover, it ruled that in the elections for this assembly the Buddhists should

---

* This is not to be confused with the junta's earlier reversal in April of the recommendations of the previous civilian body, whose membership it had also appointed.

not be barred from using as an electoral symbol the red lotus, a traditional emblem, with great drawing power among an often unsophisticated rural electorate.

However, Premier Ky promptly made clear that these recommendations were unacceptable. On June 15, 1966, his government announced publicly that the constituent assembly to be chosen in the elections would be dissolved upon the promulgation of a constitution and would not be permitted to assume the role of a lawmaking body. While the constituent assembly deliberated (a period that was to last for as long as six months), governmental power would remain in the hands of the junta's National Leadership Committee. Even after the constitution had been promulgated this army-dominated Committee would for a period continue to govern and would be "entrusted with endowing the country with the various institutions provided by the constitution." Only in the autumn of 1967, after a legislative assembly had been established following a second election, would the Ky regime surrender its power.[57]

On June 19, 1966, the National Leadership Committee issued a revised version of the electoral law and published the decree law on the constituent assembly itself.[58] The terms under which the elections of September 11, 1966, were held demonstrated the dominating role of the army. It is therefore important that the key provisions of these decree laws be carefully studied.

Following the example of the elections of May 30, 1965, the electoral districts in September 1966 were divided into 25 single-member constituencies and 27 multiple-member constituencies, wherein a system of proportional representation was used.[59] Since many multimember constituencies were established in areas of greatest Buddhist strength, the number of candidates that the Buddhists could expect to elect was thereby reduced. Contrary to the draft electoral law that the junta rejected, Article 29 of its decree law expressly forbade the use of "any familiar religious emblem"—another undisguised move to undercut Buddhist drawing power. The size of the constituent assembly was changed from the electoral commission's proposed membership of 171 to 117, thereby insuring that the expected bloc of government supporters would be all the more effective.*

Article 10 of the electoral law excluded as possible candidates: "Civil servants, servicemen, government personnel of all levels who are dismissed or discharged for disciplinary reasons" and those "who work directly *or indirectly* for Communism or neutralism." (Emphasis added.) † As was observed above, the government's addiction to labeling virtually any serious opposition "communist" or "neutralist" permitted nearly automatic elimination of candidates whom it suspected of favoring discussions with the NLF and a negotiated settlement or whom it found politically objectionable for any other reason.[60] Despite the rigorous limitations on the conditions for candidacy, of the 735 who first filed in accordance with those conditions on July 11, approximately 200 had been removed from candidacy by election day.[61] Moreover, if any one candidate on a "list" in a multimember constituency was disqualified on the above grounds, all other candidates on that list were to be barred from participating in the elections (Article 16). This guilt-by-association provision effectively insulated the assembly from neutralist sympathizers and individuals suspected of favoring a negotiated settlement of the war.

---

* Nine of these 117 seats were reserved for Montagnards, including "North Vietnamese Montagnard refugees" and individuals of Cham descent and were to be filled subsequent to the elections through an "allocation" which was to be "fixed by the enactment of a subsequent decree law, and in accordance with the traditions and customs of these compatriots" (Article 3).

† According to another translation (one distributed through the U.S. Department of State) available to the authors, this sentence (paragraph 9 of Article 10) reads: "Those who have directly or indirectly worked for the communists and pro-communist neutralists, or neutralists whose actions are advantageous to the communists."

Even should neutralists or Buddhist-nationalist elements somehow have slipped through this electoral Maginot Line, the junta's decree law on the workings of the constituent assembly forms an effective second line of defense. Under Article 5 of the decree law, with concurrence of two-thirds of the Assembly any member may be "sued, arrested, incarcerated, or sentenced" for having made statements or cast a vote "instrumental to the promotion of communist or pro-communist Neutralist policies or activities." [62]

If, despite all these obstacles, any unwelcome provision should later find its way into the draft constitution, the junta, so long as it has the support of 40 of the assembly's 117 members, may redraft it without restriction. The chairman of the National Leadership Committee is explicitly empowered to make any modifications he chooses, and the assembly can reject these only by mustering against them a "vote of two-thirds of the total number of Deputies" (Article 20). Should the assembly fail to achieve a two-thirds majority, the chairman's modifications are considered automatically *approved*. In other words, if as many as 65 per cent of this rigorously screened assembly should vote against a measure sponsored by the military leadership, this would be regarded as approval. Thus, General Thieu, with only 40 out of a membership of 117, will have total control of drafting the new constitution. As has already been shown, the conditions governing the elections virtually assured the junta of at least this many adherents in the assembly.*

---

* The Saigon government has reported that on September 11, 80.8 per cent of the registered voters (4,274,812 out of 5,288,512) went to the polls. Contrary to prediction, the number of incidents of Vietcong terror were minimal even though Saigon labeled every infraction of the law as an anti-election "sabotage effort." [63] The vast majority of those chosen were from the cities: 23 were reported to be educators, 22 businessmen-industrialists, 18 civil servants, 18 military men, 8 lawyers, 6 retired individuals, 5 doctors, 5 elder statesmen, and 5 unknown. Seven were farmer-landowners. The government classified 34 of those elected as "Buddhists" (the

It is scarcely surprising that the Buddhists decided to boycott elections held under such conditions.[64] The terms of the election law constituted, then, one part of the junta's strategy of breaking the Buddhists' power—a combination of physical repression and quasi-legal obstruction and disqualification.

The perspectives first opened up by the Buddhist movement thus seem to have been closed. Military suppression and manipulation in drafting and executing the electoral law are likely to ensure the continuation of a pro-war government. The Buddhist defeat over the issue of free elections caused the downfall, at least temporarily, of the relatively pro-American, Buddhist leader Tam Chau, who had staked his reputation on the sincerity and good intentions of Ky and Washington.[65] His replacement at the head of the Buddhist Institute, Thich Thien Hoa, stated on July 28, 1966: "The Buddhists have much sympathy for the Americans but oppose their mistaken policy here. They have not helped the Vietnamese people as such, but only individuals or cliques, who did nothing but oppress the people." [66] The gentleness of these words should not conceal the bitterness behind them. In indicating plans to boycott the rigged elections, Thien Hoa, on August 6, accused the United States of backing unpopular governments and called for foreign support to save his people from religious persecution by Ky's regime.[67]

The earlier promise of a real change of course in South

---

elections had been boycotted by adherents of the Buddhist Institute); of the remainder it listed 30 Catholics, 10 Hoa Hao, 7 Confucianists, 5 Cao Dai, and the rest unknown. Categorized on a regional basis, 27 of those elected were Northerners, 28 from central Vietnam (an ambiguous category that includes both Northerners and Southerners if defined in terms of the present demarcation line), and 44 Southerners. From the evidence revealed publicly as of November 15, 1966, it is impossible to estimate the number of votes the Ky-Thieu government can safely count on within the newly formed constituent assembly. These figures are from an information release of October 1966, distributed through U.S. Government agencies in Saigon.

Vietnam had, even before the elections were held, been nullified. The "drama" of September 11, like the Manila Conference of October 24 and 25, was to become an essential part of the Administration's preparations for its own November congressional elections.[68] The Johnson Administration on the eve of the congressional elections could tell the American public that Saigon's elections and the President's meetings with Asian leaders at Manila provided assurance that the reason the United States was in Vietnam was to protect and promote freedom and democracy there.

However the Vietnamese elections were viewed in the United States, for the cynical and apathetic Vietnamese public, dragooned into going through the motions of participating in them, they evoked no enthusiasm and were seen as a politically irrelevant gesture made in compliance with the demands of local officials acting for Saigon.[69] The political polarization imposed upon the population was being maintained, leaving little opening that might permit access to a third course—some other road that might lead to a peaceful resolution of the conflict they have suffered under for more than two decades.

So long as the United States planted itself so firmly behind the army leadership, this polarization was likely to endure. But if this could be considered stability, it was an artificial one and in all probability would collapse as soon as American power had withdrawn. For that power was being applied in a way that obstructed internal evolution toward a government capable of winning popular support. If thereby the United States was buying time, in the end it would be the Vietcong that would be most likely to benefit.

Notes to Chapter X

1. U.S. Senate, *Supplemental Foreign Assistance, Fiscal Year 1966—Vietnam,* 89th Congress, 2nd Session (Washington: U.S. Government Printing Office, 1966), pp. 120–122.

2. For a statement of American interests in this period, see *Department of State Bulletin* (Washington, March 15, 1965), pp. 362–371, and (March 22, 1965), pp. 398–403. By mid-June the number of American troops in South Vietnam had reached 53,500, compared to 16,500 the summer before.

3. For relevant statements see *New York Times,* February 27 and 28, 1965, and April 1, 1966.

4. See Robert Shaplen, *The Lost Revolution* (New York: Harper & Row, 1965), pp. 341–343. See also *New York Times,* May 10, 1965.

5. Shaplen, *op. cit.,* pp. 343–345; *New York Times,* May 21 and 22, 1965.

6. *New York Times,* June 20, 1965.

7. *Ibid.,* June 20 and 27, and July 1, 1965.

8. *Ibid.,* June 25, 1965.

9. *Ibid.,* November 12, 1965. In July 1966 Ky called for a confrontation with China now, because, in his words, it was the "real enemy." *Ibid.,* July 26, 1966.

10. *New York Times,* July 16, 1966. According to the Vietnamese Ambassador to Washington, Vu Van Thai, who asked Premier Ky for a clarification concerning this allegation, Ky stated: "I want to infuse in our youth the same fanaticism, the same dedication, the same fighting spirit as Hitler has infused in his people." Public lecture, Cornell University, March 3, 1966.

11. For example, see *ibid.,* September 1 and October 19, 1965.

12. *Ibid.,* November 12, 1965.

13. Full text broadcast on Saigon Radio, January 15, 1966.

14. See, for instance, *New York Times,* June 18 and 22, 1965, and March 14, 1966.

15. Charles Mohr in *ibid.,* February 6, 1966.

16. *Department of State Bulletin* (Washington, February 28, 1966).

17. *New York Times,* April 6 and 15, 1966.

18. Talks of one of the authors with General Nguyen Chanh Thi, October 5, 1966.

19. Details of this perspective have been derived from the Vietnamese press and from private interviews with Buddhist leaders, which have been shown to the authors. The authors confirmed

them with a leading Buddhist, Thich Nhat Hanh, in interviews on May 23 and 24, 1966, at Cornell University. For Hanoi's reaction to Buddhist perspectives see, for example, the comment on Thich Nhat Hanh, Hanoi Radio, May 24, 1966.

20. Tran Van Dinh, "Elections in Vietnam," *The New Republic,* July 2, 1966, p. 20. For a broad discussion of Buddhist aims, see also Max Clos, "The Karma of Vietnam's Buddhists," *New York Times Magazine,* August 21, 1966, pp. 28ff.

21. For a CIA assessment of Vietcong strength, see George A. Carver, Jr., "The Faceless Viet Cong," *Foreign Affairs,* Vol. XLIV, No. 3, April 1966, pp. 347–372.

22. Joseph Kraft, "Politics in Vietnam," *The New York Review of Books,* June 23, 1966, p. 5.

23. For reports on how this can happen, see *New York Times,* September 5, 1965, and August 11 and 17, 1966.

24. According to Buddhist spokesmen: "Most of the so-called Viet Cong areas are those where the Viet Cong and the government are contending with one another for domination. Almost all the inhabitants, except for five or six, in any given area are not Viet Cong. Once the government troops move in and secure such areas, elections can be held under satisfactory conditions. The current military government has no legal basis or legitimate background." *Mainichi,* April 12, 1966.

25. *Vietnam Press,* April 12, 1966.

26. *Mainichi,* April 12, 1966.

27. Statement by Chief of State Nguyen Van Thieu in *Luan Zan Moi,* April 21, 1966.

28. Kraft, *op. cit.,* p. 6.

29. See above, Chapters 3 and 4.

30. Kraft, *op. cit.,* p. 6.

31. *New York Times,* February 21, 1965. For a more recent speech by the Pope, see *ibid.,* June 25, and September 20, 1966. On September 19, Pope Paul VI declared: "We cry to them in God's name to stop. Men must come together and work out concrete plans and terms in all sincerity. A settlement should be reached now, even at the expense of some inconvenience or loss, for it may have to be made later in the train of bitter slaughter and involve great loss." For one Catholic discussion of the war, see *La Croix,* April 7, 1965, republished in *The Viet-Nam Reader,* ed. by Marcus G. Raskin and Bernard B. Fall (New York: Vintage, 1965), pp. 276–278.

32. *New York Times,* March 26, 1966. In his January 15, 1966, State of the Union address, Ky pledged that elections for a national legislature would be held in 1967. Saigon Radio, January 15, 1966.

33. *New York Times,* March 26, 1966.

34. *Ibid.,* March 30, 1966.

35. *Ibid.,* April 1, 1966.

36. *Ibid.,* April 6, 1966.

37. Moreover, as Seymour Topping noted, a side effect of the massive buildup was that "the country is more stable militarily because of the presence of United States troops" than it was in 1964. *New York Times,* April 5, 1966.

38. *Ibid.,* April 5, 1966, and Max Frankel in *ibid.,* April 7, 1966.

39. *Ibid.,* April 9, 1966.

40. *Vietnam Press,* April 14, 1966.

41. *Saigon Post,* April 11, 1966.

42. *New York Times,* April 16, 1966.

43. *Ibid.,* April 14 and 15, 1966.

44. *Ibid.,* April 16, 1966.

45. This comes out clearly in Tri Quang's appeal of April 18, when he exhorted the residents of Hué to "stop all activities causing disturbances" and declared further that "the present government may remain in power till a constitutional assembly is set up." Saigon Radio, April 18, 1966. See also *Vietnam Press,* April 19 and 21, 1966.

46. *New York Times,* April 23 and May 5 and 7, 1966.

47. See *ibid.,* May 15–25, 1966, for a full account of these actions. For the campaign to retake Hué, see *ibid.,* June 10–20, 1966. Even journals as sympathetic to the U.S. and Ky position as the London *Economist* stated: "In a war like Vietnam's a man can play dirty tricks and still qualify as a leader. But the really important thing that has been destroyed in this week's mess is Marshal Ky's standing as a leader capable of pushing ahead with the fight to keep South Vietnam out of communist hands." *Economist,* May 21, 1966, p. 797.

48. Saigon Radio, May 16, 1966.

49. *New York Times,* April 18 and May 15, 1966.

50. *Ibid.,* May 22, 1966.

51. Saigon Radio, May 21, 1966.

52. *Ibid.,* May 24, 1966.

53. *Ibid.*

54. Letter by Nguyen Cao Ky, Saigon Radio, May 16, 1966.

55. Saigon Radio, May 24, 1966.

56. *New York Times,* June 6 and 11, 1966.

57. *Ibid.,* June 15 and 20, 1966.

58. The texts of these two laws have been provided to the authors by a reliable source in Saigon.

59. *New York Times,* July 17, 1966. See also these key provisions of the voting law:

Article 44:

In case of voting for a group list the number of seats will be divided among the group lists in proportion to the votes obtained. Firstly, the Committee in charge of the voting room will calculate the quotient of election of the constituency by dividing the total number of voters who have voted by the number of seats in the constituency. Then the number of seats won by each group list will be computed by dividing the number of ballots for the group list by the quotient of election; and there are as many seats for the group list as the quotients of election obtained by dividing the total number of votes by the number of seats.

If after the division, there still remain a number of seats, this number of seats will be gradually added to any ticket which has the greatest factor.

Any ticket receiving less than five per cent of the total number of ballots in the constituency will not be elected.

In each constituency, the candidates will be declared elected following the order stated in the list of candidates provided for in Art. 17.

In case one candidate elected on the ticket dies, resigns or gives up his duties for whatever reason, the candidate who wins the next largest number of votes on the ticket will replace him.

No candidate who runs in several constituencies or on several tickets may be declared elected in any constituency.

As for those constituencies which have seats reserved for Vietnamese of Cambodian descent, the results of the election must be calculated separately for candidates of Cambodian ancestry and for others of Vietnamese ancestry; and among the candidates of Cambodian descent themselves. [4 seats were to be reserved for those of Cambodian ancestry.]

60. See *New York Times*, August 15, 1966.

61. As of the date of first filing (July 11), there were 735 candidates. This number was reduced to 635 by the extended filing deadline (July 14) and to 542 at the end of the screening process (August 12). On the day of the elections there were "slightly less than 540" candidates. Most of those eliminated were removed by the local screening boards. These facts are taken from an information release of October 1966, distributed through U.S. Government agencies in Saigon.

62. Since any such expression of opinion violates Paragraph 9 of Article 10 of the electoral law (as cited above), under Article 7 of the decree law any deputy found guilty will be "considered to have automatically resigned." Typical of Ky's reasoning with regard to infiltration of these elements into the assembly is his statement to a "seminar" that was held on the elections on August 1: "Since the elections of the constituent national assembly aims at advancing toward a democratic regime, a regime of which the communists are afraid and which they have often sought every means possible

to sabotage, appropriate measures must be taken to prevent any infiltration by the communist or the procommunist neutralist elements into the constituent national assembly or any collusion on their part with the deputies of the constituent national assembly." Saigon Radio, August 1, 1966.

63. A total of 42 "Vietcong terrorist and harassing incidents" were officially reported in the hours of the election, bringing death to 19 Vietnamese and wounding 120. In May 1966, an average of 817 incidents were reported weekly. By July 2, the weekly number was reported to be 642 and for later weeks as follows: week of July 16: 582; week of July 30: 426; week of August 13: 400; and week of September 3: 517. The daily average for the week of September 3 was 74 incidents, almost twice the number of incidents as were recorded on election day. By definition an "incident" includes harassment, terrorism, attacks, sabotage, propaganda, and anti-aircraft fire. Saigon gives no reason why on election day all incidents were regarded automatically as "anti-election" incidents. *New York Times* correspondent Charles Mohr noted in this regard: "There has been a shameful amount of hoopla about these elections. American and South Vietnamese officials have outdone even the Vietcong in trying to spread the impression that the guerrillas are determined to disrupt the voting—the better to argue later that the guerrillas have been thwarted." *New York Times,* August 24 and September 9 and 11, 1966. For official figures concerning Vietcong incidents on election day, see the information release of October 1966, distributed through U.S. Government agencies in Saigon.

64. *New York Times,* July 29, August 7 and 17, and September 7, 1966. Emotional hostility to the Ky-Thieu regime was also a factor. See Tri Quang's statement of June 3, 1966, where he opposed elections "organized by the bloody hand of those who have killed people in Danang . . . [to] establish a militaristic national assembly." *New York Times,* June 4, 1966.

65. *Saigon Daily News,* July 13, 1966; on September 17, 1966, the *New York Times* reported that Tam Chau had returned to Saigon from "sick leave" and that Tri Quang had ended his long fast. Both monks were expected to begin the task of rebuilding the power of the Buddhist Institute.

66. *New York Times,* July 29, 1966.

67. *Ibid.,* August 7, 1966.

68. For the principal speeches and documents of the Manila Conference, see *New York Times,* October 24–26, 1966.

69. *Ibid.,* August 15 and 21, and September 11, 1966. Charles Mohr reported on August 21: "There is, in fact, little likelihood that the vote will be light. Provincial chiefs, military commanders, rural-development teams and other officials are expected to make

an all-out effort to turn out large numbers of voters. This may not take the form of intimidation of the almost 5 million eligible voters, but few peasants are likely to risk offending officials by refusing to vote even though, according to diplomatic sources, there is considerable apathy regarding the elections."

CHAPTER XI

China and Vietnam

1: **American views on Vietnam** have been conditioned strongly by the American attitude toward China and interpretations of past Chinese actions. Because of this it is important to assess those elements in the record that have helped shape Communist China's policy toward Vietnam and have influenced its present and potential role there.

The costly and dangerous conflict in Korea from 1950 to 1953 led the Chinese to question their previous judgments on the effectiveness of armed force in pursuit of their national goals. The Soviet Union's unwillingness to support China in that war also made Mao Tse-tung dubious of placing reliance on the Russian military deterrent as a defense for his country.[1] By 1953 Peking was convinced that the protracted struggle in Korea was against its interests and should be ended through a truce.[2] As a consequence of the Korean experience China began after the armistice to reappraise its partnership with Moscow and to incorporate in its external policies the numerous military and political lessons derived from the three-year struggle.

One central lesson was caution. Peking recognized that its intervention in Korea had come close to precipitating an American retaliation against China itself. As later congressional testimony revealed, Mao Tse-tung had good reason to heed seriously the threats of U.S. military leaders in Korea. This testimony disclosed that pressure had been building up in General Douglas MacArthur's command and in Washington to expand the war by bombing bases and supply facilities in mainland China, using Chinese Nationalist troops against it, and imposing a naval blockade.[3] Although by preserving communist North Korea as a political entity China had attained its primary strategic objective, its leaders understood the magnitude of the risk taken, and they began to display caution in their international dealings.

A second lesson for Peking was that, contrary to the stereotype it had come to accept, the neutrals of Asia and Africa had demonstrated that they were not puppets of the United States. For example, despite strong American persuasion the Burmese and Indians had refused to sign (and the Indonesians to ratify) the 1951 Japanese peace treaty. The neutrals firmly suppressed their local communist uprisings, and the efficacy of communist subversive techniques and revolutionary warfare was negated in country after country. At the same time as a consequence of Washington's antagonism toward neutralist regimes and the inapplicability of its strategies of "massive retaliation" and "liberation," China was provided with an unparalleled opening to promote friendly relations with the states of Africa and Asia. Under these circumstances, the Chinese concluded that favorable results might sometimes accrue from a policy of backing neutralist leaders as well as local communists.

Finally, a third important lesson pertained to the internal development of China. By the end of the Korean War, the Chinese recognized the overwhelming need to transform their economy from its "poor and blank" condition. Although the First Five-Year Plan (1953–57) had technically been initiated prior to the Korean armistice, actual implementation had been deferred until 1955. China's domestic economic goals had partially supplanted ideologically dictated objectives, so Peking became less willing to risk costly losses in the international sphere.

These considerations led the Chinese leaders to moderate their previous line of policy and embark upon what they called "peaceful coexistence." *

---

* As was to become clear, China and Russia meant somewhat different things by the term "peaceful coexistence." For the Chinese, it applied principally to the relations between China and

2: **During the period 1949–54,** China's assistance to the Vietminh in their war against France was never wholehearted. Although beginning in late 1949 Peking provided Ho Chi Minh with some weapons and other aid, until late 1953 this was largely restricted to light arms. Peking apparently feared the possibility of U.S. retaliation should China's aid become substantial.

After the signing of the truce in Korea, Peking deliberately moved to secure a prompt conclusion to the Indochina conflict. This course was dictated by the lessons of the Korean War and by the fact that if peace were achieved in Southeast Asia China would be able to devote more attention to its own internal problems. Thus, while continuing to render aid—which included heavy artillery for the Vietminh buildup against Dienbienphu—from at least as early as September 1953 China recommended that the warring parties negotiate.[4]

With the fall of the Dienbienphu fortress to the Vietminh on May 7, 1954, the Chinese delegation at Geneva adjusted realistically to the psychological climate produced by France's military defeat and by the threat of American military intervention. Premier Chou En-lai, China's chief delegate, moved deftly and decisively to gain his principal objectives of ensuring the neutrality of the Indochinese states, as a barrier against the establishment of American bases or alliances there. He withdrew his insistence that the communist movements in Cambodia and Laos be granted equal status with the Viet-

---

its neighbors, while Moscow emphasized the need for "peaceful coexistence" in East-West relations. In April 1954, Peking, in signing a treaty with India on trade with Tibet, gave formal expression for the first time to the so-called "five principles of peaceful coexistence." These principles—mutual respect for each other's territorial integrity and sovereignty, nonaggression, noninterference in each other's internal affairs, equality and mutual benefit, and peaceful coexistence—were confirmed in joint statements between Chou En-lai and Nehru (June 28, 1954) and Burmese leader U Nu (June 29, 1954).

minh in the meetings and agreed to the withdrawal of all foreign troops (including those of the Vietminh) from Cambodia and Laos on condition that no United States bases would be established in those countries.[5]

At the same time, Chou En-lai told British Foreign Secretary Anthony Eden that his government was extremely worried over the possibility that American-sponsored military alliances in Asia would "split South-East Asia in two. . . ."[6] The Chinese premier was "particularly insistent," Eden added, that the three Indochinese states should be "independent, sovereign and neutral." To help guarantee this, he proposed a membership for the envisaged international control commission in Indochina acceptable to all three Western powers. The Chinese also urged the Vietminh to make concessions on the provisional demarcation line and the date for the elections.

The final agreements reached at Geneva accorded with Peking's essential objectives in stipulating the neutrality of the three Indochina states, forbidding foreign military aid—except on a replacement basis—and barring the establishment of foreign military bases. The Geneva Conference marked Communist China's entrance into the international community. There its diplomats demonstrated political moderation and gained acceptance from all powers represented, with the exception of the United States. In the face of American opposition the Chinese had enlarged their political influence and could, on balance, be satisfied with the results of the meetings.

3 : In his final statement to the Geneva Conference, Chou En-lai said: "What the peoples of Asia desire is, unquestionably, not splits or antagonism, but peace and cooperation. In the interest of safeguarding the collective peace of Asia, it is our opinion that the nations of Asia should consult among themselves and cooperate with each other."[7] The attitude of moderation that this statement reflected characterized China's approach to the conference of Asian and African countries held at Bandung, Indonesia, in April 1955. By the end of the

Bandung sessions, the suspicious neutrals had been much more assured of the sincerity of China's avowed desire to live in peace and reach compromise agreements with its Asian neighbors.

In the opening round at Bandung, Chou En-lai demonstrated his determination to "set the record straight" on China's potential role in Asia. In his "supplementary speech" on April 19, he told the assemblage that his delegation had "come here to seek common ground, not to create divergence." [8] He insisted that the communist nations could live in harmony with noncommunist governments, that though atheistic, his own country would respect the religious beliefs of its Asian neighbors, and he attempted to mitigate the fears of various delegates concerning Chinese-instigated subversion. Concern with the latter had been of central importance in the formation of the Southeast Asia Treaty Organization (SEATO) at Manila the year before. On the last day of the Manila Conference Secretary of State Dulles had remarked: "There is little doubt but what in this Southeast Asia area, as elsewhere, the main purpose of those who are hostile to freedom is to attempt to frighten us into a division so that we shall be more vulnerable to either open aggression or to indirect subversive aggression." [9] In reply to such charges, Premier Chou stressed the internal nature of the communist revolution, stating, "It is by the efforts of the Chinese people that the Chinese revolution won its victory. It is certainly not imported from without." In order to allay the fears of countries with large Chinese minorities, Chou denied that his government would use these ethnic brothers for subversive purposes. He undertook to demonstrate China's seriousness by drafting a treaty on dual nationality for Chinese residents in Indonesia that met Jakarta's terms.[10]

As an earnest of peaceful intent, the Chinese premier told the assemblage at Bandung that his government was fully prepared to reach a détente with the United States. No other single act at the meetings so profoundly affected the delegates.

Though Peking did continue to rail against the United States, its representative made specific and concrete proposals aimed at easing international tensions in the Pacific and improving its relationship with the United States. After accusing Washington of creating such tensions, Chou En-lai said, "The Chinese people do not want to have a war with the United States of America. The Chinese Government is willing to sit down and enter into negotiations with the United States Government to discuss the question of relaxing tension in the Far East, and especially the question of relaxing tension in the Taiwan area." [11] The sponsors (Burma, Ceylon, India, Indonesia, and Pakistan) and many of the participants at Bandung saw this Chinese gesture toward Washington as one of the conference's paramount achievements.

It was significant that the delegate from the principal Asian member of SEATO—Pakistan—responded to Chou's speeches at Bandung, stating: "China is by no means an imperialist nation and she has no satellites. Therefore, when the Prime Minister of Ceylon [Sir John Kotelawala] raised this issue with which some of us are in complete agreement, he was directing his criticism against the Soviet form of imperialism by which many countries have been made satellites. . . . We have the friendliest relations with China; China is certainly not imperialistic; she has not brought any other country under her heels." [12]

Although India had been the first to suggest that China should attend the conference, many in New Delhi did not "think China can take her proper place in Asia so long as she is in [the] Sino-Soviet Pact." [13] Following the conference, however, Pandit Nehru stated that "Chou believes in and will honor the five principles [of peaceful coexistence]." China, he added, "should be given as much chance as possible to have 'other windows' to the outside world and not be restricted to looking out the window of Soviet Russia." [14] Many of the other Asian leaders agreed. China would not exert direct or indirect pressure on them, they believed, if they left China alone, did not seek the outside support of the Western governments against her, and were willing to seek compromise settlements of any outstanding problems with Peking.

Ten years later, U Thant summarized the results for his own country, Burma, that had placed some faith in Peking's words and reached a favorable border solution with it in 1960. "As you know," he said, "the Burmese Communist Party is still underground after 17 years and still illegal. But let me tell you: there is not a single instance of outside help to the Burmese Communists inside Burma in the last 17 years. . . . As you know, Burma has over 1,000 miles of land frontier with mainland China. If only the Burmese Government had decided at some stage to seek outside military assistance to suppress the internal insurrections and revolutions, then I am sure that Burma would have experienced one of the two alternatives: either the country would be divided into two parts or the whole country would have become communist long ago." [15] Because of U Thant's deep knowledge of Asia and because his country has more to lose than the United States should his interpretation prove false, his opinion should not be discounted.

4 : The reverberations of Chou En-lai's offer to ease international tensions by reaching a wide-ranging accord with the United States on Pacific problems profoundly challenged American statesmanship in the Afro-Asian world. Washington had to find out whether or not China had genuinely set its course onto a new path of conciliation and friendship. On the basis of Peking's initiative at Bandung, Sino-American bilateral talks were started at Geneva in August 1955. On September 10, 1955, the talks produced an agreement on the repatriation of civilians between the two sides. But thereafter the meetings deteriorated into a fruitless round of proposals on the renunciation of the use of force in the Taiwan area. [16] The following year Chou again announced that his government was "not against the issuance jointly with the United States of an announcement on mutual renunciation of the use and threat of force in Sino-American relations." [17] Qualifying this, he added that "any announcement concerning the renunciation of the use of force between China and the United States must be capable of leading to the relaxation and elimination of the tension, and must not imply acceptance of the United States occupation of Taiwan." This need not constitute a major obstacle, he indicated. "If a statement is to be specifically included in the Sino-American announcement that the disputes between the two countries in the Taiwan area will be settled through peaceful negotiations without resorting to force, then it must also be explicitly provided that a Sino-American conference of the Foreign Ministers be held so as to implement this statement." The Eisenhower Administration rejected these conditions, thereby ending hope for an agreement proscribing the use of force in the Taiwan Straits.

It cannot be known what might have happened had Washington reacted favorably to these Chinese conditions.[18] Also, since the full record of the Sino-American ambassadorial talks is highly classified, it is uncertain how far the United States in fact went beyond the published record in an attempt to reach an accord with Peking on the renunciation of the use of force.[19] In public statements, however, despite its talks with Chinese representatives, the United States gave no hint of its intention to negotiate with a government that, in the words of the then Assistant Secretary of State, Walter S. Robertson, "flagrantly violated the international obligations assumed by responsible governments" and was "an outlaw-gangster regime, unpurged of its crimes and aggressions, and unfit to sit in any respectable family of nations." [20] Mr. Robertson later asserted that the Chinese only appeared to be moderate and had gone "into an accommodating switch when the signal came [from Moscow]." [21] It must be remembered that in this period following the Korean War the "Chinese menace" dominated the thinking of the Department of State, which had yet to recover from Senator Joseph R. McCarthy's attacks.

As the United States concluded security alliances with China's neighbors, its hostility to the government in Peking became more marked. In 1958, Secretary Dulles set American policy squarely on a collision course with the interests of Communist China.* In December of that year, he declared that U.S. policy was, in the words of President Eisenhower, "a noble strategy of victory." [22] That "strategy of victory" produced an unpromising climate for any pursuit by China of a moderate course of action with respect to the United States in Asia. The United States had added country after country to its system of military alliances with Asian states rigidly opposed to Peking—Japan, South Korea, Taiwan, the Philippines, Thailand, and South Vietnam—and in addition during 1957–58 was providing military aid to antigovernment rebels in Laos and Indonesia. The fact that the United States was busily renovating Chiang Kai-shek's military establishment as well as arming and supporting anti-Peking Chinese units in Burma and elsewhere [23] made it all the more difficult for China to pursue a policy of peaceful coexistence. The failure of America's clandestine incursions into Laos and Indonesia did not change Peking's conclusion that the object of United States policy was to encircle China militarily. At the same time Moscow was moving ever closer to a détente with Washington. Isolated and under pressure from the United States,

---

* In a Department of State press release of August 11, 1958, that probably came in large measure from Dulles' pen, these key passages appeared: "It is true that there is no reason to believe that the Chinese Communist regime is on the verge of collapse; but there is equally no reason to accept its present rule in mainland China as permanent. . . . Dictatorships often create an illusion of permanence from the very fact that they suppress and still all opposition, and that of the Chinese Communists is no exception to this rule. The United States holds the view that communism's rule in China is not permanent and that it one day will pass. By withholding diplomatic recognition from Peiping it seeks to hasten that passing." *Department of State Bulletin* (Washington, September 8, 1958), p. 389.

the Chinese began to take a less conciliatory position and to abandon the line of foreign policy they had adopted in 1953.

But despite a gradual shift in line China did not develop a domestic capability sufficient to undertake expansionist actions abroad. Its moves, moreover, accorded with its capabilities and not with its more strident pronouncements on "national liberation." China withdrew its remaining armed forces from Korea in 1958 and regularized its boundaries with Afghanistan, Nepal, Burma, Mongolia, and Pakistan on a mutually satisfactory basis (and accepted the existing boundaries with Vietnam and Laos). With the announcement of the "Great Leap Forward" in 1958 and the program for the establishment of rural communes, China turned dramatically inward.

Since the Korean War, the Communist Chinese have used military force on three important fronts: in Tibet (1959),[24] the Taiwan Straits (1954 and 1958),[25] and India (1962).[26] These applications of force were on a limited basis, and Peking was evidently intent on avoiding a major military confrontation. Peking sent its troops into Tibet in 1950 at almost the same time that it intervened in Korea. After several years of unsuccessful attempts at "peaceful liberation," its repressive measures then provoked a rebellion in 1959. Most governments, including India's,* have affirmed China's claim to sovereignty over Tibet but have deplored its use of brute force there. President Chiang Kai-shek has always insisted that Tibet is part of China, and accordingly a Chinese Nationalist official in the Ministry of External Affairs told one of the authors in 1959, "Those Communist bandits are wrong on most things, but we completely agree with their policy on Tibet." Since the United States recognizes Taipei as the *de jure* government of all China, Washington presumably agrees that legally Tibet is a part of China.

---

* In the "Agreement Between the Republic of India and the People's Republic of China on Trade and Intercourse Between the Tibet Region of China and India" (April 29, 1954), India acknowledged China's sovereignty over Tibet.

From 1959 to 1962, both India and China resorted to military measures in their common border area; and on October 12, 1962, a week before the Chinese invaded the disputed border territory held by India, Prime Minister Nehru stated that the Indian army was "to free Indian territory in the Northeast Frontier Agency of Chinese intruders." After defeating the Indian army in the border region and penetrating well beyond it, Peking withdrew its armed forces from most of the area that they had just invaded and established a demilitarized zone on either side of the line of control.

Finally, a communist bombardment of Quemoy in the Taiwan Straits in 1954 and 1958 followed major Nationalist Chinese military buildups on the island. On September 3, 1954, communist batteries shelled Quemoy (which is about 1,000 yards from communist-controlled territory at the nearest point). As one result of the ensuing crisis, the United States and the Republic of China signed a mutual defense treaty that covered Taiwan and other Nationalist-held islands. After the Bandung Conference, Peking changed its tactic to one of "peaceful liberation" of Taiwan, holding to this policy until early 1958. In August of that year Peking resumed the artillery bombardment of Quemoy and on August 28 broadcast an ultimatum demanding the surrender of the island's Nationalist garrison. After a prolonged exchange of fire, both sides agreed by loudspeaker that they would continue firing according to specially arranged schedules, thereby maintaining Quemoy as the international symbol of the unfinished Chinese civil war.

5: **During the period 1954–61,** China's attitude toward the situation in Vietnam remained largely consonant with the pledges made at Bandung. Peking called for the strict implementation of the Geneva Agreements, giving particular emphasis to the provisions concerning foreign alliances and the holding of elections. In a letter of October 31, 1955, Premier Chou En-lai told the British Foreign Secretary that Saigon's position in refusing elections was "untenable" because, "when

France signed the Geneva Agreement, it signed also on behalf of the southern part of Viet-Nam." He reiterated Indian Prime Minister Nehru's remark that Saigon could not "enjoy the benefits brought about by the agreement while attempting to reject other aspects of the agreement." To this statement he added a strong plea that the "competent authorities of two zones in Viet-Nam" immediately convene a consultative conference on the matter of general elections.[27] With Diem's refusal to respond to Hanoi's call for the preelection consultation stipulated in the Geneva Agreements, Chou, on January 25, 1956, addressed a letter to Britain in her capacity as Co-Chairman (and presumably to Russia as well) stating that "the Chinese Government deems it necessary that another Geneva Conference on Indo-China be convened by the Co-Chairmen of the Geneva Conference, to discuss the question of implementation of the Geneva Agreements in Viet-Nam. The Chinese Government also holds that the three member countries of the International Commission in Viet-Nam—India, Poland and Canada—should be invited to take part in this conference." [28] When Saigon and Washington refused to consider a conference, the Chinese did not resort to force but merely censured the United States for championing the "Ngo Dinh Diem clique of South Viet-Nam in violating the Geneva agreement provisions for holding consultations on all Viet-Nam general elections, and in obstructing the peaceful unification of Viet-Nam." [29]

The likelihood that China was sincere in its stated objective of seeing the Geneva Agreements strictly implemented in Vietnam is strengthened by its actions regarding Laos. There, as in Vietnam, Peking's overriding consideration was to insulate the country from any American military presence. In May 1959 the Chinese demanded the resumption of the activities by the International Commission for Supervision and Control in Laos, which had, over communist protest, adjourned in 1958.[30] Later, the Chinese joined other communist governments in accepting Cambodia's proposal of January 1, 1961, for a Geneva Conference on Laos. They adopted its plan for the neutralization of Laos and signed a declaration to that effect on July 23, 1962.[31] There is no evidence that the Chinese have in any significant way violated this neutrality,* although the same cannot be said for Hanoi [32] or the United States. Available evidence indicates that Peking believed that Chinese interests would be sufficiently served through a neutralization of Laos guaranteed by an international control commission and that this would remove the threat of U.S. power based across her southern border. Though the Chinese obviously

---

* The correctness of China's position on Laos is further substantiated by the data given in the important "secret Military Papers," released by the Department of State on August 5, 1963. The Military Papers are a set of twenty-nine issues of a secret military journal (*Kung-tso t'ung-hsün* [*"Bulletin of Activities"*]), which covers the period January 1–August 26, 1961. They were published by the General Political Department of the People's Liberation Army. In these papers, the Chinese write a rather factual account of the history of communist political fortunes in Laos and describe with considerable accuracy how a neutralist government there had been destroyed by American intervention.

In violation of the Geneva Agreements, the United States had attempted in 1958 to fashion Laos into an anticommunist bastion, a labor that was not abandoned until 1961. In attempting to do this, Washington—and not Peking—managed to thrust the anticommunist neutralist troops of Prime Minister Souvanna Phouma into a marriage of convenience with forces of the procommunist Laotian Pathet Lao and thereby provoked Hanoi into giving the latter greater assistance. It was the open American backing of the rightwing army generals in Laos who sought to overthrow Souvanna Phouma that induced him to enter into diplomatic relations with Moscow and request the Soviet arms that were soon airlifted to his forces via Hanoi. Subsequent to this counterproductive American effort to topple a Laotian government officially recognized by Washington, the Chinese were able to conclude in the Military Papers that "the Laotian revolutionary strength is greater now than before and there is a strong desire to have a government that wants peaceful neutrality. If we support this government we are actually supporting the revolutionary strength." See J. Chester Cheng, ed., *The Politics of the Chinese Red Army* (Stanford, Cal.: Hoover Institution, 1966), pp. 365–369, 485, 585–588.

hoped for the ultimate success of procommunist Laotians, they showed no willingness to participate in Laos' domestic political struggle except on the diplomatic level.

During the period 1958–61, the Chinese—consistent with the priorities they assigned to their domestic policies—strictly circumscribed their commitments to Vietnam. Mao's government supported Premier Pham Van Dong's proposal of March 7, 1958, that "the authorities of North and South Viet-nam meet at an early date to discuss the reduction of troops of both sides and work out ways of mutual trade so as to promote the peaceful unification of Viet-nam." [33] In the main, however, from 1958 to 1961 Peking displayed only a slight interest in Vietnam. Chinese statements over these years stressed that the Geneva Agreements must be upheld and charged that the United States, in violation of the agreements, was building up a military base in Vietnam.[34] China continued with its economic assistance to the Hanoi regime, though its loan agreement signed on January 31, 1961, actually cut the annual level of Chinese aid to North Vietnam in half.[35]

From late 1961 China became keenly worried by the flow of American troops into Laos and Vietnam.[36] The Staley Plan for South Vietnam, which was designed to wipe out the Vietcong in eighteen months, aroused special concern. Peking officially demanded that the International Control Commission and the Geneva Conference parties act to prevent further American incursions into Indochina.[37] It then moved to expand its military aid to the North, although the level of expansion was still limited. Fearing that the struggle in Vietnam might threaten its own security, Peking stated: "U.S. imperialist aggression in south Viet Nam is spearheaded against both the Democratic Republic of Viet Nam and the People's Republic of China. The security of China and Viet Nam is indivisible." [38]

Virtually silent in 1961 on the newly created Liberation Front, Peking the following year grew more wholehearted in its endorsement of the NLF campaign to oust Diem as it became convinced that only a decisive political reversal would make the United States relinquish its military position in South Vietnam.[39] Its judgment in this respect initially seemed to be confirmed by the events of 1963. As discussed earlier, during this year the Diem regime was overthrown and American-devised plans for counterinsurgency were discredited. In spite of overwhelming superiority in both numbers and military equipment, Saigon's forces had suffered one reverse after another, bearing out for Peking Mao Tse-tung's thesis that no army, however well equipped, could operate when whole sections of the population shielded the guerrillas. It was at this time that Mao Tse-tung issued a highly publicized "manifesto" of August 29, 1963, on Vietnam expressing China's support of the Buddhist-led struggle in the South against President Diem.[40] When Diem and his brother perished several weeks later, the Chinese said that the American effort "to throttle the revolutionary struggle and convert South Vietnam into a permanent colony and military base for the United States" had been smashed by the political struggle of "the people."

The American air strikes against North Vietnam in August 1964 increased Peking's concern over the possible expansion of the war. Nevertheless, the Chinese held to the position that "the Vietnamese could cope with their [own] situation" [41] and implied that an American defeat at the hands of indigenous guerrillas would be all the more dramatic if conducted without Chinese military assistance.[42]

6 : **For the past seventeen years** Peking's policies have been directed toward enhancing China's influence in Asia and eventually consolidating its status as an industrial power with a commensurate voice in international affairs.[43] Considerable argument has existed in the West as to whether or not China can attain these goals peacefully. One of the most persistent arguments supporting the thesis that China's territorial expansion is inevitable centers around the ever-growing disparity between its population and arable land. With a population of at least 700 million people living on less than 17 per cent of her land area, it is argued that the Chinese cannot survive without a major expansion into the "land-rich" areas of South-east Asia.[44] This disregards the fact that it is only within China itself that a sufficiently large economic potential exists for remedying the currently unfavorable ratios of land to people and people to food production.*

China now requires approximately 200 million metric tons of food grains each year, and to meet annual deficiencies in its own production Peking has occasionally needed to import as much as 12 million metric tons of grain a year from Canada and Australia. While it is possible for China substantially to raise its total food production through massive internal development, no part of Southeast Asia in the foreseeable future could supply more than a small fraction of the needed imports. When the current total rice surplus figures for all of Southeast Asia are combined, they do not even equal the amount China now imports.† It does not seem reasonable, therefore, to expect Peking in its search for food to wager China's national survival in a major military aggression when greater economic return could be obtained through internal programs of development and trade. §

---

* Western specialists estimate that China could produce truly sizable increases in basic food grains by making substantial technological improvements particularly in the scientific application of water and chemical fertilizers. One of the most promising regions for development is the upper Yellow River basin, which traverses a large undeveloped area of North China.

† According to one source, in 1937–38, all of Vietnam produced 7.74 million metric tons of rice "with an exportable surplus of perhaps 1.2 million tons." Elsewhere in the area, Malaya and Indonesia are net importers of grain; the only current exporters of food grains in Southeast Asia are Burma and Thailand, whose combined total export of rice in 1965 has been estimated at less than 2.5 million metric tons. See Bernard B. Fall, *The Two Viet-Nams,* rev. ed. (New York: Praeger, 1964), pp. 292 and 294; and *Far Eastern Economic Review Yearbook, 1966* (Hong Kong, 1966), pp. 101, 333, and 334.

§ China's foreign minister, Ch'en Yi, has stated the food problem in these terms: "To feed the 650 million people, we have to increase production by every means, and cannot rely on imports of grain. The reason is clear. An additional consumption of ten kilo-

The sheer weight of the American military might arrayed against it since the end of the Korean War has caused China to avoid actions that might lead to a possible direct confrontation with the United States. Consequently, in pursuit of their aims the Chinese have come to place maximum emphasis on indirect, less risky political tactics. Chinese leaders firmly believe that the presence of U.S. military power in the area threatens the security of China and obstructs what they regard as the normal evolution of political forces in Asia. Mao has staked his prestige on the hope that Asian peoples will achieve the removal of that presence by employing revolutionary methods against American-supported local governments and that they would replace them with neutralist or communist regimes. While encouraging such movements, China does not intend to commit its own forces to these revolutionary wars,* though it does hope to derive national security and prestige from their success.

Thus far, Chinese expectations that "revolutionary" or neutralist states would come to replace pro-American regimes in Asia and Africa have been frustrated. Except in Vietnam, the very reverse has occurred. During the last two years in several countries in Africa as well as in Indonesia, Cuba, and North Korea political developments have taken place adverse to China's interests and which the Chinese have been powerless to control. Communist China's inability to realize its hopes for revolution abroad has been dramatized by this train of unending foreign-policy failures. Peking's leaders have not demonstrated that they possess the knowledge or the power to generate successful communist-dominated revolutions abroad and thus have been unable to turn the civil conflicts of our time to their own ends.[45]

The most significant in a long series of Chinese manifestos

---

grammes of grain by everyone in our country each year would mean a total additional need of 6,500,000 tons, and no foreign country can meet such a big demand." *Peking Review,* No. 28, 1961, p. 10.

* For a discussion of China's military aid to Vietnam, see above, pp. 189–190, 227–238.

on "national liberation" wars was written by Peking's Minister of Defense Lin Piao. His statement, delivered in commemoration of the twentieth anniversary of the defeat of Japan in the Second World War, was entitled: "Long Live the Victory of People's War" (September 3, 1965).[46] When read as one of many doctrinal pronouncements issued by the Chinese on this subject, the Lin Piao thesis appears as a *moderation* rather than a hardening of the Chinese line. As a recent Rand Corporation study has pointed out, the previous Chinese threats to enter the Vietnam war are completely absent in this thesis, and there is significantly greater emphasis on the need for self-reliance in national-liberation wars.[47] Lin argues that popular insurrections cannot succeed if they place reliance on substantial foreign assistance—whether from China or elsewhere. To the extent that indigenous rebels depend on outside support they inevitably loosen their bonds with the local populace. In 1965 and 1966 this line of argument helped China rationalize its decision against participation in the Vietnam war.

Reinforcing this inference is Lin Piao's stress on the importance of broad popular alliances or "united fronts" to include communists and noncommunists in achieving revolutionary aims. Whenever the Chinese have wished to moderate their policies and to employ a more cautious approach they have enthusiastically endorsed these "united fronts," and any knowledgeable observer of the Chinese communist movement would recognize that in this thesis Lin Piao was not arguing for expansion of the Chinese effort but for a temporary tactical retreat.* Subsequent events have reinforced this conclusion.

The Administration, however, has chosen to single out those portions of the Lin Piao article that accord with domestically acceptable anticommunist assumptions and that appear to illustrate Chinese extremism. Even though Lin's prognostica-

---

* The article perhaps also aimed at placing the army in a more favorable position in the domestic political crisis that was just beginning behind the scenes in Peking.

tions of communist-led revolutions in other underdeveloped countries were shown to bear little relationship to reality, President Johnson nearly a year later asserted that U.S. policy toward the third world had to be based on the assumption that Lin's prediction of future revolutionary changes in these underdeveloped countries might be correct.*

China today is in the phase of development roughly corresponding to that era in Soviet history that Stalin called "socialism in one state." In this period Mao hopes to construct an industrialized state with Party control left unchallenged and with the outlook of the Chinese people, particularly the youth, kept consonant with Marxist-Leninist ideas.[48] An atmosphere of external threat bolsters the contrived "struggle campaigns" and thereby helps overcome public apathy and instill the drive for national development and revolutionary zeal.

Mao's principal aim, his self-proclaimed "great strategic task," is to mold the communist man within an industrialized society. His obsession with this objective overrides all his foreign-policy goals. In this endeavor he has thus far failed, for since shortly after 1949 many youths in China as well as intellectuals and nonparty bureaucrats have adopted a view of the world that differs profoundly from Mao's revolutionary clichés. Indoctrination has not succeeded in controlling their view, and societal changes have proceeded faster than the Party's efforts to alter them. This has made it more difficult for Mao to work out a solution to the problem of political succession that is satisfactory to him. The way that problem is resolved will determine the character of the next generation of China's leadership.

---

* In describing their model of revolution for propaganda purposes, the Chinese regularly do great violence to their own civil-war history. They also attempt to convey a general message of communist solidarity and triumph in obvious contradiction to the actual situation prevailing within the faction-ridden communist movement and to the nationalist, antiforeign strain in virtually every dissident or insurrectionist group.

The outcome is already being affected by the war in Vietnam. Mao's efforts to sustain a domestic environment of intense activity and xenophobia have received an added boost from the concrete American threat on China's southern border. In the well-publicized communist leadership shake-up that came to the surface in April 1966, the threat of war with the United States severely handicapped the more moderate, younger elements of the society and helped open the way for the regimentation symbolized by the youthful bands of zealots, the "Red Guards." [49] Where anti-American campaigns heretofore had only limited success, their promise has seemed brighter as the Peking leadership is able to blend indoctrination programs with patriotic appeals. For the first time since the Korean War the Party has found a genuine cause—an immediate American threat to Chinese security—which lends urgency to its plans for enforcing domestic conformity. At the very time when the succession to Mao's leadership may be coming to a head, the wartime atmosphere has robbed the younger generation and other dissident elements of their grounds for arguing in favor of internal changes.

So long as the Vietnamese war remains unsettled—and continues to be fought beyond their borders—the leaders of Mao's generation will, therefore, welcome the "vigorous opposition" of their American enemies. Although Mao Tse-tung presumably opposes an all-out conflict, which would destroy large parts of China and indefinitely set back its economic development, a peaceful settlement in Southeast Asia also would be contrary to his interests as he understands them. It would seriously weaken one of the principal means of propaganda for mobilizing the unquestioning allegiance of his people to the present leadership and to a domestic program of sustained revolutionary communism. A settlement in Vietnam would also threaten Peking's hopes of discrediting American power in Asia. For Mao that goal will be achieved most easily if China is able to point to an endless, costly fight that the United States can neither win conclusively nor translate into an effective political solution, but that nevertheless results in tremendous devastation and loss of life for Asians.

7 : **Peking has indicated** that it will regard any drastic American escalation of the Vietnam war as endangering China's vital national interests and will thus take defensive action. Although Chinese troops are not engaged in combat in Vietnam, an estimated 50,000 Chinese (mostly engineering troops)[50] have been sent into the North, primarily if not exclusively on reconstruction assignments. It is likely, however, that Chinese combat troops would move into action in response to an American ground campaign north of the 17th parallel. Peking could not easily tolerate the loss of the North to an American army, and it is questionable whether it could accept the collapse of the North Vietnamese state from a prolonged bombing of the North's cities, dikes, and food supplies.

Despite the care the Peking leadership has taken in Vietnam to do nothing that might invite an American attack, the United States may still choose to enlarge its theater of operations to include China.[51] A decision to do this would probably derive from the belief that a war with China is inevitable and should be waged soon, before China grows stronger and attains a real nuclear capacity.[52] Although this view is still confined to a minority, it probably was strengthened in the 1966 debates on China when Secretary of Defense McNamara stated that China is moving to support its bellicose "words with instruments of war of the most terrible kind." [53]

Once the United States attacks China—with or without nuclear weapons—the whole context of the American effort in Vietnam would be drastically altered. It is certain that, if attacked, China would retaliate and in so doing would not confine herself to the present areas of conflict. American actions, the Chinese hold, "have turned this entire region [of Southeast Asia] into a battleground." [54] Peking has promised that if the United States attacks China, American troops will be engaged by its forces on a vast front in "Indochina, Southeast Asia and the Far East." [55] In April 1966 Premier Chou En-lai told a reporter, "Once the war breaks out, it will have no boundaries. . . . If you can come from the sky, why can't we fight back on the ground?" [56] And in their reaction to the June 1966 air raids on the Hanoi-Haiphong fuel depots, the Chinese reiterated that if the United States directly assaulted their country their own troops would not be "subject to any restrictions." [57]

Discussions of strategy in the Peking press indicate that if their country were invaded the Chinese would not attempt an all-out defense of their borders but would wage prolonged guerrilla campaigns in China itself [58] as well as in adjacent countries that the United States has pledged to defend. Conduct of such military operations would not be dependent upon centrally directed, massive Chinese logistical support. Whether confined to Southeast Asia or extending into China as well, such a situation would be far more difficult for the United States than the Korean War, where Chinese troops were confined to a narrow peninsula and highly vulnerable to American sea and air power. China could be expected to mount guerrilla operations simultaneously at many points along a thousand-mile jungle and mountain front, deploying in addition to its regular army troops or "volunteers" some of the 10 to 15 million people in China who are ethnically akin to the Thai, Lao, and Vietnamese.[59]

U.S. power could neither gain a decisive victory over these forces nor compel them to withdraw. Even though American air power could achieve the destruction of China's industry and major cities, the United States—unless prepared to assume the responsibility for nuclear devastation—would be totally unable to subdue the country.

Notes to Chapter XI

1. *Two Different Lines on the Question of War and Peace* (Peking: Foreign Languages Press, 1963), p. 27.

2. The year 1953 was also a time of great internal trouble for Mao. On July 1, 1966, *Jen-min Jih-pao ("People's Daily")* said: "The first [of three big struggles against Mao's leadership] was against the antiparty alliance of Kao Kang and Jao Shu-shih. This struggle took place in 1953, at the crucial moment when China's socialist revolution began to develop on a large scale."

3. U.S. Senate, *Military Situation in the Fast East,* 82nd Congress, 1st Session (Washington: U.S. Government Printing Office, 1951), Vol. I, p. 13.

4. *Jen-min Jih-pao,* September 2, 1953.

5. Anthony Eden, *Full Circle* (London: Cassell, 1960), p. 129. Several years later, Anthony Eden, the British Foreign Secretary at the time of the Geneva Conference, wrote that he had "received a strong impression" from this act that Chou wanted a settlement.

6. *Ibid.,* p. 140.

7. *People's China,* No. 15, August 1, 1954, Supplement, p. 6.

8. Text in George McT. Kahin, *The Asian-African Conference, Bandung, Indonesia, April 1955* (Ithaca, N.Y.: Cornell University Press, 1956), pp. 52–56; and *People's China,* No. 10, May 16, 1955, Supplement, pp. 11–13.

9. *Department of State Bulletin* (Washington, September 20, 1954), p. 392.

10. For the text of the treaty, see *People's China,* No. 10, May 16, 1955, Supplement. A discussion of the way this treaty was carried out may be found in David Mozingo, "The Sino-Indonesian Dual Nationality Treaty," *Asian Survey,* Vol. I, No. 10, December 1961, pp. 25–31.

11. Text of remark of April 23, 1955, in *People's China,* No. 10, May 16, 1955, Supplement, p. 13.

12. This and other uncited quotations are from the unpublished verbatim records of the conference.

13. Interview of author (Kahin) with V. K. Krishna Menon, New Delhi, May 30, 1955.

14. Interview of author (Kahin) with Pandit Nehru in New Delhi, May 28, 1955.

15. For full text, see Appendix 11.

16. For texts of these proposals and the Department of State's discussion, see U.S. Department of State, *Renunciation of Force:*

U.S. and Chinese Communist Positions (Washington: U.S. Government Printing Office, 1956).

17. Chou En-lai, *On Present International Situation, China's Foreign Policy, and the Liberation of Taiwan* (June 28, 1956) (Peking: Foreign Languages Press, 1956), pp. 25ff.

18. Secretary of State Dean Rusk almost ten years later said that it was now a major objective of the United States "to try to persuade the Chinese Communists to join with us in renouncing the use of force in the area of Taiwan." U.S. House, *United States Policy Toward Asia,* 89th Congress, 2nd Session (Washington: U.S. Government Printing Office, 1966), Vol. II, p. 533.

19. For Washington's official comment at the time, see *Department of State Bulletin* (Washington, March 19, 1956), p. 451; (June 25, 1956), pp. 1070–1071; (August 13, 1956), pp. 267–268; (August 20, 1956), p. 312; (August 27, 1956), p. 355; and (November 12, 1956), p. 774.

20. Speech of July 30, 1954, in *Department of State Bulletin* (Washington, August 23, 1954), p. 262.

21. Text in *Department of State Bulletin* (Washington, August 13, 1956), p. 264. Robertson accused the Chinese of being unwilling to renounce the use of force in the achievement of their political objectives. He did not mention the Chinese willingness to sign such a declaration that would not imply the permanent political separation of Taiwan from the mainland and was backed up by a foreign ministers' meeting.

22. The Eisenhower statement is in *Department of State Bulletin* (Washington, January 6, 1958), p. 6; and the Dulles statement is in *ibid.* (December 22, 1958), p. 994.

23. On Burma, see below, pp. 311–313.

24. See George Ginsburgs and Michael Mathos, *Communist China and Tibet: The First Dozen Years* (The Hague: Martinus Nijhoff, 1964). This book, one of the first on the subject, is of uneven quality.

25. John W. Lewis, "Quemoy and American China Policy," *Asian Survey,* Vol. II, No. 1, March 1962, pp. 12–19. For a contrasting viewpoint see Tang Tsou, "The Quemoy Imbroglio: Chiang Kai-shek and the United States," *The Western Political Quarterly,* Vol. XII, No. 4, December 1959, pp. 1075–1091.

26. Lewis, "China's Invasion of the Indian Frontier: The Framework of Motivation," in *This Is China: Analyses of Mainland Trends and Events,* ed. by Francis Harper (Hong Kong: Dragonfly Books, 1965), pp. 253–266. More comprehensive studies are: Alastair Lamb, *The China-India Border: The Origins of the Disputed Boundaries* (London: Oxford University Press, 1964); G. N. Patterson, *Peking versus Delhi* (London: Faber and Faber,

1963); and W. F. van Eekelen, *Indian Foreign Policy and the Border Dispute with China* (The Hague: Martinus Nijhoff, 1964).

27. Text of letter in *Documents Relating to British Involvement in the Indo-China Conflict, 1945–1965,* Command 2834 (London: Her Majesty's Stationery Office, 1965), pp. 113–114.

28. Text of letter of January 25, 1956, in *ibid.,* p. 118.

29. Chou, *On Present International Situation,* p. 11.

30. Text of Ch'en Yi's letter of May 25, 1959, in *Documents Relating to British Involvement,* pp. 139–140.

31. For the text of the declaration and its protocol, see *ibid.,* pp. 178–186.

32. See Royal Government of Laos, *North Vietnamese Interference in Laos* (Vientiane: Ministry of Foreign Affairs, 1964). No mention is made in this document of Chinese interference. For a discussion of U.S. involvement in Laos since 1962, see Arthur J. Dommen, *Conflict in Laos: The Politics of Neutralization* (New York: Praeger, 1964).

33. Text of Chinese statement of March 9, 1958, in *Peking Review,* No. 3, 1958, p. 22.

34. See for example the articles in *Peking Review,* No. 11, 1959, pp. 5–7; No. 15, 1959, pp. 16–18; No. 30, 1959, pp. 6–8; No. 36, 1959, pp. 13–14; No. 20, 1960, pp. 22–29; No. 29, 1960, p. 17; No. 30, 1960, pp. 11–15; and No. 12, 1961, pp. 12–15.

35. *Ibid.,* No. 5, 1961, p. 9. According to some estimates this long-term loan of over 141.75 million rubles constituted a 50 per cent reduction in the annual amount of Chinese aid to North Vietnam. China had been providing assistance from 1955 to 1961 at an annual level of $50 million. The amount dropped to $22.5 million per year from 1961 through 1964. See Alexander Eckstein, *Communist China's Economic Growth and Foreign Trade: Implications for U.S. Policy* (New York: McGraw-Hill, 1966), pp. 162 and 306.

36. See *Peking Review,* No. 21, 1961, p. 11; and No. 43, 1961, pp. 12–13.

37. *Ibid.,* No. 43, 1961, pp. 12–13; and No. 49, 1961, pp. 9–10.

38. *Ibid.,* No. 30, 1962, p. 10; and see also *ibid.,* No. 18, 1964, p. 22.

39. *Ibid.,* No. 39, 1962, pp. 16–17; No. 41, 1962, pp. 5–6; and No. 52, 1962, pp. 12–13.

40. Text in *ibid.,* No. 36, 1963, p. 6. In May 1963, Liu Shao-ch'i while in Hanoi stated: "The Chinese people firmly support the heroic south Vietnamese people's just and patriotic struggle against U.S. imperialism and the Ngo Dinh Diem clique and regard this struggle as a brilliant example for the oppressed nations and peoples in the world in fighting for liberation. The Chinese people

resolutely support all the Vietnamese people in their sacred struggle for the peaceful reunification of their fatherland and are firmly convinced that this struggle will surely win final victory." *Ibid.,* No. 21, 1963, p. 13.

41. Quote from Mao Tse-tung in Edgar Snow, "Interview with Mao," *New Republic,* February 27, 1965, p. 22.

42. As Mao Tse-tung told reporter Edgar Snow in early 1965, "China gave support to revolutionary movements but not by sending troops. Of course, whenever a liberation struggle existed China would publish statements and call demonstrations to support it." He added: "It was precisely [those statements] which vexed the imperialists." *Ibid.*

43. For a cross-section of interpretations of Chinese foreign policy, see Morton H. Halperin, "Chinese Nuclear Strategy," *The China Quarterly,* No. 21, January–March 1965, pp. 74–86; A. M. Halpern, "China in the Postwar World," *ibid.,* pp. 20–45; Harold C. Hinton, *Communist China in World Politics* (Boston: Houghton Mifflin, 1966), especially Part I; and Allen S. Whiting, *China Crosses the Yalu* (New York: Macmillan, 1960), Ch. 1.

44. For a useful analysis of Chinese population statistics see John S. Aird, *The Size, Composition and Growth of the Population of Mainland China* (Washington: U.S. Department of Commerce, Bureau of the Census, 1961).

45. See the editorial in the *New York Times,* September 5, 1966.

46. Lin Piao, *Long Live the Victory of People's War* (Peking: Foreign Languages Press, 1965), written in commemoration of the 20th anniversary of the victory over Japan. For an authoritative comment see D. P. Mozingo and T. W. Robinson, *Lin Piao on "People's War": China Takes a Second Look at Vietnam* (Santa Monica, Cal.: Rand Corporation, 1965), p. vii. In this study the authors state, "There is a striking absence of threats of possible intervention, such as those Peking made on several occasions in the months preceding publication of Lin's article."

47. Mozingo and Robinson, *op. cit.*

48. This discussion is based on John W. Lewis, "Revolutionary Struggle and the Second Generation in Communist China," *The China Quarterly,* No. 21, January–March 1965, pp. 126–147; and Lewis, "The Study of Chinese Political Culture," *World Politics,* Vol. XVIII, No. 3, April 1966, pp. 503–524.

49. For a discussion, see John W. Lewis, *Communist China— Crisis and Change* (New York: Foreign Policy Association, 1966), esp. pp. 40–50. On April 6, 1966, *People's Daily* warned: "So long as U.S. imperialism exists, we of this generation must be prepared, and so should be the second and third generation." The period from late July through October 1966 witnessed an intensification of the so-called cultural revolution in China. American military

actions in Vietnam were often used to whip up revolutionary fervor on behalf of this "cultural revolution." Thus on July 30 Peking Radio stated that U.S. leaders "are frenziedly expanding their war of aggression in our neighboring country Vietnam. Under this situation . . . the study of Chairman Mao's ideas on people's war bears a significant meaning." Subsequently the Red Guards in their agitational activity have sporadically castigated the United States role in Vietnam and have quite consciously used this theme to promote an anti-foreign, and specifically anti-American, sentiment. Typical of their statements was that carried by Peking Radio on October 12: "Vietnam is our brother. Whoever bullies Vietnam is bullying us. We shall fight him to the end."

50. See above pp. 189–190, 227–228.

51. An official Chinese government report of March 12, 1965, commented on remarks in the U.S. press that China would not be allowed to remain a sanctuary as it did in the Korean War. It added: "In plain language, this means it [the U.S.] would bomb China." Peking Radio, March 13, 1965. During the 1966 debate on China held by the Senate Foreign Relations Committee, the Chinese could see little to choose between the two sides. They said: "Some shout that the American forces should fight their way to North Vietnam or even 'bomb all the way to Peking,' and others express fear at the prospect of a big land war in Asia." *Jen-min Jih-pao,* March 3, 1966.

52. See University of Michigan, Survey Research Center, *The American Public's View of U.S. Policy Toward China* (New York: Council on Foreign Relations, 1964), pp. 19–21.

53. *New York Times,* March 8, 1966.

54. *Jen-min Jih-pao,* June 1, 1965. The Chinese gave a country-by-country analysis of U.S. moves in Southeast Asia on Peking Radio, November 29, 1965. The following month, Chinese protests against the U.S. announcement that American troops would be permitted to pursue communist forces into Cambodia carried the additional threat of Chinese involvement. *Jen-min Jih-pao,* December 24, 1965, said: "Should U.S. imperialism dare to attack Cambodia, the 650 million Chinese people will firmly support the Cambodian people to utterly defeat the U.S. aggressors."

55. *Ibid.,* February 9, 1965.

56. Peking Radio, May 9, 1966.

57. See the official Chinese government statement in *New York Times,* July 4, 1966. On July 19, 1966, Peking reiterated its earlier statement that China could be considered "the rear area of the Vietnamese people" and that a destruction of the Vietnamese air arm would bring Chinese planes into the war. *New York Times,* July 20, 1966.

58. In 1965, it was stated: "If U.S. imperialism should impose a

war upon us . . . millions of people and millions of militia will shoot from all directions, lay mines, blockade the enemy, cut off the enemy's rear, and drown the enemy in the ocean of a people's war." *Jen-min Jih-pao,* September 21, 1965.

59. The possibility of China using these minority people has been suggested by the intensive militia campaigns conducted with particular fervor during 1964 and 1965 in Yunnan, Kwangsi, and Kwangtung—all provinces that border Southeast Asian states.

CHAPTER XII

The Global Context

1 : **The U.S. decision** to commit and deploy so much of its power in Vietnam has exerted an important influence on its relationships and commitments throughout the world. "Not only are great and potentially more important questions of world affairs not receiving, as a consequence of our involvement in Vietnam, the attention they should be receiving," George F. Kennan told the U.S. Senate in February 1966, "but in some instances assets we already enjoy and hopefully possibilities we should be developing are being sacrificed to this unpromising involvement in a remote and secondary theater." [1]

One of the major casualties of the present Vietnam policy has been America's relationship with the Soviet Union. The promising rapprochement with Russia, begun by President Eisenhower and continued by President Kennedy, has deteriorated under the pressures of the Vietnam war and will be further undermined by continuation of the conflict. Early in this decade the United States decided that its most basic interests required the avoidance of measures likely to damage its relationship with the Soviet Union and the tacit agreement between the two countries on the restraint of Chinese power. By choosing to escalate the Vietnam war, however, Washington has seriously jeopardized the possibilities for improving its relations with Moscow. [2] The Administration has openly acknowledged that as a consequence of America's Vietnam policy the Soviet Union is constrained from cooperating with the United States on global matters of paramount and long-term significance. [3] This delays further progress in efforts to reduce the dangers of nuclear war; at a crucial point in history the opportunity to stem further proliferation of nuclear arms is being lost. Recognizing this, President Johnson, in a speech on August 26, 1966, expressed his concern that Russia's strong feelings on Vietnam might impede any agreement on halting the spread of nuclear weapons. He appealed to the Soviet leaders to join in "rational acts of common endeavor" despite the Vietnam war, and he tried to reassure the Russians that American objectives in South Vietnam "do not threaten the vital interests of the Soviet Union or the territory of any of her friends." [4]

Such a plea is unrealistic while United States planes are bombarding on a daily basis an ally, not just a friend, of the Soviet Union. Since the air strikes on North Vietnam began, Moscow has strengthened its commitments to Hanoi rather than forfeit its trust and that of other states whom the Soviet Union has publicly agreed to defend. Washington is not the only capital concerned with its international image, with "keeping its word," and with the credibility of its global commitments.*

After World War II the United States devoted nearly twenty years to marshaling multilateral support against Soviet military intervention in the affairs of other states only to end up by arrogating to itself the right to unilateral intervention in Vietnam. [5] This action, undertaken with such disregard of Soviet prestige, of UN opinion and the efforts of the UN Secretary General to prepare the ground for a peaceful settlement, has not only led to a serious deterioration in Russo-American relations but also contributed to a decrease in the overall effec-

---

* In defending its involvement in Vietnam Washington has usually placed this aspect of the problem merely in the special context of the Sino-Soviet dispute rather than in the setting of United States-Soviet relations. Thus it is sometimes argued that the Vietnam war has helped enlarge the gulf between Peking and Moscow and has exacerbated Sino-Soviet frictions. Such considerations of the Sino-Soviet dispute, however, are peripheral to the basic pattern of American-Soviet relations. The crucial consequence of American escalation in Vietnam has been a marked deterioration in these relations.

tiveness of the United Nations and to a weakening of American leadership in international affairs generally.

Through its absorption in Vietnam, Washington is also losing the initiative with respect to many pivotal developments affecting other outstanding global issues of critical long-term importance to the United States. Its influence with old European allies in particular is being jeopardized. Rather than limiting support of Saigon to conform with the general pattern of America's worldwide alliance structure, the Johnson Administration has attempted to adapt that alliance system to its own deepening involvement in Vietnam. Defense arrangements with forty-two allies—the heart of the United States postwar system for maintaining international peace and security—have been fundamentally reinterpreted in accordance with the Administration's unilateral commitment in Vietnam, one that is now in practice accorded priority over all previous obligations. This mortgaging of so much of America's power to a single conflict has been undertaken without prior consultation with the allies to whom it had already pledged assistance.*

In defending this position Secretary Rusk has asserted that the credibility of American promises elsewhere would be destroyed if the United States failed in Vietnam, and he has admonished America's allies that they would lose confidence in this country if it did not win there. Few of these allies agree with Mr. Rusk's assessment of their own conclusions, and many disapprove of U.S. actions in Vietnam,[6] fearing that these will lead to an expansion of the war that, despite their opposition to it, may engulf them. Nevertheless, Washington

---

* The Administration has sometimes referred to advocates of alternative policies in Vietnam as "neo-isolationists." Arthur Schlesinger, Jr., in this regard notes: "The Administration has called the critics of its Vietnam policy 'neo-isolationists.' But surely the real neo-isolationists are those who have isolated the United States from its allies and raised the tattered standard, last flourished 15 years ago by Douglas MacArthur, of 'going it alone.'" "A Middle Way Out in Vietnam," *New York Times Magazine,* September 18, 1966.

expects them to reorder and adapt their security arrangements in accordance with a radically altered scale of American global priorities resulting from United States policies in Vietnam over which they have no influence. America's prior pledges to them have become seriously dependent on the redemption of its subsequent commitment in Vietnam.

2: **The arguments the United States has chosen to use** in defending the legality of its Vietnam actions have also led to apprehension on the part of its alliance partners.[7] In attempting to legitimize its policies in Vietnam (as much in the eyes of the American public as in those of the international community), the Administration began in 1966 to stress not only that the United States is entitled to take unilateral action but that the Southeast Asia Treaty of 1954 obliges it to act unilaterally in South Vietnam.* In Dean Rusk's words, "It is this fundamental SEATO obligation that has from the outset guided our actions in South Viet-Nam." [8]

In considering the actual U.S. commitment under SEATO it must be recalled that in Article IV of the pact the Eisenhower Administration envisaged two forms of threat: "armed aggression and . . . the danger of subversion and indirect aggression." [9] In the case of "aggression by means of armed attack" each party was "to meet the common danger in ac-

---

* Speaking of the treaty on February 18, 1966, Secretary Rusk said: "The language of this treaty is worth careful attention. The obligation it imposes is not only joint but several. That is not only collective but individual. The finding that an armed attack has occurred does not have to be made by a collective determination before the obligation of each member becomes operative. Nor does the treaty require a collective decision on actions to be taken to meet the common danger. If the United States determines that an armed attack has occurred against any nation to whom the protection of the treaty applies, then it is obliged 'to act to meet the common danger' without regard to the views or actions of any other treaty member." U.S. Senate, *Supplemental Foreign Assistance Fiscal Year 1966—Vietnam,* 89th Congress, 2nd Session (Washington: U.S. Government Printing Office, 1966), p. 567.

cordance with its constitutional processes." [10] In the case of a threat "in any way other than by armed attack" (i.e., subversion), the parties were to "consult immediately in order to agree on the measures which should be taken for the common defense." The discussion of the treaty at the time makes very clear that the situation in Vietnam does not fall under the category of "armed attack" as then defined by the United States and its SEATO allies.[11] This type of aggression, Dulles said, was "based upon the Monroe Doctrine principle"—that is "open and armed attack" coming from outside the treaty area. To Dulles, the Korean War exemplified the "armed attack" type of aggression; Indochina represented a second type of aggression covered by paragraph 2 of Article IV.[12]

In the hearings on SEATO these significant exchanges took place: [13]

Senator Green. Then we are obliged to help put down a revolutionary movement.

Secretary Dulles. No. If there is a revolutionary movement in Vietnam or in Thailand, we would consult together as to what to do about it, because if that were a subversive movement that was in fact propagated by communism, it would be a very grave threat to us. But we have no undertaking to put it down; all we have is an undertaking to consult together as to what to do about it.

. . . . . .

Senator Ferguson. In other words, the words "armed attack" in paragraph 1 of article IV are the ordinary armed attack rather than a subterfuge of penetration or subversion.

Secretary Dulles. Yes, sir.

As Secretary of State Dulles further explained to the Senate: ". . . article IV, paragraph 2, contemplates that if that situation [of subversion] arises or threatens, that we should consult together immediately in order to agree on measures which should be taken. That is an obligation for consultation. It is not an obligation for action." [14]

In his recent effort to argue for a unilateral American obligation under the SEATO treaty, Secretary of State Rusk was obliged for the sake of consistency to extend this to all of America's far-flung treaty commitments. Thus, in Secretary Rusk's present view the United States must act individually in order to fulfill the obligations of an alliance, regardless of the position that other allies take. An American response depends solely on actions taken by an enemy and not on whether any of its allies are willing to contribute to the undertaking. As James Reston assesses this new "Rusk Doctrine" * it is a formidable one that "goes well beyond Vietnam in space and time. Mr. Rusk has asked the Senate to contain the expansion of communism all along the periphery of the Communist empire, by force of arms and without allies if necessary, and the Congress cannot oppose him in present circumstances without opposing its own men in Vietnam, which it obviously will not do." [15]

There are other arguments advanced by the Johnson Administration in defense of its Vietnam policy that most of America's European allies also find quite unacceptable. One of these is the proposition that the United States must fight communist-led forces in Vietnam because "freedom is indivisible." These allies of the United States are not, however,

---

* For a time, the Secretary of State dismissed some of the implications of the Rusk Doctrine, but on August 25, 1966, he extended the range of potential defense action by the United States to include all nations, whether bound to the United States by treaty or not. The same day, Secretary Robert McNamara assured Congress that the United States had the strength to meet such global commitments. Some members of Congress reportedly "were taken aback by Mr. Rusk's statement . . . that the United States regarded itself as not limited to the defense of those nations [with which it had treaties], but as more generally bound to uphold the peace-keeping work of the United Nations throughout the world." One senator, John F. Stennis of Mississippi, voiced the concern of many of his colleagues by saying: "The old lines are all gone, the old tests and safeguards, the caution we used to have, are all gone." *New York Times,* August 26 and 31, 1966. See also *Department of State Bulletin* (Washington, April 4, 1966), pp. 516–517.

disposed to equate anticommunism with freedom, and they do not regard South Vietnam under Marshal Ky as an example of a free country. They realize that had the Vietcong and North Vietnamese been anything but communist, they could have pursued their course of action as ruthlessly as they wished without the Johnson Administration's having thought of responding militarily. It is also understandable that America's European allies should question why the United States, while accepting and living in peace with communist regimes in Eastern Europe and elsewhere, cannot tolerate a communist Vietnam. And certainly these allies cannot be expected to regard the experience of Munich as in any sense applicable in Vietnam.[16] Attempts to draw an analogy between developments in Vietnam and Hitler's aggression in Europe or the characterization of political compromise in Vietnam as another "Munich" are without real relevance to either Vietnamese or European history.*

---

* In 1938 Germany possessed the strongest military machine on the continent, if not in the world, while today it is the United States and Soviet Russia—not North Vietnam, the Vietcong or even China—who hold such power. In 1938 the issue was the refusal of Britain and France to abide by a formal military alliance made to a politically unified state under the effective leadership of a genuinely representative, fairly elected government that had the will to fight against external German aggression but was abandoned by its allies.

In Vietnam we are not witnessing a case of external aggression and conquest by an outside power. This is a struggle within Vietnam itself—one between Vietnamese factions (each with adherents drawn from both geographic halves of the country) for political mastery of their own, with both committed to its ultimate reunification. It is basically a civil war, which is an outgrowth of a nine-year anticolonial conflict that was indeed marked by "outside aggression"—the effort of France, backed by the United States, to reassert her dominance over one nationally conscious people. The civil war temporarily halted twelve years ago by a military armistice has broken out again because key political provisions of the truce were flouted. It is still being fought between contending groups of the same nation, except that the outside military power supporting the weaker of the indigenous factions is now predominantly American rather than French.

3: President Johnson has described **Vietnam** as the entrance to Southeast Asia at which the United States must mount guard. "We did not choose to be the guardians at the gate," he declared in July 1965, "but there is no one else." [17] The President did not explain whether the gate was being held against the spread of communism or against Chinese expansion, thereby reinforcing his Administration's frequent confusion of the broad but nationally differentiated force of communism with a threat of specifically Chinese power. There is, of course, a basic difference.

There is no one gate to any southern thrust of China's armies. Vietnam—North or South—is hardly as important in this respect as Burma or India, each of whose frontiers with China is many times that of Vietnam. The primary restraining factor, should Peking develop the disposition to order its armies across China's southern borders, is the threat of American power poised to retaliate by sea and air (with Soviet power possibly constituting an additional deterrent).

The potentialities of communism in South and Southeast Asia do not depend on Chinese power, nor on any mere projection of Maoist ideology. Throughout Asia, every bit as much as in the West, communism has been obliged to come to terms with indigenous nationalism or else remain politically impotent. Noncommunist Asian leaders appreciate the character of their own nationalism sufficiently well to recognize that if a communist party is to attract adherents in their country, it will do so because of its appeal to the local people and not because of any championing by Peking. They know that where a communist movement is identified with an outside power it inevitably conflicts with nationalism and thereby loses its political effectiveness.* Where communism takes root

---

* Thus, when during the postwar period communists in Burma, Indonesia, Malaya, and the Philippines attempted to seize power by force they could not develop sufficient nationalist support, and their efforts failed.

in Asia its strength arises, not through subversion directed from China or Russia, but because of locally generated social, economic, and political factors. Against the spread of communism the only effective gate-keepers are the indigenous peoples themselves. No foreign power can man the gate successfully, and its very presence will range the force of local nationalism against it and against whatever local faction it supports.

4 : While there is no indication that most Asian leaders consider South Vietnam the Far Eastern fulcrum of communism or China's southern gateway, they do share a deep concern over the outcome of the war there and earnestly hope for a peaceful solution. The extent of U.S. involvement in Vietnam has added immeasurably to their concern, particularly since they recognize that only the Vietnamese themselves can provide an enduring solution. Throughout Asia apprehension has risen over the possibility that Washington's commitment of American prestige in Vietnam has become so great that the increasing weight of its military and political presence there may make it impossible for North Vietnam's allies—the Soviet Union or China—to remain out of the conflict.

In Asia, "face" is not a term reserved for the United States. If it is true as one writer has argued that the preservation of face with respect to a country's "reputation for action" is "one of the few things worth fighting over," [18] this surely applies to the Soviet Union and Communist China as well. Most Asian leaders, in fact, regard the Russian and Chinese commitments to Hanoi as quite as legitimate and firm as that of the United States to Saigon, and they realize that Moscow and Peking must find it enormously difficult not to match American escalation against North Vietnam with an escalation of their own assistance to Hanoi. In this Asian view, the war will not determine the outcome of political unrest in other Asian countries, but it may soon compel the Russians and Chinese drastically to increase their involvement in the area. In this sense a gate has been opened that Asian leaders had hoped was closed.

5: The Johnson Administration asserts that other Asian governments regard Vietnam's future as crucial to their own and that the presence of American power in Vietnam strengthens their otherwise faltering will to resist communism—both external and local. In his speech of July 12, 1966, President Johnson went so far as to suggest that, because of America's stand in Vietnam peoples elsewhere in Asia had "taken new heart" and that a great many changes favorable to the United States were "taking shape behind our defense of South Viet-Nam." [19] In conjunction with these assertions he listed a series of developments "in the last year" that had actually either begun long before the United States intervened in Vietnam or were a consequence of internal factors totally dissociated from the war there. One development was in fact primarily the result of Soviet rather than American diplomatic efforts.* Such Administration statements may help make U.S. policy in Vietnam more acceptable to many Americans, but from most Asian leaders this type of argument evokes indigna-

---

* The major achievements (the first five) listed by the President were the following: "Japan and Korea have settled their long-standing disputes and established normal relations with promise for closer cooperation [a development completely divorced from the American stand in Vietnam]; one country after another has achieved rates of economic growth that are far beyond the most optimistic hopes we had a few years ago; Indonesia and its more than 100 million people have already pulled back from the brink of communism and economic collapse [for the situation in Indonesia see pp. 308–310 below]; Our friends in India and Pakistan—600 million strong—have ended a tragic conflict and have returned to the immense work of peace [the recrudescence of this conflict took place after the American escalation of the Vietnam war, and the Soviet Union, not the United States, played the major role in achieving the ceasefire and disengagement]; Japan has become a dramatic example of economic progress through political and social freedom and has begun to help others [a development that had gotten well under way over a decade previously and for which Presidents Truman and Eisenhower might feel the right to take some credit]." See *Department of State Bulletin* (Washington, August 1, 1966), pp. 160–161.

tion, and it is regarded by them as arrogant and patronizing, as well as untrue.

All four of the largest noncommunist states of Asia—India, Indonesia, Japan, and Pakistan—accord first priority to their own domestic and international problems, matters of much greater immediate concern to them than the rights or wrongs of the Vietnam war. For India and Pakistan their bitter differences over Kashmir, erupting in actual warfare during the summer of 1965, decisively overshadow their interest in Vietnam. It is notable that even Pakistan, the largest Asian member of SEATO, has refused to evince any support or sympathy with American policy in Vietnam, much less to respond to Washington's request through SEATO for a contribution of troops.[20]

Like Pakistan, India and Indonesia are desperately dependent upon American economic assistance. Although the Johnson Administration has given the impression that it will be less likely to respond favorably to New Delhi's and Djakarta's requests for aid if their protests against American actions in Vietnam are audible,[21] their leaders have been remarkably forthright in public condemnation of American Vietnam policy.

Until mid-1966 open criticism of American policy was muted in New Delhi because of India's desperate food crisis and the acute need for emergency American aid. But, despite her country's continuing need for additional American economic assistance, on July 7, 1966, Prime Minister Indira Gandhi expressed blunt disapproval of the U.S. bombings of the Hanoi-Haiphong fuel depots. She stated: "Recent events [in Vietnam] have regrettably added to the grave danger of escalation that might embroil the world in a larger conflict. There can be no military solution in Vietnam; there is no alternative to a peaceful settlement. The parties must be brought to the negotiating table within the framework of the Geneva Agreements." [22] During her visit to Moscow, Mrs. Gandhi expressed even stronger criticism in a joint Soviet-Indian communiqué of July 16, 1966, where both sides called for an immediate cessation of the bombing of North Vietnam.[23] On

July 21, the United States made strong representations to the Indian Government over aspects of the communiqué, particularly the call for ending the bombing and the use of such phrases as "aggressive actions of imperialist and other reactionary forces." Evidently Mrs. Gandhi was disinclined to change her views as she showed on October 24, when she joined with Tito and Nasser in calling on the United States to stop the bombing of North Vietnam immediately and "without any preconditions." [24]

Without significant armed forces of its own, Japan is still completely dependent upon the United States for protection. Although the Japanese government has adopted a cautious attitude toward American policies in Vietnam, it has been under pressure from the general public's opposition to the war.[25] The recently retired American Ambassador to Tokyo, Edwin O. Reischauer, considered Vietnam to be the central issue undermining American-Japanese relations and stated that "the relationship between the United States and Japan is being eroded by Vietnam strains and stresses." [26] His view was endorsed by George Kennan when he told the U.S. Senate that the war is causing us to sacrifice "the confidence and good will of the Japanese people." [27] The Japanese have been struck by the discrepancy between U.S. objectives and the violent measures employed to attain them.[28] Japanese critics reject the attempt to equate Hanoi's military intervention with that of the United States and would agree with the unidentified Asian statesman who remarked: "The two actions look to us very different. *They* are not just Asian: they are *Vietnamese*. And you cannot contend that the military behavior of one half of a small country toward its other half resembles closely the intervention, some 10,000 miles away, of the world's greatest military power." [29]

In justifying its policy in Vietnam during the past year, Washington has argued that the American stand there has decisively tipped the internal political balance within Indonesia, emboldening the army to move against and liquidate the

Indonesian Communist Party. There is, however, no evidence that external influences played any part whatsoever in the abortive coup of September 30, 1965, and its aftermath. This was precipitated by long-maturing and purely domestic internal pressures. It was an inevitable culmination of a struggle for political ascendancy among three major power centers—the army, the Communist Party, and President Sukarno—which had been shaping up and intensifying over the course of a decade.[30] Insofar as the American actions in Vietnam had any appreciable effect on this struggle, it was only to benefit the Communist Party, permitting it (until its liquidation in early 1966) to capitalize on the widely based Indonesian opposition to American policies in Vietnam. Indeed, opposition to U.S. military involvement in Vietnam constituted one of the few aspects of foreign policy wherein there was a congruence of viewpoint between the Indonesian army, the Indonesian communists, and President Sukarno.

Both before and subsequent to the attempted coup, Indonesian army commanders have been strong in their criticism of U.S. policy in Vietnam.[31] Today, not only the army but the new civilian leadership and all noncommunist political factions still consider Washington's actions in Vietnam as "intervention" and "aggression" and call upon the United States to cease its propping up of Saigon regimes, withdraw its military forces, and permit the Vietnamese people to work out a settlement themselves.[32]

Indonesia's foreign minister, Adam Malik, has summed up the current Indonesian dilemma of genuinely desiring better relations with the United States and desperately needing American aid but at the same time being unwilling to abandon a conviction so firmly held by Indonesians of all political casts of mind. In addressing Parliament on May 5, 1966, he said:[33]

. . . Indonesia intends to smooth relations [with the United States], particularly with regard to economic, trade, and technical matters. But the Indonesian Government is still firmly of the opinion that it supports the struggle of the Vietnamese people against U.S. military intervention. The settlement of the Vietnamese problem must be performed on the basis of the freely expressed will of the people of Vietnam, without intervention from any quarter. Indonesia maintains her demand that the U.S. withdraw its military forces from Vietnam, and leave the settlement of the Vietnamese problem to the Vietnamese people themselves.*

6: **There has been little appreciation** by the Johnson Administration of the extent to which the views of Southeast Asians toward the U.S. involvement in Vietnam have been conditioned by their reactions to earlier American intervention in the area. In reviewing events of the past decade, Southeast Asians see the United States, not Communist China or Soviet Russia, as the outside power that has attempted most frequently to direct their political destinies. In the countries of the area, the American presence has been consistently more substantial and obvious than that of either major communist power.

In the Philippines and Thailand, local governments have invited a substantial American involvement—military as well as economic. Although U.S. actions in the Philippines have probably been for the most part enlightened and effective, the same does not hold for Indonesia, Burma, Cambodia, or Laos. The way in which the United States in recent years intervened in their affairs has heightened their sensitivity to the introduction of American power elsewhere in Asia, including Vietnam.

---

* On July 11, 1966, Foreign Minister Malik further stated: "The government and people of Indonesia strongly condemn the escalation of the war by the U.S. in Vietnam. The recent daily bombings carried out in the environs of Hanoi and Haiphong have gone beyond the bounds of humanity; therefore, the Indonesian Government calls on the U.S. to stop these bombings immediately. . . ." The attitude of Indonesia towards Vietnam, he said, remained the same as it always had been: wishing for a peaceful settlement by putting the Geneva Agreements sincerely into practice, which do not permit any foreign intervention, let alone intervention in the form of military force. *Berita Yudha,* July 13, 1966.

The episode that most adversely affected Indonesian attitudes toward the United States was American backing of a rebellion in Sumatra and the Celebes in 1957–59, aimed not only at Sukarno's government but also against the army leadership of General A. H. Nasution and other currently dominant Indonesian officers.* The flagrancy of this intervention produced an enduring suspicion of the United States among Indonesians of all political persuasions, including the anticommunist army leaders as well as the communists. (It has weighed much more heavily with Indonesians than the considerable economic assistance previously provided by the United States or Washington's subsequent support of Indonesia in the dispute with the Netherlands over West Irian.)

The Burmese have much justification for their adverse sensitivity toward the U.S. role in Southeast Asian affairs. Regarding American policy as having subordinated Burmese national interests to those of Chiang Kai-shek and of the United States, Rangoon has remained alienated from Washington and wary of its motives. Beginning in 1950, the United States, at first directly and later indirectly through Taiwan, supported the remnant Chinese Nationalist (Kuomintang) forces of Chiang Kai-shek that ravaged much of northeast Burma after their retreat from mainland China.[34] In addition to a continuing flow of modern American arms, Chiang's forces in Burma received by air from Taiwan reinforcements of officers, non-coms and technicians.† Despite repeated and

---

* This American action was carried out through the Central Intelligence Agency (CIA) and involved sending large amounts of U.S. military equipment to the rebels by sea and air; CIA pilots flew combat missions for the rebel command, bombing Indonesian naval vessels and the city of Ambon.

† The Burmese Minister of Defense bitterly remarked to one of the authors in 1955 that in view of the U.S. opposition to communism it seemed to him ironic that the American-supplied Nationalist Chinese troops in Burma were keeping his army too preoccupied to deal effectively with the country's own dissident communist troops. This view was consistent with the statement on

urgent pleas from the Burmese government,[35] the U.S. allowed this flow to continue until 1961.[36]

The Burmese have remained grateful that even though Chiang's forces made limited probes into China from their sanctuary in Northeast Burma, Peking did not use this as a pretext for ordering Communist Chinese troops into Burma to subdue them. In 1960, despite Rangoon's continuing inability to restrict Chiang Kai-shek's marauding bands, it reached what the Burmese have regarded as an eminently fair settlement of their boundary dispute with China, one wherein Peking waived previous substantial territorial demands.[37] The Nationalist Chinese government on Taiwan, on the other hand, has never abandoned these claims and has in fact denounced the settlement secured by the Burmese in their negotiations with Peking.

Despite belated American efforts to arrange for the repatriation of some of the Kuomintang forces to Taiwan, several thousand of these well-equipped troops still operate in northeast Burma. Since the Burmese see Taiwan's military policy as completely dependent upon the United States, the continuing presence of Kuomintang troops serves to remind them that thus far the United States, not Communist China, has been the intruder in their domestic affairs. The Burmese are uncertain how long Peking will be restrained in its reactions, particularly since the remaining Kuomintang troops in Burma maintain close links with other Kuomintang forces operating out of

---

January 25, 1954, of Senator H. Alexander Smith, then Chairman of the Sub-Committee on the Far East of the Senate Committee on Foreign Relations: "Certainly the Burmese government, which is busily engaged in fighting Communist uprisings within its borders, should not have to dissipate its resources and its energy chasing troops and trouble makers who claim to be on the side of the free world." See his report on his Far East trip, U.S. Senate, *Congressional Record,* Vol. 100, February 9, 1954, p. 1548. At that time most of the Burmese Army's nongarrison forces were still tied down in trying to contain Chiang Kai-shek's forces in Burma's Shan states.

northwest Thailand—a country that China increasingly regards as an American military base for use against China as well as against Vietnam. The Burmese feel themselves walking on a dangerous tightrope between Peking and Washington.[38]

While no such palpable impingement of American power has existed in Cambodia, Prince Norodom Sihanouk's keen distrust of the United States has shaped his country's stand on American actions in Vietnam.[39] Fundamental to Cambodia's foreign policy is its fear of Vietnamese encroachment—both noncommunist and communist. This is one reason for Cambodia's long interest in international guarantees of its borders and its consequent resentment at Washington's unwillingness to participate in such guarantees. Convinced also that less than a decade ago the Central Intelligence Agency cooperated with the South Vietnamese and Thai governments to overthrow him, Prince Sihanouk has interpreted U.S. policy toward Cambodia as a product of America's plan to strengthen his traditional enemies, Vietnam and Thailand, at his expense. Sihanouk has countered this buildup across his frontiers by seeking closer relations with China, even while severely suppressing local communists and closely controlling resident Chinese within his own country. He presumably hopes that if Vietnamese and Thai pressures on his little kingdom become excessive, he can turn to Peking for assistance.

Any realistic discussion of Laos must begin with the acknowledgment that the area so designated does not constitute a nation.* Whatever potential it may have for nationhood has hardly been strengthened by American policy there in the last decade. Moreover there can be no durable settlement in Laos so long as the Vietnam war is in progress. U.S. intervention in Laos (briefly discussed in the earlier context of China) has

---

* The French did not give Laos administrative unity until 1946–47. Before they took over the area at the end of the 19th century, much of the western half was controlled directly or indirectly by Bangkok, while parts of the eastern highlands were subject to varying degrees of Vietnamese authority.

on balance been highly counterproductive. The actions of the
United States in 1958–60—in contravention to the country's
neutralization under the 1954 Geneva Agreements—succeeded in weakening the power of the right-wing generals,
whose position it initially built up; undermining the political
base of the neutralists under Souvanna Phouma, whom it later
belatedly backed; and concurrently providing tremendous
political capital to the procommunist Pathet Lao.[40] In recent
years the present Prime Minister, Souvanna Phouma, has had
good reason to be antagonized by North Vietnamese incursions
into Laos arising out of their efforts to keep open the "Ho
Chi Minh trail" to the backdoor of South Vietnam. But he
can scarcely have forgotten that an earlier U.S. intervention
was openly aimed at toppling his government. The political
backlash from this American involvement (as well as some
aspects of more recent American policy in Laos) has been of
importance in recruiting support for the Pathet Lao. Undoubtedly, however, the principal reason for the Pathet Lao's
growing strength has been its championing of many non-Lao
highlanders who have long been discriminated against by the
ruling valley-dwelling aristocracy.* Thus, it is not surprising
that most of the approximately half of Laotian territory currently dominated by the Pathet Lao is inhabited by the
non-Lao uplanders.

7: **Peking predicted** early in 1964 that the United States
could not offset by military escalation the political defeat it
had suffered with the collapse of the Diem regime.[41] The
Chinese argued that after American power was committed

---

* Culturally and linguistically the population of Laos is about
evenly divided between the Lao and non-Lao hill-dwelling peoples.
Nearly all the Lao live in the river valleys in the western part of the
country adjacent to Thailand (whose Lao population is at least
four times as large as that of Laos). Most of the non-Lao peoples
live in the eastern highland regions and have close ethnic and
linguistic ties with non-Vietnamese hill-dwelling minorities of Vietnam.

and discredited in Vietnam, revolutionaries elsewhere would no longer be "frightened by the seemingly powerful American imperialists, [and would] dare to struggle. . . . In this sense, the victory of the South Vietnamese people has universal significance." American imperialism, they argued, would then be "exposed for the paper tiger it is." [42] The same argument led China to describe the American escalation in Vietnam as a necessary prelude to the shattering of U.S. global prestige.[43]

The Johnson Administration has accepted this Chinese propagandistic thesis unquestioningly and at face value. The Chinese would undoubtedly be delighted to see this thesis hold true, but in fact it is quite inconsistent with the highly localized factors governing political developments outside Vietnam and with Peking's own acknowledgment that revolutions cannot be exported. In accepting the Chinese assertion that the future of the underdeveloped world is on trial in Vietnam and by committing American troops and prestige in accordance with this proposition, the Johnson Administration has lent its own authority to Chinese propaganda and given it a credence before an American and world audience that it in no sense deserves.

Secretary of State Rusk could not have been more helpful in sustaining the myth that Peking has hoped to promote than in his repeated assertion that if the technique of "national liberation . . . succeeds in South Viet-Nam, it can succeed anywhere in the world . . . [A]ll small nations have a vital stake in the defeat of this aggression."[44] It would, of course, be just as sensible (or fatuous) to observe that if revolution can succeed in one country it can succeed in another—or that if it can be crushed in one country it can be crushed in another.

Peking's proposition means, among other things, subscribing to the idea that nationalism is already harnessed to communism throughout the underdeveloped world—a judgment that does violence to the most evident facts. In terms of nationalism Vietnam is, as we have seen, a case apart and cannot

provide the basis for generalizations as to the course and outcome of revolutionary movements elsewhere. But neither the
Secretary of State nor the President give evidence of appreciating this and continue to evaluate nationalism's revolutionary
potential in Asia and Africa in accordance with Peking's
hopes.

Washington's disposition to regard Vietnam as a test case
has done much to nurture the "domino theory," or what General Maxwell Taylor calls the "bandwagon effect." [45] Basic to
this concept and a common denominator to all of its variations
is the apocalyptic expectation that a communist political victory in Vietnam or in any state will automatically incline noncommunist regimes in other countries to yield to communist revolutionary movements. This concept can, in fact, be
rendered plausible only through ignorance, or studious disregard, of the differences among the individual states of Southeast Asia and an assumption that Asians and their governments
react in a different way toward outside threats than do Westerners and their governments. The domino analogy has not
been applied to the countries of Europe, for here are countries
of traditional U.S. concern, where most Americans would
quickly grasp its irrelevance. They understand the great di-
versity of the European states and recognize that the European
peoples have qualities that run counter to any simplistic
chain-reaction dynamic of the domino theory. Europeans, they
know, can generally be expected to respond to an outside
threat—whether physical or ideological—by standing up to
it and closing their ranks against it.

The Administration argues, however, that in Asia such a
chain reaction would be set in motion should a communist
regime come to power in Saigon. But in Asia, as in Europe,
geographical propinquity is not equivalent to political vulnera-
bility. When the largest Asian "domino"—China—fell in
1949, the rest of Asia did not collapse, and even China's communist neighbors—North Vietnam and North Korea—have
resisted Peking's embrace. Nationalism is as strong a force in

Asia as in Europe, and because of their recent colonial status the Asian nations are all the more sensitive and alert to any threat of foreign domination. Opposition to foreign encroachment, real or threatened, has been a primary generator of national consciousness and a major factor in strengthening political cohesion. The states of Cambodia and Thailand clearly demonstrate this. In harmony with their countries' traditions and nationalism, neither of their governments has faced any strong local communist movement.

It has only been with Thailand's increasing involvement in the Vietnamese war that local dissidents in parts of that country have during the last few years appeared to be developing significant communist ties. The U.S. intervention in Vietnam and the injection of a substantial American military presence in Thailand, however, has not as yet significantly altered the political situation in the latter country. The proximity of the warfare in Laos and Vietnam has probably served to tighten the hold of the Thai military on the political system, and this may have further retarded any possible move toward greater popular participation in political decisions. The king remains the symbol of Thai nationalism, and the military and bureaucratic elite of Bangkok still benefit by their ability to work closely with the throne.

Not yet extensive, the incipient political disaffection in the country is largely concentrated in northeast Thailand where the majority are Lao-speaking and have traditionally been treated as second-class citizens by Bangkok.[46] Political dissidence has a long history in this area of Thailand, and its increase thus far has actually been slight. Insofar as it has assumed a procommunist cast, this appears to be a predictable reaction to the buildup of American military power in Thailand (35,000 troops by November 1966) and the construction of a major network of air bases, particularly in the northeastern provinces.[47] Many of the American raids against the Pathet Lao areas of Laos and approximately half of the American bombing missions sent over North Vietnam originate from these air bases.[48] Thus, it is not surprising that Lao-speaking agents from the Pathet Lao and possibly agents from North Vietnam have infiltrated areas of northeast Thailand and begun agitation, exploiting local grievances and supplying arms. Only after Thailand, on May 8, 1966, announced its decision to dispatch a contingent of naval and air units to Vietnam did the clandestine communist radio in Thailand pointedly link the Thai and Vietnamese insurrections.[49] So long as northeast Thailand remains a strategic base of American military operations, Hanoi and the Pathet Lao will undoubtedly strive to incite the people of this area to rebellion in order to reduce the effectiveness of that base.

Beyond this, the greatest danger to the Thai nation is that the magnitude of U.S. military and economic aid will create an increasingly artificial political situation where the army-dominated government can rule without feeling obliged to maintain and develop sufficient popular backing. Overly heavy reliance on outside aid might well insulate the Thai leaders from economic and political realities outside Bangkok and reduce their sensitivity and responsiveness to a growth of discontent within the country.

Contrary to President Johnson's assertion that "what happens in South Vietnam will determine—yes, it will determine—whether ambitious and aggressive nations can use guerrilla warfare to conquer their weaker neighbors," [50] developments in Vietnam do not have a significant political effect upon the rest of Southeast Asia or in the underdeveloped world as a whole. Revolutions will develop there wherever local conditions warrant, regardless of the outcome in Vietnam. And in every case the principal responsibility for meeting the challenge of insurrection, whether communist or not, must rest with the governments of these countries themselves. No outside power has the wisdom or the influence to solve their internal problems.

Notes to Chapter XII

1. U.S. Senate, *Supplemental Foreign Assistance Fiscal Year 1966—Vietnam,* 89th Congress, 2nd Session (Washington: U.S. Government Printing Office, 1966), p. 333. See also Mr. Kennan's astute article in the *Washington Post,* December 12, 1965.

2. For evidence of this greater Russian hostility, see *New York Times,* June 10 and 18, 1966. The Russians in their comment on the Warsaw Pact communiqué in early July said: "The statement of the Warsaw Pact member states concerning U.S. aggression in Vietnam, unanimously adopted by the meeting, has the full approval and emphatic support of the Soviet Union. The Politburo of the CPSU Central Committee and the Soviet Government instructed competent government agencies to take all necessary steps flowing from this statement in support of the heroic Vietnamese people, including those connected with rendering economic and military aid to repel American aggression, with due account of the requirements caused by the new phase of the war in Vietnam." TASS, July 11, 1966. On August 5, 1966, Secretary Rusk said: "I would have to say that the Soviet position, with respect to bilateral relations and the general situation, is a difficult one under the circumstances of the Vietnam situation. We regret that. We would like to find ways to improve our bilateral relations with the Soviet Union, but we cannot do so by giving away South Vietnam." *New York Times,* August 6, 1966.

3. See Rusk's statements on Soviet-American relations in *Department of State Bulletin* (Washington, August 2, 1965), p. 190; (November 29, 1965), p. 861; (December 13, 1965), p. 934; (February 7, 1966), p. 193.

4. *New York Times,* August 27, 1966. The Russians, in reply to President Johnson's speech, said that Johnson's assertion that the war in South Vietnam is a local conflict "that in no way infringes on the interests of the Soviet Union is very strange. It is more illogical to state that a war that involves one of our closest allies, the Democratic Republic of Vietnam, and as you know the United States is daily and systematically bombing the country, is of no consequence to us." Moscow Radio, August 30, 1966. *Pravda,* on September 1, 1966, stated that "the expansion of the U.S. aggression in Vietnam which aggravated international tensions is responsible for the obvious deterioration of Soviet-American relations. As for the Soviet Union, it has never believed and does not now believe that Soviet-American relations cannot be different

from what they are now through the fault of the United States. For their improvement, it is necessary for the United States to observe the norms of international law and not interfere in the internal affairs of other countries and peoples."

Following a major and well-publicized effort in early October 1966 by the Johnson Administration to bring about an over-all improvement in United States-Soviet relations and, in particular, to break the deadlock on achieving an agreement on the prevention of the spread of nuclear weapons, Leonid Brezhnev, First Secretary of the Communist Party of the Soviet Union, stated: "Once more we have to deal with the attempt by the U.S. policy leaders to put the matter in such a way as though relations between the United States and the Soviet Union and other socialist European countries could develop unimpeded despite the U.S. aggression against Vietnam and the interference by the Americans into the affairs of other states—a strange and persistent delusion. We have declared more than once that if the United States wants to develop mutually advantageous relations with the Soviet Union—and we, too, would like this—it is necessary for this purpose to remove the major obstacles from the road, cease the bandit raids on a socialist country—the Democratic Republic of Vietnam; cease the aggression against the sovereignty and territorial integrity of other countries and peoples not in words but in deeds." *New York Times,* October 11–16, 1966; and Moscow Radio, October 15, 1966.

5. This point is eloquently put by Charlton Ogburn, Jr., "Our 'Misjudgment' in Vietnam," *Washington Post,* January 2, 1966.

6. See the comments of British Prime Minister Harold Wilson on the bombing of the fuel depots outside Hanoi and Haiphong in *New York Times,* June 30, 1966.

7. U.S. Department of State, *The Legality of U.S. Participation in the Defense of Viet-Nam* (Washington: U.S. Government Printing Office, 1966). A legal statement that questions the legality of the American policy in Vietnam may be found in *Supplemental Foreign Assistance Fiscal Year 1966—Vietnam,* pp. 687–713.

8. Statement of February 18, 1966, in *Department of State Bulletin* (Washington, March 7, 1966), p. 349.

9. U.S. Senate, *The Southeast Asia Collective Defense Treaty,* 83rd Congress, 2nd Session (Washington: U.S. Government Printing Office, 1954), Vol. I, p. 3. See above, pp. 61–63, and Appendix 3 for text of treaty.

10. Words such as "external aggression" and "armed attack" are not clear and unambiguous, and in such cases under international law resort must be made to the *travaux préparatoires* on their reasonable interpretation. Hans Kelsen states that "It may be doubted whether the action of insurgents against the legitimate government can be an 'armed attack' within the meaning of Article

51 [of the UN Charter]." *The Law of Nations* (New York: Praeger, 1950), p. 930. On the difficulties of defining aggression, see, for example, Leland M. Goodrich and Edvard Hambro, *Charter of the United Nations: Commentary and Documents,* 2nd rev. ed. (Boston: World Peace Foundation, 1949), pp. 94, 104, 207, 263, and 300. The United Nations from the beginning attempted without success to define aggression. It requested the International Law Commission to construct a workable definition and then in 1950 established an interim special committee for the task of defining aggression.

11. *The Southeast Asia Collective Defense Treaty,* pp. 1–40.

12. *Ibid.,* pp. 3, 13, and 21–22. See address by Secretary of State John Foster Dulles, June 11, 1954, in *Department of State Bulletin* (Washington, June 28, 1954), p. 972.

13. *The Southeast Asia Collective Defense Treaty,* pp. 28 and 33.

14. *Ibid.,* p. 25.

15. *New York Times,* February 20, 1966.

16. *Department of State Bulletin* (Washington, August 16, 1965), p. 263. Secretary Rusk stated: "We do ourselves no service by insisting that each source of aggression or each instance of aggression is unique." U.S. House, *United States Policy Toward Asia,* 89th Congress, 2nd Session (Washington: U.S. Government Printing Office, 1966), Vol. II, p. 528. President Johnson, on July 28, 1965, said: "Nor would surrender in Viet-Nam bring peace, because we learned from Hitler at Munich that success only feeds the appetite of aggression." *Department of State Bulletin* (Washington, August 16, 1965), p. 263.

17. *Department of State Bulletin* (Washington, August 16, 1965), p. 263.

18. Thomas C. Schelling, *Arms and Influence* (New Haven, Conn.: Yale University Press, 1966), p. 124.

19. *Department of State Bulletin* (Washington, August 1, 1966), p. 161.

20. For typical statements by President Ayub Khan on Pakistan's attitude toward Vietnam see *Dawn,* May 4, 1966, and President Ayub Khan, *Pakistan's Domestic and Foreign Policies* (Washington: Information Division, Embassy of Pakistan, 1966), p. 4.

21. For Pakistan and India see *New York Times,* December 13 and 17, 1965.

22. New Delhi Radio, July 7, 1966.

23. *New York Times,* July 17, 1966. For text of the Soviet-Indian communiqué of July 16 see *Times of India,* July 17, 1966.

24. *New York Times,* July 22, and October 25, 1966.

25. See "The *Asahi* Poll on Vietnam," *Japan Quarterly,* Vol.

XII, No. 4, October–December 1965; and R. P. Dore, "How Asian is Japan?" *New Society,* Vol. V, No. 139, pp. 14–15.

26. Quote from article by United Press correspondent Arthur Dommen, *Bangkok Post,* September 11, 1965. See also *New York Times,* November 19, 1965. In January, Japanese Premier Eisaku Sato asked the United States to continue the bombing pause in order to facilitate Japanese peacemaking efforts. The United States evidently rejected this request. *New York Times,* January 22, 1966.

27. *Supplemental Foreign Assistance Fiscal Year 1966—Vietnam,* p. 333.

28. As the well-known chairman of the Board of Directors of the International House of Japan, Shigeharu Matsumoto, has put it, "The Japanese government realizes the many difficulties confronting current American undertakings in the Vietnamese area. It has provided medical aid to the Vietnamese. . . . Most Japanese, however, have been inclined to believe that Chinese incitement of, and ideological and military assistance to, the Pathet Lao, the Viet Cong, and North Vietnam have been unduly dramatized, and that until recently the indigenous origin and growth of the Communist forces in Southeast Asia have not been properly evaluated by the American public." "Japan and China," *Policies Toward China: Views from Six Continents,* ed. by A. M. Halpern (New York: McGraw-Hill, 1966), p. 151. Professor Nobutaka Ike adds: ". . . by August [1965] Prime Minister Sato was telling the Diet that, while Japan supported the United States in Vietnam because it was fighting communism, it did not support the bombing of north Vietnam." *Asian Survey,* Vol. VI, No. 1, January 1966, p. 23.

29. Emmet John Hughes, "A View of Vietnam," *Newsweek,* May 30, 1966, p. 22.

30. See G. McT. Kahin, "Indonesia," *Major Governments of Asia,* 2nd ed., ed. by G. McT. Kahin (Ithaca, N.Y.: Cornell University Press, 1963). For some of the relevant documents on the coup, see *Indonesia* (Ithaca, N.Y.: Cornell Modern Indonesia Project), Vol. I, April 1, 1966, pp. 131–204.

31. The few editorials devoted to Vietnam in the Army newspaper *Berita Yudha* are harsh in their denunciation of American policy there. See the issues of *ibid.,* November 6 and 26, 1965. The stance taken in these editorials is also reflected in the news reporting on the area; see for example *ibid.,* November 20 and 23, 1965, February 3, July 16, and August 5, 1966. See also *ibid.,* August 10 and 11, 1966, which carried two commentaries by former Foreign Minister Sunario on the Vietnam problem depicting the United States as the "violator of the letter and spirit of the Geneva Agreements" and as deserving the label "aggressor for its current policy."

32. For the views of Islamic, Catholic, and other groups see, for

example, *Indonesian Herald,* January 27, 1966, and April 18, 1966; *Antara,* July 19, 1966; and *Duta Masjarakat,* September 13, 1966. It is also noteworthy that in Sukarno's speech of August 17, 1966, the militant anticommunist Action Command of Indonesian Students (KAMI), while booing and generally expressing disapproval of most of what he said, singled out for approval his statement in English, "Please, America, get out of Vietnam." *New York Times,* August 18, 1966.

33. *Berita Yudha,* May 6, 1966.

34. *New York Times,* July 24, 1953, and January 17, 1954. See text of Burma's note to the UN accusing the Chinese Nationalists of aggression, *ibid.,* March 27, 1953. For a comprehensive account of the Kuomintang Chinese involvement in Burma, see Oliver E. Clubb, Jr., *The United States and the Sino-Soviet Bloc in Southeast Asia* (Washington: Brookings Institution, 1962).

35. *New York Times,* February 18, 1961.

36. *Ibid.,* March 3, 1961. In a series on the CIA in April–May 1966 the *New York Times* stated: "A sorry episode in Asia in the early nineteen-fifties is a frequently cited example. C.I.A. agents gathered remnants of the defeated Chinese Nationalists armies in the jungles of northwest Burma, supplied them with gold and arms and encouraged them to raid Communist China. One aim was to harass Peking to a point where it might retaliate against Burma, forcing the Burmese to turn to the United States for protection." *New York Times,* April 25, 1966.

37. See Daphne E. Whittam, "The Sino-Burmese Boundary Treaty," *Pacific Affairs,* Vol. XXXIV, No. 2, Summer 1961, pp. 174–183.

38. For a discussion of Burmese neutralism, see *New York Times,* June 20, 1966.

39. It should be unnecessary to document Cambodia's mounting hostility toward U.S. policy in Vietnam in view of the American decision in mid-December 1965 to allow U.S. troops to pursue communist forces from Vietnam into Cambodia. *New York Times,* December 21, 1965. Recent samples of Sihanouk's views on U.S. Vietnam policy are represented in the broadcasts of Phnom Penh Radio, October 26 and December 27, 1965; and January 4 and 31, May 9, and June 18, 20, and 21, 1966. The following quote is typical of his attitude: "We repeat that we support the National Liberation Front in its legitimate claims, in the name of the Vietnamese people who have the right to settle their own affairs, to independence, and to demand the unconditional withdrawal of the Americans. They even have the right to engage in a civil war among themselves, that is among the Vietnamese. We support these legitimate rights." Phnom Penh Radio, June 20, 1966.

40. See Arthur J. Dommen, *Conflict in Laos* (New York:

Praeger, 1964), especially chs. 7–9; and Roger M. Smith, "Laos," *Governments and Politics of Southeast Asia*, 2nd ed., ed. by George McT. Kahin (Ithaca, N.Y.: Cornell University Press, 1964), especially pp. 544–556.

41. *Jen-min Jih-pao ("People's Daily")*, March 4, 1964.

42. *Ibid.*

43. *Ibid.*

44. Dean Rusk, *Guidelines of U.S. Foreign Policy*, Department of State Publication 7921 (Washington: U.S. Government Printing Office, 1965), p. 8.

45. General Taylor told the U.S. Senate: "There is always a danger of a sort of bandwagon movement, I am afraid, among these very weak countries." *Supplemental Foreign Assistance Fiscal Year 1966—Vietnam*, p. 509.

46. See the articles in the *New York Times*, July 10 and 12, 1966. For a symposium on Thailand's northeast, see *Asian Survey*, Vol. VI, No. 7, July 1966.

47. For a description, see *New York Times*, July 7, 1966.

48. These raids are discussed in *ibid*.

49. *Ibid.*, July 12, 1966.

50. *Ibid.*, July 1, 1966.

CHAPTER XIII

Limits of Power

1: **Many advocates of American policy in Vietnam** argue that the past is irrelevant to the pursuit of present U.S. objectives in Southeast Asia. But in Vietnam past is present, and previous American actions have shaped and helped set in motion forces and attitudes that today bear decisively on the situation there. If the United States is to undertake a political approach consistent with current realities, the pervading influence of recent Vietnamese history cannot be ignored and American policies must accommodate to the fundamental political limits it imposes.

By mid-1949, when Mao Tse-tung came to power in China, nationalism and communism in Vietnam had already largely fused and the main body of the nationalist movement had passed under communist leadership. Although even at this early date there was little solidarity between the communist movements in China and Vietnam and American efforts to contain China might have found an ally in Vietnamese nationalism, Washington felt unable to cooperate with a communist-led movement and backed France's attempts to reassert her authority in Vietnam. Preoccupied with the spread of communism, the United States did not differentiate between Chinese power (then assumed to be a projection of Soviet power) and the national communist movements in Southeast Asia. Considering Vietnamese and Chinese communism as simply different facets of one world monolith and alarmed by the entry of Chinese troops into the Korean War, Washington became more inclined to regard the Franco-Vietminh conflict as another front in the containment of China. This and the need for France's cooperation in the development of the European alliance system made Washington easily susceptible to the French argument that American interests necessitated increased support to France in Vietnam. Thus between 1950 and 1954 the United States underwrote most of the cost of the French military campaign against the Vietminh. But unstinting American financial and material aid proved futile and could not compensate the French and the small group of Vietnamese who collaborated with them for their lack of significant indigenous backing.

Washington's refusal to recognize the individual character of the Vietnamese communist movement was in part a result of domestic political pressures within the United States. The election campaigns of 1950 and 1952 had centered on the Truman Administration's alleged responsibility for the loss of China to the communists, and the Eisenhower Administration was naturally sensitive lest a similar allegation be leveled against it over Vietnam. Disregarding the fact that Vietnam, no more than China, was not America's to lose, Washington was disposed to oppose any communist movement there, irrespective of its relationship with Moscow or Peking.* Consequently, before it sufficiently appreciated that communism on a global basis was not monolithic, the United States had committed itself in Vietnam in a way whereby it could not benefit from the nationalist emphasis of Vietnamese communism. American support of France forced Ho Chi Minh's Vietminh

---

* Since President Johnson's Administration has stated publicly that a communist takeover in Vietnam would constitute a loss of American security, his Administration has made itself more vulnerable to such a charge than was ever the case with that of President Truman. In both cases indigenous forces, which the United States could not possibly control, were essentially responsible for the fact that communists developed the power to win political ascendancy. However groundless the allegation that a particular administration "lost" a country to communism, this does not alter the fact that such allegations have tremendous relevance for American domestic politics. They were made a major campaign issue in 1950 and 1952 and could easily have become so in 1968.

into an unwelcome dependence upon China and denied the movement the freedom to act in accordance with the historically conditioned, anti-Chinese proclivity of Vietnamese nationalism. So long as the United States continued to oppose the major thrust of Vietnamese nationalism, which the Vietminh in fact constituted, Vietnam could not fully reassert its traditional role as one of the strongest Southeast Asian ramparts on China's southern flank.*

For the twelve years following the Geneva Conference of mid-1954 the United States tried to establish a separate state in the southern part of Vietnam under an anticommunist government. The terms of the Geneva Agreements granted this new government under Ngo Dinh Diem a period of reprieve from political competition with the revolutionary forces that had defeated the French. Moreover, the noncommunist nationalists in the South had been less clearly allied with the communists than had most of those in the North, and pursuit of enlightened policies might have secured substantial popular backing for a noncommunist Saigon government. Yet, Diem made no effective use of the period of political insulation for mobilizing this latent political strength—despite the fact that he faced no communist competition for double the two years stipulated at Geneva. Instead, because of his heavily repressive measures, Diem gradually alienated the very political forces with whom he might have allied. Ultimately his government's base of support was confined to virtually the same Vietnamese who had worked with the French. Refusing to tolerate political opposition and resorting to increasingly dictatorial actions, he

---

* While the obsolescence of the previously deep-rooted American concern with the threat of a worldwide, coordinated communist conspiracy is now appreciated in Washington and has had some effect upon American policy, understanding of this has only slightly percolated down into the bulk of the American population. There the previous perception of "international communism" remains so strong that in terms of domestic political exigencies the Administration must still be sensitive to it and respond accordingly, particularly in election years.

antagonized noncommunist as well as procommunist nationalists, driving some into exile and many in the rural areas into insurgency.

The United States initially provided Diem with a shield against armed attack from the North and encouraged him in his refusal to resolve through elections the military power struggle suspended at Geneva. During subsequent years, Washington moved beyond this position of guaranteeing the new state against outside attack and undertook to defend the Saigon government against communist-led insurrection within its own borders.* To this end it provided additional war matériel and American military advisors. It was only in mid-1963, on the eve of Diem's fall, that American backing of his government was withdrawn. Since that time the United States has had a series of opportunities for influencing South Vietnam's political development in a way that might have enabled it to secure a government in Saigon with a wider popular following. The most recent opportunity occurred in the spring of 1966, when the Buddhists headed a major upsurge against the military junta led by Marshal Ky. By this time, however, American policy in Vietnam had moved to a new phase of involvement. The United States no longer confined itself to guaranteeing South Vietnam from external aggression or to protecting the Saigon government against communist subversion but was dedicated to the preservation of army rule in Saigon against any internal political challenge from whatever quarter.

By mid-1966 a political polarization existed in South Viet-

---

* As George Kennan put it, "[H]ere is an obligation on our part not only to defend the frontiers of a certain political entity against outside attack, but to assure the internal security of its government in circumstances where that government is unable to assure that security by its own means." U.S. Senate, *Supplemental Foreign Assistance Fiscal Year 1966—Vietnam,* 89th Congress, 2nd Session (Washington: U.S. Government Printing Office, 1966), Part I, p. 335.

nam quite as extreme as under Ngo Dinh Diem. Its population was left with no effective political alternatives outside of the military junta and the National Liberation Front. Nationalist groups that might have worked for a popularly based, non-communist solution in the South were denied the necessary scope for such action. Essentially, then, the United States in 1966 was facing the same problem that it had confronted a decade earlier; it was still refusing to acknowledge the actual character and relative strength of the political forces in South Vietnam and failing to tailor its policies accordingly.

And, as before, Washington was undertaking to compensate for the weakness of the anticommunist political elements in Saigon by strengthening the American military presence. Thus, in order to avert the imminent collapse of the Saigon government in 1965, the United States introduced massive increments of military force until, by October of the following year, the number of American troops actually exceeded those of the regular South Vietnamese army. Today it is as evident as ever that the increased infusions of this military power are politically fruitless and are not compensating for the dwindling support of the Saigon military government. More pronounced than ever is the absence of any significant anticommunist nationalist base that could provide the United States with an effective fulcrum for the application of its power.

2 : Today the United States deploys enough armed might in Vietnam to prevent the Vietcong from winning a military victory and to stop them from overrunning Saigon, the other cities, and most major towns. But to attain and keep the military initiative outside these urban strongholds, the United States has had to resort to warfare of a kind that is destroying the rural Vietnamese society it hopes to deny the Vietcong and win for Saigon. Although Washington has declared that the first essential is to give the people security, it feels that this can only be achieved by eradicating the Vietcong from their midst. This social surgery requires military actions in contested areas

on a nonselective basis, and, while the civilian survivors may blame the Vietcong for attracting destruction to their homes, this cannot lessen their hatred for those directly responsible— the Saigon government and the United States. For the preponderant majority of the peasants, a period of security has become rarer today than before American military operations began, and, as the scope and scale of the fighting have expanded, the areas of safety for the peasants have shrunk. After weathering American "search and destroy" campaigns they can still generally anticipate that the Vietcong will again return within days if not hours.

The consequences of aerial bombardment are similar. In 1965 alone, over one ton of bombs, napalm, and rockets fell for each known Vietcong soldier; by the end of 1966 the tonnage-to-Vietcong ratio will have more than doubled. Assigned to drop such a weight of bombs, American and South Vietnamese pilots cannot be expected to discriminate between their Vietcong adversaries and Vietnamese civilians. The type of counterguerrilla warfare that relies so heavily on air power and artillery tends to be directed against pieces of territory and involves the destruction of whole villages suspected of harboring the enemy.[1] In view of the character of these operations it is understandable why a congressional report should conclude that "In the final analysis it appears that a ratio of two civilians [casualties] to one Vietcong [casualty] is likely." [2]

Fear of the bombing and the destruction of their lands have caused huge numbers of the rural population to flee their home villages. The refugees have sought sanctuary in the bases of American power, assuming that the United States will not bomb or shell its own troops or those of its Vietnamese allies. By mid-1966 over 1,000,000 men, women, and children had "voted with their feet" against escalation.[3] Abandoning their homes and villages, they fled to the Saigon-administered base areas in order to survive and thus came with great initial resentment. Their subsequent treatment is unlikely to temper their bitterness, for the flow of the homeless and orphaned has proceeded at a pace far beyond the capacity of the pacification programs to care for them.

Against this background of devastation and social disintegration, efforts at reconstruction must perforce remain relatively inconsequential. The billion dollars for Indochina's economic development that President Johnson has promised was undoubtedly intended to be a generous gesture. As measured against the physical destruction that military operations have entailed, however, it appears pathetically meager. Indeed, it can only begin to compensate for the results of a military effort that costs much more than that to mount each month. Moreover, even this billion-dollar program will not commence until the war ends, and thus whatever benefits it may bring are being deferred to that still indefinite time.

Nevertheless, the Johnson Administration speaks of carrying out a "social and political revolution" in Vietnam even while the fighting is in progress. This "revolution" is not, however, permitted to obstruct the prosecution of the war, nor is it directed toward eradicating those underlying causes of the conflict that over the years have been a product of Saigon's own policies. In any case, because of the vested interests it represents, the Saigon government has remained unwilling to give more than token implementation to any program involving genuine social change. Efforts to ameliorate this situation by American-financed and directed crash-basis reconstruction programs are artificial and bear no relation to a social revolution.

Thus the application of American military power that was originally intended to offset Saigon's inadequate political support has progressively weakened the remaining potential for social cohesion.* The ensuing social disruption makes any

---

* If the South Vietnamese army once constituted an island of social cohesion within the country, this has ceased to be the case over the last two years. In 1965 alone 113,000 men, or more than 15 per cent of its total number, deserted from Saigon's forces. Desertions

lasting political solution all the more remote. In the broad contested zones of the South, unending military campaigns destroy the possibility of effective political reconstruction. Although they prevent the Vietcong from establishing its own authority in these zones, they also deny this possibility to Saigon. As a consequence of search-and-destroy operations, the political no-man's-land in South Vietnam is expanding. American military power can probably succeed in overcoming all significant military opposition to Saigon, but the accompanying destruction of Vietnamese lives and society can only ensure that any Saigon regime allied to the United States will appear as the very symbol of this foreign-inflicted devastation.

3: **Once having decided** to rely primarily upon a military strategy, the Administration felt compelled to demonstrate the efficacy of such a policy. Its new commitment, however unwise, was dramatically visible—both to a global audience and to the American public. It was in this wider context of its commitment that the term "credibility" began to receive so much more attention. Indeed, the heart of the Administration's defense of its Vietnam policy has been the argument that its actions there have been necessary to maintain America's worldwide credibility and justify the faith placed in it by others. There are two applications of this concept—the credibility of U.S. *commitment* to South Vietnam and the credibility of U.S. *power*.

The initial commitment that President Eisenhower made to South Vietnam was modest, cautious, conditional, and specifi-

---

from the regular army in 1965 nearly doubled those of the previous year and ran from five to ten times higher than the number of Vietcong defections. In mid-May 1966, the American Defense Secretary testified that the desertion rate from the Saigon army had reached between 10,000 and 12,000 a month. See *New York Times,* February 24 and May 12, 1966. It should be noted that there is a wide range of estimates on desertion rates.

cally to the government of President Ngo Dinh Diem. Although President Kennedy widened the scope of the American commitment, it remained limited and based on the realization that any salvation for the South Vietnamese depended in the final analysis on their own efforts. Under President Johnson, the limits were removed and the commitment was extended to open-ended American backing of the Saigon military leadership irrespective of its political performance. Now related primarily to a global and American audience, the U.S. commitment in South Vietnam has become less and less directly related to conditions in that country or to the wishes of its people. Washington's commitment to South Vietnam has in fact become progressively overshadowed by the Administration's concern for the global credibility of American military power.

At the onset of the military escalation in 1965, the Vietcong's imminent victory over the South Vietnamese army did not challenge the credibility of U.S. military power, because at that time the military role of Americans was still primarily advisory, and American ground troops were not yet engaged in offensive combat. The credibility at issue then was that of the U.S. reliability in honoring a pledge to a beleaguered ally by providing it with all possible means for fighting a communist enemy. The conviction that the credibility of America's military capability was at stake became explicit only after the introduction of its own troops for combat purposes. Even so, there was never any likelihood that the Vietcong could eject U.S. forces from Vietnam but only doubt as to whether American military power could attain a preconceived political solution. Unable to translate military superiority into effective political power, the Johnson Administration has committed ever larger increments of American military strength in the hope of achieving some sort of political breakthrough that would vindicate its policies.

The establishment of military credibility in this sense came to mean the attainment of a position of strength whereby the communists would be forced to agree to a settlement on American terms. In order to achieve this position the United States felt obliged to demonstrate its tenacity of will and determination; as a consequence these have almost become ends in themselves. This led to an emphasis on American military credibility to a degree whereby credibility for peaceful intent was progressively undermined and with it the foe's disposition to negotiate. So long as military means had remained subordinate to limited political ends, American policy could remain flexible and in tune with U.S. interests, and Washington could disengage militarily with honor. But when vindication of the American military presence took precedence over attainable political objectives, the conditional character of the U.S. presence was lost.

Thus, one is brought to inquire whether the United States is laying such great stress on maintaining its military credibility that it has become blind to other attributes of power that are at least as important to American world leadership. And here, even if the concern is exclusively with *Realpolitik,* political effectiveness—as distinguished from military power alone—derives from an ability to bring military capabilities into line with objective political factors rather than with wishful political thinking. This is true even if one disregards those criteria of moral credibility and humanitarian concern so widely regarded as necessary qualities for any nation that aspires to responsible international leadership. In maintaining its influence, even a major power must recognize the limited effectiveness of military strength in achieving national goals and must shun the use of military means where politically requisite conditions are absent. It involves the maturity to acknowledge that where no sufficient and friendly political base exists, American military power, no matter how great, cannot achieve political solutions desired by Washington. Credibility for political wisdom will have a greater influence on the world Washington aspires to lead than credibility for disposing of overwhelming military might.

4: **If the United States** is to reestablish the credibility for political wisdom that it has been losing in Vietnam and have any chance of extricating itself from the present impasse there, it must subordinate its military means to its political ends and adapt those ends to existing Vietnamese realities.

One of the central realities is that Vietnam is a single nation, not two. The 1954 Geneva Agreements explicitly prohibited its political division, and the construction of a separate state in the South was made possible only through the injection of American military and economic aid. Despite Vietnam's regional differences, national consciousness was and remains strong. Though the American effort to establish an anti-communist state in the South resulted in an enduring de facto division, this cannot overcome the fact that to the Vietnamese their country, North and South, is a single nation and that South Vietnam constitutes an artificial creation whose existence depends on the sustained application of American power.

Washington's insistence that Vietnam is composed of two states has made more plausible the thesis of aggression from the North. In fact, however, the struggle in Vietnam is basically a civil war. The present conflict began within the South primarily as a reaction to the repressive measures of the American-backed Saigon regime. Only when this insurgency had built up a momentum of its own did Hanoi begin to assist the Southern insurgents, and the civil war resumed its Vietnam-wide, pre-Geneva dimension. It was not until after the United States had injected substantial American military forces into the struggle that Northern support of the Vietcong became significant. Yet, a crucial distinction remains between American and Northern intervention: while American support of Saigon is critical in that Saigon would quickly collapse were it withdrawn, the NLF, even if it received no assistance from Hanoi, could probably sustain a widely based guerrilla resistance for many years against both American and Saigon forces and could on its own overcome Saigon if the latter lost the financial and military backing of the United States.

Washington nevertheless persists in the assertion that the National Liberation Front is so politically and militarily dependent upon Hanoi that it cannot function on its own. This has led to the conclusion that by bombing North Vietnam the United States can persuade the Vietcong to sue for peace and accommodate to American demands for a settlement. It also gives rise to the contention that the NLF has no right to assume a significant political role either in negotiating such a settlement or in any ensuing South Vietnamese government. Thus the United States refuses to consider reaching an accord with its principal opponent in the field while applying "strategic persuasion" against a secondary adversary.

The United States has adopted a parallel argument concerning the government in South Vietnam, maintaining that Saigon speaks for the majority of the South Vietnamese and has the necessary influence to mobilize the noncommunist political forces in the South. By pursuing a strategy in accordance with these assumptions, Washington has helped bring about a polarization that permits noncommunists no other political channel except that controlled by the army leadership. So long as the United States persists in maintaining this polarization, it denies noncommunist South Vietnamese any scope for working out their own destiny.

Thus, the Administration has been left with a conceptual context that inhibits its formulation of a policy consistent with the situation in Vietnam. This constrains it from working effectively toward a political solution and helps convince its communist adversaries that the United States is not prepared to make the compromises necessary for a peaceful settlement. Indeed, the Administration is unwilling to consider compromise on what are actually the basic issues of the conflict— in particular, the political character of the South. Washington apparently continues to hold that communists cannot be considered as indigenous to South Vietnam and that American troops there are no more alien than those of Hanoi or even the NLF. Not viewing the political composition of South Vietnam as a matter for compromise and insisting that its separate and anticommunist status is fundamental and nonnegotiable, Washington regards the negotiable issues as commencing with the timing and modalities for the withdrawal of those forces which it considers alien—American and communist.

At the Manila Conference of October 24–25, 1966, the United States undertook to withdraw its troops from South Vietnam within six months after certain ambiguously defined conditions had been fulfilled by both the Vietcong and Hanoi. These included withdrawal of the forces of "the other side" to the North, the cessation of infiltration, and a consequent subsidence of "the level of violence." * Presumably the relevant context for interpreting this undertaking was provided by President Johnson's statement a few days later that American and allied troops would depart "just as soon as the infiltration, the aggression and the violence ceases." [4] With regard to the Manila communiqué South Vietnam's Chief of State, General Nguyen Van Thieu, stated that withdrawal of American and allied troops would commence "when there is a firm guarantee and a supervisory group has proved that all armed forces of all types have withdrawn from South Vietnam and all acts of sabotage, terrorism, and murder have been stopped throughout South Vietnam. Six months after there is such a guarantee and supervision, the allied troops who have come to help us will withdraw from Vietnam." In a press conference immediately afterwards, General Thieu emphasized that no distinc-

---

* Paragraph 29 of the Manila communiqué stated: "In particular, they declared that allied forces are in the Republic of Vietnam because that country is the object of aggression and its Government requested support in the resistance of its people to aggression. They shall be withdrawn, after close consultation, as the other side withdraws its forces to the North, ceases infiltration, and the level of violence thus subsides. Those forces will be withdrawn as soon as possible and not later than six months after the above conditions have been fulfilled." *New York Times,* October 26, 1966.

tion was to be made between the Vietcong and Hanoi forces.[5] These statements lend credence to the *New York Times* conclusion that the United States is demanding the withdrawal from the South not only of North Vietnamese but also of Vietcong forces as a prior condition for an American withdrawal.[6]

The U.S. insistence on such preconditions helps explain why the NLF and Hanoi have become so intransigent toward American proposals for negotiations. They are not only convinced that Washington demands both the capitulation of the Vietcong and the withdrawal of Hanoi's forces before entering into any political settlement. They also fear that the United States will insist upon the retention of permanent military bases in the South and that any armistice agreement would be susceptible to subsequent violation by the United States.

In arguing for the prior (or concurrent) withdrawal of communist forces from the South, Washington fails to appreciate the past conditioning of the Southern communists. The post-Geneva withdrawal of Vietminh troops to the North was dependent on a compromise political settlement, and because this was never enforced the communists lost an ascendant position that they had won on the battlefield. Remembering this, they will neither risk obliteration again through a settlement that afterwards leaves them at the mercy of an American-supported Saigon government, nor countenance an agreement that obliges them to yield even temporarily at the conference table a political position built up through long struggle and sacrifice. Doubting that the United States will accept the terms of a compromise settlement permanently, the communists can be expected to insist that any formula for returning to the Geneva Agreements (or any other negotiated resolution of the conflict) provide strong guarantees enforced by an effective international supervisory body and by an unequivocal commitment of the United States to the agreed political settlement that is to follow an armistice. Whereas after Geneva the provisions for the interdependence of the political settlement and the military armistice were not enforceable, at any future conference the communists will demand guarantees for ensuring that inter-dependence.

If the United States wishes to achieve a peaceful political settlement in Vietnam, it must recognize that any lasting solution must be worked out by the Vietnamese themselves and cannot be imposed from outside. For the principal Vietnamese factions in the South to have any chance of arriving at such a solution, they must be able to engage in political activity under conditions in which the American presence is not dominant and the conduct of military operations is not the overriding consideration. In order to provide these conditions, it is necessary to set in motion a progressive de-escalation of the warfare.

The continuing American insistence that the war in the South is simply a case of aggression from the North has led to erroneous conclusions concerning de-escalation. Principal among these is that an American de-escalation against the North must be reciprocated by an equivalent de-escalation by the North. But there is no equivalency in the capacities of Hanoi and Washington for de-escalation. Since Hanoi was unable to match the American bombing of North Vietnam with its own bombing of the United States, it similarly lacks the capacity to provide the military equivalent of an American cessation of this bombing. The disparity in military positions and capacities leads Washington to insist upon Hanoi's responding to a cessation of American bombing of the North by the withdrawal of Northern troops from the South and a decrease of Vietcong activity there—actions which in fact constitute fundamental political concessions. Even if Hanoi were disposed to reciprocate in accordance with this American demand, the Vietcong would be unlikely to scale down its actions unless there were at least an equivalent de-escalation in the South by both the United States and Saigon.

The major arguments for a cessation of the bombing of the North stand quite apart from the question of any possible military equivalency in the Northern response. An unconditional cessation of the bombing of the North would be the first earnest of American peaceful intent necessary to secure the active participation of the Soviet Union and other Geneva powers in setting up the negotiations that must precede any political solution. It would also be an indispensable condition for the North to consider a subsequent disengagement from the South, and it would be of indirect benefit in helping to create a general climate within Vietnam conducive to eventual peaceful discussions. While a cessation of the bombing of the North would produce no settlement in itself, it is an antecedent and necessary step to any future peaceful resolution of the conflict in the South.

The crucial de-escalation would have to take place in South Vietnam. There, a steady decrease in the offensive military operations of the United States, whether coincident with or followed by that of the North Vietnamese, would best be accompanied by a progressive buildup of an impartial international political presence, preferably endowed with significant military attributes. A principal objective of this process would be to reach a situation where the suppressed political forces in the South could reassert themselves and also begin working out a political accommodation among themselves and with Saigon and the NLF. To promote this freedom of political activity, it would be necessary for the United States to oblige the Saigon regime to yield to the decisions of an international supervisory body charged with protecting the interests of all parties in the South. Along such lines the United States can help provide the means for the Vietnamese to work out their own settlement. The Vietnamese themselves must be free to determine the ends that any settlement is to secure.

While military de-escalation could make this possible, progress toward a peaceful solution would be slow and unpredictable. The wall of mutual mistrust that has grown up between the belligerents will not be broken down overnight. The history of the United States in Vietnam has shown how the relationships of the various parties have become entangled in emotional and incompatible commitments. For this reason alone any policy of de-escalation must be accompanied by a patience and statesmanship wherein the United States is willing to work for political compromise with the same perseverence and energy that it has displayed in pursuing its military ends. If the United States is prepared to fight additional years for a military victory, it must similarly be prepared to strive as long and hard for a peaceful political settlement.

In the end this will require Washington's willingness to accept an outcome in Vietnam that is reasonably representative of the balance of political forces that actually exists there. It is improbable that such a settlement would mirror the pattern most congenial to the United States or that it would be attuned to the exigencies of American domestic politics. But it would be more likely to be politically viable and lasting than any settlement imposed by American power.

Notes to Chapter XIII

1. On March 9, 1966, the Department of State also revealed that "about 20,000 acres of South Vietnamese crops had been destroyed with herbicides to deny food to the guerrillas." This figure did not include the use of defoliants to deny cover to the guerrilla forces. *New York Times,* March 10, 1966. On September 10, 1966, the *Times* reported that the military is taking steps to triple its efforts at chemical defoliation and crop destruction.

2. U.S. Senate, *U.S. Policy with Respect to Mainland China,* 89th Congress, 2nd Session (Washington: U.S. Government Printing Office, 1966), p. 349. See also Neil Sheehan, "Not a Dove, But No Longer a Hawk," *New York Times Magazine,* October 9, 1966, pp. 134–137.

3. *New York Times,* July 5, 1966.

4. *Ibid.,* November 5, 1966.

5. Saigon Radio, October 26, 1966. The Manila communiqué did not make clear what fate lay in store for the remaining locally based Vietcong guerrillas and sympathizers. According to the *New York Times,* Marshal Ky insisted that "South Vietnam will be left free to deal with its purely internal problems—including the mopping-up of local guerrilla resistance—and that these internal questions will not be made part of an agreed international solution to the war." *New York Times,* October 30, 1966.

6. *Ibid.,* November 13, 1966. Also relevant was the statement made in behalf of Mr. McNamara in late October by Assistant Secretary of Defense Townsend Hoopes. Referring to what previously had been thought a relatively moderate position described by the U.S. Ambassador to the United Nations, he stated that the Defense Department "believes Ambassador Goldberg's speech includes the intent that Vietcong military units would be deactivated in any proposed withdrawal of external forces from South Vietnam." Officials reportedly interpreted this statement as meaning the departure of some 60,000 main-force Vietcong guerrilla fighters as well as the 47,000 North Vietnamese regulars then estimated to be in the South.

CHAPTER XIV

1967-1969

1: **The Johnson Administration** went into 1967 convinced that it was marshalling military power in Vietnam sufficient to ensure the NLF's capitulation.* The uncompromising position laid down by the President at the Manila Conference of October 1966 remained unaltered.

During January, however, there were several indications that Hanoi was prepared to enter into talks with the U.S. in return for a cessation of the bombing of the North. A small element within the Department of State centering around Averell Harriman hoped that an understanding might be reached whereby Hanoi would be permitted to avoid any public acceptance of military reciprocity. They believed that if this could be arranged, the North Vietnamese might be willing to agree to mutual de-escalation of military activity in the South following a halt in American bombardment of the North. It appeared that Soviet Premier Kosygin and British Prime Minister Wilson saw some promise in this approach when they discussed it in London in early February.

---

* At the beginning of the year the U.S. had 385,000 men in Vietnam, the main combat units of which were organized into 256 maneuver battalions. U.S. forces were committed to two large engagements as the year began—Operations Cedar Falls and Junction City. On January 12, 1967, the Commander in Chief Pacific, Admiral U. S. G. Sharp told General Earle G. Wheeler, Chairman of the Joint Chiefs of Staff, that the objective of the bombing of the North for 1967 (Operation Rolling Thunder) was "to cause North Vietnam to cease supporting, controlling, and directing insurgencies in Southeast Asia." Commander in Chief Pacific and Commander, U.S. Military Assistance Command, Vietnam, *Report on the War in Vietnam (As of June 1968)* (Washington: U.S. Government Printing Office, 1969), p. 31.

But the possibility of Premier Kosygin's using his good offices with Hanoi following these discussions was destroyed when President Johnson ruled out such an approach and instead sent a letter to Ho Chi Minh tying very strong conditions to any American bombing halt.[1] In his letter of February 8, 1967,[2] the first day of a brief Tet truce, the President stipulated that the U.S. would not cease its bombing of the North until after Hanoi had stopped all infiltration into South Vietnam; only then would the U.S. be willing to stop increasing its own forces. For Washington, "infiltration" by Hanoi meant not only the sending of additional troops to the South, but also the supply of ammunition and other materiel to Northern soldiers already fighting there. President Johnson's willingness to freeze the level of American troops in South Vietnam (now approximately eight times as numerous as North Vietnamese troops there) in return for a pledge by North Vietnam to halt its infiltration did not mean that the United States would stop the flow of arms, ammunition and rations to American and Saigon forces. The United States was thus reserving the right to continue its supplies on the massive scale made possible by American shipping and air power, while denying the North Vietnamese government the right to resupply the Vietcong and its own forces previously sent to the South.

President Johnson apparently expected such terms to be unacceptable to Ho Chi Minh since he ordered a resumption of the bombing on February 14, before receiving the Vietnamese leader's response to his letter.* In fact, the President de-

---

* On February 11, the Vietnamese Ambassador in Moscow informed the U.S. Ambassador there that President Johnson's letter of February 8 had been received in Hanoi and that a response was currently being prepared. The American bombing was resumed on February 14, the day before the date of Ho Chi Minh's letter replying to President Johnson, and well before it could be delivered. In his letter of February 15 Ho did not insist that before peace talks could start a cessation of American bombing of

layed the renewal of air strikes, suspended for the three-day Tet (Lunar New Year's) truce, only long enough to permit Premier Kosygin to return to Moscow from his London talks with Prime Minister Wilson.[3]

2 : The flexibility of U.S. policies was seriously limited by Washington's unquestioning support for the Saigon military leadership. This had intensified the polarization in South Vietnamese politics and blocked virtually all possibilities for the exercise of political influence by any element outside the military. American backing for the junta stemmed basically from the Administration's desire for stability in Saigon and its belief that only a military regime could achieve this and at the same time prosecute the war in accordance with American objectives. Conversely, the Administration feared and opposed the creation of any representative civilian government, for it recognized that any government commanding broad popular support would make its first priority a peaceful settlement, an objective that necessarily involved negotiations and accommodation with the NLF. By the beginning of 1967 the Saigon military leadership was convinced that it could count on unquestioned American backing, not only against the NLF but against all noncommunist civilian challengers, whether Buddhist or other elements excluded from power in Saigon. Civilians shared this view and the dejected Buddhist leadership now considered American power to be so decisive in Vietnamese politics that it would be futile for them to make any moves unless these were at least tacitly favored by the Americans—a prospect which the Buddhists had now come to regard as completely unrealistic.

---

the North would have to be "permanent" (as President Johnson in his letter of February 8 had indicated Hanoi was demanding), but he continued to insist that the cessation would have to be "unconditional." For the text of Ho's reply see *New York Times,* March 22, 1967.

The position of the generals and colonels who dominated the Saigon regime was wholly dependent on sustained U.S. military and economic backing. They were confident that the United States would maintain a military shield for them and bear the brunt of the fighting against the Vietcong for an indefinite period. Thus protected, the Saigon military leadership hoped ultimately to build up for itself sufficient political as well as military power to compete effectively with the NLF. Their assumption of a continuing American military shield was generally evident among top military leaders. Thus, General Pham Xuan Chieu, Secretary General of the National Leadership Committee, an officer generally regarded by American officials as politically the most astute of the junta, said in January 1967 to one of the authors:

> We are very weak politically and without the strong political support of the population which the NLF have. Thus, now even if we defeat them militarily, they can come to power because of their greater political strength. We now have—thanks to the support of our allies—a strong military instrument. But we are without a political instrument that can compete with the communists in the South. Such a political instrument we must now begin to create, a process that will take a generation. It is unrealistic to speak of a cease-fire until after we have built up our political strength to a point where we can compete with the communists successfully—a decade from now at least. Thus your President's statement at Manila that U.S. troops would begin withdrawal within six months of a settlement makes no sense. We must have military victory *plus* political superiority first.

Confident of American backing, Saigon's military leaders felt free to manage and control the process of constitution-making and elections in the months that followed. They forced through a constitution and organized elections in ways calculated to ensure their continuing control of all the levers of real political power.

Within this process, the American role was largely confined to ensuring that the generals cooperated with each other and agreed to a single military ticket in the presidential elections scheduled for September 1967.[4] Ellsworth Bunker on replacing Henry Cabot Lodge as U.S. Ambassador to Saigon in mid-March 1967 showed less partiality than his predecessor for Premier Ky but was equally wed to the formula of unstinting American support for the military junta as the basis for political stability in South Vietnam.

During the first half of 1967 the constituent assembly, under the watchful eye of the military leaders,* completed the drafting of a new constitution (which was promulgated April 1, and took effect on May 1) and drew up a set of laws for the election of a President, a Senate and a Lower House, to take place the following September and October.

Within the constituent assembly there was a small but determined minority which was willing to challenge the junta openly in an effort to write a constitution and an election law designed to establish a civilian-controlled government. However, Chief of State Thieu and Premier Ky had such a solid endorsement from their military colleagues as to render these efforts ineffective.

The ardor of dissident members of the assembly in pressing for civilian supremacy was also dampened by a series of intimidating incidents. On December 7, 1966, Tran Van Van, one of its most forceful and articulate members, was assassinated just after advocating a constitutional measure to prevent anyone less than forty from serving as president, thereby ruling out Premier Ky, who was only thirty-seven. Van's

---

* All provisions of the constitution were drafted only after being approved by the military's National Leadership Committee. Regular unpublicized meetings were held between delegates of the constituent assembly and members of the junta, with General Pham Xuan Chieu, Secretary General of the Committee, serving as liaison with the assembly.

widow publicly blamed his murder on General Nguyen Ngoc Loan, a principal lieutenant of Ky and head of the national police, a judgment that was widespread among Western correspondents as well as members of the constituent assembly.[5] The assembly backed down and accepted an age limit of thirty-five. Many also blamed Loan for the subsequent unsuccessful efforts to assassinate Buddhist leader Thien Minh and Dr. Phan Quang Dan, another critic of Premier Ky. These two incidents, along with a host of minor ones, combined to produce an atmosphere of fear and caution in the assembly, which was reinforced by steady, though for the most part unpublicized, pressure from the generals. Repeatedly the assembly capitulated on key issues and accepted their views.

Principal among these issues was the constitutional provision for the future presidency. Expecting that one of their own number would occupy that office, the military leaders insisted that it be a powerful one, capable of dominating the Premier and the legislative branch. As finally written, Article 64 of the constitution endowed the President with wide emergency decree powers that could be invoked largely at his own discretion, and Article 114 stipulated that for the four-year term of the first president all province chiefs would be appointed by him rather than elected.

Military leaders also prevented candidates unacceptable to them from running in the elections. The most easily eliminated were the 10,000–20,000 political prisoners already in jails and concentration camps.* Many of these were noncommunist, including politically active Buddhists and their

---

* Furthermore, the rate of arrests and detentions in the months before the elections grew appreciably. Shortly after the elections the Saigon government disclosed that it was releasing 6,270 prisoners of various categories; it refused to reveal how many remained in prison but a "ranking official" described the 6,270 as only a "tiny fraction" of the total. A little over a year later, on December 21, 1968, in the course of a plenary session of South Vietnam's Senate it was disclosed that in 1968 a total of some 32,000 people had

adherents who had been rounded up by Ky following his suppression of the Buddhist struggle movement in mid-1966.

Equally important in screening out candidates unacceptable both to the military leadership and the assembly's ultra-conservative membership*   was a provision which in effect permitted courts appointed by the government to determine which of those Vietnamese nationalists arrested "for political reasons" by the French, Diem, or subsequent governments would be permitted to stand for election. (A similar provision was incorporated in the election laws for the Senate and Lower House.)[7] With the "legal" sanction of such provisions, a government led by military leaders who had fought for the French against the Vietminh was empowered to decide which of those nationalists who had fought against France would be permitted to compete in the election.†

---

been detained, of whom about half, approximately 16,000, were political prisoners. In the course of this discussion one senator stated that expenditures on food in prisons had risen because "many persons are kept in jail for six or seven months without trial." *Chinh-Luan* ("*Right Opinion*"), December 23, 1968. This newspaper is strongly anticommunist and owned by Dang Van Sung, a major leader of the Dai Viet Party. See above, p. 110. Of the freed prisoners 1,120 were described as "political detainees," individuals who had been held, generally without trial, for periods up to three years. However, few if any of those freed were students and Buddhists arrested in the 1966 demonstrations. *New York Times*, November 4, 1967. Finally in December 1967, many of these Buddhists were brought to trial. See Robert Shaplen, "Letter from Saigon," *The New Yorker,* January 20, 1968.

* The narrow socio-economic representation of the assembly was dramatized when one of its few members of any stature, Dr. Phan Quang Dan, attempted to introduce a constitutional provision providing for land reform. This measure would have vested ownership of land with the peasants who worked it and was regarded by Dr. Dan as essential if Saigon were to have any chance of competing with the NLF for the allegiance of the peasantry.[6] From the assembly's 117 members it received just three votes.

† A similar provision, couched in almost identical language, had been incorporated into the election law for the constituent assembly, but when the authors wrote the first edition of this book they did not appreciate its significance, as was evidently also the case

In drafting the election laws, it was, of course, unlikely that constituent assembly members whose own selection had been so tightly screened[8] would accept a more open electoral process for the new institutions of government. The mesh in the screen for keeping out any proponents of a negotiated peace settlement would predictably be just as tight. In addition, the junta's Leadership Committee would not countenance any relaxation that would permit peace candidates in the election, whether they were anticommunist, procommunist or neutralist. Thus, the final election laws for the President, Senate and Lower House all stipulated that no one could stand as a candidate who had "directly or indirectly worked for communism or pro-communist neutralism or worked in the interests of communism."[9] As had been anticipated, the junta insisted that this provision be interpreted so as to eliminate all candidates known to advocate a peaceful settlement and negotiations with the NLF.

Finally the military prescribed that there would be no runoff election and that the President would be elected by a simple plurality, regardless of the percentage of votes secured by the winning candidate.[10] If, as was anticipated, no individual received a majority in the initial voting, civilian candidates would thereby be prevented from joining forces on a second ballot against the military candidate. The junta was not disposed to test the firmness of its support against any individual civilian ticket.

3 : Notwithstanding the procedural safeguards that had been established for the election, the political solidarity of the military was initially threatened by the competing presidential candidacies of Ky and Thieu.

---

with American correspondents in Saigon. It was only in talking with political leaders in Saigon in December 1966 and January 1967 that the importance of this feature of the constituent assembly election law was understood. In fact, this feature of the law received particular attention in Saigon's underground press.

At the end of June an emergency meeting of the National Leadership Committee ended this rivalry by uniting behind Thieu as its presidential choice. Over the previous months, General Thieu had been patiently and skillfully building up among the top military officers a position of ascendancy over Ky, a process in which he was widely believed to have been encouraged by Ambassador Bunker. In thrusting himself forward as the army's candidate,* Premier Ky had apparently not realized the extent to which his previous backing by the most influential officers had been eroded. Finding the balance within the Committee inclined against him, he was obliged to abandon his presidential aspirations and stand instead as the vice-presidential candidate on the Thieu ticket. Ky agreed to this, however, only after securing a number of important concessions through which he hoped to retain considerable power in any new government.

Apparently the same meeting of the Leadership Committee also dealt with the threat posed by General Duong Van Minh's candidacy for the Presidency. Minh, a Southerner in exile in Bangkok,† was known to have a popular following far broader than any other military figure, and it was generally expected that he could easily outpoll any other military candidate. His intention to run for President was made public on June 28, and Premier Ky promptly forbade his return. The Leadership Committee approved this decision. §

---

* Although the election law forbade campaigning prior to August, already in May Ky had announced substantial cash bonuses for all government employees and was using full governmental facilities to promote his election. When radio and television carried spot messages lauding him, Ky defended this breach of the election law by saying: "What is the use of TV and radio if not to serve the propaganda of the government." *New York Times,* June 16, 1967. See also *Saigon Post,* June 16, 1967.

† It was Minh who had taken over after the assassination of Diem, but was himself ousted by a coup in January 1964. (See above, pp. 151–152.)

§ Premier Ky also persisted in his refusal to permit the return of another popular general, Nguyen Chanh Thi, who still com-

This action was in flagrant disregard of the assembly and the Central Election Council, which under the election laws had full authority for approving candidates and supervising the elections. In defiance of the junta, the constituent assembly on July 7 approved General Minh's candidacy by the overwhelming majority of 72 to 13. But it could not withstand pressure from the generals and later rescinded this decision.

Meantime, another source of concern for the military was presented by the prospective candidacy of Au Truong Thanh, a prominent Southerner and previously a Minister for Economic Affairs in the Ky cabinet. Thanh had led a cabinet revolt in the fall of 1966 against the lack of Southern representation in the government and later publicly challenged the right of Thieu and Ky to run for office while controlling the government.[11] Not only was Thanh prominent in his own right, but also he had based his platform on a cease-fire and a bombing halt. The military was so aware of the great popularity of the peace issue that the press, in reporting Thanh's candidacy, was forbidden to print his election symbol, a bomb with an "X" superimposed on it, or his motto of "ceasefire." The government quickly mounted a campaign to discredit Thanh. The police alleged that they had a confession made by him in 1960 admitting to Marxist views, and in the constituent assembly supporters of Ky accused Thanh of being a communist.[12] Thanh replied that these allegations were a bit incongruous in view of the fact that Ky had previously appointed him Minister of Economic Affairs and had had plenty of opportunity at that time to review his record. Despite the government's attacks, it appeared that a majority of the constituent assembly would approve Thanh's candidacy

---

manded substantial support at least in the I Corps Area, and who had been obliged to leave the country for Washington in 1966 and not permitted to return. Evidently the junta also supported Ky in this decision.

and that he would benefit in the upcoming campaign from the widespread sentiment for peace.

On July 18, 1967, the constituent assembly met to consider the Central Election Council's recommendations on candidacies. The Council had just refused to approve the Thieu and Ky ticket because they had violated the provision requiring them to resign from public office prior to running for election. Maximum pressure was now mounted by the military to bend the assembly to its will. Most of this pressure was exerted behind the scenes, but there was abundant visible evidence of the junta's determination. Police and troops in Saigon were put on alert, and around the balcony within the constituent assembly, fully visible to all its members, strode Police General Loan flanked by two armed guards.[13] Both the Central Election Council* and the assembly backed down. Of the 75 out of 117 deputies attending the assembly's session, 56 voted to approve the Thieu-Ky ticket and a majority voted to disqualify the candidacies of both General Minh and Au Truong Thanh. † Out of the seventeen presidential slates

---

* As to the pressure exerted on the Central Election Council, one should also note the following: The assembly's representative on the Council resigned shortly afterwards, contending that the Council had been subjected to so much pressure from the government while screening presidential and senatorial tickets that it had been unable to do its job. *New York Times*, August 11, 1967. The member of the Central Election Council who had the reputation for being the most independent-minded in this official-dominated body was the President of the Saigon Bar Association. His secretary was murdered the night before the Council made its recommendations on the candidates to the constituent assembly. This fact received little or no attention in the press, but was subsequently corroborated to one of the writers by a high U.S. official, who as late as October 1967 stated that nothing more was known about the assassination and that it was still "being looked into."

† Minh's candidacy was refused on the ground that his running mate had at one time held French citizenship, but in any case, Ky had still refused to permit his return to South Vietnam; Au Truong Thanh was charged as "procommunist and neutralist."

submitted to it, the constituent assembly validated eleven.

Thus the outcome of the presidential election was easily predictable; so long as the antagonism between Thieu and Ky could be kept submerged and their ticket intact, the military was assured of victory. With the strongest civilian candidates eliminated, with the military united behind a single ticket, and with the outcome to be decided by a simple plurality, the actual process of balloting seemed of relatively small importance.* For with the anti-Thieu vote split between ten candidates, no one civilian ticket could expect to outpoll the military's ticket, even if a fair ballot were permitted.

The only unforeseen factor was the linking of one civilian candidate's name to the peace issue. Shortly after his candidacy had been validated by the Election Council and the constituent assembly, Truong Dinh Dzu, a relatively unknown Saigon lawyer without much public following or previous political experience, announced a peace platform (with a dove as his election symbol) and advocated negotiations with the NLF. It was significant that by running on such a platform a political unknown such as Dzu was able to outpoll all other civilian candidates.

Initially Thieu and Ky appeared confident of victory. However, in the final week before the elections their confidence turned to alarm, causing them to make open threats and reprisals against supporters of the opposition. Their principal concern was that the army was not remaining sufficiently

---

He was arrested on Ky's orders on September 22, but, after strong representations from the U.S. Embassy, was released. In late 1968, following more than a year of intermittent harassment, he was permitted to leave the country.

* Realizing the predetermined outcome, the civilian candidates spent almost as much of their time in trying to demonstrate that the election was unfair as in discussing the issues. "The probable result on September 4," the *New York Times* observed in advance, will be "the same regime, 'legitimized' by a process the world already considers illegitimate." (*New York Times,* August 14, 1967.)

united behind them, with some officers throwing their support to one or another of the most prominent civilian candidates. Just before the election a reorganization of the army was proposed, two opposition newspapers were closed,[14] and there were several arrests,* removals and transfers of officers regarded as opposed to the government ticket.[15]

South Vietnamese were generally aware of the extent of irregularities and government manipulation in the voting. They were made all the more cynical by President Johnson's dispatch of twenty-two prominent Americans to observe and report back on the election. To many Vietnamese it seemed preposterous that a group of foreigners, ignorant of the Vietnamese language, history and politics, led by ex-Ambassador Henry Cabot Lodge and shepherded by members of the American Embassy staff and Premier Ky's Information Ministry, should presume to judge the honesty of these elections.[16] The object of this exercise seemed attuned more to American than Vietnamese politics, with its major purpose to make U.S. policy in Vietnam more respectable to an American audience.[17]

The Johnson Administration pointed to the high popular turnout, a reported four and three-quarter million voters (83 per cent of those classified as eligible) going to the polls, as an indication of the popular base and democratic character of the government in Vietnam. The size of the vote, however, bore little relation to popular interest in the elections. Since the government officials who administered the balloting stamped each individual's voting card as proof of his having voted, the belief was widespread that one courted trouble if he lacked this symbol of loyalty to Saigon. †

---

* Among those officers placed under house arrest was the influential Colonel Pham Van Lieu, who had been working for the return of General Thi and in support of the candidacy of Phan Khac Suu.

† This belief was the stronger because of memories from the Diem years, when a somewhat similar system of card stamping had been employed in elections.

On September 5, 1967, the government announced its final official tabulation of the election returns. The Thieu-Ky ticket had won a clear plurality, 1,649,561 votes or 35 per cent of the 4,735,404 votes cast. The slate led by Truong Dinh Dzu, as noted above, ran a surprising second, and secured a total of 817,120 or 17 per cent of the vote.* The third largest total was that of Phan Khac Suu and Dr. Phan Quang Dan, whose ticket won 513,374 votes, or 11 per cent. The fourth largest total—474,100 or 10 per cent—was for the presidential ticket led by Tran Van Huong.[19]

Many gross incongruities in the election results reinforced the popular conclusion that balloting irregularities and pressures by the junta had been widespread.[20] Following publication of the results, opposition candidates joined with students and Buddhists in a series of demonstrations against these irregularities. †

These demonstrations reportedly provided Ky with useful leverage in bargaining with Thieu[21] for a greater role in the

---

* Ten days later the junta visited reprisal on Dzu by convicting him for alleged violation of currency regulations five years before. The following year a military court sentenced him to five years hard labor for having "weakened the fighting spirit of the Vietnamese armed forces" through statements wherein he was alleged to have urged formation of a coalition government as a step toward peace.[18]

† The constituent assembly reported that irregularities involved 2,724 out of 8,954 ballot boxes containing 1,449,647 votes. Although they accepted these figures, the adherents of Thieu and Ky opposed invalidation of the elections, arguing that if these numbers were subtracted from the totals of the leading candidates Thieu would have led by an even larger percentage. *Washington Post*, October 3, 1967, and *New York Times,* October 3, 1967.

It has remained difficult to analyze and form an overall judgment as to the extent of such electoral irregularities because both the Saigon government and the U.S. Department of State have refused to make public the district-by-district breakdown of votes. Presumably this is because of the widely made charge that there were a number of serious discrepancies between the statistics for provincial election totals and the district returns.

new government. At a secret session of the junta a compromise was worked out between the two leaders so that the military could present a solid front to the constituent assembly when that body voted on the validity of the elections. At the close of the junta's session on September 30, a spokesman reported that Thieu and Ky were now in accord, and that despite the modest position assigned to the Vice-President under the constitution, Ky would in fact be given a "greatly expanded" role.* With this assured, Ky then instructed his delegates in the assembly to join with the minority who already supported validation of the elections.

Meanwhile, the Central Election Council had conveyed to the assembly all the contents of its files on the presidential elections. A special committee of the assembly then convened to cross-check its own figures with those of the Council, and make its recommendations to the entire assembly.[22] On September 30, this committee voted 16 to 2, with one abstention, to recommend invalidation of the election results.[23] As the assembly began the process of debating this recommendation the U.S. mission in Saigon, "having now been apprised of the Thieu-Ky rapprochement and utterly reconciled to its implications, made it unmistakably clear to the delegates that America's commitment to South Vietnam would be endangered were the elections to be invalidated."[24] With Ky having won his concessions from Thieu, General Loan moved to disperse the demonstrations that had been mounted to protest the irregularities in the elections.

---

* In return for receiving Ky's public support, Thieu was reported to have agreed to keep several close Ky aides in the government. *Washington Post*, October 1, 1967. This was made clear when in the formation of the new government on October 31, his candidate, Nguyen Van Loc, was appointed Premier, and on November 3 when three of Ky's closest aides were appointed Ministers respectively of Defense, Interior, and Pacification. In addition, Nguyen Ngoc Loan, head of the national police force, was promoted to the rank of permanent brigadier general.

As the assembly met to vote on whether or not the elections should be validated, the junta did its best to determine the outcome.[25] With General Loan and two riot policemen again pacing the balcony inside the assembly chamber, the delegates voted to take a secret ballot. However, General Loan's men kept a running tally of this "secret" vote by peering down into the voting booths. By a vote of 58 to 43, the assembly agreed to validate the election. A month later Thieu and Ky were sworn in as President and Vice-President.*

The elections for the Senate (which had been held concurrently with those for the Presidency) were also attended by widespread irregularities. The outcome of these elections hardly contributed to any broadening of the government's political base. † A screening committee ruled out 16 slates, including two identified with Buddhists close to Thich Tri Quang and one with the labor unions. All slates led by advo-

---

* Nguyen Van Thieu was born on April 5, 1923, in Phan Rang, a provincial capital 150 miles northeast of Saigon. He graduated in 1949 from the French-run Vietnamese Military Academy and under the French had by 1954 attained the rank of colonel. As a Catholic convert, Thieu rose rapidly under Ngo Dinh Diem's regime to become commander of the Fifth Infantry Division, a unit that played a decisive part in the anti-Diem coup of 1963. In the years that followed Thieu became one of the few leaders of that coup to remain in a position of power. He had been Premier Quat's Minister of Defense and along with other members of the military junta was instrumental in ousting him in favor of Air Marshal Ky in June 1965. When Ky became Premier, General Thieu was appointed Chief of State by the junta's National Leadership Committee of which he had emerged as chairman. For an account of Thieu's career, see Kevin P. Buckley, "No One Can Be Sure What Thieu is Thinking," *New York Times Magazine*, March 2, 1969.

† On October 22, 1967, elections held for the Lower House returned a somewhat more representative membership than was the case with the Senate. In the 137-member Lower House, 30 were military and 29 civil officials. Of those whose religious affiliations could be determined 46 were reported to be Buddhists, 35 Catholic, 13 Hoa Hao and 5 Cao Dai.[26]

cates of a negotiated peace settlement were excluded. The composition of the Senate was strongly conservative; approximately half its sixty members were Catholic (even though Catholics constitute only 10 per cent of the population) and about one-quarter were former members of Diem's Can Lao party. Twenty-seven of the total reportedly were former refugees from North Vietnam.[27]

With the elections over, President Johnson could now assure the American public that the sacrifices they were making in Vietnam were in support of a "legitimate," freely elected government representing the will of the South Vietnamese people. However farcical the election appeared at the time, henceforth Washington in defending its policies would refer to "the elected government of South Vietnam." The opportunity for effectively broadening the base of the Saigon regime had been lost. Whatever leverage it gained in dealing with opposition to the war in the United States, the Johnson Administration was now tied even closer to the Thieu-Ky leadership. As a consequence, in any future negotiations Washington's options would be narrowly restricted by the predictably rigid viewpoint of a highly unrepresentative South Vietnamese government, whose popular base was so narrow that it could not risk any meaningful compromise without courting its own destruction. The Administration, instead of using its influence and power to help develop greater political strength for non-NLF South Vietnamese in meeting the challenge of future negotiations, had, in fact, helped perpetuate Saigon's political weakness. The majority of noncommunists in Saigon-controlled areas had been excluded from any effective participation in their own government, and an overall political polarization had been rigidified between a narrowly based military clique in Saigon and the NLF.

4: The National Liberation Front seemed well aware of this situation and of how narrow the popular base of the

Saigon government continued to be. On September 1, 1967, the very eve of the balloting, the Front made public a detailed new program, consistent with previous ones[28] but with greater emphasis upon the broadest possible appeal.* According to this program, the NLF was "prepared to invite and welcome all patriotic forces and individuals who oppose U.S. aggressors to join its ranks, and to shoulder together the common duties." But it did not insist that those sharing its goals join the NLF; it proposed that they take "joint action . . . against the common enemy—the U.S. aggressors and their lackeys," even if "for one reason or another" they did not elect to become part of the NLF. † In directives to its own forces a specific appeal was made to encourage the defection of Saigon's military personnel and civilian officials.

To bring about a new South Vietnamese government the

---

* This program stated: "The tasks and objectives of the South Vietnamese people in the struggle for national salvation are now as follows: To unite the entire people, resolutely defeat the U.S. imperialists' war of aggression, overthrow their lackey puppet administration, establish a broad national union and democratic administration and build an independent, peaceful, neutral, and prosperous South Vietnam and proceed towards the peaceful reunification of the fatherland." For text of this program adopted officially in "mid August 1967" see Hanoi Radio, September 1, 1967.

† In elucidating the NLF's position on cooperation with other groups, Nguyen Van Hieu, a top official of the NLF, and formerly its Secretary-General, stated on August 11, 1967, to one of the authors: "The NLF is willing to cooperate in a common action program and work parallel with representative groups which share at least some of its objectives, and for this it is not necessary for them to join the NLF." It would be possible, he said, to work with the militant Buddhists "towards common goals such as do exist. There does not have to be organizational linkage for the NLF to work with them and other genuinely representative groups for common action programs. Such common action programs could, for instance, be in any of the areas relating to the five basic goals of the NLF, for some of these goals are shared by such representative groups still standing outside of the NLF. These goals are five: peace, independence, democracy, neutrality, reunification."

NLF called for the following steps: (1) abolish the existing Saigon regime and "overthrow its puppet administration"; (2) "hold free general elections to elect a national assembly in a really democratic way in accordance with the principle of universal, equal, direct suffrage and secret ballot"; (3) as the "state body with the highest authority in South Vietnam" this national assembly "will work out a democratic constitution" which will "guarantee the establishment of a broad, progressive, democratic state structure"; and (4) "set up a national union democratic government including the most representative persons among the various social strata, nationalities, religious communities, patriotic and democratic parties, patriotic personalities, and forces which have contributed to the national liberation." This new government would be "independent" and "neutral." It would "trade with all countries," "establish diplomatic relations with all countries" and "accept economic and technical assistance" from them, "regardless of their social and political systems." It would "join no military alliance" and "accept no military personnel or military bases of foreign countries on South Vietnamese territory." Emphasizing that "Vietnam is one," and that "Vietnam must be unified," the NLF appeared once again to be indicating that unification would take time and come about from a process of negotiations between equals.*

---

* Nguyen Van Hieu stated to one of the authors: "Reunification is a basic aim of the NLF, but the character of the reunification and the amount of time necessary to undertake it are not clear. Certainly, it is not something that could be carried out in two or three years, but might well take ten years. In the first place, the differences between the two Vietnams are so great that it will take a long time to accommodate the differences. The North is a socialist system and the South is an economic system still based upon private property. It will take a long time to shave down the differences between the two systems. The objective must be a normalization of relations, certainly involving commerce between the two parties." When asked whether the process of accommodation between the two Vietnams would eventuate in unity, federation,

By these provisions and its timing the NLF's program seemed calculated to appeal to those South Vietnamese whose sense of isolation from the Saigon government had been reinforced by the electoral process then underway. The program continued to serve as the fundamental statement of NLF aims, and provided the basis in May 1969 for the Front's "ten points" put forward at the Paris talks. †

5: **During the course of 1967** the Johnson Administration assured the American public that U.S. power was steadily weakening the political and military capacity of the North Vietnamese and Vietcong forces to continue the war. At the beginning of the year an increased effort was being made in the rural areas to develop a pacification program designed to secure the villages and win the peasants' loyalty to Saigon. This effort was dependent upon a military strategy which put great emphasis upon "search and destroy" operations, carried out largely by U.S. and South Korean troops. Their missions were to be followed up with complementary action by the South Vietnamese Army (ARVN) which was assigned the responsibility to "clear and hold" the territory already penetrated by American and Korean forces. ARVN units were supposed to carry out mopping-up operations by clearing out the shattered remnants of enemy forces; then with the help of specially trained pacification teams they were to organize the rural population against any future enemy penetrations.

Overall, this strategy failed. In the first place, the NLF

---

or confederation, he said it was not clear but this was something that had to be worked out step by step over a long period of time, and the ultimate outcome could not be foreseen. "It might," he said, "eventuate in two separate economies and it might eventuate in two separate governments." He added that the NLF remained "strongly in favor of a neutralization of South Vietnam, but since North Vietnam is a socialist state it could not be neutralist." Interview in Phnom Penh, August 11, 1967.

† See below, p. 394 and text in Appendix 17.

and Hanoi adapted to the American strategy and, despite heavy manpower losses, continued to deploy their forces in large concentrations so that the "search and destroy" sweeps did not effectively remove the enemy's presence from those provinces they chose to contest. As a consequence, American casualties were much higher than had been expected. The most important reason for the failure of General Westmoreland's strategy, however, was the incapacity of the South Vietnamese Army to carry out its assigned mission.[29] Although U.S. forces were capable of penetrating any Vietcong-controlled areas, their actions alone could not secure such areas for Saigon. In terms of either military or political control, U.S. deployments could have no more than transitory effect, unless they were supplemented by strong South Vietnamese "clear-and-hold" operations and an effective political follow-up.

On those occasions when South Vietnamese forces did follow in the wake of U.S. firepower, they were usually ineffective in their clearing operations. Most ARVN units refused to conduct "active patrolling," thus relaxing pressure on enemy units and failing to gain knowledge of Vietcong movements. Their posture was for the most part defensive, and they frequently lived off the rural population, rather than working with it, usually acting more like conquerors of an alien people than as their friendly protectors.[30] The brief penetration of U.S. or South Korean* troops into an area did no more than reduce temporarily the NLF's political control.

---

* By mid-1967 there were in South Vietnam approximately 50,-000 South Korean troops, approximately equal in number to the North Vietnamese troops operating there. These Korean soldiers were paid (directly or indirectly) from American funds much more than they received in Korea. South Korea's annual Vietnam dollar earnings (remittances from soldiers and several thousand civilian workers; service and construction contracts in Vietnam; and U.S. purchase of Vietnam military supplies in Korea) reached $200,000,000 in 1968. Meanwhile, the U.S. continued to station more than 50,000 of its own troops in South Korea.

Thus in terms of political impact, American operations often tended to benefit the Vietcong, for "search and destroy" missions antagonized rural populations which so often were badly mauled by them.

Official U.S. spokesmen consistently minimized the number of civilian casualties, but these were in fact high. The staff of the Senate Subcommittee on Refugees and Escapees, after having conducted an extensive survey in Vietnam at the end of 1967, estimated the total as being "between 150,000 to 200,-000,"[31] as against the Administration's official estimate of 50,000 total casualties. In addition to these casualty estimates, a substantial number of those killed who were reported as Vietcong soldiers were actually civilians unfortunate enough to be in the fighting zones. South Vietnamese government hospital statistics indicated in December 1967 that civilian casualties for the year could be expected to reach 76,000 wounded and 24,000 killed.[32] Hospital statistics, of course, reflected only a part of the casualties, for a great many of the wounded were unable even to reach them. Moreover, many of the most seriously wounded, particularly victims of napalm,[33] soon died. Of those who did reach hospitals, the majority were casualties of U.S., South Korean, and ARVN "harassment and interdiction" tactics* and attacks against whole villages from which the communists operated or were suspected to be based.[34]

Especially in the five provinces of the I Corps† an important additional cause for the ineffectiveness of pacification efforts and for the growth of the NLF's control stemmed from Premier Ky's smashing of the Buddhists' political organization in the spring and summer of 1966. For the most part, Ky removed as politically unreliable the civilian administrative officials who had sided with the local Buddhists or

---

* See below, p. 368.

† I Corps is the northernmost military region of South Vietnam. The five provinces are given on the map on p. 76.

had simply supported their ally, General Nguyen Chanh Thi. Thereby in these critical northern provinces, the existing noncommunist administrative infrastructure was largely demolished. Most of it was not rebuilt, for Ky seldom could find appointees of his own capable of securing the loyalty of the local populace. His harsh suppression of the Buddhists, and the students and civil administrators who had backed them, simply left the field open to the Front in most of this area.

This put the American Marines, who had the major military responsibility in the I Corps, at an unusual disadvantage, leaving them to face a situation much worse than they had encountered upon their arrival in mid-1965. The political context within which their military operations had to be conducted was, thus, drastically altered. For when they had first landed in 1965, there was some semblance of a coherent noncommunist rural administration in much of I Corps, but by the beginning of 1967 this area was predominantly under NLF influence.

Indeed, in January 1967, U.S. Marine officers calculated that in Quang Nam Province, out of a total of 549 hamlets, only 18 were "secure." A total of 246, with a population of 171,241, were considered as outright NLF-controlled, with the balance designated as "contested." It was estimated that there were over 150,000 refugees in Quang Nam, a large proportion of them settled in Danang, whose population had more than doubled to nearly 300,000 during the previous year.[35]

Although I Corps was an area where communist power was particularly strong, the Vietcong was dominant throughout most of the rural South.* By early 1967 it had become

---

* Even in extensive areas adjacent to Saigon itself the Vietcong was clearly ascendant. This was particularly so in Long An Province just to the south of the capital where in January 1967 American officials estimated that out of approximately 600 hamlets only 90 were controlled by the government, control being reckoned by

abundantly clear that despite the massive presence of U.S. troops, General William Westmoreland's strategy was still not succeeding. Neither were Saigon's fifty-nine-man "rural development" teams in 1967 motivated or capable of carrying out an actual program of development in the handful of villages in which they were able to work.* Regardless of the size of the American forces, the pacification program which the U.S. urged Saigon to mount in the rural areas was inherently dependent upon an effective South Vietnamese military presence. Whatever the qualifications of the Vietnamese pacification teams upon which the U.S. had counted so

---

the willingness of government-appointed officials to stay there at night. (Eighteen months later, after the introduction of new guidelines for measurement of pacification, the U.S. Army estimated that only 88 of the hamlets in Long An Province could be designated as "secure," with 268 Vietcong-controlled and 188 "contested." Col. E. R. Brigham, *Pacification Measurement in Vietnam* [Prepared for SEATO Internal Security Seminar, Manila, June 3–10, 1968], p. 16.) For additional discussion of these problems, see U.S. House of Representatives, *Measuring Hamlet Security in Vietnam*, 91st Congress, 1st Session (Washington: U.S. Government Printing Office, 1969). Apart from Vietcong village forces, two full Vietcong battalions plus two heavy companies regularly operated in the province. In the late fall of 1966, two American battalions had been introduced in order to bolster ARVN units which had proven increasingly ineffective. When one of the authors visited Long An in January 1967, one of its district capitals was just recovering from a heavy Vietcong attack and at least one other could be reached only by helicopter, an entire ARVN battalion being tied down to its static defense. In the ARVN's 25th Division, most of which was assigned to the province's defense, the desertion rate was calculated at approximately 1,000 per month. This loss involved officers as well as enlisted men, with the division's effective strength standing at 70 per cent.[36]

* The "rural development" or RD teams consisted of 34 soldiers for security and 25 trained in various phases of development work. The attrition rate of these teams from all causes was about 35 per cent in 1967. According to one U.S. report, "Of Vietnam's 12,722 hamlets, 562 were worked in by RD cadre [in 1967]. . . ." U.S. Senate, *Stalemate in Vietnam,* 90th Congress, 2nd Session (Washington: U.S. Government Printing Office, 1968), p. 15.

heavily, they were generally without the minimal ARVN military protection necessary if they were to contest politically with the NLF for the peasantry's allegiance. In effect, the tide of the political battle in the countryside continued to run heavily in favor of the NLF. As a consequence, General Westmoreland began to abandon his basic strategy of employing U.S. military power to open the way for Saigon's political control and came to concentrate on using this power simply to deny the NLF as much rural territory as possible. This in fact constituted a wholly new strategy, involving a dramatic break with the pacification goals which the U.S. had previously tried to attain, and which officially it still was pursuing. Although the official, publicized line did not change, the substance of U.S. policy was basically altered.

For planning and evaluation purposes, and to assess for the American people the political and military balance in South Vietnam, the Johnson Administration made wide use of maps and charts purporting to show the relative degree of population control exercised by the two sides. Initially, three categories were used: white, designating areas controlled by Saigon and American forces; black, designating areas controlled by the Vietcong; and grey, indicating contested territory. But by the end of 1966 this threefold cartography no longer sufficed.* Except in the Mekong Delta, an addi-

---

* In addition to these color-coded maps, the U.S. since 1966 has used a system of computer-tabulated monthly reports on the extent of Saigon's control relating to approximately 12,650 hamlets. Rating is made for only 8,650, the rest considered permanently under Vietcong control. Hamlets are rated "A," "B," or "C" if reasonably secure, "D" or "E" if contested, and "V" if under the NLF. A copy of the worksheet used in the Hamlet Evaluation System is in *Measuring Hamlet Security in Vietnam, op. cit.* According to Senator Joseph Clark: "There is pressure from above to upgrade the hamlets. One senior U.S. adviser told me frankly, 'I'm in trouble with [then Deputy Ambassador] Komer because I'm not gobbling up hamlets—making them "A," "B" or "C." ' " *Stalemate in Vietnam,* p. 13.

tional dimension to the conflict was being added, making it necessary to superimpose on the old maps a new and expanding fourth category. This was made up of "harassment and interdiction" or "free-fire" zones—the frequently extensive areas that U.S. artillery and planes intermittently bombarded in order to render them uninhabitable and thus deny them to enemy control.[37] This tactic, along with the "search and destroy" operations, created the majority of South Vietnam's swelling refugee population.

Orginally the designation of free-fire zones was prompted, exclusively, by military exigencies—to harass Vietcong units and deny them staging areas for preparing assaults on towns and military camps. In 1967, however, these free-fire zones were authorized for the additional and specific purpose of denying the enemy military forces access to the manpower and food resources of inhabited territory. Faced with the increasing inability of Saigon to assert its authority throughout rural South Vietnam, American and ARVN commanders concluded that many villages, willingly or not, were supporting the Vietcong and must therefore become targets of allied bombing and shelling. While in many cases efforts were made by American commanders either to warn the villagers or to remove them before artillery or air strikes, often this was not regarded as feasible, and it was even rarer that ARVN military commanders were concerned to save lives in this way. This bombardment was supplemented by the widespread use of chemical defoliants to deny the communists food supplies as well as cover. The peasants of course suffered most from the resulting loss of crops and many were driven by starvation to the cities.

Thus, in wide areas of South Vietnam American strategy gradually abandoned efforts to develop popular allegiance to Saigon through measures of social and political reform and instead relied on efforts to deny the guerrillas a social environment in which they could live. In practice, what was referred to as "rooting out the NLF's infrastructure" amounted to the destruction of much of South Vietnam's rural society.

When Administration spokesmen announced, as Ambassador Bunker did in November 1967, that the population under Saigon's control was growing,[38] the reported increase actually reflected the augmented number of refugees—a population which was under physical control, but for the most part scarcely to be considered loyal to Saigon or disposed to back it or the U.S. This phenomenon explains the seeming paradox that while during 1967 the number of hamlets under Saigon's control shrank, U.S. spokesmen were able to claim that the number of people under its control had grown. During this period, by the Saigon government's own figures, the number of refugees had swollen to more than two million, and these statistics did not include the tremendous number in and around Saigon and Danang.[39] Following a field study of the refugee problem in late 1967, Senator Edward Kennedy, acting in his capacity as chairman of the Senate subcommittee on refugees, concluded that refugees constituted about 25 per cent of the entire population of South Vietnam, or approximately four million. Of the refugees he and his staff encountered, over 80 per cent "claimed they were either deposited in camps by the Americans* or fled to camps in fear of

---

* Part of the program for separating the rural populace from the Vietcong involved sizeable resettlement projects such as the village of Ben Suc, the Edap Enang program in the Central Highlands, and the DMZ. Ben Suc had been a Vietcong fortified village providing rear service support to the communists and was also used as the headquarters for the Vietcong Long Nguyen secret base. The widespread publicity on the maltreatment of the Ben Suc refugees after the evacuation and obliteration of their village by American and ARVN units finally forced Saigon to build a new village, though not before destroying all hope of winning the loyalties of the peasants involved.[42] As late as March 1969, the same mistakes were being repeated in such resettlement efforts as the removal of 11,367 people from the Batangan peninsula to camps in Quang Ngai.

American airplanes and artillery. Only a handful claimed they were driven from their homes by the Vietcong."[41]

Among the people forced from the countryside there were many who no doubt had suffered from Vietcong military activities or resented its control. This segment of the population might, therefore, have been expected to respond positively to enlightened social measures. But after the trauma of their uprooting and the misery of living in the squalid "refugee camps,"[42] whatever the limitations of the NLF rule that they had previously experienced, for many of them the communists could only look the better by comparison with Saigon.

6: It was in this way that the armed forces of the U.S. and Saigon were building up large islands of hostile peasants in their rear, many of them forcibly settled in camps at the periphery of provincial and district capitals. The presence of these camps next to vital urban areas greatly augmented the ability of the Vietcong during the spring and summer of 1967 to penetrate Danang as well as all five provincial capitals in I Corps, including Hué. Although American military authorities played down the significance of these attacks—in some instances failing to report them until well after the event—in fact, they were evidence of a new dimension in the war. Despite the massive U.S. military presence in I Corps, the Vietcong had now developed the capacity to assault and penetrate any of its cities. In fact, the Vietcong was able to hold on long enough in some of these cities to release large numbers of prisoners from the jails, more than 2,000 reportedly being freed during the attacks on Hoi An, Quang Tri and Quang Ngai.[43]

The Vietcong's success in attacking these towns and cities was partly due to the presence of strong North Vietnamese forces in Quang Tri and Quang Nam provinces which diverted some of the American forces away from the cities and towards the Demilitarized Zone and the Laotian border. A particularly heavy concentration of American forces was ultimately drawn into the defense of Khe Sanh, one of a series of fortified strong points in the extreme northwest corner of South Vietnam which sat astride one of Hanoi's major supply routes from Laos.* It is not clear whether or not the enemy's actions at Khe Sanh were designed as a feint, calculated to draw more American units away from the cities.[44] In any case, the Tet offensive, begun at the end of January 1968, found a large, hastily marshalled number of American forces in the area of Khe Sanh (or poised as reserves nearby) and thus too far from focal points of the enemy's offensive to be of help quickly enough to prevent the almost simultaneous assaults against Saigon and most of the provincial capitals.

The fighting around Khe Sanh had begun on January 21, 1968, and had become intense by January 27, the first day of the seven-day nationwide Tet truce proclaimed by the Vietcong. On the 27th, 15,000 American troops were ordered to areas near Khe Sanh as covering reinforcements for the 5,000 U.S. Marines defending the base. Meantime, the South Vietnamese government had proposed a 36-hour Tet cease-fire to begin January 29.[45] However, less than an hour before it was due to commence, Saigon, citing the perilous situation at Khe Sanh and the extensive buildup of North Vietnamese forces around it, announced its cancellation of the truce in the five northern provinces of I Corps. The next day the forces of the Vietcong and Hanoi opened their biggest offensive of the war, with almost concurrent attacks on thirty-six of South Vietnam's forty-four provincial capitals. The Tet offensive caught the American and Saigon commands by

---

* According to General Westmoreland, the Marines had devised these strong points to serve as "observation posts, patrol bases and fire support bases." They were meant to canalize communist movements. "It was an effort to counter both enemy infiltration and direct invasion by increasing the enemy's cost and minimizing our own." *Report on the War in Vietnam*, p. 145.

surprise. Indeed, initially in referring to it General Westmoreland stated: "In my opinion, this is a diversionary effort to take attention away from the northern part of the country."[46]

In the initial assaults Vietcong troops penetrated to the heart of Saigon. They attacked and briefly overran part of the U.S. Embassy compound, bombarded three U.S. Army officer billets, and for approximately two days occupied part of both the South Vietnamese Army General Staff and Armored Command Headquarters. For several days they rendered inoperative the great American military airport at Tan Son Nhut, and for twenty-four hours held the Saigon radio station. Subsequently, it was estimated that in the days prior to their attack the Vietcong had infiltrated some 5,000 men into the Saigon area, the relaxed atmosphere of the Tet holidays having made this much easier. Upon arriving in the capital, they were put in touch with local Vietcong agents and were issued arms and rations previously brought in and hidden. ARVN forces in the Saigon area, though numerous and well equipped, were unable to turn the tide. Communist units continued to hold major portions of the capital, the most extensive being in the Cholon district for more than two weeks, until superior American firepower, including extensive artillery and aerial bombardment, drove them out. When the Vietcong was finally compelled to withdraw, large sections of Saigon lay in ruins and more than 133,000 were homeless.

Vietcong and North Vietnamese forces overran a number of other cities and succeeded in freeing thousands of political prisoners before being forced to retreat. Numerous American military positions were attacked, including the city of Danang, and much American military equipment was destroyed. The Vietcong launched major attacks against eleven of the principal towns in the Mekong Delta, and some of these were largely demolished in the allied reoccupation. The city of My Tho was reported to have been half destroyed.

In the fighting for Ben Tre much of the city was razed to the ground, with more than a thousand civilians reported killed. The U.S. officer in command of the operation stated, "It became necessary to destroy the town to save it."[47]

Probably the most intensive fighting of all was in Hué, South Vietnam's third largest city, where Vietcong main force units and North Vietnamese regulars smashed the ARVN garrison, overran most of the city and held much of it for three weeks. Like the Saigon battle, American forces had to be brought in to recapture it. In the process they were obliged to make extensive use of nausea gas, bombs, rockets, napalm, and even naval artillery support from the Seventh Fleet, before they regained control over the Citadel at Hué on February 24. During the fighting approximately 3,600 civilians were killed. General Westmoreland has reported that some 1,000 of these were executed by the Vietcong. Approximately 70 per cent of civilian homes were destroyed, and 116,000 of 145,000 residents became refugees in their own city.[48]

Three days after it had begun, President Johnson announced that the Tet offensive had been "a complete failure." He declared that "the stated purposes of the general uprising have failed. Communist leaders counted upon popular support in the cities for their effort. They found little or none."[49] No doubt the communists received less active support from the population than they hoped for, just as they found more support than American officials conceded. Clearly the Vietcong had underestimated the reluctance of urban dwellers to commit themselves to either side in the midst of intense fighting and while the ultimate outcome of the war seemed so uncertain. Moreover, the political cadres of the Vietcong assigned to operate in the urban areas were apparently unprepared to cope with American tactics predicated on the destruction of whole sections of towns and cities as the means employed for their recapture.

It was presumably in the expectation that their offensive

enlarged the possibility of organizing greater political strength in the urban areas that the NLF sponsored the establishment of an "Alliance of National and Peace Forces" in Saigon and the "Front of National, Democratic and Peace Forces of Hué City."* Whether or not these new organs were endowed with logistical and administrative functions, as reported, they apparently were to have linked the NLF-controlled rural zones to new pockets of insurgent support in the cities.[50]

In Washington, Administration spokesmen stated that whatever psychological success the communists had achieved through demonstrating their capacity to penetrate Southern cities, this had been accomplished at a devastating cost in casualties. The Vietcong's losses were held to have been so extensive and critical as to weaken greatly its fighting potential and overall military strength relative to the ARVN and U.S. forces. Although exact statistics on these casualties may never be known—and there is no doubt that the figures

---

* This Saigon alliance and the organization in Hué should not be confused with the country-wide "South Vietnam Alliance of National, Democratic and Peace Forces" established a few months later. This later Alliance had rather different objectives, as will be described below, pp. 382 - 384. These earlier local alliances were not intended to set up "governments," as such, in Saigon and Hué. Rather their purpose seems to have been to mobilize general political support in the cities and to set the stage for an expected eventual NLF-dominated administration. Where it proved possible to maintain control over urban areas, interim administration was apparently to be carried out by the NLF's "people's revolutionary committees." The first such organization to emerge on a provincial basis after the Tet offensive was the Thua Thien-Hué "people's revolutionary committee," its membership being the same as that of the Hué alliance. As the Vietcong and Hanoi forces were driven from Saigon and Hué, however, the visible presence of these two city alliances and of the Thua Thien-Hué people's revolutionary committee virtually disappeared. For an account of these organizations and their role, see John W. Lewis and Jayne S. Werner, "The 'New Stage' in Vietnam," *Bulletin of the Atomic Scientists*, January 1969.

were often exaggerated[51]—the extent of these losses did not appear fundamentally to impair communist morale or fighting capacity, as later intense fighting was to show. In subsequent months the Vietcong was able to replace many of its losses with new recruits drawn primarily from the Mekong Delta. Even official U.S. reports conceded that, despite the Tet losses, the defection rate of Vietcong and North Vietnamese forces had, in fact, fallen to the lowest in months. Whatever the long-range impact of the offensive on the relative military power of the two sides, the initial success of the attacks clearly resulted in a massive diversion of allied forces from the rural front to protect the exposed urban sector, a shift that obviously favored the NLF. As a result, the latter was able to extend its authority over a much wider region of the countryside than before. Many rural pacification teams, as well as the South Vietnamese armed forces assigned to defend them, were pulled back into towns and cities, and in extensive areas Saigon's pacification program collapsed.[52] Clearly the Tet campaign further reduced Saigon's already tenuous authority outside the cities. Moreover it shifted the main battleground from the NLF-dominated rural areas to the urban centers, the major base of Allied power.

7: Perhaps the greatest significance of Tet was its impact on the American public. It had now become obvious that even the 535,000 American troops then in the South could not provide the Thieu government with sufficient strength to compete effectively with the Vietcong. The public trust in the Johnson Administration sharply sagged as the credibility gap widened. For right up until the Tet offensive, American military and civilian officials had assured the American people that the military and political strength of the U.S. and Saigon were steadily increasing, while that of the enemy was being eroded.[53]

During the autumn previous to Tet, increasing popular

discontent with the war and criticism of President Johnson's Vietnam policy had encouraged Senator Eugene McCarthy to announce on November 30, 1967, his candidacy for the Presidency. For many Americans this move had seemed quixotic and futile in the face of the Administration's continuing ability to convince so much of the public that its eventual success in Vietnam was assured. However, the shattering impact of the Tet offensive suddenly made Senator McCarthy's views much more plausible and those of President Johnson more discredited. This public reaction was symbolized on March 12 by the Senator's strength in the New Hampshire primaries, an outcome which signalled to the President himself the depth of popular disaffection with his policy. The entry into the Presidential race four days later of Senator Robert Kennedy, another strong critic of the Administration's Vietnam policy, apparently further diminished the President's self-confidence. It was now unmistakably clear that Lyndon Johnson would face mounting criticism in the impending campaign.

As a consequence of the Tet offensive the President directed a major review of policy. This began on February 28, 1968, on the return of the Chairman of the Joint Chiefs of Staff, General Earle G. Wheeler, from a post-Tet inspection tour to South Vietnam. Initially the focus of debate was restricted to consideration of the unexpected and upsetting request of General Westmoreland, conveyed by General Wheeler, for American forces there to be increased by three more combat divisions plus the necessary supporting troops. This would involve an overall increase of 40 per cent in the existing American military strength of 535,000 men. It amounted to a request for 206,000 more men, an increment which clearly could not be met without exacerbating popular opposition to the war.

As head of a task force to advise him on this troop request the President chose his long-time friend and advisor,

Clark Clifford, whom he had recently appointed to replace
Robert McNamara as Secretary of Defense, and who was to
assume his new office on March 1, 1968. Although Clifford
entered the Pentagon with the reputation of a "moderate
hawk," what he learned about the actual situation in Vietnam caused his views to change. Initially the President was
adamantly against any bombing halt, but Clifford finally
won approval for a proposal limiting American bombing to
areas south of the 20th parallel, that is, somewhat more than
200 miles north of the 17th parallel and some 70 miles south
of Hanoi and Haiphong. Reflecting the by now broadly held
belief in the limited effectiveness of the bombing,* this proposal also reflected the hope that if the United States made
such an initial de-escalatory move, Hanoi might tacitly
match it, and that thereafter step by step, each side could
move in a de-escalatory direction, without any necessity for
prior negotiations. The initial opposition by a number of
military advisors was apparently lessened by their general expectation that Hanoi would not respond and that therefore
within a month or two the President would probably order a
resumption of bombing against the whole of North Vietnam.[54]

---

* Arguments for a bombing halt were strengthened by the testimony before the Senate Armed Services Committee in August
1967. Secretary Robert McNamara had then revealed that the
"quantity of externally supplied material, other than food, required to support the VC/NVA forces in South Vietnam at about
their current level of combat activity is very, very small. The reported figure is 15 tons per day, but even if the quantity were five
times that amount it could be transported by only a few trucks."
Stopping this essential flow, Mr. McNamara stated, was next to
impossible. He added that out of the 359 targets recommended for
air attack by the Joint Chiefs of Staff, all but 57 had been authorized and that striking these remaining 57 would "not materially
shorten the war." Finally, the Secretary refuted the arguments of
those who felt that expanded use of air power would accomplish
anything significant. U.S. Senate, *Air War Against North Vietnam*, 90th Congress, 1st Session (Washington: U.S. Government Printing Office, 1967), pp. 277-283.

In his television address of March 31, 1968, President
Johnson reiterated the conditions for a bombing halt which
he had described in a speech at San Antonio on September
29, 1967.[55] He recalled that under this formula* "the United
States would stop its bombardment of North Viet-Nam when
that would lead promptly to productive discussions—and
that we would assume that North Viet-Nam would not
take military advantage of our restraint." The President
stated that he was now renewing this earlier offer. He said:

> We are prepared to move immediately toward peace through
> negotiations. So tonight, in the hope that this action will lead

---

* President Johnson's San Antonio formula was generally regarded as more moderate than his letter to Ho Chi Minh of February 1967 (see above, p. 344). Whereas in that letter he had insisted that the North Vietnamese end all infiltration before the
U.S. stopped bombing North Vietnam, at San Antonio he said
that it would stop the bombing "when this will lead promptly
to productive discussions," and that the U.S. "would assume that
while discussions proceed North Vietnam would not take advantage of the bombing cessation or limitation." The President had
also cited the San Antonio formula in his State of the Union speech
on January 17, 1968, but had then slightly altered it so that one
key element was rendered in somewhat more moderate language
and another in a considerably harsher tone: "The bombing would
stop if talks would take place promptly and with reasonable hopes
they would be productive. And the other side must not take advantage of our restraint as they have in the past." *New York
Times*, January 18, 1968. The least stringent of the interpretations
of the San Antonio formula had been made by incoming Defense
Secretary Clark Clifford in his confirmation hearings before the
Senate Armed Services Committee on January 25, 1968. He
stated that he did not expect the North Vietnamese to stop military activities in the South and that he would not regard them as
taking advantage of a pause in bombing if they continued "to
transport the normal amount of goods, munitions, men to South
Vietnam." *New York Times*, January 26, 1968. This reflected
the fact that Clifford had arrived at the same conclusion as Robert McNamara; namely that the bombing had not been effective in
significantly reducing the flow of men and supplies from North to
South Vietnam.

to early talks, I am taking the first step to deescalate the conflict. We are reducing—substantially reducing—the present level of hostilities. And we are doing so unilaterally and at once. Tonight I have ordered our aircraft and naval vessels to make no attacks on North Viet-Nam, except in the area north of the demilitarized zone where the continuing enemy buildup directly threatens Allied forward positions and where the movements of their troops and supplies are clearly related to that threat. . . . Even this limited bombing of the North could come to an early end if our restraint is matched by restraint in Hanoi.

At the same time the President announced that 13,500 additional support troops were being sent to Vietnam to augment 11,000 Marine and airborne troops added at the height of the Tet offensive; and he also announced that since the beginning of the year a program for re-equipping the South Vietnamese armed forces had been underway. He reaffirmed the Manila formula,[56] thereby indicating that basic American terms for a settlement remained unchanged. Finally, to the astonishment of all but a few of his closest advisors, he stated that he would not seek or accept the nomination of his party for another term as President, a statement which may well have induced Hanoi to believe that the de-escalatory step taken by the President reflected a serious desire to move toward negotiations.

To the surprise of the Administration, on April 3, 1968, three days after the President's speech, Hanoi agreed to meet with American representatives for preliminary talks.[57] These would have to be restricted, they insisted, to just one subject—a determination of the time when the United States would bring to an end unconditionally all bombing and other acts of war against the North.* Hanoi had, in

---

* In its response Hanoi stated: "The U.S. Government has not seriously and fully met the legitimate demands of the Government of the Democratic Republic of Vietnam, of progressive American

effect, undertaken to meet Washington partway, agreeing to a limited range of talks in return for the limited suspension of bombing, but making explicit that full talks and actual negotiations on matters of substance could not take place before the cessation of American bombing of the North was complete and unconditional.

Initially, however, it appeared unlikely that even such preliminary talks would take place. The inducement for Hanoi to participate was undermined because the area of North Vietnam which was actually free of bombardment was considerably less than had been suggested in the March 31 speech, and there was a sizeable increase in the tonnage dropped on this more restricted area. Moreover, for more than a month, Washington and Hanoi were unable to agree on a mutually acceptable site for their talks until finally on May 3 they settled on Paris. On May 13, an American delegation, led by Averell Harriman, began talks with a North Vietnamese delegation led by Xuan Thuy, a former Foreign Minister of the North Vietnamese government.

From the very outset, the American delegation's basic position was that a full end of the bombing would require a reciprocal de-escalatory move by Hanoi in South Vietnam. Xuan Thuy's delegation reiterated the fundamental position of the North Vietnamese and the NLF, that Vietnam being their country, it was impossible to agree to such reciprocity. "As the victim," their representatives stated repeatedly, "we cannot accept the American view of reciprocity." That demand, they stated, "puts the victim and the aggressor on a plane of equality"; they insisted that they would never submit

---

opinion and of world opinion. However, for its part, the Government of the Democratic Republic of Vietnam declares its readiness to appoint its representative to contact the United States representative with a view to determining with the American side the unconditional cessation of the United States bombing raids and all other acts of war against the Democratic Republic of Vietnam, so that talks may start." *New York Times*, April 4, 1968.

to any demand limiting their "struggle against aggressors." Moreover, Hanoi's representatives held that they could not accept the proposition that they abandon support of their countrymen in the South while the United States continued to conduct unrestricted military operations there.*

Nevertheless, American officials hoped that despite this publicly announced position Hanoi would tacitly move towards some *de facto* de-escalation in the South in the expectation that this would elicit some matching de-escalatory step there by the United States. Thus American officials and the American press watched closely for such a sign. Some had been disposed to see this in the enemy's lifting of its seige of Khe Sanh in early April.[58] However, U.S. military spokesmen had promptly dismissed any such interpretation, stating that superior American power had forced the enemy to withdraw.

When the first session of the Paris talks began on May 13, there was no evidence that either side was practising military restraint in South Vietnam. At midnight on May 4, when the Vietcong initiated a major new offensive with rocket and mortar attacks on Saigon it was already being reported that American forces were conducting major offensives in South Vietnam and that allied units were operating "at near-peak capacity in search-and-destroy sweeps."[59]

The new enemy offensive lasted until the end of the month. Again the Vietcong demonstrated its ability to penetrate and briefly hold parts of Saigon until sufficient U.S. firepower was massed to drive it out. Damage to that city was again extensive with additional people left homeless. Elsewhere in South Vietnam enemy forces attacked more than

---

* This view was not limited to Hanoi, the *New York Times* observing editorially on May 15: "The United States insists on 'a sign' that American de-escalation has been 'matched by restraint on the other side' . . . Leaving its own hands free in the South, the United States is demanding—for a cessation of bombing in the North—limitations on Hanoi's operations in the South the bombing could never impose."

twenty provincial and district capitals and mounted heavy assaults against American military outposts, at least one of which was overrun. The number of American soldiers who were killed soared to an all-time weekly high of 562 and 549 respectively for the second and third weeks of May.[60] General Westmoreland, serving out the last month of his Vietnam command before taking his new assignment in Washington as the Army's Chief of Staff, reported to President Johnson in a familiar vein that the enemy appeared to be "approaching a point of desperation" with his forces "deteriorating in strength and quality."[61]

8 : On April 20–21, 1968, a group of prominent non-communist South Vietnamese known for their previous advocacy of a peace settlement, established the Alliance of National, Democratic and Peace Forces. This new Alliance was not confined to particular cities, but was represented as speaking for all South Vietnam. Although its leaders had not previously been known as supporters of the NLF, their organization was undoubtedly launched with its encouragement, and probably at its initiative. The Chairman of the Alliance was Trinh Dinh Thao, a leading Saigon attorney who numbered among his clients the Japanese Embassy, and who had in mid-1945 served as Minister of Justice in a cabinet set up under Bao Dai during the last months of the Japanese occupation. He had been arrested in 1954, 1959, and 1965, because of his participation in groups advocating a peace settlement, and had close connections with the Buddhist opposition to Thieu and Ky.[62] The Alliance's two Vice-Chairmen were the influential Hué Buddhist leader Thich Don Hau and Lam Van Tet, a Saigon engineer, previously a member of the civilian Council of Notables set up to advise the military directorate just after the fall of Diem. Lam Van Tet was reported to have close connections with the Cao Dai, and in 1964 had been Chairman of the All-Religions Citizen's Front, a quasi-political religious organization which undertook to bring the major religious groups of South Vietnam into closer harmony.[63] The Alliance's Secretary General, Ton That Duong Ky, had been a professor of history at Saigon and Hué Universities and a prominent lay Buddhist. He had been arrested in 1965 on charges of "advocating false peace" and forced to cross the 17th parallel into North Vietnam. The Hanoi government had given him facilities to go to Europe and later he had managed to return to Saigon.[64] Other members of the Alliance leadership were also well known, particularly among academic and religious groups in the South.

As an organization the Alliance could only operate in NLF-controlled areas, and in July the ten members of its Central Committee were tried *in absentia* by the Saigon government and found guilty on charges of treason, all of them being sentenced to death and their property confiscated.[65] But this was a hollow gesture and simply underlined the political importance of the fact that such individuals stood in open opposition to Saigon. Their alignment with the NLF served to provide something of a bridge from the latter to previously uncommitted urban elements. Indeed, both the NLF and Hanoi described the Alliance as a means of broadening the anti-American and anti-Thieu-Ky struggle by incorporating additional sectors of the urban population. The political and economic program of the Alliance was almost identical to that of the NLF, but its appeal seemed to be particularly pitched to an urban audience. It may also have been perceived as relevant to possible patterns of settlement centering about a coalition government. In some cases the Alliance provided a rallying point for those seeking escape from the upsurge of political detentions and arrests carried out by Saigon following Tet. This mounting repression was precipitated by the increased feeling of insecurity among government leaders arising out of the clear demonstration during the Tet offensive of the scope of the NLF's urban intelligence network. The repression was sustained as Thieu moved to consolidate his power against rivals such as Vice-President Ky and those leaders of the continuing and widespread peace movement, particularly the Buddhists.

9: For two months following the commencement of the Paris talks on May 13, 1968, the United States, through Ambassador Averell Harriman and officials in Washington, stressed that a full end of the bombing would depend upon tangible indications of Hanoi's military restraint in the South. As appropriate acts of restraint, they called repeatedly for a cessation of rocket and mortar attacks on Saigon and restoration of the DMZ's buffer status. On June 21, Secretary of State Dean Rusk stated that Washington's conditions for a complete cessation of bombardment of the North could be met by Hanoi if in the South it moved toward *de facto* de-escalation: "it could be done by some indication, either directly or indirectly, that such a step is being taken by the other side."[66]

After the middle of June there were increasing signs of a substantial reduction in enemy military activity in South Vietnam. Beginning June 21, the rocket and mortar attacks on Saigon, which U.S. military commanders had stated they were powerless to prevent, were halted for more than two months.[67] A considerable number of communist troops withdrew from the Saigon area, and offensive enemy military activity in many other parts of South Vietnam substantially declined; from one-quarter to one-third of the estimated 80,000 North Vietnamese troops in the South were pulled out, and it became evident in many areas that enemy forces were avoiding contact with U.S. troops.[68] This was reflected in a dramatic reduction in U.S. casualties over this two-month period, a drop from a weekly high of 562 on May 11 to the year's low of 157 in the week ending July 20.[69] In talking with American correspondents during the last two weeks of July, the North Vietnamese delegation to Paris pointed to these developments as examples of military restraint having political significance in terms of American expectations concerning reciprocity.[70] The second ranking Hanoi delegate, Colonel Ha Van Lau, in an interview, stated that President Johnson must be aware of the decline in Hanoi-NLF military activity and asked why the President did not take advantage of this development if he genuinely wanted an end to the war. This position was reiterated by the North Vietnamese in the official talks at Paris with Xuan Thuy finally stating for the record on August 28: "For more than three months now, by words and by deeds, we have fully shown our good will and readiness to move towards such a [negotiated] solution."[71]

In view of the enemy's military restraint in the South, Ambassador Harriman urged Washington to end all bombing of North Vietnam and argued that this would open the way for substantive negotiations. Despite Harriman's persistent appeals, the Johnson Administration refused to interpret these battlefield developments as evidence of the military restraint it had been demanding. The President alone had the power of interpretation; he alone could decide whether or not his condition of *de facto* reciprocal restraint was being met. Apparently he was still persuaded that a continued application of military power could yield greater concessions from the enemy, and he was to wait another three months before deciding to interpret a somewhat similar reduction in offensive military activity as fulfilling the requirements for a total bombing halt against the North.

Indeed, on July 20 in a well-publicized conference in Hawaii between President Johnson and President Thieu, the joint communiqué stated that "there had been no response to the major limitation of bombing put into effect on March 31,"[72] and they reasserted the rigorous terms for a political settlement set forth at Manila. The American position was further spelled out by Secretary Rusk in a press conference on July 30, when he made clear that the United States would no longer be content with simple *de facto* restraint and that it now needed to have advance assurance of what Hanoi would do if the United States ended the bombing completely. What was vital, he stated, was not yesterday's lull but "what will happen tomorrow, next week, next month."[73] This appeared to be a stiffening of the San Antonio formula, a change in the American position noted by the North Vietnamese as well as the American press.

Following this in mid-August there was a major upsurge in offensive actions by Vietcong and North Vietnamese units. On August 22, Saigon was shelled for the first time in two months. The next day rocket attacks were launched against Danang and Hué, and several other towns and military bases were attacked. Over a four-week period, communist troops partly overran Tay Ninh city and launched several major attacks against and into Danang. American casualties rose sharply. During the last week of August, 408 American soldiers were killed (the highest weekly loss since the end of May) and 2,513 were wounded.[74]

10 : Unproductive though the first four months of the Paris talks actually were, the Johnson Administration made important political capital out of them. Especially during the Republican and Democratic conventions, it was able to reduce domestic criticism of its Vietnam policy by giving the American public the impression that real progress was being made in the Paris talks and that the United States was now finally on the path to peace. With these talks underway, many Americans tended to disengage from their sense of anxious concern over the war and to settle back with a sense of relief. Moreover, the proposition that delicate diplomatic proceedings were taking place and that in the ongoing election campaign untutored candidates had a patriotic duty to refrain from interfering served to deflect the criticism of

Senator Eugene McCarthy and provided Hubert Humphrey and Richard Nixon with an excuse for not developing their views on a Vietnam settlement.

The Vietnam planks of both the Republican and Democratic parties were essentially in accord with President Johnson's policies. However, in both conventions this affinity reflected the attitudes of the parties' organizations much more than it did the views of their rank and file. This was demonstrated in the Democratic Party's convention at Chicago in late August, when a plank introduced by supporters of Senators Eugene McCarthy, George McGovern and Edward Kennedy, which departed sharply from the President's Vietnam policy, won approximately 40 per cent of the votes. In view of the tight control exerted by the President's supporters over the organization of the convention and the limited role of his opponents in its conduct, the size of this vote was a dramatic indication of the extent of the opposition to the President's Vietnam policy within his own party. Noting that the Vietnam war would not end in military victory, the minority plank called for an unconditional end to all bombing of North Vietnam, followed by a reduction in offensive operations in South Vietnam and the negotiation of a mutual withdrawal of all United States and North Vietnamese forces. The Saigon government and the National Liberation Front were to be encouraged "to negotiate a political reconciliation" which would be "broadly representative of these and all elements in South Vietnamese society."[75]

The imminence of the American elections as well as the knowledge that after them Lyndon Johnson would be a lame-duck President probably helped precipitate the diplomatic moves that culminated in late October 1968 in the next major step toward negotiations. Since it was now clear that continuing United States military pressure would not induce Hanoi to pledge military restraint in the South as a condition for a bombing halt, American representatives sought another formula. Beginning in the second week of October, they undertook initiatives in Paris and Saigon aimed at moving the talks on to the level of negotiations. In doing so, Washington was mindful of Hanoi's insistence that the NLF would itself have to be party to any negotiations on matters relating to the South. Although no meaningful negotiations concerning an armistice or political settlement could take place without the NLF, its representation at the conference table would constitute tacit recognition of its political importance, carrying the implication that it would share power in any Southern government issuing from the negotiations. To get such negotiations started the President now for the first time appeared prepared to accept the NLF's full participation in the talks, conditional, of course, on Hanoi's willingness to agree to the presence of a Saigon delegation there.

President Johnson met the central and perennial issue of whether a full bombing halt would be unconditional or dependent upon reciprocal military de-escalation by Hanoi and the NLF with calculated ambiguity. His formula was, in fact, very simple and might have been utilized four months earlier when Ambassador Harriman had so strongly urged such a halt. Essentially it called for a cessation of all American aerial and naval bombardment of the North, without any promise from Hanoi of a military *quid pro quo,* but with the U.S. stating unilaterally that the bombing halt "simply could not be sustained" if there were "abuses" of the Demilitarized Zone or "attacks on the cities." The American delegation sought, and apparently obtained, from Hanoi's delegates an indication that they understood this position to be the basis on which Washington was ending the bombing. There was, however, no pledge from Hanoi that it would carry out such acts of restraint or undertake any sort of military de-escalation in the South. As the *New York Times* put the matter editorially: "there can be no doubt that Hanoi 'understands' the basis on which Washingon acted. But that is quite different from asserting that Hanoi entered into an 'understanding' in the sense that it pledged itself to refrain from such military operations."[76]

President Johnson in his broadcast to the nation on October 31, 1968, announcing the bombing halt drew upon the ambiguity of this formula as a means of making less obvious the diplomatic retreat from his earlier stand on reciprocity.[77] He also made his position seem more consistent in terms of earlier pronouncements by stating that participation of the Saigon government in the talks ensured that they would be "productive" and that attendance by representatives of the NLF "in no way 'involved' recognition of the National Liberation Front in any form." He had been assured, he said, by the Joint Chiefs of Staff and General Creighton Abrams (who had succeeded General Westmoreland as the U.S. Commander in Vietnam) that "in their military judgment" the total bombing halt "would not result in any increase in American casualties," and that it had been made "clear to North Vietnam that a total bombing halt must not risk the lives of our men." The United States, the President stated, had "made clear to the other side that such talks cannot continue if they take military advantage of them. We cannot have productive talks in an atmosphere where the cities are being shelled and where the Demilitarized Zone is being abused." Part of the reason why it had been possible to order the full bombing halt, he said, was that American military efforts had "produced truly remarkable results" in the South and that the government of South Vietnam had grown "steadily stronger" and its armed forces "substantially increased" with a million men under arms whose effectiveness had "steadily improved."

Within the week, the North Vietnamese and the NLF accepted President Johnson's proposals for four-sided talks. Both reiterated their long-standing positions for a settlement in the South, but now agreed to sit down with Saigon's delegation.[78]

The Saigon government held back from joining the

negotiations, originally scheduled to begin on November 6.*
It procrastinated even over sending a delegation to Paris, and
remained for more than two months generally obstructionist
in working out the modalities for the negotiations. In particular, Saigon resisted any conference table arrangement that might reinforce the impression that the NLF was
participating, as Hanoi insisted, as a fully equal party. In
Washington the feeling grew that this uncooperativeness
reflected the belief of Thieu's government that the incoming
Nixon Administration would prove more sympathetic than
President Johnson to its point of view. Finally, after the
President-elect had publicly backed the outgoing Administration in insisting that all delegations take their seats so that
negotiations could be started, Saigon reluctantly went along,
consenting to the compromise of a round conference table
set up so as to hint at a two-sided format, with Saigon and
the United States on one side and Hanoi and the NLF on the
other. On January 24, 1969, for the first time the four delegations sat down together at the same table.

11 : **Richard M. Nixon entered the Presidency** pledged to
find an honorable end to the conflict in Vietnam. His Administration came into office appreciating what the Johnson
Administration had only come to perceive in its final months,
that a military victory was not feasible. However, the new
Administration was politically and psychologically limited in

---

* In his speech to the National Assembly on November 2, 1968,
Thieu declared: "The Republic of Vietnam Government agrees to
talk only with the North Vietnamese authorities. To state it
more clearly, the Republic of Vietnam does not agree to talk with
what the communists call NFLSV, because the Republic of
Vietnam so far has asserted that it will never recognize the NFLSV
as an entity separate and independent from the North Vietnamese
Government [because] it is only their tool." Saigon Radio, November 2, 1968. See also his news conference on the talks, Saigon
Radio, November 27, 1968.

selecting alternative policies by its acceptance of past U.S. assumptions and policy premises. Still hoping that the pursuit of new tactics might somehow induce the communists to make greater concessions and accept the broad objectives of his predecessor, President Nixon hesitated to enunciate any clear break with the past.*

Initially, North Vietnam had responded to the bombing halt of November 1, 1968, by a major de-escalation of its own. Hanoi ordered 22 of its 25 regiments in the northernmost parts of the South back across South Vietnam's borders,[79] and communist attacks on urban targets soon sharply declined. President Johnson, however, had instructed General Abrams to apply "all-out pressure on the enemy,"[80] and the U.S. troops released by the North's pullback were reassigned to offensive missions further south. In the two months after the bombing halt, the number of American and ARVN battalion-sized operations jumped by more than one-third, from 800 to 1,077,[81] small-unit actions initiated by the U.S. doubled between November 1968 and the following March,[82] and U.S. bombing raids over South Vietnam and Laos were similarly stepped up. In the first six months after his election in November, the leader of the incoming Administration endorsed these actions of the U.S. Command and, after his inauguration, he did not modify President Johnson's instructions for maintaining maximum military pressure.[83]

The Saigon leadership clearly assumed that in dealing with Hanoi and the NLF the new Administration in Washington would take a more uncompromising stand than that

---

* At his first news conference, President Nixon said: "We have a new team in Paris, with some old faces, but a new team. We have new direction from the United States. We have a new sense of urgency with regard to the negotiations. There will be new tactics. We believe that those tactics may be more successful than the tactics of the past." *New York Times,* January 28, 1969.

indicated in Johnson's October 31 speech. In its actions Thieu's government gave every sign of greater intransigence. Saigon insisted that if a peace settlement were to be achieved the only course open to the communists would be their complete and unilateral withdrawal. In his New Year's Eve address,[84] Thieu taunted them for lacking the capacity and courage to launch another major offensive* and announced that assassinations of Vietcong village leaders, under the "Phoenix program," would be greatly accelerated in the coming year. †

With the Nixon Administration in office, Thieu was also emboldened to take even stronger measures to eliminate all criticism of his regime within Saigon-controlled areas. He moved to repress all opposition, whether from noncommunist students or anticommunist Buddhists. On February 23, 1969, Saigon police arrested the militant Buddhists' most effective political organizer, Thich Thien Minh, Director of the Buddhist Youth Center, along with some fifty members of the Center. On March 15, a military court sentenced Minh to ten years hard labor, but subsequently under public pressure reduced this to a three-year jail sentence.[85] Prior to Thien Minh's seizure, there had been a whole series of political

---

* On February 22, communist forces did launch a new spring offensive. Though less dramatic than that at Tet in 1968, it exacted a large toll of Vietnamese and U.S. casualties. They relied heavily on rocket attacks and quick assaults over widely scattered areas, particularly against U.S. military installations. As a consequence, Vietnamese civilian casualties were proportionately fewer, while U.S. military casualties were relatively high. The Vietcong itself sustained far fewer losses than the year before.

† President Thieu claimed that the joint U.S.-Saigon "Phoenix program" for assassinating Vietcong village officials had caused the deaths of 18,393 communist cadres. Saigon Radio, December 31, 1968. Increasingly the NLF has reacted to these losses and organized its own local security programs to meet the threat. See, for example, Liberation Radio, December 3, 1968, and March 3, 1969.

arrests of Buddhist monks, youth leaders and students. But the jailing of a man of his stature and popular following was indicative of how far Thieu was willing to go in throttling any criticism of his government.[86]

12: Between January 24 and April 30, 1969, in the first fifteen sessions of the four-sided talks in Paris, no real progress was registered. These weekly meetings were so fruitless that there was a tendency for the press to speculate that secret talks were underway and that significant matters were being discussed in them. Presumably as a means of offsetting the growing feeling that the negotiations had reached an impasse, the Nixon Administration encouraged this idea.*

---

* Almost immediately after taking office the Nixon Administration stressed the importance of private talks, a theme soon picked up by the Saigon delegation. In calling for these on February 3, Ky said his delegation would meet only Hanoi's representatives. However, his position changed the following week when he said that he would meet with the NLF if Hanoi would first withdraw its troops from the South. On March 25, President Thieu, going further, stated that he now was willing for Saigon's delegates to conduct secret talks with the Vietcong's representatives. While the U.S. sought to enter into private discussions with Hanoi it refused to conduct them with the Front, insisting that Saigon should assume this role. For its part, the NLF rejected the idea of private discussions and stressed that all matters could be raised in the public sessions and that if there were to be any progress it would be achieved in them. While there is some reason to believe that in the first weeks of the Nixon Administration private discussions may have taken place between the North Vietnamese and U.S. delegations, there is no evidence that they produced anything significant. The absence of further private talks between Washington and Hanoi might have reflected Hanoi's unwillingness to discuss bilaterally, over the head of the NLF, matters concerning the South. For reports on these developments, see *New York Times*, January 28, February 4–15 and March 10–15 and 22–31, 1969, *passim*. On March 4, President Nixon suggested a possible shift in emphasis from secret talks in Paris to dealing indirectly with the Vietnamese communists through Moscow. *Department of State Bulletin* (Washington, March 24, 1969), pp. 242 and 245.

The impression was given that Washington was following a carefully conceived strategy and timetable and that, given time, its plan would yield real progress toward a settlement.

The prospect of finding the common ground necessary for such a settlement seemed dim, however, when on April 7, President Thieu outlined in detail his government's terms for peace.[87] Thieu's point of departure was explicitly the position taken in his joint communiqué with President Johnson at Manila in October 1966, and in his own public elucidation immediately thereafter.[88] He insisted that the North Vietnamese "must end their aggression" and that "all North Vietnamese troops and cadres and their auxiliary forces be withdrawn." Only after their departure would Saigon "urge the Allied nations to withdraw their forces." Former adherents of the NLF could participate in the political process of South Vietnam provided they turned in their arms, renounced communism and agreed to abide by Saigon's constitution,[89] an instrument which proscribed communist political activity.[90] He added that any new elections would have to be conducted under the terms of the existing constitution and that no new elections for the Presidency could be held until September 1971 (Article 52)—a position that he strongly reiterated eight weeks later.[91]

Another month was to elapse before any of the parties further clarified or developed its negotiating position. The first significant movement came at the sixteenth session of the Paris talks on May 8, 1969, when Tran Buu Kiem, the head of the NLF's delegation, set forth a comprehensive ten-point proposal giving the "Principles and Main Content of an Overall Solution to the South Vietnam Problem to Help Restore Peace in Vietnam."[92] The Front stated that these points formed "an integrated whole," but its reference to them as "the basis" on which "the parties shall reach an understanding" seemed to suggest a measure of flexibility on at least some issues. While this statement was generally consistent with past positions taken by the National Liberation Front, there were several new and important elements.

As before, the NLF demanded the unconditional withdrawal from South Vietnam of all troops of the United States and its non-Vietnamese allies, but for the first time it advocated international supervision of this process. (It did not, however, extend this supervision to the removal of North Vietnamese forces from the South.) In what was generally interpreted as an oblique reference to Hanoi's troops in the South, point three stated that questions relating to "the Vietnamese armed forces in South Viet Nam shall be resolved by the Vietnamese parties among themselves." The Front appeared to envisage that a South Vietnamese "provisional coalition government" with authority over all the South would work out, with Hanoi, terms for the removal of North Vietnamese forces.

Of major importance, and in contrast with its earlier position, the NLF now dropped its explicit demand that the Saigon regime be overthrown before a political settlement could be reached among all South Vietnamese parties. As a first stage it called for a provisional coalition government that could serve as a bridge to a definitive coalition government to be formed following elections throughout the South. The provisional coalition would be set up through negotiations by the "political forces representing the various social strata and political tendencies in South Viet Nam, that stand for peace, independence and neutrality, including those persons who, for political reasons, have to live abroad."[93] While thus limiting participation in this process to those standing for "peace, independence and neutrality," the Front wished to keep the door open to those civil and military officials currently working for the Saigon government whom it regarded as meeting this condition. Subsequently, in elucidating this point, the NLF has indicated that this definition would exclude Thieu, Ky, and Saigon's Premier Tran Van Huong.[94]

As proposed, the provisional coalition government would not simply be an agency for coordinating the administrations and economies of NLF-and Saigon-controlled areas but, according to Tran Buu Kiem, would "cover the whole territory of South Vietnam in all aspects; our view is that this government would be an organization that would insure the unification of all activities in South Vietnam—administrative, economic, and so forth—over the whole territory."[95] (This view appears to take into account the contested character of much of South Vietnam's territory where so frequently Saigon and NLF administrations overlap and compete for control of the same populations. Because of the impossibility of drawing clearcut boundaries in these contested areas, it would be difficult, if not impossible, to conceive of a coalition government whose mandate was restricted to coordinating two autonomous, administratively discrete regimes.) The NLF is convinced that a Saigon government led by Thieu and Ky would be unwilling to consider the compromises necessary for achieving such a coalition, and would remain opposed to ending the war and to anything more than a partial U.S. military withdrawal. The Front believes, however, that a more broadly based Saigon government led by noncommunists other than these military leaders would oppose further fighting and would support the compromises necessary to create a reasonably balanced interim coalition. Thus, it has tried to encourage those who seek to create a "peace cabinet" in Saigon, such as the Buddhists and the Alliance of National, Democratic and Peace Forces.

The NLF's new statement assigned the following tasks to the provisional coalition government: implementation of the agreements on withdrawal of American and other foreign troops; achievement of "democratic freedoms" such as speech, press, the formation of political parties, and the freeing of political prisoners; the prohibition of all "reprisal and discrimination against people who have collaborated with either side";* restoration of the economy; and, finally, the holding of "free and democratic general elections in the whole of South Viet Nam. . . ." A second, definitive coalition-type government is envisaged as the appropriate outcome of these elections, for the Front believes that the coalition formula would make possible representation of the diverse political and religious groupings in the South, which could be counted upon to secure representation in any free electoral process. Providing for minority representation in the post-election government, it asserts, will ensure an ultimate "national concord" consistent with the pluralistic nature of South Vietnamese society.

For almost four months President Nixon's view of the Vietnam question was marked by ambiguity, and the first public clarification of his position came only after the Front had published its ten points. Until then, his Administration had issued a series of often contradictory statements regarding its military strategy † and approach to negotiations. One of its few consistent themes was that the South Vietnamese

---

* The sharing of power involved in the coalition concept which the NLF has put forward in the ten points appeared to offer the possibility for safeguards against reprisals.

† The new Administration released a number of such statements after the communists launched their spring offensive on February 22. Referring to this new assault, President Nixon spoke of making an "appropriate response" without defining what such a military riposte might entail. It was in this context of a threatened retaliation that former Ambassador Averell Harriman called the communist offensive "essentially a response to our actions rather than a deliberate, reckless attempt to dictate the peace terms or torpedo the talks." *New York Post*, March 7, 1969. The President, echoed by the Secretary of Defense and the principal U.S. negotiators at Paris, blamed the escalation in the South solely on the communists. On March 14, the President contradicted hints given by his Secretary of Defense to the effect that at least 50,000 Americans would be pulled out of the South in 1969. Mr. Nixon noted that "in view of the current offensive on the part of the North Vietnamese and the Vietcong, there is no prospect for a reduction of American forces in the foreseeable future." *New York Times*, March 9, 15 and 20, 1969.

army was being strengthened as quickly as possible so that it could assume more and more responsibility for the fighting, thereby releasing American forces from combat. Commenting on this in late February, Senator George McGovern— the first major Democratic leader to speak out against the Nixon Administration's failure to move toward a resolution of the Vietnam conflict—stated that to turn "the war over to the South Vietnamese army only if we are certain it is able to carry the load . . . is the same as proposing that we stay in Vietnam indefinitely."[96] He called at this time for an immediate "offensive ceasefire" and for a "carefully phased withdrawal of our troops, beginning now," providing that this be "accompanied by a change to a defensive strategy designed to reduce danger to the remaining troops, while negotiations proceed." On May 1, this latter theme was taken up by the senior Republican on the Senate Foreign Relations Committee, George D. Aiken,[97] who was joined the following day by Hugh Scott, assistant Senate Republican leader.[98] In the meantime, on April 3, it was noted that the duration of the Vietnam war now exceeded that of any previous conflict in U.S. history and that the number of American soldiers killed there had surpassed the number killed in Korea, with combat deaths the third highest in any U.S. foreign conflict. This, together with the maintenance of high draft levels and the evident fiscal difficulty of the Nixon Administration in meeting the country's increasingly critical domestic problems, was creating a perceptible public pressure to which the President had by May become highly sensitive.

On May 14, 1969, in a televised speech to the nation, President Nixon stated that his Administration had recently completed a lengthy review of the Vietnam problem. He presented his assessment of military and political developments and outlined the kind of settlement his Administration hoped to negotiate at Paris.[99] Stressing that his proposals were "not offered on a take-it-or-leave-it basis," he seemed to indicate a disposition to be flexible. "We are willing," he said, "to talk about anybody's program—Hanoi's four points, the NLF's 10 points. . . ." However, there were important stipulations. His proposals were to be regarded as "consistent with President Thieu's six points,"[100] and responses by the United States to the proposals of its adversaries would have to conform with certain "basic principles." These included: the South Vietnamese people must be allowed "to determine their own political future without outside interference"; the U.S. as a "great nation cannot renege on its pledges" to South Vietnam; and the U.S. must demonstrate in Vietnam that "confrontation with the United States is costly and unrewarding."

In several respects President Nixon's position departed from that of his predecessor. He made no explicit commitment, as had Johnson, to maintain Thieu's government in power and appeared no longer to oppose the concept of a coalition government as such. Further, President Nixon did not now insist, as he had initially, that the internal political future of South Vietnam be left to bilateral negotiations between Saigon and the NLF, but said that if requested the United States would be willing to join with Hanoi in such negotiations.

In his speech the President reaffirmed that the U.S. sought no bases in South Vietnam and would agree to its neutrality if its people so desired. American withdrawal was made conditional, however, on the "mutual withdrawal" of the North Vietnamese, with the U.S. willing to commence removal of its forces simultaneously with the departure of North Vietnamese forces in accordance with a "mutually acceptable timetable." To meet Hanoi's public position concerning its troops in the South, the President added: "If North Viet-Nam wants to insist that it has no forces in South Viet-Nam, we will no longer debate the point—provided that its forces cease to be there and that we have reliable assurances that they will not return." To initiate the process, he proposed the following measures:

> Over a period of 12 months, by agreed-upon stages, the major portions of all U.S., Allied, and other non-South Vietnamese forces would be withdrawn. At the end of this 12-month period, the remaining U.S., Allied, and other non-South Vietnamese forces would move into designated base areas and would not engage in combat operations.

This proposal left unspecified the amount of time that would then elapse before "the remaining United States and Allied forces would complete their withdrawals" along with North Vietnam's remaining forces. For the purpose of verifying troop withdrawals and arranging "supervised cease-fires" an international supervisory body would be created.

President Nixon stated that the final political settlement "is an internal matter which ought to be decided among the South Vietnamese themselves, and not imposed by outsiders." That settlement would guarantee "the interests of all major South Vietnamese groups" and "permit all persons and groups that are prepared to renounce the use of force to participate freely in the political life of South Vietnam." Calling for "a process that would allow the South Vietnamese people to express their choice," he proposed that elections "be held under agreed procedures and under the supervision of the international body." This vague proposal bypassed the central problem of achieving a reasonably neutral transitional administration under which elections could be conducted. Thus, the inference to be drawn from the Nixon proposals was that South Vietnam's elections would be held under the aegis of the Thieu government.

13: **The exchange of proposals in May** formally reduced the negotiating positions of the four parties to two. The North Vietnamese endorsed the ten points of the NLF, and Washington and Saigon stressed the consistency of their own approaches to a settlement. The statements by President Nixon and the Front disclosed little additional common ground but, despite their ambiguities, did help to clarify the principal differences between the two positions and exposed the distance that separated them.

The views on troop withdrawal constituted one major difference between the Nixon and NLF proposals. The two formulas reflected the incompatibility in outlook of the two sides concerning the origins of the war in the South and the right of the disputants to determine the outcome.[101] The U.S. President—and President Thieu in Saigon—rejected "a one-sided withdrawal" from South Vietnam, insisting that the departure of U.S. and allied non-Vietnamese troops be accompanied by the departure of North Vietnam's forces. North Vietnam and the Front refused to equate the right of North Vietnamese and American (and other foreign allied) troops to operate in the South in much the same way as they rejected Washington's equating North Vietnam and the United States as countries foreign to the South. Thus both Hanoi and the NLF repudiated any suggestion of mutual troop withdrawal as an infringement on Vietnam's "fundamental national rights" and demanded "total and unconditional U.S. withdrawal."*

Considering the problem of Vietnamese armed forces in South Vietnam to be a domestic matter and therefore appropriate for joint solution by the Vietnamese parties alone, the communists indicated their unwillingness to accept President Nixon's proposal for the international supervision of North Vietnamese troop withdrawal. They interpreted Nixon's formula of maintaining a reduced American military

---

* Some observers, however, foresaw the possibility of a tacit understanding whereby unpublicized North Vietnamese withdrawals might take place in conjunction with the withdrawal of American and allied non-Vietnamese forces.

presence for an indeterminate period after the 12-month phase of partial mutual withdrawal as revealing a U.S. intention to retain a foothold in Vietnam and sustain the Thieu regime by force of arms. The communists were convinced that without American support Thieu's regime would crumble, and that no de-Americanization strategy* could succeed in building up ARVN strength sufficiently for it to stand up alone to the Vietcong. Thus they suspected that Washington was planning for a continuing, if somewhat diminished, U.S. presence in South Vietnam. The NLF, however, was unwilling to countenance the continuing presence of even a much reduced and territorially restricted American military force in the South. They stated: "If American troops still occupy part of South Vietnam, the fighting will continue."[102]

Another point of basic disagreement exposed by the May 1969 proposals related to the method of achieving self-determination in South Vietnam, particularly who would govern there during the holding of country-wide elections. The deep-rooted distrust between Thieu's government and the Front precluded the running of these elections under the aegis of only one of them, and their mutual antipathy clouded any prospect of agreement on a sharing of power during such a politically decisive period. In his statement, President Nixon appeared reluctant to trust the outcome of the voting to any electoral process not ultimately controlled by the Saigon government. By subscribing to Thieu's six-point program of April 7, Nixon allied the United States with Thieu's demand that the Front be disarmed before its members could vote,

---

* At the outset of the Midway conference on June 8, 1969, President Nixon announced that approximately 25,000 of the 540,000 U.S. troops then in Vietnam would be withdrawn by the end of August 1969. Adding his concurrence, President Thieu noted that this was possible because "the armed forces of Vietnam [ARVN] are now able to start the process of the replacement of American forces." *New York Times*, June 9, 1969.

while Thieu's army would remain intact. Having witnessed Saigon's organization of the 1967 elections and Washington's certification of them as being free and democratic, the NLF predictably ridiculed Nixon's proposal as a call for "general elections to be held at gunpoint."[103] Thus the Front continued in its demand that the Thieu-Ky government be replaced by a "peace cabinet" composed of Buddhists and other "third force" elements.[104] Only such a governing body, the Front argued, could reduce the polarization in Southern politics and make possible the transition to the requisite neutral pre-election government. The NLF could see no basis of compromise with men it considered "shameless traitors"[105] and decisively dependent on an outside power.

Saigon, which took a rather similar view of the Front, rejected outright any possibility of a coalition government with it.[106] Under U.S. prodding, Thieu had in late March gone on record as being willing to hold direct talks with the NLF.* Apart from increasing his acceptability to the American public, this was an empty gesture. He offered no realistic basis for compromise, and the NLF themselves publicly rejected such talks. President Thieu and his military colleagues insisted upon maintaining their political dominance in Saigon throughout the period leading up to and including country-wide elections. They were quite unwilling to share power with any Vietnamese who were prepared to negotiate with the NLF for the establishment of a transitional coalition administration under whose aegis these elections

---

* After the authors completed this manuscript, President Thieu on July 11, 1969, announced that he was prepared to permit the NLF to participate in internationally supervised elections so long as its members did not stand as communists or make communist propaganda. He also agreed to the American proposal for a joint Saigon-NLF commission to supervise the election, but he made very clear that any elections held in South Vietnam would have to be organized by his government. See the *New York Times*, July 12 and 13, 1969.

could be held. Having for so long found its policies best served by the military's control of the Saigon government, the U.S. was now hardly in a position to persuade the generals to widen their government's political base when such a course would inevitably result in a major reduction of their power. It was the continuing protection of American troops that enabled Saigon's leaders to refuse the very steps that might finally lead to a negotiated compromise. Thus, in the areas controlled jointly by U.S. and ARVN forces, the South Vietnamese people were still obliged to accept the unrepresentative military junta as their only spokesman.

President Nixon appeared fearful of risking the unpredictable consequences that would attend a withdrawal of U.S. support from President Thieu. At the Midway Island conference of June 8 between the two heads of government President Nixon indicated a continuing commitment to the dominance of Thieu's regime all the way through the crucial period leading up to elections.* The refusal of the United States to

---

* Soon after announcement at the Midway Island Conference of an initial U.S. troop withdrawal of 25,000 men, the broad outlines of President Nixon's strategy for incremental disengagement in Vietnam were disclosed. The Administration was reported to have plans for additional withdrawals in August and October of 45,000 to 75,000 U.S. troops contingent upon the reaction of Saigon and Hanoi to the departure of the initial 25,000 men. William Beecher of the *New York Times* Washington Bureau, quoting "authoritative sources," wrote:

If South Vietnamese forces move aggressively and if North Vietnamese and Vietcong troops either do not try, or try and fail, to launch successful military offensives, the rest of this year's withdrawal plan probably will be carried out, these sources assert. . . .

A progressive schedule of American withdrawals, the sources contend, should reduce antiwar pressure at home while demonstrating that even with smaller forces, the allies are capable of fending off the enemy on the battlefield.

If North Vietnam becomes persuaded of this, the hope is that it will agree, formally or tacitly, to a mutual withdrawal plan

accept the formula of a pre-election coalition government in the South may well have been a decisive factor in the NLF's announcement just after the Midway conference that it was now establishing its own transitional government, the Provisional Revolutionary Government of South Vietnam.*

14: Thus the Vietnam conflict continued, with no fundamental changes in the positions of the major parties. The same erroneous premises that provided the rationale for the

---

that would see the bulk of both North Vietnamese and American troops out of South Vietnam at a much faster rate than under unilateral United States withdrawals.

But if Hanoi refuses to consider mutual reductions, the strategy looks toward removal of 340,000 American troops over the next three years, leaving behind "indefinitely" enough of a force to so bolster South Vietnamese troops that they could contend with anything the enemy could throw at them.

This would involve a residual force of about 200,000 Americans.

New York Times, June 18, 1969.

* In the year preceding the formation of this provisional regime, the Front set up "over 1,000 people's revolutionary councils and people's revolutionary committees at village, district, province, and municipal levels" (see above, p. 374 n). Liberation Radio, May 1, 1969. In May a number of local revolutionary congresses were convened, including a "congress of Saigon-Cholon people's delegates" at the end of the month. Liberation Radio, May 27, 28 and June 4 and 5, 1969. From June 6 to 8, representatives from the Front, the Alliance of National, Democratic and Peace Forces and other "patriotic organizations" held a national congress, which formed the "Provisional Revolutionary Government of the Republic of South Vietnam." Huynh Tan Phat, a former deputy head and secretary-general of the NLF, was named as the new regime's President. Other senior officials included Mrs. Nguyen Thi Binh, second in rank on the Front's delegation at the Paris talks, as Foreign Minister; Phung Van Cung, another NLF deputy head, as Vice-President and Interior Minister; Tran Nam Trung as Defense Minister; Tran Buu Kiem as Minister in the Office of the President; Nguyen Huu Tho, the NLF's president, as head of the Advisory Council; and Trinh Dinh Thao, the head of the Alliance, as vice-chairman of the Advisory Council. The twelve-point "program of action" announced by the provisional govern-

faulty judgments of those whose decisions led the United States to project its power into Vietnam still governed American policies. Although President Nixon clearly wished to disengage from Vietnam, six months after he assumed office there was little indication that his understanding of the situation there was any more profound than that of President Johnson. Like his predecessor, he evidenced little appreciation of the actual balance and character of indigenous political forces in South Vietnam. Nor did he seem aware of the extent to which the attitudes of America's Vietnamese adversaries remained conditioned by the impact of past U.S. actions. Without this understanding, and with the premises underlying American policies still so far removed from Vietnamese realities, it was difficult to see how a negotiated settlement could soon be achieved.

---

ment substantially mirrored the Front's 1967 program (see above, pp. 359-362) and also emphasized the NLF's ten points as the basis for settling the war. *New York Times*, June 11, 12 and 13, 1969; Liberation Radio, June 10, 11 and 12; Hanoi Radio, June 11 and 12; and *Nhan Dan* (*"The People"*), June 11, 15 and 16, 1969. By June 14, the NLF's Provisional Revolutionary Government had been accorded diplomatic recognition by Algeria, Bulgaria, Congo, Cuba, Czechoslovakia, East Germany, Hungary, North Korea, Poland, Rumania, Soviet Union, Syria, North Vietnam, and Yugoslavia. *New York Times*, June 13 and 14, 1969.

Notes to Chapter XIV

1. The fullest, though somewhat controversial, account of these developments and of other aborted efforts at opening up negotiations during 1967 and early 1968 can be found in David Kraslow and Stuart H. Loory, *The Secret Search for Peace in Vietnam* (New York: Vintage Books, 1968).

2. *New York Times,* March 22, 1967.

3. *Ibid.,* February 14, 1967.

4. *Ibid.,* July 1 and October 15, 1967.

5. One of the authors, then in Saigon, made a wide canvass of opinion concerning this matter. See also the *New York Times,* December 7, 15 and 18, 1966; *Washington Post,* December 20, 1966; and *Vietnam Guardian,* December 9, 1966. The latter Saigon newspaper managed to convey the idea by a photograph that a number of inconsistencies attended the government's efforts to pin the blame for Van's assassination on the Vietcong and it was indefinitely suspended from publication on orders from Premier Ky on December 12, 1966. See the *New York Times,* April 1, 1967, and a comment by the editor of the *Vietnam Guardian* in Don Luce and John Sommer, *Viet Nam: The Unheard Voices* (Ithaca: Cornell University Press, 1969), p. 158.

6. This is not to say that the only or even major opposition to land reform came from the Vietnamese. According to former Agriculture Secretary Orville L. Freeman, the U.S. Embassy in Saigon strongly opposed land reform after the Honolulu Conference in early 1966. *Washington Star,* March 16, 1969.

7. This provision was incorporated in the final section of paragraph 9, Article 11, of the presidential election law and reads: "Those who have been sentenced for criminal or light offenses of political character or for political reasons before April 1, 1967, may appeal by June 15, 1967, for a Council's decision that the sentence passed upon them is one which would not prevent them from running. This Council will be presided over by the President of the Supreme Court of Appeal, assisted by two Assistant Judges of the same Court serving as members and will have to issue a decision within two weeks following the date of appeal." See also paragraph 9, Article 11 of the Senate and Lower House election laws.

8. See above, pp. 255–260.

9. Paragraph 9, Article 11 of "Presidential Election Law," "Up-

per House [Senate] Election Law" and "Lower House Election Law."

10. *New York Times,* May 17, 1967.

11. See *Saigon Post,* July 18, 1967; and *New York Times,* July 9, 1967.

12. *New York Times,* July 8 and 9, 1967.

13. *New York Times,* July 19, 1967.

14. Although press censorship had been officially lifted on July 20, *Than Chung* (*"Sacred Bell"*) and *Sang* (*"Light"*) were suspended on September 2 for "an indefinite period." See *New York Times,* August 13 and September 3, 1967.

15. See, for example, the *New York Times,* August 26, 1967.

16. In those limited areas where President Johnson's observer group was given facilities for observation, its members reported few irregularities. Lt. Col. William Corson, however, states that even in one "model" polling place visited by members of the group, Kien Hoa Province, some 120,000 registered voters produced approximately 150,000 ballots. *The Betrayal* (New York: W. W. Norton, 1968), p. 112. Although, according to the *New York Times,* NLF control was considered so widespread in this province that it had been possible previously for Saigon to hold elections in only six out of 115 villages, in the presidential election Thieu and Ky were reported to have carried it by a margin of 26,000 votes. *New York Times,* April 3 and September 3, 1967.

17. This conviction grew when President Johnson publicly congratulated Thieu and Ky on their election victory three weeks before either the Central Election Board or the constituent assembly had validated the outcome of the election. See *Department of State Bulletin* (Washington, October 2, 1967), p. 421.

18. *New York Times,* September 29, 1967; *Saigon Daily News,* May 3 and July 27, 1968.

19. *New York Times,* September 5 and 6, 1967. The votes for the seven other civilian candidates totaled 1,282,249, two of them receiving approximately 7 per cent each and the other five all well under 4 per cent.

20. With respect to election irregularities and pressures exerted by military and civil administrators, see also Charles A. Joiner, "South Vietnam: Political, Military, and Constitutional Arenas in Nation Building," *Asian Survey,* Vol. VIII, No. 1, January 1968.

21. See the *New York Times,* September 25, 1967.

22. Word leaked out to an anti-government newspaper, *Thoi Dai,* that the assembly's election committee would recommend invalidation of the elections to the assembly on the grounds of irregularities in both the conduct of the elections and tabulation of

the vote. On September 27, four days after the story's publication, the government closed down the paper. See *Saigon Post,* September 22, 1967, and *New York Times,* September 27, 1967.

23. *New York Times,* September 30, 1967.

24. Francis H. Craighill III and C. Robert Zelnick, *Vietnam from Elections to Negotiations and Beyond* (Washington, D.C., mimeo, 1968), p. 45. The two Washington lawyers who wrote this report were in Saigon at the time and made an intensive study of this phase of the election. United Press International reported from Saigon: "The U.S. diplomatic mission here was working behind the scenes to assure certification of the election." *Washington Post,* October 3, 1967. With respect to Ambassador Bunker's attitude, see *New York Times,* September 30, 1967.

25. See Craighill and Zelnick, *op. cit.,* p. 48, and *Washington Post,* October 3, 1967. Reports were widespread that Ky dispensed considerable funds in order to ensure sufficient votes for validation of the elections. See *Washington Post,* October 1 and 3, 1967.

26. Charles A. Joiner, *op. cit.*

27. *New York Times,* September 19, 1967. The unrepresentative character of the Senate stemmed from the organization and discipline of Catholic voters as well as from the high incidence of election irregularities. Concerning the Senate election and composition, see also Robert Shaplen, "Letter from Saigon," *The New Yorker,* January 20, 1968; and Charles A. Joiner, *op. cit.*

28. For a discussion of the Front's previous programs, see above, pp. 118–119, 134–137, 208–209.

29. The then Commander in Chief Pacific, Admiral U. S. G. Sharp describes this failure in more opaque official language as follows: "Although the Vietnamese Armed Forces had the primary mission of supporting pacification, United States forces reinforced their efforts by direct support. Vietnamese Army units were redeployed and retrained to support these programs, but providing the motivation was difficult and progress in orienting those forces was slow." Commander in Chief Pacific and Commander U.S. Military Assistance Command Vietnam, *Report on the War in Vietnam (As of June 1968)* (Washington: U.S. Government Printing Office, 1969), p. 9.

30. For an illuminating account of the performance of South Vietnam's armed forces, see Lt. Col. William R. Corson, *The Betrayal,* esp. pp. 83–106.

31. U.S. Senate, *Civilian Casualty and Refugee Problems in South Vietnam,* 90th Congress, 2nd Session (Washington: U.S. Government Printing Office, 1968), p. 17.

32. *New York Times,* December 12, 1967.

33. Hospital administrations were so controlled as to make it

difficult for visiting American congressmen ever to see napalm victims, but in fact even in Saigon hospitals they were numerous. If one visited these hospitals on major holidays when administrative personnel were off duty, one could relatively easily with the help of concerned doctors and interns visit wards where there were many such casualties. On December 25, 1966, when one of the authors visited the central hospital in Saigon, he was led to six back wards where at least 35 individuals were clearly napalm victims. A visit on the same day to Saigon's children's hospital disclosed three cases of napalm who had just been admitted. The Johnson Administration mounted a campaign to assure the American public that what had been taken to be burns from napalm were for the most part caused by kerosene stoves. Since Dr. Howard Rusk in his reports, given such wide publicity by the Johnson Administration (see *New York Times*, March 12 and 19 and December 31, 1967, and *Time*, March 24, 1967), stated that he saw little evidence of napalm injuries in the hospitals he visited, one can only surmise that he must have been given the sort of prepared and guided tour that often makes it so difficult for official visitors to see much that is significant.

34. Corroboration for this view, widely held by American correspondents, was found by one of the writers in visiting South Vietnamese hospitals in late December 1966 and January 1967. European and American medical personnel at the hospitals in Hué and Quang Ngai attributed respectively 90 per cent and 70 per cent of their civilian casualties to U.S. and Korean aerial and artillery bombardment.

35. Briefings of one of the authors by U.S. Marine officers in the area.

The concentration of Vietnamese in the cities led to extreme problems of overcrowding. In March 1969, Saigon was reportedly the "world's most crowded city" with more than twice the population density of Tokyo. *Vietnam Guardian*, March 22, 1969.

In Quang Ngai Province, the southernmost in the I Corps area, military officers informed one of the authors in January 1967 that in Son Tinh district adjacent to the provincial capital, out of a population of slightly over 108,000, a total of 26,587 were refugees. Eleven hamlets were designated as "secure," 65 as "VC controlled," with the remaining 23 classified as "contested." Most of the clearing operations were being undertaken by Korean forces operating from bases to the north, whose actions U.S. military officers described as "brutal" and as having been responsible for "generating" many of the refugees. For a copy of the official map of all South Vietnam, showing the relative balance of control on December 31, 1967, see U.S. Senate, *Stalemate in Vietnam,* 90th Congress,

2nd Session (Washington: U.S. Government Printing Office, 1968).

36. This was the estimate of several U.S. Embassy officials and U.S. Army officers in the area encountered by one of the authors. According to a Congressional source, 84,000 ARVN troops deserted in 1967, a total that exceeded the number drafted; *Stalemate in Vietnam*, p. 10.

37. The fullest published account of this phenomenon can be found in Jonathan Schell, *The Military Half* (New York: Vintage Books, 1968).

38. See, for example, *New York Times*, November 15, 1967.

39. The total number of refugees, not including those in these (and probably several other) cities was officially listed by the Saigon government as 2,084,640 on October 31, 1967.

40. See Jonathan Schell, *The Village of Ben Suc* (New York: Knopf, 1967). In his report, General Westmoreland comments as follows on Ben Suc: "Unfortunately, the resettlement phase was not as well planned or executed as the actual evacuation. For the first several days the families suffered unnecessary hardships." *Report on the War in Vietnam*, p. 148.

41. Address of January 25, 1968, before World Affairs Council of Boston, reprinted in *Civilian Casualty and Refugee Problems in South Vietnam*, pp. 33–38. See also U.S. Senate, *Civilian Casualty, Social Welfare, and Refugee Problems in South Vietnam*, 90th Congress, 2nd Session (Washington: U.S. Government Printing Office, 1968). Senator Kennedy's estimates concerning refugees were based on visits by him and his staff to more than 25 refugee camps.

42. With regard to administration of the camps, Senator Edward Kennedy estimated that of the $30 million a year given by the U.S. for refugee relief only one-half ever reached the refugees, with South Vietnamese government officials keeping much of the goods and money for themselves. Although each refugee was supposed to receive the equivalent of $45 for resettlement, a U.S. official advisor to the refugee program estimated that "75 percent of this amount is siphoned off before it reaches these people." Senator Kennedy concluded that in the field of refugee care "the government of South Vietnam has been engaged in the systematic looting of its own people." *Civilian Casualty and Refugee Problems in South Vietnam*, p. 36. See also *New York Times*, October 12, 1967.

43. See *New York Times*, September 18, 1967. Four of these capitals were attacked at least twice during this period—Hué: May 16 and May 29; Hoi An: July 15 and August 27; Quang Ngai: August 7 and August 30; and Tam Ky: September 2 and September 18. In his report on this period General Westmoreland

does not mention these attacks. He states: "After the end of the southwest monsoon in October, they [the communists] began to move their main forces into the populated areas throughout the entire country. We became aware of this movement in November and December through our intelligence, and as the number of incidents rose in the populated areas, the rate of ralliers returning to government authority fell off sharply, while pacification progress virtually stopped." *Report on the War in Vietnam*, p. 136.

44. This seems more likely than the official U.S. judgment. According to General Westmoreland, "Judging from the size of his buildup, and from his own statements, he [the enemy] was hoping to achieve a military-political victory similar to the one 14 years earlier at Dien Bien Phu." *Report on the War in Vietnam,* p. 163.

45. *New York Times*, January 27, 1968.

46. *New York Times,* February 11, 1968. The following year in his section of the *Report on the War in Vietnam* (pp. 157–158), General Westmoreland states: "During January we began to receive numerous reports about a major offensive to be undertaken just before or immediately after *Tet*. . . . In response to this changed enemy situation, just before *Tet,* well over half of the maneuver battalions plus most of the Regional and Popular Forces in the III Corps were either defending the immediate approaches to Saigon, interdicting the corridors which lead to Saigon from War Zones C and D and the Plain of Reeds, or defending villages and hamlets. Even though by mid-January we were certain that a major offensive action was planned by the enemy at *Tet*, we did not surmise the true nature or the scope of the countrywide attack." While asserting that large-scale efforts were undertaken to put U.S. and Vietnamese troops on full alert before Tet, he notes: "Notwithstanding efforts to increase the state of alert, large numbers of Vietnamese soldiers were on leave for *Tet* and their units were, in most cases, about half strength." *Ibid*, p. 159.

47. *New York Times*, February 5–6, 1968; and *Time*, February 16, 1968.

48. *Report on the War in Vietnam*, p. 160. As is the case with all statistics from Vietnam, figures on the losses in Hué vary widely.

49. For the text of President Johnson's remarks, see *New York Times*, February 3, 1968.

50. See John W. Lewis and Jayne S. Werner, "The 'New Stage' in Vietnam." *Bulletin of the Atomic Scientists*, January 1969.

51. According to General Westmoreland, "Between 29 January and 11 February the Communists lost some 32,000 men killed and 5,800 detained, out of an estimated force of 84,000

committed to the offensive. . . . By the end of February the number of enemy killed had risen to more than 45,000." *Report on the War in Vietnam*, p. 161.

52. By late February it was reported that 18 ARVN battalions of the 51 committed to support of the pacification teams had been withdrawn to the cities. Half of the 535 teams of pacification workers had also been removed. Official U.S. reports estimated that the offensive had a "serious impact" on 13 of the 44 provinces, "moderate effect" in 16 provinces and "slight effect" in 15 provinces. *New York Times*, February 25, 1968.

53. See *ibid.*, December 27, 1967, and February 13, 1968.

54. For a comprehensive and remarkably enlightening account of the discussions involved in the President's March reassessment of Vietnam policy, see the two articles prepared by staff members of the *New York Times* which appear in its issues of March 6 and 7, 1969.

55. For the text of the March 31, 1968, speech, see *Department of State Bulletin* (Washington, April 15, 1968), pp. 481-486. The San Antonio speech is in *ibid.* (October 23, 1967), pp. 519-522.

56. See above, pp. 262, 337–338.

57. On December 29, 1967, North Vietnamese Vice Premier and Foreign Minister Nguyen Duy Trinh had stated, "After the United States has ended the bombing and all other acts of war against the DRV, the DRV will hold talks with the United States on questions concerned." This led to a flurry of discussion on communist "willingness" to talk, but no action resulted at the time. For the text of Trinh's remarks, see Hanoi Radio, January 1, 1968.

58. The *New York Times* had previously suggested that such a move would provide an earnest of Hanoi's desire to move further along the road of reciprocal de-escalation. See *New York Times*, April 4 and 10, 1968.

59. *Ibid.*, May 5, 1968; see also *ibid.*, May 31, 1968.

60. *Ibid.*, May 6, 7, 12 and 24, 1968.

61. *Ibid.*, May 31, 1968.

62. One of the authors talked with Trinh Dinh Thao in early 1967.

63. Douglas Pike, *War, Peace and the Vietcong* (Cambridge, Mass.: M.I.T. Press, 1969), pp. 26 and 27.

64. *Ibid.*, p. 27.

65. See *Washington Post*, July 28, 1968.

66. *Department of State Bulletin* (Washington, July 8, 1968), p. 35.

67. *New York Times*, August 25, 1968.

68. *Ibid.*, July 29 and August 4, 1968.

69. *Ibid.*, May 17 and July 26, 1968.

70. See in particular interviews with David Schoenbrun of ABC and Murray Marder of the *Washington Post*, August 3 and 4, 1968; see also *New York Times*, August 4 and 11, 1968.

71. Transcript of the 19th Session. On September 6, in talking to one of the authors, members of the North Vietnamese delegation at Paris again pointed to the two-month suspension of rocket attacks against Saigon after June 21 and the reduction in military activity by the Vietcong and Hanoi, despite increased American ground sweeps, with an attendant decline in American casualties and stated: "Tell the people of America the truth as it is; tell them to look at the objective reality of reduced hostilities on our part."

72. *New York Times,* July 21, 1968.

73. *Ibid.*, July 31 and August 4, 1968.

74. *Ibid.*, August 19 and September 13, 1968.

75. *Ibid.*, August 24, 1968.

76. *Ibid.*, November 17, 1968.

77. *Ibid.*, November 1, 1968.

78. Major statements were issued by Hanoi, the Front and the Alliance and jointly by the NLF and the Alliance on November 2, 3, 4 and 5, respectively. For texts of these documents and Ho's appeal, see Hanoi Radio, November 2, 3 and 4, 1968, and Liberation Radio, November 4 and 5, 1968.

79. *New York Times,* March 9, 1969.

80. *Ibid.*, March 9 and 23, 1969.

81. *Ibid.*, March 9, 1969.

82. *Ibid.,* May 23, 1969 and *Newsweek,* June 9, 1969.

83. On April 18, 1969, Mr. Nixon stated: "I have not ordered and do not intend to order any reduction of our own activities. We will do what is necessary to defend our position and to maintain the strength of our bargaining position in the Paris peace talks." *New York Times,* April 19, 1969. This policy was reiterated in May, and in June a U.S. general was quoted as saying, "In terms of guidance from Washington, we have received nothing new except to hurry up." *New York Times*, May 23, 1969, and *Newsweek*, June 9, 1969.

84. Saigon Radio, December 31, 1968.

85. On February 4, 1969, the Ministry of Interior in Saigon had given Minh a stern warning for allegedly "distorting the truth" and "libelling the government" in a sermon. In his sentencing on March 15, he was charged with giving refuge to traitors and with illegal possession of weapons and documents. *New York Times,* February 24 and 26, and March 13, 16 and 18, 1969. See also *Saigon Daily News*, *Vietnam Guardian* and *Saigon Post,* February 26 through March 21, 1969. On the reduction of Minh's sentence, see Saigon Radio, May 25, 1969.

86. As a culmination of these moves Thieu on April 7 announced that he was forming a new pro-government political party and laid down the conditions for the formation of a "loyal" and "responsible" opposition party. Saigon Radio, April 7, 1969. On May 25, he accepted the leadership of the new government party, the National Social Democratic Front. See *New York Times,* May 26, 1969.

87. Saigon Radio, April 7, 1969.

88. See above, pp. 262, 337–338.

89. Article 5 of the constitution states: "(1) The Republic of Vietnam opposes communism in every form. (2) Every activity designed to propagandize or carry out communism is prohibited."

90. On March 25, Thieu had stated that in order to become a legitimate party, the Front would have to dissolve itself and become "another political party." *New York Times*, March 27, 1969.

91. *Ibid.*, May 28–31, 1969. The following week, on the eve of the Midway Island meeting, both Saigon and Washington hinted that the date for the presidential or any special elections might be subject to negotiation. *Ibid.*, June 6, 8 and 9, 1969.

92. This is the formal title of the ten-point NLF proposal, the text of which is found in Appendix 17. Although a text of this document is in *New York Times*, May 9, 1969, an official translation provided by the NLF delegation in Paris is the one used here. The following analysis of the text is based in part on a verbal explanation provided one of the authors by Tran Buu Kiem in Paris on May 25, 1969.

93. The details of how this coalition would be set up are further elaborated in a broadcast by Liberation Radio, May 26, 1969.

94. See, for example, *ibid.*; interview of Tran Buu Kiem on May 24, 1969, and June 14, 1969; and Hanoi Radio, May 27 and 29, 1969.

95. Interview of one of the authors with Tran Buu Kiem, May 25, 1969.

96. Senator McGovern's speech of February 23, 1969, at the University of Arkansas.

97. *New York Times,* May 2, 1969.

98. *Ibid.*, May 3, 1969.

99. A text of the major part of this speech is found in Appendix 18.

100. For a discussion of these six points see above, p. 394.

101. For typical communist views on "mutual troop withdrawal" see Hanoi Radio, May 16 and June 1, 1969; *Nhan Dan* ("*The People*"), May 17, 1969; and Liberation Radio, May 24, 1969. Part of this analysis is based on an interview by one of the authors with Tran Buu Kiem in Paris, May 25, 1969.

102. Interview with Tran Buu Kiem, May 25, 1969.

103. Liberation Radio, May 17, 1969.

104. In Tran Buu Kiem's interviews in late May he consistently stressed the importance of a peace cabinet.

105. Hanoi Radio, May 30, 1969.

106. See, for example, Thieu's press conference in Korea as broadcast on Seoul Radio, May 30, 1969.

Appendices

INTRODUCTORY NOTE: *We have not undertaken to provide a coverage of the documents that gives equal emphasis to the points of view of all the parties to the Vietnam conflict. Apart from a few basic documents such as the Geneva Agreements, we have selected those important materials that are not easily available to the general reader. Thus, there is a relatively large number of documents relating to the National Liberation Front.*

Appendix 1[*]

DECLARATION OF INDEPENDENCE OF THE DEMOCRATIC REPUBLIC OF VIET NAM

(EXCERPTS)

All men are created equal. They are endowed by their Creator with certain inalienable rights, among these are Life, Liberty and the pursuit of Happiness.

This immortal statement was made in the Declaration of Independence of the United States of America in 1776. In a broader sense, this means: All the peoples on the earth are equal from birth, all the peoples have a right to live, to be happy and free.

The Declaration of the French Revolution made in 1791 on the Rights of Man and the Citizen also states: "All men are born free and with equal rights, and must always remain free and have equal rights."

Those are undeniable truths.

Nevertheless, for more than eighty years, the French imperialists, abusing the standard of Liberty, Equality and Fraternity, have violated our Fatherland and oppressed our fellow-citizens. They have acted contrary to the ideals of humanity and justice.

In the field of politics, they have deprived our people of every democratic liberty.

They have enforced inhuman laws; they have set up three distinct political regimes in the North, the Centre and the South of Viet Nam in order to wreck our national unity and prevent our people from being united.

---

[*] SOURCE: Ho Chi Minh, *Selected Works* (Hanoi: Foreign Languages Publishing House, 1961), Vol. III.

They have built more prisons than schools. They have mercilessly slain our patriots; they have drowned our uprisings in rivers of blood.

They have fettered public opinion; they have practised obscurantism against our people.

To weaken our race they have forced us to use opium and alcohol.

In the field of economics, they have fleeced us to the backbone, impoverished our people and devastated our land.

They have robbed us of our ricefields, our mines, our forests and our raw materials. They have monopolized the issuing of bank-notes and the export trade.

They have invented numerous unjustifiable taxes and reduced our people, especially our peasantry, to a state of extreme poverty.

They have hampered the prospering of our national bourgeoisie; they have mercilessly exploited our workers. . . .

The truth is that we have wrested our independence from the Japanese and not from the French.

The French have fled, the Japanese have capitulated, Emperor Bao Dai has abdicated. Our people have broken the chains which for nearly a century have fettered them and have won independence for the Fatherland. Our people at the same time have overthrown the monarchic regime that has reigned supreme for dozens of centuries. In its place has been established the present Democratic Republic.

For these reasons, we, members of the Provisional Government, representing the whole Vietnamese people, declare that from now on we break off all relations of a colonial character with France; we repeal all the international obligation[s] that France has so far subscribed to on behalf of Viet Nam and we abolish all the special rights the French have unlawfully acquired in our Fatherland.

The whole Vietnamese people, animated by a common purpose, are determined to fight to the bitter end against any attempt by the French colonialists to reconquer their country.

We are convinced that the Allied nations which at Teheran and San Francisco have acknowledged the principles of self-determination and equality of nations, will not refuse to acknowledge the independence of Viet Nam.

A people who have courageously opposed French domination for more than eighty years, a people who have fought side by side with the Allies against the fascists during these last years, such a people must be free and independent.

For these reasons, we, members of the Provisional Government of the Democratic Republic of Viet Nam, solemnly declare to the world that Viet Nam has the right to be a free and independent country—and in fact it is so already. The entire Vietnamese people are determined to mobilize all their physical and mental strength, to sacrifice their lives and property in order to safeguard their independence and liberty.

September 2, 1945

Appendix 2[*]

GENEVA AGREEMENTS

A. Agreement on the Cessation of Hostilities in Viet Nam

July 20, 1954

Chapter I

Provisional Military Demarcation Line and Demilitarised Zone

Article 1

A provisional military demarcation line shall be fixed, on either side of which the forces of the two parties shall be regrouped after their withdrawal, the forces of the People's Army of Viet Nam to the north of the line and the forces of the French Union to the south.

The provisional military demarcation line is fixed as shown on the map attached, see Map No. 1.(1)

It is also agreed that a demilitarised zone shall be established on either side of the demarcation line, to a width of not more than 5 kms. from it, to act as a buffer zone and avoid any incidents which might result in the resumption of hostilities.

Article 2

The period within which the movement of all forces of either party into its regrouping zone on either side of the provisional military demarcation line shall be completed shall not exceed three

---

(1) Map not printed. (The demarcation line is shown on Maps 2 and 3, pp. 6 and 7.)

*Source: *Further Documents Relating to the Discussion of Indo-China at the Geneva Conference, June 16–July 21, 1954.* Miscellaneous No. 20 (1954), Command Paper 9239 (London: Her Majesty's Stationery Office, 1954).

hundred (300) days from the date of the present Agreement's entry into force.

Article 3

When the provisional military demarcation line coincides with a waterway, the waters of such waterway shall be open to civil navigation by both parties wherever one bank is controlled by one party and the other bank by the other party. The Joint Commission shall establish rules of navigation for the stretch of waterway in question. The merchant shipping and other civilian craft of each party shall have unrestricted access to the land under its military control.

Article 4

The provisional military demarcation line between the two final regrouping zones is extended into the territorial waters by a line perpendicular to the general line of the coast.

All coastal islands north of this boundary shall be evacuated by the armed forces of the French Union, and all islands south of it shall be evacuated by the forces of the People's Army of Viet Nam.

Article 5

To avoid any incidents which might result in the resumption of hostilities, all military forces, supplies and equipment shall be withdrawn from the demilitarised zone within twenty-five (25) days of the present Agreement's entry into force.

Article 6

No person, military or civilian, shall be permitted to cross the provisional military demarcation line unless specifically authorised to do so by the Joint Commission.

Article 7

No person, military or civilian, shall be permitted to enter the demilitarised zone except persons concerned with the conduct of civil administration and relief and persons specifically authorised to enter by the Joint Commission.

Article 8

Civil administration and relief in the demilitarised zone on either side of the provisional military demarcation line shall be the responsibility of the Commanders-in-Chief of the two parties in their respective zones. The number of persons, military or civilian, from each side who are permitted to enter the demilitarised zone for the conduct of civil administration and relief shall be determined by the respective Commanders, but in no case shall the total number authorised by either side exceed at any one time a figure to be determined by the Trung Gia Military Commission or by the Joint Commission. The number of civil police and the arms to be carried by them shall be determined by the Joint Commission. No one else shall carry arms unless specifically authorised to do so by the Joint Commission.

Article 9

Nothing contained in this chapter shall be construed as limiting the complete freedom of movement, into, out of or within the demilitarised zone, of the Joint Commission, its joint groups, the International Commission to be set up as indicated below, its inspection teams and any other persons, supplies or equipment specifically authorised to enter the demilitarised zone by the Joint Commission. Freedom of movement shall be permitted across the territory under the military control of either side over any road or waterway which has to be taken between points within the demilitarised zone when such points are not connected by roads or waterways lying completely within the demilitarised zone.

Chapter II

Principles and Procedure Governing Implementation of the Present Agreement

Article 10

The Commanders of the Forces on each side, on the one side the Commander-in-Chief of the French Union forces in Indo-China and on the other side the Commander-in-Chief of the People's Army of Viet Nam, shall order and enforce the complete cessation of all hostilities in Viet Nam by all armed forces under their control, including all units and personnel of the ground, naval and air forces.

Article 11

In accordance with the principle of a simultaneous cease-fire throughout Indo-China, the cessation of hostilities shall be simultaneous throughout all parts of Viet Nam, in all areas of hostilities and for all the forces of the two parties.

Taking into account the time effectively required to transmit the cease-fire order down to the lowest echelons of the combatant forces on both sides, the two parties are agreed that the cease-fire shall take effect completely and simultaneously for the different sectors of the country as follows:—

Northern Viet Nam at 8:00 a.m. (local time) on July 27, 1954.
Central Viet Nam at 8:00 a.m. (local time) on August 1, 1954.
Southern Viet Nam at 8:00 a.m. (local time) on August 11, 1954.

It is agreed that Peking mean time shall be taken as local time.

From such time as the cease-fire becomes effective in Northern Viet Nam, both parties undertake not to engage in any large-scale offensive action in any part of the Indo-Chinese theatre of operations and not to commit the air forces based on Northern Viet Nam outside that sector. The two parties also undertake to inform each other of their plans for movement from one regrouping zone to another within twenty-five (25) days of the present Agreement's entry into force.

Article 12

All the operations and movements entailed in the cessation of hostilities and regrouping must proceed in a safe and orderly fashion:—

(*a*) Within a certain number of days after the cease-fire Agreement shall have become effective, the number to be determined on the spot by the Trung Gia Military Commission, each party shall be responsible for removing and neutralising mines (including river- and sea-mines), booby traps, explosives and any other dangerous substances placed by it. In the event of its being impossible to complete the work of removal and neutralisation in time, the party concerned shall mark the spot by placing visible signs there. All demolitions, mine fields, wire entanglements and other hazards to the free movement of the personnel of the Joint Commission and its joint groups, known to be present after the withdrawal of the military forces, shall be reported to the Joint Commission by the Commanders of the opposing forces;

(*b*) From the time of the cease-fire until regrouping is completed on either side of the demarcation line:—

    (1) The forces of either party shall be provisionally withdrawn from the provisional assembly areas assigned to the other party.

    (2) When one party's forces withdraw by a route (road, rail, waterway, sea route) which passes through the territory of the other party (see Article 24), the latter party's forces must provisionally withdraw three kilometres on each side of such route, but in such a manner as to avoid interfering with the movements of the civil population.

Article 13

From the time of the cease-fire until the completion of the movements from one regrouping zone into the other, civil and military transport aircraft shall follow air-corridors between the provisional assembly areas assigned to the French Union forces north of the demarcation line on the one hand and the Laotian frontier and the regrouping zone assigned to the French Union forces on the other hand.

The position of the air-corridors, their width, the safety route for single-engined military aircraft transferred to the south and the search and rescue procedure for aircraft in distress shall be determined on the spot by the Trung Gia Military Commission.

Article 14

Political and administrative measures in the two regrouping zones, on either side of the provisional military demarcation line:—

(*a*) Pending the general elections which will bring about the unification of Viet Nam, the conduct of civil administration in each regrouping zone shall be in the hands of the party whose forces are to be regrouped there in virtue of the present Agreement.

(*b*) Any territory controlled by one party which is transferred to the other party by the regrouping plan shall continue to be administered by the former party until such date as all the troops who are to be transferred have completely left that territory so as to free the zone assigned to the party in question. From then on, such territory shall be regarded as transferred to the other party, who shall assume responsibility for it.

Steps shall be taken to ensure that there is no break in the transfer of responsibilities. For this purpose, adequate notice shall be given by the withdrawing party to the other party, which shall make the necessary arrangements, in particular by sending administrative and police detachments to prepare for the assumption of administrative responsibility. The length of such notice shall be determined by the Trung Gia Military Commission. The transfer shall be effected in successive stages for the various territorial sectors.

The transfer of the civil administration of Hanoi and Haiphong to the authorities of the Democratic Republic of Viet Nam shall be completed within the respective time-limits laid down in Article 15 for military movements.

(*c*) Each party undertakes to refrain from any reprisals or discrimination against persons or organisations on account of their activities during the hostilities and to guarantee their democratic liberties.

(*d*) From the date of entry into force of the present Agreement until the movement of troops is completed, any civilians residing in a district controlled by one party who wish to go and live in the zone assigned to the other party shall be permitted and helped to do so by the authorities in that district.

Article 15

The disengagement of the combatants, and the withdrawals and transfers of military forces, equipment and supplies shall take place in accordance with the following principles:—

(*a*) The withdrawals and transfers of the military forces, equipment and supplies of the two parties shall be completed within three hundred (300) days, as laid down in Article 2 of the present Agreement;

(*b*) Within either territory successive withdrawals shall be made by sectors, portions of sectors or provinces. Transfers from one regrouping zone to another shall be made in successive monthly instalments proportionate to the number of troops to be transferred;

(*c*) The two parties shall undertake to carry out all troop withdrawals and transfers in accordance with the aims of the present Agreement, shall permit no hostile act and shall take no step whatsoever which might hamper such withdrawals and transfers. They shall assist one another as far as this is possible;

(*d*) The two parties shall permit no destruction or sabotage of any public property and no injury to the life and property of the civil population. They shall permit no interference in local civil administration;

(*e*) The Joint Commission and the International Commission shall ensure that steps are taken to safeguard the forces in the course of withdrawal and transfer;

(*f*) The Trung Gia Military Commission, and later the Joint Commission, shall determine by common agreement the exact procedure for the disengagement of the combatants and for troop withdrawals and transfers, on the basis of the principles mentioned above and within the framework laid down below:—

1. The disengagement of the combatants, including the concentration of the armed forces of all kinds and also each party's movements into the provisional assembly areas assigned to it and the other party's provisional withdrawal from it, shall be completed within a period not exceeding fifteen (15) days after the date when the cease-fire becomes effective.

The general delineation of the provisional assembly areas is set out in the maps (2) annexed to the present Agreement.

In order to avoid any incidents, no troops shall be stationed less than 1,500 metres from the lines delimiting the provisional assembly areas.

During the period until the transfers are concluded, all the coastal islands west of the following lines shall be included in the Haiphong perimeter:

meridian of the southern point of Kebao Island,

northern coast of Ile Rousse (excluding the island), extended as far as the meridian of Campha-Mines,

meridian of Campha-Mines.

2. The withdrawals and transfers shall be effected in the following order and within the following periods (from the date of the entry into force of the present Agreement):—

Forces of the French Union

Hanoi perimeter	80 days
Haiduong perimeter	100 days
Haiphong perimeter	300 days

Forces of the People's Army of Viet Nam

Ham Tan and Xuyenmoc provisional assembly area	80 days
Central Viet Nam provisional assembly area—first instalment	80 days
Plaine des Joncs provisional assembly area	100 days
Central Viet Nam provisional assembly area—second instalment	100 days
Pointe Camau provisional assembly area	200 days
Central Viet Nam provision assembly area—last instalment	300 days

---

(2) Maps not printed.

CHAPTER III

Ban on the Introduction of Fresh Troops, Military Personnel, Arms and Munitions. Military Bases

Article 16

With effect from the date of entry into force of the present Agreement, the introduction into Viet Nam of any troop reinforcements and additional military personnel is prohibited.

It is understood, however, that the rotation of units and groups of personnel, the arrival in Viet Nam of individual personnel on a temporary duty basis and the return to Viet Nam of the individual personnel after short periods of leave or temporary duty outside Viet Nam shall be permitted under the conditions laid down below:—

(a) Rotation of units (defined in paragraph (c) of this Article) and groups of personnel shall not be permitted for French Union troops stationed north of the provisional military demarcation line laid down in Article 1 of the present Agreement during the withdrawal period provided for in Article 2.

However, under the heading of individual personnel not more than fifty (50) men, including officers, shall during any one month be permitted to enter that part of the country north of the provisional military demarcation line on a temporary duty basis or to return there after short periods of leave or temporary duty outside Viet Nam.

(b) "Rotation" is defined as the replacement of units or groups of personnel by other units of the same échelon or by personnel who are arriving in Viet Nam territory to do their overseas service there;

(c) The units rotated shall never be larger than a battalion— or the corresponding échelon for air and naval forces;

(d) Rotation shall be conducted on a man-for-man basis, provided, however, that in any one quarter neither party shall introduce more than fifteen thousand five hundred (15,500) members of its armed forces into Viet Nam under the rotation policy.

(e) Rotation units (defined in paragraph (c) of this Article) and groups of personnel, and the individual personnel mentioned in this Article, shall enter and leave Viet Nam only through the entry points enumerated in Article 20 below;

(*f*) Each party shall notify the Joint Commission and the International Commission at least two days in advance of any arrivals or departures of units, groups of personnel and individual personnel in or from Viet Nam. Reports on the arrivals or departures of units, groups of personnel and individual personnel in or from Viet Nam shall be submitted daily to the Joint Commission and the International Commission.

All the above-mentioned notifications and reports shall indicate the places and dates of arrival or departure and the number of persons arriving or departing;

(*g*) The International Commission, through its Inspection Teams, shall supervise and inspect the rotation of units and groups of personnel and the arrival and departure of individual personnel as authorised above, at the points of entry enumerated in Article 20 below.

Article 17

(*a*) With effect from the date of entry into force of the present Agreement, the introduction into Viet Nam of any reinforcements in the form of all types of arms, munitions and other war material, such as combat aircraft, naval craft, pieces of ordnance, jet engines and jet weapons and armoured vehicles, is prohibited.

(*b*) It is understood, however, that war material, arms and munitions which have been destroyed, damaged, worn out or used up after the cessation of hostilities may be replaced on the basis of piece-for-piece of the same type and with similar characteristics. Such replacements of war material, arms and ammunitions shall not be permitted for French Union troops stationed north of the provisional military demarcation line laid down in Article 1 of the present Agreement, during the withdrawal period provided for in Article 2.

Naval craft may perform transport operations between the re-grouping zones.

(*c*) The war material, arms and munitions for replacement purposes provided for in paragraph (*b*) of this Article, shall be introduced into Viet Nam only through the points of entry enumerated in Article 20 below. War material, arms and munitions to be replaced shall be shipped from Viet Nam only through the points of entry enumerated in Article 20 below.

(*d*) Apart from the replacements permitted within the limits laid down in paragraph (*b*) of this Article, the introduction of war material, arms and munitions of all types in the form of unassembled parts for subsequent assembly is prohibited.

(*e*) Each party shall notify the Joint Commission and the International Commission at least two days in advance of any arrivals or departures which may take place of war material, arms and munitions of all types.

In order to justify the requests for the introduction into Viet Nam of arms, munitions and other war material (as defined in paragraph (*a*) of this Article) for replacement purposes, a report concerning each incoming shipment shall be submitted to the Joint Commission and the International Commission. Such reports shall indicate the use made of the items so replaced.

(*f*) The International Commission, through its Inspection Teams, shall supervise and inspect the replacements permitted in the circumstances laid down in this Article, at the points of entry enumerated in Article 20 below.

Article 18

With effect from the date of entry into force of the present Agreement, the establishment of new military bases is prohibited throughout Viet Nam territory.

Article 19

With effect from the date of entry into force of the present Agreement, no military base under the control of a foreign State may be established in the re-grouping zone of either party; the two parties shall ensure that the zones assigned to them do not adhere to any military alliance and are not used for the resumption of hostilities or to further an aggressive policy.

Article 20

The points of entry into Viet Nam for rotation personnel and replacements of material are fixed as follows:—

—Zones to the north of the provisional military demarcation line: Laokay, Langson, Tien-Yen, Haiphong, Vinh, Dong-Hoi, Muong-Sen;

—Zone to the south of the provisional military demarcation line: Tourane, Quinhon, Nhatrang, Bangoi, Saigon, Cap St. Jacques, Tanchau.

CHAPTER IV

Prisoners of War and Civilian Internees

Article 21

The liberation and repatriation of all prisoners of war and civilian internees detained by each of the two parties at the coming into force of the present Agreement shall be carried out under the following conditions:—

(*a*) All prisoners of war and civilian internees of Viet Nam, French and other nationalities captured since the beginning of hostilities in Viet Nam during military operations or in any other circumstances of war and in any part of the territory of Viet Nam shall be liberated within a period of thirty (30) days after the date when the cease-fire becomes effective in each theatre.

(*b*) The term "civilian internees" is understood to mean all persons who, having in any way contributed to the political and armed struggle between the two parties, have been arrested for that reason and have been kept in detention by either party during the period of hostilities.

(*c*) All prisoners of war and civilian internees held by either party shall be surrendered to the appropriate authorities of the other party, who shall give them all possible assistance in proceeding to their country of origin, place of habitual residence or the zone of their choice.

CHAPTER V

Miscellaneous

Article 22

The Commanders of the Forces of the two parties shall ensure that persons under their respective commands who violate any of the provisions of the present Agreement are suitably punished.

Article 23

In cases in which the place of burial is known and the existence of graves has been established, the Commander of the Forces of either party shall, within a specific period after the entry into force of the Armistice Agreement, permit the graves service personnel of the other party to enter the part of Viet Nam territory under their military control for the purpose of finding and removing the bodies of deceased military personnel of that party, including the bodies of deceased prisoners of war. The Joint Commission shall determine the procedures and the time limit for the performance of this task. The Commanders of the Forces of the two parties shall communicate to each other all information in their possession as to the place of burial of military personnel of the other party.

Article 24

The present Agreement shall apply to all the armed forces of either party. The armed forces of each party shall respect the demilitarised zone and the territory under the military control of the other party, and shall commit no act and undertake no operation against the other party and shall not engage in blockade of any kind in Viet Nam.

For the purposes of the present Article, the word "territory" includes territorial waters and air space.

Article 25

The Commanders of the Forces of the two parties shall afford full protection and all possible assistance and co-operation to the Joint Commission and its joint groups and to the International Commission and its inspection teams in the performance of the functions and tasks assigned to them by the present Agreement.

Article 26

The costs involved in the operations of the Joint Commission and joint groups and of the International Commission and its Inspection Teams shall be shared equally between the two parties.

Article 27

The signatories of the present Agreement and their successors in their functions shall be responsible for ensuring the observance and enforcement of the terms and provisions thereof. The Commanders of the Forces of the two parties shall, within their respective commands, take all steps and make all arrangements necessary to ensure full compliance with all the provisions of the present Agreement by all elements and military personnel under their command.

The procedures laid down in the present Agreement shall, whenever necessary, be studied by the Commanders of the two parties and, if necessary, defined more specifically by the Joint Commission.

Chapter VI

Joint Commission and International Commission for Supervision and Control in Viet Nam

Article 28

Responsibility for the execution of the agreement on the cessation of hostilities shall rest with the parties.

Article 29

An International Commission shall ensure the control and supervision of this execution.

Article 30

In order to facilitate, under the conditions shown below, the execution of provisions concerning joint actions by the two parties, a Joint Commission shall be set up in Viet Nam.

Article 31

The Joint Commission shall be composed of an equal number of representatives of the Commanders of the two parties.

Article 32

The Presidents of the delegations to the Joint Commission shall hold the rank of General.

The Joint Commission shall set up joint groups, the number of which shall be determined by mutual agreement between the parties. The joint groups shall be composed of an equal number of officers from both parties. Their location on the demarcation line between the re-grouping zones shall be determined by the parties whilst taking into account the powers of the Joint Commission.

Article 33

The Joint Commission shall ensure the execution of the following provisions of the Agreement on the cessation of hostilities:—

(*a*) A simultaneous and general cease-fire in Viet Nam for all regular and irregular armed forces of the two parties.

(*b*) A re-groupment of the armed forces of the two parties.

(*c*) Observance of the demarcation lines between the re-grouping zones and of the demilitarised sectors.

Within the limits of its competence it shall help the parties to execute the said provisions, shall ensure liaison between them for the purpose of preparing and carrying out plans for the application of these provisions, and shall endeavour to solve such disputed questions as may arise between the parties in the course of executing these provisions.

Article 34

An International Commission shall be set up for the control and supervision over the application of the provisions of the agreement on the cessation of hostilities in Viet Nam. It shall be composed of representatives of the following States: Canada, India and Poland.

It shall be presided over by the Representative of India.

Article 35

The International Commission shall set up fixed and mobile inspection teams, composed of an equal number of officers appointed by each of the above-mentioned States. The mixed teams shall be located at the following points: Laokay, Langson, Tien-Yen, Haiphong, Vinh, Dong-Hoi, Muong-Sen, Tourane, Quinhon, Nhatrang, Bangoi, Saigon, Cap St. Jacques, Tranchau. These points of location may, at a later date, be altered at the request of the Joint Commission, or of one of the parties, or of the International Commission itself, by agreement between the International Commission and the command of the party concerned. The zones of action of the mobile teams shall be the regions bordering the land and sea frontiers of Viet Nam, the demarcation lines between the re-grouping zones and the demilitarised zones. Within the limits of these zones they shall have the right to move freely and shall receive from the local civil and military authorities all facilities they may require for the fulfilment of their tasks (provision of personnel, placing at their disposal documents needed for supervision, summoning witnesses necessary for holding enquiries, ensuring the security and freedom of movement of the inspection teams, &c. . . . .). They shall have at their disposal such modern means of transport, observation and communication as they may require. Beyond the zones of action as defined above, the mobile teams may, by agreement with the command of the party concerned, carry out other movements within the limits of the tasks given them by the present agreement.

Article 36

The International Commission shall be responsible for supervising the proper execution by the parties of the provisions of the agreement. For this purpose it shall fulfil the tasks of control, observation, inspection and investigation connected with the application of the provisions of the agreement on the cessation of hostilities, and it shall in particular:—

(*a*) Control the movement of the armed forces of the two parties, effected within the framework of the regroupment plan.

(*b*) Supervise the demarcation lines between the regrouping areas, and also the demilitarised zones.

(*c*) Control the operations of releasing prisoners of war and civilian internees.

(*d*) Supervise at ports and airfields as well as along all frontiers of Viet Nam the execution of the provisions of the agreement on the cessation of hostilities, regulating the introduction into the country of armed forces, military personnel and of all kinds of arms, munitions and war material.

Article 37

The International Commission shall, through the medium of the inspection teams mentioned above, and as soon as possible either on its own initiative, or at the request of the Joint Commission, or of one of the parties, undertake the necessary investigations both documentary and on the ground.

Article 38

The inspection teams shall submit to the International Commission the results of their supervision, their investigation and their observations, furthermore they shall draw up such special reports as they may consider necessary or as may be requested from them by the Commission. In the case of a disagreement within the teams, the conclusions of each member shall be submitted to the Commission.

Article 39

If any one inspection team is unable to settle an incident or considers that there is a violation or a threat of a serious violation, the International Commission shall be informed; the latter shall study the reports and the conclusions of the inspection teams and shall inform the parties of the measures which should be taken for the settlement of the incident, ending of the violation or removal of the threat of violation.

Article 40

When the Joint Commission is unable to reach an agreement on the interpretation to be given to some provision or on the appraisal of a fact, the International Commission shall be informed of the disputed question. Its recommendations shall be sent directly to the parties and shall be notified to the Joint Commission.

Article 41

The recommendations of the International Commission shall be adopted by majority vote, subject to the provisions contained in Article 42. If the votes are divided, the chairman's vote shall be decisive.

The International Commission may formulate recommendations concerning amendments and additions which should be made to the provisions of the agreement on the cessation of hostilities in Viet Nam, in order to ensure a more effective execution of that agreement. These recommendations shall be adopted unanimously.

Article 42

When dealing with questions concerning violations, or threats of violations, which might lead to a resumption of hostilities, namely:—

(*a*) Refusal by the armed forces of one party to effect the movements provided for in the regroupment plan;

(*b*) Violation by the armed forces of one of the parties of the regrouping zones, territorial waters, or air space of the other party;

the decisions of the International Commission must be unanimous.

Article 43

If one of the parties refuses to put into effect a recommendation of the International Commission, the parties concerned or the Commission itself shall inform the members of the Geneva Conference.

If the International Commission does not reach unanimity in the cases provided for in Article 42, it shall submit a majority report and one or more minority reports to the members of the Conference.

The International Commission shall inform the members of the Conference in all cases where its activity is being hindered.

Article 44

The International Commission shall be set up at the time of the cessation of hostilities in Indo-China in order that it should be able to fulfil the tasks provided for in Article 36.

Article 45

The International Commission for Supervision and Control in Viet Nam shall act in close co-operation with the International Commissions for Supervision and Control in Cambodia and Laos.

The Secretaries-General of these three Commissions shall be responsible for co-ordinating their work and for relations between them.

Article 46

The International Commission for Supervision and Control in Viet Nam may, after consultation with the International Commissions for Supervision and Control in Cambodia and Laos, and having regard to the development of the situation in Cambodia and Laos, progressively reduce its activities. Such a decision must be adopted unanimously.

Article 47

All the provisions of the present Agreement, save the second subparagraph of Article 11, shall enter into force at 2400 hours (Geneva time) on July 22, 1954.

Done in Geneva at 2400 hours on the 20th of July, 1954, in French and in Vietnamese, both texts being equally authentic.

For the Commander-in-Chief of the French Union Forces in Indo-China:

DELTIEL [Delteil],
Brigadier-General.

For the Commander-in-Chief of the People's Army of Viet Nam:

TA-QUANG-BUU,
*Vice-Minister of National Defence
of the Democratic Republic of Viet Nam.*

B. Final Declaration of the Geneva Conference on the Problem of Restoring Peace in Indo-China, in Which the Representatives of Cambodia, the Democratic Republic of Viet Nam, France, Laos, the People's Republic of China, the State of Viet Nam, the Union of Soviet Socialist Republics, the United Kingdom and the United States of America Took Part

July 21, 1954

1. The Conference takes note of the agreements ending hostilities in Cambodia, Laos and Viet Nam and organising international control and the supervision of the execution of the provisions of these agreements.

2. The Conference expresses satisfaction at the ending of hostilities in Cambodia, Laos and Viet Nam; the Conference expresses its conviction that the execution of the provisions set out in the present declaration and in the agreements on the cessation of hostilities will permit Cambodia, Laos and Viet Nam henceforth to play their part, in full independence and sovereignty, in the peaceful community of nations.

3. The Conference takes note of the declarations made by the Governments of Cambodia and of Laos of their intention to adopt measures permitting all citizens to take their place in the national community, in particular by participating in the next general elections, which, in conformity with the constitution of each of these countries, shall take place in the course of the year 1955, by secret ballot and in conditions of respect for fundamental freedoms.

4. The Conference takes note of the clauses in the agreement on the cessation of hostilities in Viet Nam prohibiting the introduction into Viet Nam of foreign troops and military personnel as well as of all kinds of arms and munitions. The Conference also takes note of the declarations made by the Governments of Cambodia and Laos of their resolution not to request foreign aid, whether in war material, in personnel or in instructors except for the purpose of the effective defence of their territory and, in the case of Laos, to the extent defined by the agreements on the cessation of hostilities in Laos.

5. The Conference takes note of the clauses in the agreement on the cessation of hostilities in Viet Nam to the effect that no

military base under the control of a foreign State may be established in the regrouping zones of the two parties, the latter having the obligation to see that the zones allotted to them shall not constitute part of any military alliance and shall not be utilised for the resumption of hostilities or in the service of an aggressive policy. The Conference also takes note of the declarations of the Governments of Cambodia and Laos to the effect that they will not join in any agreement with other States if this agreement includes the obligation to participate in a military alliance not in conformity with the principles of the Charter of the United Nations or, in the case of Laos, with the principles of the agreement on the cessation of hostilities in Laos or, so long as their security is not threatened, the obligation to establish bases on Cambodian or Laotian territory for the military forces of foreign Powers.

6. The Conference recognises that the essential purpose of the agreement relating to Viet Nam is to settle military questions with a view to ending hostilities and that the military demarcation line is provisional and should not in any way be interpreted as constituting a political or territorial boundary. The Conference expresses its conviction that the execution of the provisions set out in the present declaration and in the agreement on the cessation of hostilities creates the necessary basis for the achievement in the near future of a political settlement in Viet Nam.

7. The Conference declares that, so far as Viet Nam is concerned, the settlement of political problems, effected on the basis of respect for the principles of independence, unity and territorial integrity, shall permit the Vietnamese people to enjoy the fundamental freedoms, guaranteed by democratic institutions established as a result of free general elections by secret ballot. In order to ensure that sufficient progress in the restoration of peace has been made, and that all the necessary conditions obtain for free expression of the national will, general elections shall be held in July 1956, under the supervision of an international commission composed of representatives of the Member States of the International Supervisory Commission, referred to in the agreement on the cessation of hostilities. Consultations will be held on this subject between the competent representative authorities of the two zones from July 20, 1955, onwards.

8. The provisions of the agreements on the cessation of hos-

tilities intended to ensure the protection of individuals and of property must be most strictly applied and must, in particular, allow everyone in Viet Nam to decide freely in which zone he wishes to live.

9. The competent representative authorities of the Northern and Southern zones of Viet Nam, as well as the authorities of Laos and Cambodia, must not permit any individual or collective reprisals against persons who have collaborated in any way with one of the parties during the war, or against members of such persons' families.

10. The Conference takes note of the declaration of the Government of the French Republic to the effect that it is ready to withdraw its troops from the territory of Cambodia, Laos and Viet Nam, at the request of the Governments concerned and within periods which shall be fixed by agreement between the parties except in the cases where, by agreement between the two parties, a certain number of French troops shall remain at specified points and for a specified time.

11. The Conference takes note of the declaration of the French Government to the effect that for the settlement of all the problems connected with the re-establishment and consolidation of peace in Cambodia, Laos and Viet Nam, the French Government will proceed from the principle of respect for the independence and sovereignty, unity and territorial integrity of Cambodia, Laos and Viet Nam.

12. In their relations with Cambodia, Laos and Viet Nam, each member of the Geneva Conference undertakes to respect the sovereignty, the independence, the unity and the territorial integrity of the above-mentioned States, and to refrain from any interference in their internal affairs.

13. The members of the Conference agree to consult one another on any question which may be referred to them by the International Supervisory Commission, in order to study such measures as may prove necessary to ensure that the agreements on the cessation of hostilities in Cambodia, Laos and Viet Nam are respected.

C. Extracts from Verbatim Record of Eighth Plenary Session

July 21, 1954

The Chairman (Mr. Eden): As I think my colleagues are aware, agreement has now been reached on certain documents. It is proposed that this Conference should take note of these agreements. I accordingly propose to begin by reading out a list of the subjects covered by the documents, which I understand every delegation has in front of them.

First, agreement on the cessation of hostilities in Viet Nam; second, agreement on the cessation of hostilities in Laos; third, agreement on the cessation of hostilities in Cambodia. I would draw particular attention to the fact that these three agreements now incorporate the texts which were negotiated separately concerning the supervision of the Armistice in the three countries by the International Commission and the joint committees.

I should also like to draw the attention of all delegations to a point of some importance in connexion with the Armistice Agreements and the related maps and documents on supervision. It has been agreed among the parties to each of these Agreements that none of them shall be made public for the present, pending further agreement among the parties. The reason for this, I must explain to my colleagues, is that these Armistice terms come into force at different dates. And it is desired that they should not be made public until they have come into force.

The further documents to which I must draw attention, which are in your possession, are: fourth, declaration by the Government of Laos on elections; fifth, declaration by the Government of Cambodia on elections and integration of all citizens into the national community; sixth, declaration by the Government of Laos on the military status of the country; seventh, declaration by the Government of Cambodia on the military status of the country; eighth, declaration by the Government of the French Republic on the withdrawal of troops from the three countries of Indochina.

Finally, gentlemen, there is the Draft [final] Declaration by the Conference, which takes note of all these documents. I think all my colleagues have copies of this Draft Declaration (3) before them. I

---

(3) See preceding document.

will ask my colleagues in turn to express themselves upon this Declaration.

The Representative of France.

M. Mendès-France (France): Mr. Chairman, the French Delegation approves the terms of this Declaration.

The Chairman: The Representative of Laos.

Mr. Phoui Sananikone (Laos): The Delegation of Laos has no observations to make on this text.

The Chairman: The Representative of the People's Republic of China.

Mr. Chou En-lai (People's Republic of China): We agree.

The Chairman: On behalf of Her Majesty's Government in the United Kingdom, I associate myself with the final Declaration of this Conference.

The Union of Soviet Socialist Republics.

M. Molotov (U.S.S.R.): The Soviet Delegation agrees.

The Chairman: The Representative of Cambodia.

Mr. Tep Phan (Cambodia): The Delegation of Cambodia wishes to state that, among the documents just listed, one is missing. This is a Cambodian Declaration which we have already circulated to all delegations. Its purport is as follows: Paragraphs 7, 11 and 12 of the final Declaration stipulate respect for the territorial integrity of Viet Nam. The Cambodian Delegation asks the Conference to consider that this provision does not imply the abandonment of such legitimate rights and interests as Cambodia might assert with regard to certain regions of South Viet Nam, about which Cambodia has made express reservations, in particular at the time of the signature of the Franco-Khmer Treaty of November 8, 1949, on relations between Cambodia and France and at the time the French law which linked Cochin-china to Viet Nam was passed. Faithful to the ideal of peace, and to the international principle of non-interference, Cambodia has no intention of interfering in the internal affairs of the State of Viet Nam and associates herself fully with the principle of respect for its integrity, provided certain adjustments and regularisations be arrived at with regard to the borders between this State and Cambodia, borders which so far have been fixed by a mere unilateral act of France.

In support of this Declaration, the Cambodian Delegation

communicates to all members of this Conference a note on Cambodian lands in South Viet Nam.

The Chairman: If this Declaration was not inscribed on the agenda on the list of documents I have read out, it is because it has only at this instant reached me. I do not think it is any part of the task of this Conference to deal with any past controversies in respect of the frontiers between Cambodia and Viet Nam.

The Representative of the Democratic Republic of Viet Nam.

Mr. Pham van Dong (Democratic Republic of Viet Nam): Mr. Chairman, I agree completely with the words pronounced by you. In the name of the Government of the Democratic Republic of Viet Nam we make the most express reservations regarding the statement made by the Delegation of Cambodia just now. I do this in the interests of good relations and understanding between our two countries.

The Chairman: I think the Conference can take note of the statements of the Delegation of Cambodia just circulated and of the statement of the Representative of the Democratic Republic of Viet Nam.

I will continue calling upon countries to speak on the subject of the Declaration. I call upon the United States of America.

Mr. Bedell Smith (United States): Mr. Chairman, Fellow Delegates, as I stated to my colleagues during our meeting on July 18, my Government is not prepared to join in a Declaration by the Conference such as is submitted. However, the United States makes this unilateral declaration of its position in these matters:—

DECLARATION

The Government of the United States being resolved to devote its efforts to the strengthening of peace in accordance with the principles and purposes of the United Nations

Takes Note

of the Agreements concluded at Geneva on July 20 and 21, 1954, between (*a*) the Franco-Laotian Command and the Command of the People's Army of Viet Nam; (*b*) the Royal Khmer Army Command and the Command of the People's Army of Viet Nam; (*c*) Franco-Vietnamese Command and the Command of the People's Army of Viet Nam, and of paragraphs 1 to 12 of the Declaration presented to the Geneva Conference on July 21, 1954.

The Government of the United States of America

Declares

with regard to the aforesaid Agreements and paragraphs that (i) it will refrain from the threat or the use of force to disturb them, in accordance with Article 2 (Section 4) of the Charter of the United Nations(4) dealing with the obligation of Members to refrain in their international relations from the threat or use of force; and (ii) it would view any renewal of the aggression in violation of the aforesaid Agreements with grave concern and as seriously threatening international peace and security.

In connexion with the statement in the Declaration concerning free elections in Viet Nam, my Government wishes to make clear its position which it has expressed in a Declaration made in Washington on June 29, 1954, as follows:—

> "In the case of nations now divided against their will, we shall continue to seek to achieve unity through free elections, supervised by the United Nations to ensure that they are conducted fairly."

With respect to the statement made by the Representative of the State of Viet Nam, the United States reiterates its traditional position that peoples are entitled to determine their own future and that it will not join in an arrangement which would hinder this. Nothing in its declaration just made is intended to or does indicate any departure from this traditional position.

We share the hope that the agreement will permit Cambodia, Laos and Viet Nam to play their part in full independence and sovereignty, in the peaceful community of nations, and will enable the peoples of that area to determine their own future.

Thank you, Mr. Chairman.

The Chairman: The Conference will, I think, wish to take note of the statement of the Representative of the United States of America.

---

(4) This paragraph of the UN Charter reads as follows: "All Members shall refrain in their international relations from the threat or use of force against the territorial integrity or political independence of any state, or in any other manner inconsistent with the Purposes of the United Nations."

I call on the Representative of the State of Viet Nam.

Mr. Tran van Do (State of Viet Nam): Mr. Chairman, as regards the final Declaration of the Conference, the Vietnamese Delegation requests the Conference to incorporate in this Declaration after Article 10, the following text:—

> "The Conference takes note of the Declaration of the Government of the State of Viet Nam undertaking:
>
> "to make and support every effort to re-establish a real and lasting peace in Viet Nam;
>
> "not to use force to resist the procedures for carrying the cease-fire into effect, in spite of the objections and reservations that the State of Viet Nam has expressed, especially in its final statement."

The Chairman: I shall be glad to hear any views that my colleagues may wish to express. But, as I understand the position, the final Declaration has already been drafted and this additional paragraph has only just now been received; indeed, it has been amended since I received the text a few minutes ago. In all the circumstances, I suggest that the best course we can take is that the Conference should take note of the Declaration of the State of Viet Nam in this respect. If any of my colleagues has a contrary view, perhaps they would be good enough to say so. (None.) If none of my colleagues wishes to make any other observations, may I pass to certain other points which have to be settled before this Conference can conclude its labours?

The first is that, if it is agreeable to our colleagues, it is suggested that the two Chairmen should at the conclusion of this meeting address telegrams to the Governments of India, Poland and Canada to ask them if they will undertake the duties of supervision which the Conference has invited them to discharge. Is that agreeable? (Agreed.) Thank you.

The last is perhaps the least agreeable chapter of all our work. Certain costs arise from the decisions which the Conference has taken. It is suggested that it should be left here to your Chairmen as their parting gift to try to put before you some proposal in respect of those costs. I only wish to add in that connexion that, as this Conference is peculiar in not having any Secretariat in the usual sense of the term, the two Chairmen with considerable reluctance are prepared to undertake this highly invidious task. The costs to which I refer are not our own but those of the International Commission.

Does any delegate wish to make any further observation? (None.)

Gentlemen, perhaps I may say a final word as your Chairman for this day. We have now come to the end of our work. For a number of reasons it has been prolonged and intricate. The co-operation which all delegates have given to your two Chairmen has enabled us to overcome many procedural difficulties. Without that co-operation, we could not have succeeded in our task. The Agreements concluded to-day could not, in the nature of things, give complete satisfaction to everyone. But they have made it possible to stop a war which has lasted for eight years and brought suffering and hardship to millions of people. They have also, we hope, reduced international tension at a point of instant danger to world peace. These results are surely worth our many weeks of toil. In order to bring about a cease-fire, we have drawn up a series of agreements. They are the best that our hands could devise. All will now depend upon the spirit in which those agreements are observed and carried out.

Gentlemen, before we leave this hospitable town of Geneva I'm sure you would wish your Chairmen to give a message of gratitude to the United Nations and its able staff who have housed and helped us in our work.

And lastly let me express our cordial thanks to the Swiss Government and to the people and authorities of Geneva who have done so much to make our stay here pleasant as well as of service to the cause of peace.

The Representative of the United States of America.

Mr. Bedell Smith (U.S.A.): If I presume to speak for my fellow delegates, it is because I know that they all feel as I do. I hope that they join me in expressing our thanks to the two Chairmen of this Conference. Their patience, their tireless efforts, and their goodwill have done a great deal to make this settlement possible. We owe them our sincere thanks.

The Chairman: The Representative of the Union of Soviet Socialist Republics.

M. Molotov (U.S.S.R.): Mr. Chairman, as one of the Chairmen at the Geneva Conference, I would like to reply to the remarks just made by Mr. Bedell Smith, who spoke highly of the work done by the Chairmen. Naturally I must stress the outstanding services and the outstanding rôle played by our Chairman of to-day, Mr. Eden, whose rôle in the Geneva Conference cannot be exaggerated. And I would also like to reply and thank Mr. Bedell Smith for his warm words of to-day.

The Chairman: Has any other delegate anything else they want to say?

The Representative of Viet Nam.

Mr. Tran van Do (State of Viet Nam): Mr. Chairman, I expressed the view of the Delegation of the State of Viet Nam in my statement and I would have this Conference take note of it in its final act.

The Chairman: As I think I explained, we cannot now amend our final act, which is the statement of the Conference as a whole, but the Declaration of the Representative of the State of Viet Nam will be taken note of.

Any other observations? (None.)

I would like to be allowed to add my thanks for what General Bedell Smith has said and also to thank M. Molotov for his words. Both were undeserved, but even if things are not true, if they are nice things it's pleasant to hear them said.

But I do want to close this Conference with this one sentence: I'm quite sure that each one of us here hopes that the work which we have done will help to strengthen the forces working for peace.

Appendix 3 [*]

SOUTHEAST ASIA
COLLECTIVE DEFENSE TREATY

The Parties to this Treaty,

Recognizing the sovereign equality of all the Parties,

Reiterating their faith in the purposes and principles set forth in the Charter of the United Nations and their desire to live in peace with all peoples and all governments,

Reaffirming that, in accordance with the Charter of the United Nations, they uphold the principle of equal rights and self-determination of peoples, and declaring that they will earnestly strive by every peaceful means to promote self-government and to secure the independence of all countries whose peoples desire it and are able to undertake its responsibilities,

Desiring to strengthen the fabric of peace and freedom and to uphold the principles of democracy, individual liberty and the rule of law, and to promote the economic well-being and development of all peoples in the treaty area,

Intending to declare publicly and formally their sense of unity, so that any potential aggressor will appreciate that the Parties stand together in the area, and

Desiring further to coordinate their efforts for collective defense for the preservation of peace and security,

Therefore agree as follows:

Article I

The Parties undertake, as set forth in the Charter of the United Nations, to settle any international disputes in which they may be

---

[*] SOURCE: *Southeast Asia Treaty Organization.* Department of State Publication 6305 (Washington: U.S. Government Printing Office, 1956).

involved by peaceful means in such a manner that international peace and security and justice are not endangered, and to refrain in their international relations from the threat or use of force in any manner inconsistent with the purposes of the United Nations.

Article II

In order more effectively to achieve the objectives of this Treaty, the Parties, separately and jointly, by means of continuous and effective self-help and mutual aid will maintain and develop their individual and collective capacity to resist armed attack and to prevent and counter subversive activities directed from without against their territorial integrity and political stability.

Article III

The Parties undertake to strengthen their free institutions and to cooperate with one another in the further development of economic measures, including technical assistance, designed both to promote economic progress and social well-being and to further the individual and collective efforts of governments toward these ends.

Article IV

1. Each Party recognizes that aggression by means of armed attack in the treaty area against any of the Parties or against any State or territory which the Parties by unanimous agreement may hereafter designate, would endanger its own peace and safety, and agrees that it will in that event act to meet the common danger in accordance with its constitutional processes. Measures taken under this paragraph shall be immediately reported to the Security Council of the United Nations.

2. If, in the opinion of any of the Parties, the inviolability or the integrity of the territory or the sovereignty or political independence of any Party in the treaty area or of any other State or territory to which the provisions of paragraph 1 of this Article from time to time apply is threatened in any way other than by armed attack or is affected or threatened by any fact or situation which might endanger the peace of the area, the Parties shall consult immediately in order to agree on the measures which should be taken for the common defense.

3. It is understood that no action on the territory of any State designated by unanimous agreement under paragraph 1 of this Article or on any territory so designated shall be taken except at the invitation or with the consent of the government concerned.

Article V

The Parties hereby establish a Council, on which each of them shall be represented, to consider matters concerning the implementation of this Treaty. The Council shall provide for consultation with regard to military and any other planning as the situation obtaining in the treaty area may from time to time require. The Council shall be so organized as to be able to meet at any time.

Article VI

This Treaty does not affect and shall not be interpreted as affecting in any way the rights and obligations of any of the Parties under the Charter of the United Nations or the responsibility of the United Nations for the maintenance of international peace and security. Each Party declares that none of the international engagements now in force between it and any other of the Parties or any third party is in conflict with the provisions of this Treaty, and undertakes not to enter into any international engagement in conflict with this Treaty.

Article VII

Any other State in a position to further the objectives of this Treaty and to contribute to the security of the area may, by unanimous agreement of the Parties, be invited to accede to this Treaty. Any State so invited may become a Party to the Treaty by depositing its instrument of accession with the Government of the Republic of the Philippines. The Government of the Republic of the Philippines shall inform each of the Parties of the deposit of each such instrument of accession.

Article VIII

As used in this Treaty, the "treaty area" is the general area of Southeast Asia, including also the entire territories of the Asian Parties, and the general area of the Southwest Pacific not including the Pacific area north of 21 degrees 30 minutes north latitude. The

Parties may, by unanimous agreement, amend this Article to include within the treaty area the territory of any State acceding to this Treaty in accordance with Article VII or otherwise to change the treaty area.

Article IX

1. This Treaty shall be deposited in the archives of the Government of the Republic of the Philippines. Duly certified copies thereof shall be transmitted by that government to the other signatories.

2. The Treaty shall be ratified and its provisions carried out by the Parties in accordance with their respective constitutional processes. The instruments of ratification shall be deposited as soon as possible with the Government of the Republic of the Philippines, which shall notify all of the other signatories of such deposit.

3. The Treaty shall enter into force between the States which have ratified it as soon as the instruments of ratification of a majority of the signatories shall have been deposited, and shall come into effect with respect to each other State on the date of the deposit of its instrument of ratification.

Article X

This Treaty shall remain in force indefinitely, but any Party may cease to be a Party one year after its notice of denunciation has been given to the Government of the Republic of the Philippines, which shall inform the governments of the other Parties of the deposit of each notice of denunciation.

Article XI

The English text of this Treaty is binding on the Parties, but when the Parties have agreed to the French text thereof and have so notified the Government of the Republic of the Philippines, the French text shall be equally authentic and binding on the Parties.

Understanding of the United States of America

The United States of America in executing the present Treaty does so with the understanding that its recognition of the effect of aggression and armed attack and its agreement with reference thereto in Article IV, paragraph 1, apply only to communist aggression but affirms that in the event of other aggression or armed attack it will consult under the provisions of Article IV, paragraph 2.

In witness whereof, the undersigned Plenipotentiaries have signed this Treaty.

Done at Manila, this eighth day of September, 1954.

PROTOCOL TO THE SOUTHEAST ASIA COLLECTIVE DEFENSE TREATY

Designation of states and territory as to which provisions of Article IV and Article III are to be applicable:

The Parties to the Southeast Asia Collective Defense Treaty unanimously designate for the purposes of Article IV of the Treaty the States of Cambodia and Laos and the free territory under the jurisdiction of the State of Vietnam.

The Parties further agree that the above mentioned states and territory shall be eligible in respect of the economic measures contemplated by Article III.

This Protocol shall enter into force simultaneously with the coming into force of the Treaty.

In witness whereof, the undersigned Plenipotentiaries have signed this Protocol to the Southeast Asia Collective Defense Treaty.

Done at Manila, this eighth day of September, 1954.

Appendix 4 [*]

LETTER FROM PRESIDENT EISENHOWER
TO PRESIDENT DIEM, OCTOBER 1, 1954[†]

Dear Mr. President:

I have been following with great interest the course of developments in Vietnam, particularly since the conclusion of the conference at Geneva. The implications of the agreement concerning Vietnam have caused grave concern regarding the future of a country temporarily divided by an artificial military grouping, weakened by a long and exhausting war and faced with enemies without and by their subversive collaborators within.

Your recent requests for aid to assist in the formidable project of the movement of several hundred thousand loyal Vietnamese citizens away from areas which are passing under a *de facto* rule and political ideology which they abhor, are being fulfilled. I am glad that the United States is able to assist in this humanitarian effort.

We have been exploring ways and means to permit our aid to Vietnam to be more effective and to make a greater contribution to the welfare and stability of the Government of Vietnam. I am, accordingly, instructing the American Ambassador to Vietnam to examine with you in your capacity as Chief of Government, how an intelligent program of American aid given directly to your Government can serve to assist Vietnam in its present hour of trial, provided that your Government is prepared to give assurances as to the standards of performance it would be able to maintain in the event such aid were supplied.

---

[*] SOURCE: *Why Vietnam?* (Washington: U.S. Government Printing Office, 1965).

[†] Delivered to Diem via U.S. Ambassador Donald R. Heath on October 23, 1954.

The purpose of this offer is to assist the Government of Vietnam in developing and maintaining a strong, viable state, capable of resisting attempted subversion or aggression through military means. The Government of the United States expects that this aid will be met by performance on the part of the Government of Vietnam in undertaking needed reforms. It hopes that such aid, combined with your own continuing efforts, will contribute effectively toward an independent Vietnam endowed with a strong government. Such a government would, I hope, be so responsive to the nationalist aspirations of its people, so enlightened in purpose and effective in performance, that it will be respected both at home and abroad and discourage any who might wish to impose a foreign ideology on your free people.

Sincerely,

DWIGHT D. EISENHOWER.

Appendix 5 [*]

DECLARATION OF FORMER
RESISTANCE FIGHTERS
on the Present Situation in South Vietnam

March 1960

(EXCERPTS)

We,

Former Resistance Fighters, leaders and members of the Viet-minh-Lien Viet Front, of organizations of the Resistance: Workers, peasants, youth, women, old people, high school and university students, Mothers of Resistance Fighters, Pioneers;

Members of *Religious Organizations:* Cao Dai, Hoa Hao, Buddhists, Catholics;

Associations of Journalist Resistance Fighters, Artist Resistance Fighters, Chinese Nationals for Liberation;

Parties: Communist or Workers' Party, Vietnamese Democrat or Vietnamese Socialist;

Cadres and *Members of State Organisms* during the Resistance; *Individuals Not Adhering to Any Party;*

comprising, therefore, the vast majority of the Vietnamese people,

CONSIDER that it is time once again to solemnly proclaim our position to internal and international opinion on the present situation in South Vietnam. . . .

In the present circumstances,

WE LAUNCH AN URGENT APPEAL to all classes, all social strata, all milieu to struggle even more courageously, even more resolutely, to oblige the South Vietnamese authorities to:

---

[*] SOURCE: Declaration transmitted to the authors by a reliable and respected French source.

458

—Change their policies, to put an end to bloody "sweeping" operations, abolish the fascist 10/59 law,[1] annul the death sentences pronounced for patriots, liberate those in prison without valid cause, dissolve the concentration camps, the "agricultural development centers," the "prosperity zones," end the coercive policies directed at the populations of cities and the country;

Stop the repression of labor unions;

Eliminate all coercive measures against intellectuals, journalists, writers and members of liberal professions;

End the policy of repression of religious sects, ethnic minorities and progressive foreign nationals.

End the discriminatory rule of former zones of resistance, and the so-called "policy toward Former Resistance Fighters";

Respect and apply democratic liberties;

Reestablish security in the countryside;

Promote an independent, democratic economic policy, not subject to the Americans, eliminate the monopolies, protect national industry and commerce, reduce the import of American-made products, and eliminate the legislation of rice prices;

Reduce taxes, abolish unjustified taxes, eliminate the fines and other methods designed to exact money from the people, forced labor; find solutions to unemployment, stop dismissals, introduce social security, be concerned with labor conditions, and female civil servants, improve the situation of artists;

End the despoiling of land and ricefields and end the inflationary cost of farming;

Respect the desires of civil servants, soldiers, city officials and refugees;

Liberate themselves from submission to America, eliminate all U.S. bases in South Vietnam, expel the American military advisors and not accept any form of American interference in South Vietnam;

End the man-hunt to swell military ranks, and the enlisting of the "dân-vê" (self defence units) in the "bao-an" (militia),

---

[1]The text of this law may be found in Marvin E. Gettleman, ed., *Vietnam: History, Documents, and Opinions on a Major World Crisis* (New York: Fawcett, 1965), pp. 256-260.

end the construction of military bases; reduce military expenditures and put into effect a budget for improving the material and cultural life of the people;

Reject the aggressive Manila Pact (SEATO) and the new "friendly economic alliance," another camouflaged aggressive pact;

Undertake realistic measures to consult with the government of the Democratic Republic of Vietnam for holding general elections for unification, and, first of all, to establish normal relations between the people of the two zones in postal, economic, cultural and travel matters, etc.

Outlaw all depraved "culture" of American origin, revitalize and develop national culture, allow liberty of artistic expression and representation; build new schools, institute new scholarships, reform the teaching curriculum, respecting national feelings and democratic spirit, use the mother tongue in all classes.

The Former Resistance Fighters and all the people of South Vietnam struggle to end the colonial regime and the fascist dictatorship of the Ngo family, in order to form a National Democratic Union government in South Vietnam, composed of representatives of diverse political opinions and all social classes, accomplishing national independence and the democratic liberties guaranteeing a decent life for the people, respecting and integrally and rigorously applying the Geneva Accords, entering conferences with North Vietnam for the peaceful reunification of the country. This government would pursue a foreign policy of peace and friendship based on the principles of the Bandung conference.

The present struggle in South Vietnam is that of all the people and includes all political opinions, from the communists to individuals who merely desire reform, in other words the great majority of patriots. The force of our union, with the active support of our northern compatriots and the progressive peoples of the world, will prevail.

As in the past, during nine years of Resistance, faithful to our anti-imperialist traditions,

We,

Former Resistance Fighters

UNITED WITH ALL COMPATRIOTS of South Vietnam,
WILL NOT SPARE OUR FORCES in the struggle for national independence, peace, democracy and a free Vietnam, united and prosperous . . .

NAM-BO,

March 1960

The Former Resistance Fighters of South Vietnam

Appendix 6 *

NATIONAL LIBERATION FRONT (NLF)

A. Resolution of the Third National Congress of the Vietnam Workers' Party on the Tasks and Line of the Party in the New Stage, September 1960 *

(EXCERPTS)

The revolution in the South is a protracted, hard and complex process of struggle, combining many forms of struggle of great liveliness and flexibility, ranging from lower to higher, and taking as its basis the building, consolidation and development of the revolutionary power of the masses. During this process we must pay special attention to the work of organizing and educating the people, first and foremost the workers, peasants and intellectuals, promoting to the highest degree the patriotism of the various strata of our people. We must unceasingly expose the perfidious schemes and acts of the U. S. imperialists and their henchmen, in order to divide and isolate them as much as possible.

To ensure the complete success of the revolutionary struggle in south Viet Nam, our people there must strive to establish a united bloc of workers, peasants and soldiers, and to bring into being a broad National United Front directed against the U. S. and Diem and based on the worker-peasant alliance. This Front must rally all the patriotic classes and sections of the people, the majority and minority nationalities, all patriotic parties and religious group-

---

*Source: A. Resolution excerpted from the *Third National Congress of the Viet Nam Workers' Party Documents* (Hanoi: Foreign Languages Publishing House, 1960), Vol. I.

ings, together with all individuals inclined to oppose the U. S. and Diem. The aims of its struggle are peace, national independence, democratic freedoms, improvement of the people's living conditions and peaceful national reunification. The Front must rally all forces that can be rallied, win over all forces that can be won over, neutralize all forces that should be neutralized and draw the broad masses into the general struggle against the U. S. and Diem for the liberation of the South and the peaceful reunification of the Fatherland. . . .

The revolutionary movement in the South plays a very important role in relation to the reunification of the country. Simultaneously with the effort to build the North and take it towards socialism, our people must strive to maintain and develop the revolutionary forces in the South and create favourable conditions for peaceful national reunification.

Our people's struggle for the achievement of national reunification is a just struggle against the American imperialists and their henchmen, who are undermining the Geneva Agreements, an international instrument recognizing the independence, sovereignty, unity and territorial integrity of our country. Our Government and people are resolutely maintaining their line of peaceful national reunification and preserving the Geneva Agreements. We stand for the achievement of national reunification step by step in accordance with the spirit of the Programme of the Viet Nam Fatherland Front. But we must constantly heighten our vigilance and be prepared for any eventuality. If the American imperialists and their henchmen venture to unleash war in an attempt to invade the North, the whole of our people will resolutely stand up to defeat them and achieve independence and national reunification.

B. The Ten-Point Program of the NLF
December 20, 1960 [*]
(EXCERPTS)

I. To Overthrow the Disguised Colonial Regime of the U.S. Imperialists and the Dictatorial Ngo Dinh Diem Administration —Lackey of the U.S.—and to Form a National Democratic Coalition Administration

The present regime in South Vietnam is a disguised colonial regime of the U.S. imperialists. The South Vietnam administration is a lackey which has been carrying out the U.S. imperialists' political line. This regime and administration must be overthrown, and a broad national democratic coalition administration formed including representatives of all strata of people, nationalities, political parties, religious communities, and patriotic personalities. We must wrest back the people's economic, political, social and cultural interests, realize independence and democracy, improve the people's living conditions, carry out a policy of peace and neutrality and advance toward peaceful reunification of the Fatherland.

II. To Bring into Being a Broad and Progressive Democracy

1. To abolish the current constitution of the Ngo Dinh Diem dictatorial administration—lackey of the U.S. To elect a new National Assembly through universal suffrage.

2. To promulgate all democratic freedoms: freedom of expression, of the press, of assembly, of association, of trade union, of movement.... To guarantee freedom of belief; no discrimination against any religion on the part of the State. To grant freedom of action to the patriotic political parties and mass organizations, irrespective of political tendencies.

3. To grant general amnesty to all political detainees, dissolve all concentration camps under any form whatsoever. To abolish

---

[*] Source: B. Ten-Point Program from *The Voice of Justice* (Hanoi: Foreign Languages Publishing House, 1963).

the fascist law 10-59 and other anti-democratic laws. To permit the return of all those who had to flee abroad due to the U.S.-Diem regime.

4. Strictly to ban all illegal arrests and imprisonments, tortures and corporal punishment. To punish unrepenting cruel murderers of the people.

III. To Build an Independent and Sovereign Economy, Improve the People's Living Conditions

1. To abolish the economic monopoly of the U.S. imperialists and their henchmen. To build an independent and sovereign economy and finance, beneficial to the nation and people. To confiscate and nationalize the property of the U.S. imperialists and the ruling clique, their stooges.

2. To help industrialists and tradespeople rehabilitate and develop industry both large and small, and to encourage industrial development. Actively to protect home-produced goods by abolishing production taxes, restricting or ending the import of those goods which can be produced within the country and reducing import taxes on raw materials and machinery.

3. To rehabilitate agriculture, and to modernize farming, fishing and animal husbandry. To help peasants reclaim waste land and develop production; to protect crops and ensure the consumption of agricultural products.

4. To encourage and accelerate the economic interflow between the town and the countryside, between plains and mountainous areas. To develop trade with foreign countries without distinction of political regimes, and on the principle of equality and mutual benefit.

5. To apply an equitable and rational tax system. To abolish arbitrary fines.

6. To promulgate labour regulations, that is: to prohibit dismissals, wage cuts, fines and ill-treatment of workers and office employees, to improve the life of workers and public employees, and to fix wages and guarantees for the health of teen-age apprentices.

7. To organize social relief:
—Jobs for the unemployed.

—Protection of orphans, the elderly and disabled.

—Assistance to those who have become disabled or are without support owing to the struggle against U.S. imperialism and its stooges.

—Relief to localities suffering crop failures, fire and natural calamities.

8. To help displaced persons return to their native places if they so desire, and to provide jobs for those who decide to remain in the South.

9. Strictly to prohibit forcible house removals, arson, usurpation of land, and the herding of the people into concentration centres. To ensure to the country-folk and urban working people the opportunity to earn their living in security.

IV. To Carry Out Land Rent Reduction and Advance Toward the Settlement of the Agrarian Problem so as to Ensure Land to the Tillers

1. To carry out land rent reduction. To guarantee the peasants' right to till their present plots of land and ensure the right of ownership for those who have reclaimed waste land. To protect the legitimate right of ownership by peasants of the plots of land distributed to them.

2. To abolish the "prosperity zones" and the regime of herding the people into "agricultural settlements". To permit those forcibly herded into "prosperity zones" or "agricultural settlements" to return home freely and earn their living on their own plots of land.

3. To confiscate the land usurped by the U.S. imperialists and their agents, and distribute it to landless and land-poor peasants. To re-distribute communal land in an equitable and rational way.

4. Through negotiations, the State will purchase from landowners at equitable and rational prices all land held by them in excess of a given area, fixed in accordance with the concrete situation in each locality, and distribute it to landless and land-poor peasants. This land will be distributed free of charge and with no conditions attached.

V. To Build a National and Democratic Education and Culture

1. To eliminate the enslaving and gangster style American cul-

ture and education; to build a national, progressive culture and education serving the Fatherland and the people.

2. To wipe out illiteracy. To build sufficient general education schools for the youth and children. To expand universities, vocational and professional schools. To use the Vietnamese language in teaching. To reduce school fees; to exempt poor pupils and students from paying fees; to reform the examination system.

3. To develop science and technology and national literature and art; to encourage and help intellectuals, and cultural and art workers to develop their abilities in the service of national construction.

4. To develop medical services in order to look after the people's health. To expand the gymnastic and sports movement.

VI. To Build an Army to Defend the Fatherland and the People

1. To build a national army to defend the Fatherland and the people. To cancel the system of U.S. military advisers.

2. To abolish the pressganging regime. To improve the material life of the armymen and ensure their political rights. To prohibit the ill-treatment of soldiers. To apply a policy of assistance to families of poor armymen.

3. To award and give worthy jobs to those officers and soldiers who have rendered meritorious services in the struggle against the domination of the U.S. imperialists and their henchmen. To observe leniency toward those who had before collaborated with the U.S.-Diem clique and committed crimes against the people but have now repented and serve the people.

4. To abolish all the military bases of foreign countries in South Vietnam.

VII. To Guarantee the Right of Equality Between Nationalities, and Between Men and Women; to Protect the Legitimate Rights of Foreign Residents in Vietnam and Vietnamese Living Abroad

1. To ensure the right to autonomy of the national minorities.

To set up, within the framework of the great family of the Vietnamese people, autonomous regions in areas inhabited by minority peoples.

To ensure equal right among different nationalities. All nationalities have the right to use and develop their own spoken and written language and to preserve or change their customs and habits. To abolish the U.S.-Diem clique's present policy of ill-treatment and forced assimilation of the minority nationalities.

To help the minority peoples to catch up with the common level of the people by developing the economy and culture in the areas inhabited by them, by training skilled personnel from people of minority origin.

2. To ensure the right of equality between men and women. Women to enjoy the same rights as men in all fields: political, economic, cultural and social.

3. To protect the legitimate rights of foreigners residing in Vietnam.

4. To defend and take care of the interests of Vietnamese living abroad.

VIII. To Carry Out a Foreign Policy of Peace and Neutrality

1. To cancel all unequal treaties signed with foreign countries by the U.S. henchmen which violate national sovereignty.

2. To establish diplomatic relations with all countries irrespective of political regime, in accordance with the principles of peaceful co-existence as put forth at the Bandung Conference.

3. To unite closely with the peace-loving and neutral countries. To expand friendly relations with Asian and African countries, first of all, with neighbouring Cambodia and Laos.

4. To refrain from joining any bloc or military alliance or forming a military alliance with any country.

5. To receive economic aid from any country ready to assist Vietnam without conditions attached.

IX. To Establish Normal Relations Between the Two Zones and Advance Toward Peaceful Reunification of the Fatherland

The urgent demand of our people throughout the country is to reunify the Fatherland by peaceful means. The SOUTH VIETNAM LIBERATION NATIONAL FRONT undertakes the gradual reunification of the country by peaceful means, on the principle of negotiations and discussions between the two zones on all forms and measures beneficial to the Vietnamese people and Fatherland.

Pending national reunification, the governments of the two

zones will negotiate and undertake not to spread propaganda to divide the peoples or in favour of war, not to use military forces against each other. To carry out economic and cultural exchanges between the two zones. To ensure for the people of both zones freedom of movement and trade, and the right of mutual visits and correspondence.

X. To Oppose Aggressive War, Actively Defend World Peace

1. To oppose aggressive war and all forms of enslavement by the imperialists. To support the national liberation struggles of peoples in various countries.

2. To oppose war propaganda. To demand general disarmament, prohibition of nuclear weapons and demand the use of atomic energy for peaceful purposes.

3. To support the movements for peace, democracy and social progress in the world. Actively to contribute to the safeguarding of peace in South-East Asia and the world.

Appendix 7 [*]

INTRODUCTION TO THE U.S.
DEPARTMENT OF STATE WHITE PAPER, 1961

On September 25, 1961, in an address to the United Nations, President Kennedy warned that body and the people of the world of the dangers of "the smoldering coals of war in southeast Asia." Nowhere do those coals glare more ominously than in South Viet-Nam. While attention is diverted elsewhere—to Berlin, to negotiations over Laos, to turmoil in the Congo, to the United Nations itself, as well as to dozens of other problems—the Communist program to seize South Viet-Nam moves ahead relentlessly.

It is a program that relies on every available technique for spreading disorder and confusion in a peaceful society. Today it may call for the murder of a village chief known to be unfriendly to the Communists; tomorrow it may produce an attack in battalion strength against an outpost of the Army of the Republic of Viet-Nam. No tactic, whether of brutal terror, armed action, or persuasion, is ignored. If mining a road will stop all transport, who cares that a school bus may be the first vehicle to pass? If halting rice shipments means that many people go hungry, perhaps they will blame it on the Government. If people object to paying taxes to both the Communists and to the Government in Saigon, they are urged to refuse the latter.

The basic pattern of Viet Cong (Vietnamese Communist) activity is not new, of course. It operated, with minor variations, in China, and Mao Tse-tung's theories on the conduct of guerrilla warfare are known to every Viet Cong agent and cadre. Most of the same methods were used in Malaya, in Greece, in the Philip-

[*] SOURCE: *A Threat to the Peace: North Viet-Nam's Effort to Conquer South Viet-Nam,* Department of State Publication 7308 (Washington: U.S. Government Printing Office, 1961).

pines, in Cuba, and in Laos. If there is anything peculiar to the Viet-Nam situation, it is that the country is divided and one-half provides a safe sanctuary from which subversion in the other half is directed and supported with both personnel and materiel.

What follows is a study of Viet Cong activities in South Viet-Nam and of the elaborate organization in the North that supports those activities. The Communists have made the most elaborate efforts to conceal their role and to prevent any discoveries that would point an accusing finger at them for causing what is happening. But their efforts have not been totally successful.

In such a large-scale operation there are always some failures. There are defections. There are human frailties and some misjudgment. In major military operations prisoners are taken and documents are seized. All these and more have occurred in Viet-Nam. Over the years the authorities in Saigon have accumulated a mass of material exposing the activities of the Viet Cong.

This report is based on an extensive study of much of that material. It relies on documentary and physical evidence and on the confessions of many captured Viet Cong personnel. Officials of the Government of the Republic of Viet-Nam gave unselfishly of their time and their expert advice in connection with this investigation. Countless individuals and agencies responsible for gathering and interpreting this kind of evidence contributed to the research that went into this report. Without their cooperation and help, it obviously would not have been possible.

The specific cases cited herein have been presented, as they occurred, to the International Control Commission in Saigon by the Government of the Republic of Viet-Nam. Most recently, that Government made an elaborate presentation to the I.C.C. on October 24, 1961, of the data available at that time of Communist-directed subversion in South Viet-Nam. The presentation was accompanied by a request that the I.C.C. investigate. The Government in Saigon generously made available this same information for the compilation of this report.

What emerges from this study is a detailed, but by no means exhaustive, picture of Viet Cong operations and of the program of the Communist government in Hanoi to win power over all Viet-Nam. The Government of the United States believes that picture should be presented to the world.

There can be no doubt that the Government of the Republic of Viet-Nam is fighting for its life. Those who would help the people of South Viet-Nam to remain outside the Communist orbit must have a thorough appreciation of the nature of that fight and of the way it is being conducted by the authorities in Hanoi and their disciplined followers in the South.

Appendix 8 [*]

NATIONAL LIBERATION FRONT STATEMENT

on Situation after Assassination of President
Ngo Dinh Diem, November 8, 1963

(EXCERPTS)

The military putsch of 1 November set for the South Vietnamese people a number of urgent problems which any Vietnamese patriot is concerned with. That is the danger of the present war being expanded with deeper and deeper aggression of the U.S. imperialists. That is, the danger of the dictatorial regime being maintained in a new form and with new elements. It is the duty for any responsible and goodwill force in South Vietnam, regardless of the tendency and affiliation, resolutely to prevent the South Vietnam situation from developing in a more dangerous way, and to strive to improve that situation. The NFLSV [NLF] deems that in the present circumstances the Vietnamese people have full conditions to take appropriate and effective measures to lessen the sufferings of the 14 million people in South Vietnam, to create a basis to stabilize step by step the South Vietnam situation in conformity with the national interests and the aspirations of all the people. . . .

In the present situation, the NFLSV deems it necessary to put forth the most urgent demands of the South Vietnamese people, after the Ngo Dinh Diem clique was deposed:

1. Unconditionally abolish the dictatorial and fascist regime of Ngo Dinh Diem as a whole, including the U.S. dependent lines, the anticommunist policies which mean antipeople policies, the dictatorial fascist and war policies, the reactionary policies in general in internal and external affairs, the reactionary political organiza-

---

[*] SOURCE: Hanoi Radio, November 17, 1963.

tions under such labels as "Labor and Human Dignity Organization," "National Revolutionary Movement," "Women's Solidarity Movement," "Association of Victims of Communism," "Association of War Martyrs Families," "Republican Youth and Women," the network of policemen and secret agents, and so on, which constitute the tools to manipulate, control, and suppress the people, the "strategic hamlets, quarters, and sectors," the policies of militarizing youths and women, the antipopular laws such as law 10-59, the fascist law concerning the press, the emergency order, the order on mobilization and requisition, and so on. Release all political detainees regardless of tendency. Bring out in the open the crimes of the U.S.-Diem regime and bring to trial and duly punish those who perpetrated bloody crimes against the people.

2. Carry out without delay real and broad democracy, in which freedom of thought, expression, the press, organization, assembly, demonstration, trade union; freedom to set up parties, political, social, culture, and professional organizations; freedom of movement, trade, religion, and worship, corporal liberties are guaranteed by law for the entire people, without any discrimination.

Stop the persecution, arrest, and detention of patriots and opposition individuals and parties; cancel the barbarous prison regime, especially torture, penitence, brain washing, and ill treatment of prisoners. Refrain from setting up in South Vietnam any form of dictatorial regime, either nepotic and militarist or set up by a group or party, and from carrying out a policy of monoparty or monoreligion, a policy of dictatorship concerning thoughts, politics, religion, and economy.

3. Put an immediate end to the U.S. aggression in South Vietnam, withdraw all U.S. advisers from the Republican Army units and military and civilian branches, in an advance toward withdrawing from South Vietnam all troops and military personnel of the United States, including the military command of Paul D. Harkins, weapons and other war means. The U.S. imperialists must respect South Vietnam's independence and sovereignty, and must not interfere in its internal affairs. The U.S. Embassy must halt spying activities to foment trouble in South Vietnam. South Vietnam must enjoy complete sovereignty in all political, military, economic, and cultural fields, in internal as well as in foreign relations. It must not be dependent on any country whatsoever and must enjoy an

international position on equal footing with other countries. Only on such a basis can the relations between South Vietnam and the United States be normalized and the interests and honor of the latter in South Vietnam be guaranteed.

4. Carry out the policy of an independent, democratic, and rational economy; gradually raise the people's living standard in an advance toward eliminating unemployment and poverty. Cancel all harsh economic laws, recognize freedom of business, and trade; abolish completely all kinds of exacting taxes, supplementary taxes, and forcible money collections; reduce other taxes and cut fines. Guarantee and encourage the national economy, check the influx of foreign goods which upset the South Vietnam market. Abolish the monopoly of the U.S. imperialists and the Diem family. Increase wages of workers, armymen, public servants, and private enterprise employees.

5. Stop at once terrorist raids, strafings, and operations; and the use of chemical poison, toxic gas, and napalm bombs; generally speaking, end the war; restore peace and security and stabilize the situation in the countryside and the other part of South Vietnam; stop bloodshed among the Vietnamese people. Halt pressganging, demobilize the soldiers of the Republican Army whose military terms have expired, and let them return to their families and earn their living. We loudly declare that 18 years of war is more than sufficient! There is no reason to drag on the state of mourning on our soil merely because of the ambition of the warlike U.S. imperialists and their followers.

6. The parties concerned in South Vietnam [should] negotiate with one another to reach a cease-fire and solve the important problems of the nation, to stabilize the basic internal and external policies, with a view to reaching free general elections to elect state organs and to form a national coalition government composed of representatives of all forces, parties, tendencies, and strata of the South Vietnamese people. South Vietnam, once independent, will carry out a policy of neutrality, will not adhere to any military bloc, and will not let any foreign country station troops or establish bases in South Vietnam. It will accept aid from all countries regardless of political regime and establish friendly relations on an equal footing with all countries. South Vietnam respects the sovereignty of all countries and is ready to form together with the Kingdom

of Cambodia and Laos a neutral zone on the Indochinese peninsula.

Concerning the reunification of Vietnam, as was expounded many times by the NFLSV, the Vietnam Fatherland Front, and the DRV Government, it will be realized step by step on a voluntary basis, with consideration [given] to the characteristics of each zone, with equality, and without annexation of one zone by the other. We believe that if the above six pressing demands are met, South Vietnam will get rid of the present disastrous state of things. Once the war is ended, our people's [life] will be normalized, the foreign enslavement will be gradually eliminated, and no form of dictatorship will be able to exist in South Vietnam.

Appendix 9[*]

JOINT RESOLUTION, U.S. CONGRESS

["Tonkin Gulf Resolution"] August 7, 1964

To Promote the Maintenance of International Peace and Security in Southeast Asia.

Whereas naval units of the Communist regime in Vietnam, in violation of the principles of the Charter of the United Nations and of international law, have deliberately and repeatedly attacked United States naval vessels lawfully present in international waters, and have thereby created a serious threat to international peace; and

Whereas these attacks are part of a deliberate and systematic campaign of aggression that the Communist regime in North Vietnam has been waging against its neighbors and the nations joined with them in the collective defense of their freedom; and

Whereas the United States is assisting the peoples of southeast Asia to protect their freedom and has no territorial, military or political ambitions in that area, but desires only that these peoples should be left in peace to work out their own destinies in their own way: Now, therefore, be it

Resolved by the Senate and House of Representatives of the United States of America in Congress assembled,

That the Congress approves and supports the determination of the President, as Commander in Chief, to take all necessary measures

---

* Source: *Department of State Bulletin* (Washington, August 24, 1964). This resolution was adopted August 7 by the House of Representatives unanimously and by the Senate by a vote of 88 to 2. It came after the incidents in the Tonkin Gulf a few days earlier.

to repel any armed attack against the forces of the United States and to prevent further aggression.

SEC. 2. The United States regards as vital to its national interest and to world peace the maintenance of international peace and security in southeast Asia. Consonant with the Constitution of the United States and the Charter of the United Nations and in accordance with its obligations under the Southeast Asia Collective Defense Treaty, the United States is, therefore, prepared, as the President determines, to take all necessary steps, including the use of armed force, to assist any member or protocol state of the Southeast Asia Collective Defense Treaty requesting assistance in defense of its freedom.

SEC. 3. This resolution shall expire when the President shall determine that the peace and security of the area is reasonably assured by international conditions created by action of the United Nations or otherwise, except that it may be terminated earlier by concurrent resolution of the Congress.

Appendix 10 [*]

INTRODUCTION TO U.S. DEPARTMENT
OF STATE WHITE PAPER, 1965

South Viet-Nam is fighting for its life against a brutal campaign of terror and armed attack inspired, directed, supplied, and controlled by the Communist regime in Hanoi. This flagrant aggression has been going on for years, but recently the pace has quickened and the threat has now become acute.

The war in Viet-Nam is a new kind of war, a fact as yet poorly understood in most parts of the world. Much of the confusion that prevails in the thinking of many people, and even many governments, stems from this basic misunderstanding. For in Viet-Nam a totally new brand of aggression has been loosed against an independent people who want to make their own way in peace and freedom.

Viet-Nam is *not* another Greece, where indigenous guerrilla forces used friendly neighboring territory as a sanctuary.

Viet-Nam is *not* another Malaya, where Communist guerrillas were, for the most part, physically distinguishable from the peaceful majority they sought to control.

Viet-Nam is *not* another Philippines, where Communist guerrillas were physically separated from the source of their moral and physical support.

Above all, the war in Viet-Nam is *not* a spontaneous and local rebellion against the established government.

There are elements in the Communist program of conquest

---

[*] SOURCE: *Aggression from the North: The Record of North Viet-Nam's Campaign to Conquer South Viet-Nam,* Department of State Publication 7839 (Washington: U.S. Government Printing Office, 1965).

directed against South Viet-Nam common to each of the previous areas of aggression and subversion. But there is one fundamental difference. In Viet-Nam a Communist government has set out deliberately to conquer a sovereign people in a neighboring state. And to achieve its end, it has used every resource of its own government to carry out its carefully planned program of concealed aggression. North Viet-Nam's commitment to seize control of the South is no less total than was the commitment of the regime in North Korea in 1950. But knowing the consequences of the latter's undisguised attack, the planners in Hanoi have tried desperately to conceal their hand. They have failed and their aggression is as real as that of an invading army.

This report is a summary of the massive evidence of North Vietnamese aggression obtained by the Government of South Viet-Nam. This evidence has been jointly analyzed by South Vietnamese and American experts.

The evidence shows that the hard core of the Communist forces attacking South Viet-Nam were trained in the North and ordered into the South by Hanoi. It shows that the key leadership of the Viet Cong (VC), the officers and much of the cadre, many of the technicians, political organizers, and propagandists have come from the North and operate under Hanoi's direction. It shows that the training of essential military personnel and their infiltration into the South is directed by the Military High Command in Hanoi. (See section I.)

The evidence shows that many of the weapons and much of the ammunition and other supplies used by the Viet Cong have been sent into South Viet-Nam from Hanoi. In recent months new types of weapons have been introduced in the VC army, for which all ammunition must come from outside sources. Communist China and other Communist states have been the prime suppliers of these weapons and ammunition, and they have been channeled primarily through North Viet-Nam. (See section II.)

The directing force behind the effort to conquer South Viet-Nam is the Communist Party in the North, the Lao Dong (Workers) Party. As in every Communist state, the party is an integral part of the regime itself. North Vietnamese officials have expressed their firm determination to absorb South Viet-Nam into the Communist world. (See section III.)

Through its Central Committee, which controls the government of the North, the Lao Dong Party directs the total political and military effort of the Viet Cong. The Military High Command in the North trains the military men and sends them into South Viet-Nam. The Central Research Agency, North Viet-Nam's central intelligence organization, directs the elaborate espionage and subversion effort. The extensive political-military organization in the North which directs the Viet Cong war effort is described in section IV.

Under Hanoi's overall direction the Communists have established an extensive machine for carrying on the war within South Viet-Nam. The focal point is the Central Office for South Viet-Nam with its political and military subsections and other specialized agencies. A subordinate part of this Central Office is the Liberation Front for South Viet-Nam. The front was formed at Hanoi's order in 1960. Its principal function is to influence opinion abroad and to create the false impression that the aggression in South Viet-Nam is an indigenous rebellion against the established government. (See section IV.)

For more than 10 years the people and the Government of South Viet-Nam, exercising the inherent right of self-defense, have fought back against these efforts to extend Communist power south across the 17th parallel. The United States has responded to the appeals of the Government of the Republic of Viet-Nam for help in this defense of the freedom and independence of its land and its people.

In 1961 the Department of State issued a report called *A Threat to the Peace*. It described North Viet-Nam's program to seize South Viet-Nam. The evidence in that report had been presented by the Government of the Republic of Viet-Nam to the International Control Commission (I.C.C.). A special report by the I.C.C. in June 1962 upheld the validity of that evidence. The Commission held that there was "sufficient evidence to show beyond reasonable doubt" that North Viet-Nam had sent arms and men into South Viet-Nam to carry out subversion with the aim of overthrowing the legal Government there. The I.C.C. found the authorities in Hanoi in specific violation of four provisions of the Geneva accords of 1954.

Since then, new and even more impressive evidence of Hanoi's aggression has accumulated. The Government of the United States believes that evidence should be presented to its own citizens and to the world. It is important for free men to know what has been happening in Viet-Nam, and how, and why. That is the purpose of this report.

Appendix 11[*]

PRESS CONFERENCE BY THE
UN SECRETARY-GENERAL U THANT
February 24, 1965
(EXCERPTS)

QUESTION: *Along what lines do you envisage a possible solution of the Viet-Nam situation? Have you any positive proposals in mind?*

THE SECRETARY-GENERAL: As you know, I have been consistently advocating the necessity and the advisability of resort to political and diplomatic methods of finding a solution. I have felt all along that military methods will not produce the desired result; they will not produce an enduring peace in Viet-Nam.

In my view, there was a very good possibility in 1963 of arriving at a satisfactory political solution. In 1964 the situation deteriorated still further, and the prospects for a peaceful solution became more remote. Today, of course, the situation is much more difficult.

Although opinions may differ on the methods of bringing about a satisfactory solution in Viet-Nam, there is, I believe, general agreement on one point: that the situation in the Republic of Viet-Nam has gone from bad to worse. I do not think that there is any difference of opinion on that.

I have always maintained the view that the prospects for a peaceful settlement of this problem will be more and more remote as time goes on and as the aggravation develops. But still I do not believe it is too late to try diplomatic and political methods of

---

[*] SOURCE: United Nations Press Services Note 3075, February 24, 1965. The portions of the press conference that have been excerpted include all statements relevant to Vietnam.

negotiation and discussion. Of course I have never advocated the immediate withdrawal of United States troops from the Republic of Viet-Nam. I am fully conscious of the fact that such a step will naturally involve questions of face and prestige, and questions of the abrogation of previous commitments, and so forth. But I feel that once the diplomatic and political methods have been tried and if there is any perceptible improvement in the situation, if an agreed formula is at hand, if some sort of stability can be restored in the country, then at that time, of course, the United States can withdraw its troops with dignity.

As I said on a previous occasion, one prerequisite for peace in any country is the existence and functioning of a stable government. As you all know, this element is completely absent in the Republic of Viet-Nam.

QUESTION: *You speak of the best way of attaining an enduring peace in Viet-Nam. In view of the fact that the last negotiated agreements failed to maintain a secure and enduring peace in Viet-Nam and in view of the fact that the agreements reached at that time were broken, what would your comment be in answer to this argument, which I think is the main one put up against negotiations, that it did not work in the past and therefore it will not work in the future? They were abrogated.*

THE SECRETARY-GENERAL: I doubt the correctness of your hypothesis. Let me elaborate a little on this theme:

When I was in Burma, prior to my departure for New York about eight years ago, I studied the situation in South-East Asia very closely. To my knowledge, there was not a single instance—let me repeat—there was not a single instance of North Vietnamese providing military assistance or arms to the Viet Cong in South Viet-Nam in 1954 and 1955. So far, no evidence has been adduced to prove that the authorities in North Viet-Nam provided *materiel* and military assistance to the Viet Cong in the Republic of Viet-Nam in 1954 and 1955. After the developments in the next few months and the next few years, I am sure that there must have been involvement by the North Vietnamese in the affairs of the Republic of Viet-Nam.

While on the subject, at the risk of its being deemed a digression, let me say this: as you all know, I was very much involved in the affairs of my country, Burma, for many years since independence in January 1948 until I left Rangoon in 1957. Immediately after Burma's independence in January 1948, the Burmese communists went underground and started a widespread insurrection. This fact is known to everybody. The Burmese Government dealt with this internal problem by its own means, without asking for any outside military assistance or outside military arms or outside military advisers—or whatever you call them. The Burmese Government dealt with this internal insurrection by its own means. As you know, the Burmese Communist Party is still underground after 17 years and still illegal. But let me tell you: there has not been a single instance of outside help to the Burmese communists inside Burma in the last 17 years; there has not been a single instance of one rifle or one bullet supplied to the Burmese communists inside Burma in the last 17 years. And Burma has maintained and still maintains the friendliest relations with all its neighbours: with Thailand, with Laos, with mainland China, with India and with Pakistan. As you know, Burma has over 1,000 miles of land frontier with mainland China. If only the Burmese Government had decided at some stage to seek outside military assistance to suppress the internal insurrections and revolts, then I am sure that Burma would have experienced one of the two alternatives: either the country would be divided into two parts or the whole country would have become communist long ago. This proves one point: that Burma's attitude and policies both in regard to domestic affairs and foreign affairs have been very appropriate in the circumstances prevailing in South-East Asia.

Not one American life has been lost in Burma. Not one American dollar has been spent in Burma in the form of military assistance in the last 17 years. We should ask the great question: Why? I just present these facts to you just to set about thinking: Why?

QUESTION: *Have you any indication from the United States Government that it might under certain conditions consider a negotiation of the Vietnamese dispute? Also have you any indication that the United States might withhold further reprisals against North Viet-Nam in order to see whether such negotiations could get under way?*

THE SECRETARY-GENERAL: I have been conducting private discussions on this question of Viet-Nam for a long time, as you all know. Of course, it will not be very helpful at this stage to reveal even some parts or some features of the negotiations I have conducted. I just want to say that I have the greatest respect for the great American leader, President Johnson, whose wisdom, moderation and sensitivity to world public opinion are well known. I am sure the great American people, if only they know the true facts and the background to the developments in South Viet-Nam, will agree with me that further bloodshed is unnecessary. And also that the political and diplomatic method of discussions and negotiations alone can create conditions which will enable the United States to withdraw gracefully from that part of the world. As you know, in times of war and of hostilities the first casualty is truth.

QUESTION: *You said that the first prerequisite is for a stable government. Perhaps you have some ideas and suggestions for the creation or the composition of an inclusive and popular regime in Saigon which might be stable.*

THE SECRETARY-GENERAL: Of course, I have certain ideas on this aspect of the problem. I have communicated these ideas to some of the parties primarily concerned in the last two years. As I said a moment ago, I do not think it will be helpful if I reveal some of these ideas publicly at this moment.

QUESTION: *Mr. Secretary-General, going back to Viet-Nam, you seem to be suggesting that it would be very desirable if the United States troops got out of South Viet-Nam, if South Viet-Nam had a stable Government and if there were negotiations to possibly neutralize the whole area. There seems to be something concrete missing in this series. How are you going to achieve that? Can you pin this thing down for us a little more?*

THE SECRETARY-GENERAL: As I have been saying, Mr. Grant, I have presented certain ideas on my own to some of the principal parties directly involved in the question of Viet-Nam. I have even presented concrete ideas and proposals. But up to this moment the results of these consultations and discussions have not been conclusive. And I do not think it would be in the public interest for me to reveal these ideas publicly at this moment.

QUESTION: *Have they been presented to the United States among the other interested parties?*

THE SECRETARY-GENERAL: Yes.

QUESTION: *May I come back to the question of Viet-Nam again? If no progress is made toward negotiations, might you feel compelled unilaterally to step into the breach and bring the matter to the Security Council?*

THE SECRETARY-GENERAL: I do not think that is a practical proposition, for reasons that are obvious and well known to you. The Government of North Viet-Nam has all along maintained that the United Nations is not competent to deal with the question of Viet-Nam since, in its view, there is already in existence an international machinery established in 1954 in Geneva. They have all along maintained that position and, as you all know, it is a position that is also maintained by the People's Republic of China. As far as the United Nations is concerned, I think the greatest impediment to the discussion of the question of Viet-Nam in one of the principal organs of the United Nations is the fact that more than two parties directly concerned in the question are not Members of this Organization. I therefore do not see any immediate prospect of a useful discussion in the Security Council.

QUESTION: *Do you still hold to your previous view that the 1954 Geneva Conference on Indo-China should be reconvened in terms of the Viet-Nam question, and do you think that such a conference should try to find means to carry out the provision in the Armistice Agreement regarding Viet-Nam whereby elections would be held in both North Viet-Nam and South Viet-Nam for the establishment of a united Viet-Nam?*

THE SECRETARY-GENERAL: As I have been saying, it may be rather belated to expect the same results as one could have expected, say, two years ago. But I think that it is worth trying.

On the twelfth of this month I advocated publicly that, if there are still difficulties on the part of some of the large Powers as regards the immediate convening of a Geneva-type conference, it could be worth while exploring the possibilities of informal, private and confidential dialogues between some of the parties directly involved, as a preliminary step towards the convening of a more formal conference. That was my appeal. Of course, I have no way of knowing what will happen if these dialogues take place or if a formal conference takes place. I do not know what will be the result of such discussions; I do not think that anyone knows. But it is worth trying. And let me repeat what I said a moment ago: the longer we delay, the more difficult will be the achievement of an enduring peace in Viet-Nam.

QUESTION: *Could I come back to the question of the elections in North Viet-Nam and South Viet-Nam, leading to the unification of the two Viet-Nams? Do you advocate that?*

THE SECRETARY-GENERAL: I do not want to go into the substance of the agreements arrived at in Geneva in 1954. I do not know the practical difficulties in the way of conducting free elections, both in North Viet-Nam and in South Viet-Nam. I do believe, however, that elections were possible at some stage.

QUESTION: *Have you had any positive or favourable responses from any of the parties, and particularly from Peking and Hanoi, to the proposal you just mentioned—that is, the proposal for preliminary contacts?*

THE SECRETARY-GENERAL: I do not think that it would be in the public interest to reveal any information at this stage on that aspect of my discussions.

Appendix 12*

STATEMENT BY THE NATIONAL
LIBERATION FRONT
March 22, 1965

(EXCERPTS)

For more than ten years now, the U.S. imperialists have continuously interfered in, and committed aggression against, South Vietnam. Of late, they have brought into South Vietnam many more units of U.S. combat troops composed of missile units, marines, B-57 strategic bombers, together with mercenary troops from South Korea, Taiwan, the Philippines, Australia, Malaya, etc. They even frenziedly ordered the air forces of the U.S.A. and its henchmen to conduct repeated air raids on North Vietnam and Laos. At present, not only are they stubbornly stepping up their criminal aggressive war in South Vietnam but are also attempting to fan up the flames of war throughout Indochina and Southeast Asia. . . .

Faced with the present situation of utmost gravity, the South Vietnam National Front for Liberation deems it necessary to reaf-

---

* Source: Excerpted from that major part of the statement reproduced in Marvin E. Gettleman, ed., *Vietnam: History, Documents, and Opinions on a Major World Crisis* (New York: Fawcett, 1965). This text has been used rather than that found in *We Will Win* (Hanoi: Foreign Languages Publishing House, 1965) because the translation is slightly clearer. However, in substance the two are completely congruent.

firm once again in a formal way its unswerving will to carry out the war of resistance against the U.S. imperialists.

1: *The U.S. imperialists are the saboteurs of the Geneva Agreements, the most brazen warmongers and aggressors and the sworn enemy of the Vietnamese people.*

As is known to everyone, in their extremely glorious war of resistance the Vietnamese people defeated the aggression of the French colonialists and the intervention and assistance of the U.S. imperialists. In fact, during the past war of resistance of the Vietnamese people the U.S. imperialists supplied to the French colonialists 2,600 million dollars, hundreds of thousands of tons of weapons, and 200 military advisers to frustrate the aspiration for independence and freedom of the Vietnamese people. . . .

The Vietnamese people are deeply aware of the value of these [Geneva] Agreements. Now as in the past they have been correctly implementing these Agreements and are resolved to have these Agreements implemented in their spirit and letters as all international agreements with full legal validity should be. On the contrary, the U.S. imperialists and their henchmen in South Vietnam have step by step and daily more brazenly trampled on the Geneva Agreements and have in fact scrapped them. They have brazenly conducted an atrocious war of aggression in South Vietnam during the past eleven years in an attempt to enslave and oppress the South Vietnamese people, turn South Vietnam into one of their colonies and military bases, and perpetuate the division of Vietnam.

Hardly had the ink dried on the Geneva Agreements when the U.S. imperialists hastily dragged their henchmen satellites into setting up the SEATO military bloc and brazenly placed South Vietnam in the "protection" area of this bloc, which amounted in reality to putting South Vietnam under the command of the United States. Ever since, the U.S.A. has undertaken deeper and more and more cynical intervention in South Vietnam. . . .

At present, the fact in South Vietnam is that the U.S. imperialists are waging a criminal aggressive war, that the U.S. imperialists are the most impudent saboteurs of the Geneva Agreements, the most dangerous war provocateurs and aggressors, and the sworn enemy [sic] of the peoples of Vietnam, Indochina, and of the other peoples of the world.

2: *The heroic South Vietnamese people are resolved to drive out the U.S. imperialists in order to liberate South Vietnam, achieve an independent, democratic, peaceful, and neutral South Vietnam and eventual national reunification.*

The South Vietnamese people have always cherished peace, but are determined not to sit with folded arms and let the U.S. aggressors and their henchmen do what they like and let them trample upon their homeland and ride on them. They had rather die than be enslaved. The fourteen million valiant South Vietnamese people have stood up as one man in a gallant struggle to defeat the U.S. aggressors and their traitors so as to liberate South Vietnam, achieve independence, democracy, peace, and neutrality in South Vietnam, in contribution to the maintenance of peace in Indochina and Southeast Asia.

The patriotic war of the South Vietnamese people is fully consistent with the most elementary and basic principles of international law concerning the people's rights to self-determination and to wage a patriotic and self-defense war against foreign aggression.

In their sacred liberation war, the South Vietnamese people have used all kinds of weapons to fight against the enemy. The chief and biggest arms supplier for the South Vietnamese people's armed forces is nobody else than the U.S. imperialists themselves who have sustained heavy and repeated setbacks over the past years.

. . . The fact that the U.S. imperialists have dispatched to South Vietnam more weapons and combat troops . . . is no indication of their strength but only of the frenzied behaviour of a truculent enemy who has gone out of his senses. It can intimidate nobody. . . .

The South Vietnamese people want to tell the U.S. imperialists and their agents this:

At present, the only way for you, U.S. imperialists, is to pull out of South Vietnam. If you stubbornly continue plunging headlong into the war you will sustain the biggest and most shameful failures. On behalf of the fourteen million valiant South Vietnamese people, the South Vietnam National Front for Liberation solemnly declares: The South Vietnamese people and their armed forces are resolved never to lose hold of their arms so long as they have not reached these goals of theirs: independence, democracy, peace, and neutrality. The South Vietnamese people are determined to go on dealing thunder blows at the U.S. aggressors and their lackeys, and they will surely win final victory. All negotiations with the U.S. imperialists at this moment are entirely useless if they still refuse to withdraw from South Vietnam all their troops and all kinds of war materials and means and those of their satellites, if they still do not dismantle all their military bases in South Vietnam, if the traitors still surrender the South Vietnamese people's sacred rights to independence and democracy to the U.S. imperialists, and if the South Vietnam National Front for Liberation—the only genuine representative of the fourteen million South Vietnamese people—does not have its decisive say.

3: *The valiant South Vietnamese people and the South Vietnam liberation army are resolved to fully accomplish their sacred duty to drive out the U.S. imperialists so as to liberate South Vietnam and defend North Vietnam.*

Vietnam is one, the Vietnamese people are one. North and South Vietnam are of the same family. This sentiment is higher than mountains and deeper than the sea. This truth is like the sun rising in the East and cannot be shaken by any force whatsoever. In the present state of blood and fire, in life-and-death struggle against the U.S. imperialists and their lackeys, the heart cannot but feel a pain when the hand is cut. That the people in North Vietnam are resolved to fulfill their duty toward their kith and kin in South Vietnam is just sense and reason.

On behalf of the fourteen million South Vietnamese people, the South Vietnam National Front for Liberation conveys to their seventeen million relatives in the North their steel-like confidence and unchanging pledge: "the heroic South Vietnamese people and the South Vietnam liberation army are determined to fully accomplish their sacred duty to drive out the U.S. imperialists, liberate South Vietnam, and defend the North, with a view to the reunification of their fatherland."

Recently, to escape from their critical situation and their inevitable collapse in South Vietnam, the U.S. imperialists and their flunkeys recklessly sent aircraft and warships to bomb, strafe, and shell North Vietnam, but they have received due punishment. Over fifty American jet planes have been shot down. The South Vietnam army and people greatly rejoice at, and warmly hail, those brilliant feats of arms of the North Vietnam army and people.

The heart feels a pain when the hand is cut! To defend the beloved North, the army and people of the South have given vent to their anger at the U.S. aggressors and their agents. If the U.S. imperialists lay hands upon the North of our fatherland once, the army and people of the South are resolved to strike twice or thrice as hard at them. . . .

The South Vietnam National Front for Liberation and the South Vietnamese people warn the U.S. imperialists and their lackeys: Should you dare expand the aggressive war to the whole of Vietnam and fan up the flames of war in the whole of Indochina, the invincible strength of the more than thirty million people of Vietnam and the strength to move mountains and drain up seas of the hundreds of millions of people in Indo-china and Asia will wipe you out and bury you.

> 4: *The South Vietnamese people express their profound gratitude to the wholehearted support of the peace- and justice-loving people all over the world and declare their readiness to receive all assistance, including weapons and all other war materials from their friends in the five continents.*

The just and patriotic struggle of the South Vietnamese people has enjoyed the sympathy, support, and encouragement of the peace- and justice-loving people throughout the world. Not only have the world peoples supported the South Vietnamese people morally, but have also assisted and are assisting them materially. Of course the South Vietnamese people and their representative— the South Vietnam National Front for Liberation—are fully entitled to accept, and greatly appreciate, such valuable assistance.

The South Vietnam National Front for Liberation has always relied mainly on its own strength and capacity, but it is ready to accept all assistance both moral and material, including weapons and all other war materials from other countries to strengthen the potential of its self-defense war . . .

The South Vietnam National Front for Liberation will [also]

call on the peoples of various countries to send young men and army men to South Vietnam to fight shoulder-to-shoulder with the South Vietnamese people and together annihilate the common enemy.

While the U.S. imperialists are constantly sowing suffering and death in South Vietnam, the South Vietnam National Front for Liberation, if need be, cannot but call back the sons and daughters of South Vietnam who regrouped to the North in observance of the cease-fire agreement and who have had to live far from South Vietnam during ten long years, to take arms to annihilate the enemy to save their country and homes. . . .

5: *The whole people to unite, the whole people to take up arms, to continue to march forward heroically, and to resolve to fight and to defeat the U.S. aggressors and Vietnamese traitors.*

The armed struggle waged by the South Vietnamese people against the U.S. aggressors and their henchmen has won very great victories. The U.S. imperialists and their lackeys are formidable in appearance but are inwardly very weak and very confused and more isolated than ever. The South Vietnamese people, bearing in mind their vow "rather to die than to be enslaved," will definitely smash the barbarous and predatory enemy.

The South Vietnam National Front for Liberation and the South Vietnamese people not only have justice on their side but have also developed and are developing rapidly their material and organizational strength. They have been and are the glorious victors. The more they fight the stronger they become and the more numerous and greater their victories.

We are worthy successors to, and have upheld to a high degree, the Dienbienphu tradition and the heroic tradition of the Vietnamese nation credited with 4,000 years of history against the invaders. Moreover, the South Vietnam National Front for Liberation and the South Vietnamese people are fighting heroically in the extremely favorable conditions of the present era, that of the revolutionary rising tide of the oppressed nations in Asia, Africa, and Latin America. The Socialist countries and the forces of democracy and peace all over the world are an important factor stimulating the advance of mankind, overwhelming and annihilating imperialism and colonialism of all brands. If the U.S. imperialists and their henchmen are rash enough to spread the flames of war all over

Indochina, the people of this area and Southeast Asia are resolved to stand up as one man and sweep them out into the ocean.

The South Vietnamese people and their only genuine representative—the South Vietnam National Front for Liberation—will undoubtedly win final victory. . . .

Even if we are to carry out the struggle for ten, twenty years or longer and have to suffer greater difficulties and hardships, we are prepared and resolved to fight and fight to the end until not a single U.S. soldier can be seen in our country.

The Vietnamese people's history is thousands of years old. That is the heroic history of a heroic nation. During the past ten years of fighting against the U.S. imperialist aggressors and their quislings, the people and liberation armed forces of South Vietnam have written a golden page in the glorious history of their people. We have won and we are winning; the U.S. imperialists and their agents have lost and are losing. This proves that our strength is invincible, that the U.S. aggressors and their agents are weak. If we have triumphed over the U.S. during the past ten years, we are now provided with far more favorable conditions to defeat them. If the U.S. aggressors and their lackeys have been defeated during the past ten years, they are now all the weaker and will suffer heavier defeats. Especially if the U.S. imperialists extend the war to the North, they will certainly incur more shameful defeats.

We are absolutely confident that victory belongs to us. We are determined to fight, hit vigorously and accurately at the U.S. aggressors and their quislings to liberate the South, defend the North, and reunify our fatherland.

Appendix 13[*]

PRESIDENT JOHNSON'S BALTIMORE SPEECH
APRIL 7, 1965

A. Text of "Pattern for Peace in Southeast Asia"

Last week 17 nations sent their views to some two dozen countries having an interest in Southeast Asia. We are joining those 17 countries and stating our American policy tonight, which we believe will contribute toward peace in this area of the world.

I have come here to review once again with my own people the views of the American Government.

Tonight Americans and Asians are dying for a world where each people may choose its own path to change. This is the principle for which our ancestors fought in the valleys of Pennsylvania. It is a principle for which our sons fight tonight in the jungles of Viet-Nam.

Viet-Nam is far away from this quiet campus [Johns Hopkins University]. We have no territory there, nor do we seek any. The war is dirty and brutal and difficult. And some 400 young men, born into an America that is bursting with opportunity and promise, have ended their lives on Viet-Nam's steaming soil.

Why must we take this painful road? Why must this nation hazard its ease, its interest, and its power for the sake of a people so far away?

We fight because we must fight if we are to live in a world where every country can shape its own destiny, and only in such a world will our own freedom be finally secure.

This kind of world will never be built by bombs or bullets. Yet the infirmities of man are such that force must often precede reason and the waste of war, the works of peace. We wish that this were

---

[*] Source: A. *Department of State Bulletin* (Washington, April 26, 1965).

not so. But we must deal with the world as it is, if it is ever to be as we wish.

The world as it is in Asia is not a serene or peaceful place.

The first reality is that North Viet-Nam has attacked the independent nation of South Viet-Nam. Its object is total conquest. Of course, some of the people of South Viet-Nam are participating in attack on their own government. But trained men and supplies, orders and arms, flow in a constant stream from North to South.

This support is the heartbeat of the war.

And it is a war of unparalleled brutality. Simple farmers are the targets of assassination and kidnaping. Women and children are strangled in the night because their men are loyal to their government. And helpless villages are ravaged by sneak attacks. Large-scale raids are conducted on towns, and terror strikes in the heart of cities.

The confused nature of this conflict cannot mask the fact that it is the new face of an old enemy.

Over this war—and all Asia—is another reality: the deepening shadow of Communist China. The rulers in Hanoi are urged on by Peiping. This is a regime which has destroyed freedom in Tibet, which has attacked India, and has been condemned by the United Nations for aggression in Korea. It is a nation which is helping the forces of violence in almost every continent. The contest in Viet-Nam is part of a wider pattern of aggressive purposes.

Why Are We in South Viet-Nam?

Why are these realities our concern? Why are we in South Viet-Nam?

We are there because we have a promise to keep. Since 1954 every American President has offered support to the people of South Viet-Nam. We have helped to build, and we have helped to defend. Thus, over many years, we have made a national pledge to help South Viet-Nam defend its independence.

And I intend to keep that promise.

To dishonor that pledge, to abandon this small and brave nation to its enemies, and to the terror that must follow, would be an unforgivable wrong.

We are also there to strengthen world order. Around the globe, from Berlin to Thailand, are people whose well-being rests in part on the belief that they can count on us if they are attacked. To leave Viet-Nam to its fate would shake the confidence of all these people in the value of an American commitment and in the value of America's word. The result would be increased unrest and instability, and even wider war.

We are also there because there are great stakes in the balance. Let no one think for a moment that retreat from Viet-Nam would bring an end to conflict. The battle would be renewed in one country and then another. The central lesson of our time is that the appetite of aggression is never satisfied. To withdraw from one battlefield means only to prepare for the next. We must say in Southeast Asia—as we did in Europe—in the words of the Bible: "Hitherto shalt thou come, but no further."

There are those who say that all our efforts there will be futile—that China's power is such that it is bound to dominate all Southeast Asia. But there is no end to that argument until all of the nations of Asia are swallowed up.

There are those who wonder why we have a responsibility there. Well, we have it there for the same reason that we have a responsibility for the defense of Europe. World War II was fought in both Europe and Asia, and when it ended we found ourselves with continued responsibility for the defense of freedom.

Our objective is the independence of South Viet-Nam and its freedom from attack. We want nothing for ourselves—only that the people of South Viet-Nam be allowed to guide their own country in their own way. We will do everything necessary to reach that objective, and we will do only what is absolutely necessary.

In recent months attacks on South Viet-Nam were stepped up. Thus it became necessary for us to increase our response and to make attacks by air. This is not a change of purpose. It is a change in what we believe that purpose requires.

We do this in order to slow down aggression.

We do this to increase the confidence of the brave people of South Viet-Nam who have bravely borne this brutal battle for so many years with so many casualties.

And we do this to convince the leaders of North Viet-Nam— and all who seek to share their conquest—of a simple fact:

We will not be defeated.

We will not grow tired.

We will not withdraw, either openly or under the cloak of a meaningless agreement.

We know that air attacks alone will not accomplish all of these purposes. But it is our best and prayerful judgment that they are a necessary part of the surest road to peace.

The Path of Peaceful Settlement

We hope that peace will come swiftly. But that is in the hands of others besides ourselves. And we must be prepared for a long continued conflict. It will require patience as well as bravery—the will to endure as well as the will to resist.

I wish it were possible to convince others with words of what we now find it necessary to say with guns and planes: armed hostility is futile—our resources are equal to any challenge—because we fight for values and we fight for principle, rather than territory or colonies, our patience and our determination are unending.

Once this is clear, then it should also be clear that the only path for reasonable men is the path of peaceful settlement. Such peace demands an independent South Viet-Nam—securely guaranteed and able to shape its own relationships to all others—free from outside interference—tied to no alliance—a military base for no other country.

These are the essentials of any final settlement.

We will never be second in the search for such a peaceful settlement in Viet-Nam.

There may be many ways to this kind of peace: in discussion or negotiation with the governments concerned; in large groups or in small ones; in the reaffirmation of old agreements or their strengthening with new ones.

We have stated this position over and over again 50 times and more to friend and foe alike. And we remain ready with this purpose for unconditional discussions.

And until that bright and necessary day of peace we will try to keep conflict from spreading. We have no desire to see thousands die in battle—Asians or Americans. We have no desire to devastate that which the people of North Viet-Nam have built with toil and sacrifice. We will use our power with restraint and with all the wisdom that we can command.

But we will use it.

A Cooperative Effort for Development

This war, like most wars, is filled with terrible irony. For what do the people of North Viet-Nam want? They want what their neighbors also desire—food for their hunger, health for their bodies, a chance to learn, progress for their country, and an end to the bondage of material misery. And they would find all these things far more readily in peaceful association with others than in the endless course of battle.

These countries of Southeast Asia are homes for millions of impoverished people. Each day these people rise at dawn and struggle through until the night to wrest existence from the soil. They are often wracked by diseases, plagued by hunger, and death comes at the early age of 40.

Stability and peace do not come easily in such a land. Neither independence nor human dignity will ever be won, though, by arms alone. It also requires the works of peace. The American people have helped generously in times past in these works, and now there must be a much more massive effort to improve the life of man in that conflict-torn corner of our world.

The first step is for the countries of Southeast Asia to associate themselves in a greatly expanded cooperative effort for development. We would hope that North Viet-Nam would take its place in the common effort just as soon as peaceful cooperation is possible.

The United Nations is already actively engaged in development in this area, and as far back as 1961 I conferred with our authorities in Viet-Nam in connection with their work there. And I would hope tonight that the Secretary-General of the United Nations could use the prestige of his great office and his deep knowledge of Asia to initiate, as soon as possible, with the countries of that area, a plan for cooperation in increased development.

For our part I will ask the Congress to join in a billion-dollar American investment in this effort as soon as it is underway. And I would hope that all other industrialized countries, including the Soviet Union, will join in this effort to replace despair with hope and terror with progress.

The task is nothing less than to enrich the hopes and existence of more than a hundred million people. And there is much to be done.

The vast Mekong River can provide food and water and power on a scale to dwarf even our own TVA. The wonders of modern medicine can be spread through villages where thousands die every year from lack of care. Schools can be established to train people in the skills needed to manage the process of development. And these objectives, and more, are within the reach of a cooperative and determined effort.

I also intend to expand and speed up a program to make available our farm surpluses to assist in feeding and clothing the needy in Asia. We should not allow people to go hungry and wear rags while our own warehouses overflow with an abundance of wheat and corn and rice and cotton.

So I will very shortly name a special team of outstanding, patriotic, and distinguished Americans to inaugurate our participation in these programs. This team will be headed by Mr. Eugene Black, the very able former President of the World Bank.

The Dream of Our Generation

This will be a disorderly planet for a long time. In Asia, and elsewhere, the forces of the modern world are shaking old ways and uprooting ancient civilizations. There will be turbulence and struggle and even violence. Great social change—as we see in our own country—does not always come without conflict.

We must also expect that nations will on occasion be in dispute with us. It may be because we are rich, or powerful, or because we have made some mistakes, or because they honestly fear our intentions. However, no nation need ever fear that we desire their land, or to impose our will, or to dictate their institutions.

But we will always oppose the effort of one nation to conquer another nation.

We will do this because our own security is at stake.

But there is more to it than that. For our generation has a dream. It is a very old dream. But we have the power, and now we have the opportunity to make that dream come true.

For centuries nations have struggled among each other. But we dream of a world where disputes are settled by law and reason. And we will try to make it so.

For most of history men have hated and killed one another in battle. But we dream of an end to war. And we will try to make it so.

For all existence most men have lived in poverty, threatened by hunger. But we dream of a world where all are fed and charged with hope. And we will help to make it so.

The ordinary men and women of North Viet-Nam and South Viet-Nam, of China and India, of Russia and America, are brave people. They are filled with the same proportions of hate and fear, of love and hope. Most of them want the same things for themselves and their families. Most of them do not want their sons to ever die in battle, or to see their homes, or the homes of others, destroyed.

Well, this can be their world yet. Man now has the knowledge —always before denied—to make this planet serve the real needs of the people who live on it.

I know this will not be easy. I know how difficult it is for reason to guide passion, and love to master hate. The complexities of this world do not bow easily to pure and consistent answers.

But the simple truths are there just the same. We must all try to follow them as best we can.

Power, Witness to Human Folly

We often say how impressive power is. But I do not find it impressive at all. The guns and the bombs, the rockets and the warships, are all symbols of human failure. They are necessary symbols. They protect what we cherish. But they are witness to human folly.

A dam built across a great river is impressive.

In the countryside where I was born, and where I live, I have seen the night illuminated, and the kitchen warmed, and the home heated, where once the cheerless night and the ceaseless cold held sway. And all this happened because electricity came to our area along the humming wires of the REA. Electrification of the countryside—yes, that, too, is impressive.

A rich harvest in a hungry land is impressive.

The sight of healthy children in a classroom is impressive.

These—not mighty arms—are the achievements which the American nation believes to be impressive. And if we are steadfast, the time may come when all other nations will also find it so.

Every night before I turn out the light to sleep I ask myself this question: Have I done everything that I can do to unite this country? Have I done everything I can to help unite the world, to try to bring peace and hope to all the peoples of the world? Have I done enough?

Ask yourselves that question in your homes—and in this hall tonight. Have we, each of us, all done all we can do? Have we done enough?

We may well be living in the time foretold many years ago when it was said: "I call heaven and earth to record this day against you, that I have set before you life and death, blessing and cursing: therefore choose life, that both thou and thy seed may live."

This generation of the world must choose: destroy or build, kill or aid, hate or understand. We can do all these things on a scale that has never been dreamed of before.

Well, we will choose life. And so doing, we will prevail over the enemies within man, and over the natural enemies of all mankind.

B. Saigon's Commentary: Communiqué of the Republic of Vietnam Government *

As the recent statement by President Johnson in Baltimore on the over-all situation in Viet Nam may have divergent interpretations, the Republic of Viet Nam Government deems it necessary to emphasize the following points:

1: Anxious to facilitate preliminary contacts prior to negotiations proper and to manifest its sincere desire to settle the Vietnamese problem in a common accord and by peaceful means, the United States of America, an ally of the Republic of Viet Nam, is disposed—in President Johnson's own words—to start unconditional "discussions." This does not imply the acceptance of a ceasefire without preconditions. It is a matter of course that negotiations proper can only take place when preconditions (the withdrawal of Communist troops and cadres) laid out by the Republic of Viet Nam during eventual preliminary talks will have been accepted and carried out.

2: As far as it is concerned, the Republic of Viet Nam government has on many occasions reiterated its eager wish to see peace restored to Viet Nam at the earliest possible time. It feels that the only way to achieve this is the suppression of the very cause of the present tension of which the entire responsibility lies with the Communists who have been engaged in subversive and hostile acts on the territory of the Republic of Viet Nam in violation of the Geneva Accords. In fact the success of eventual negotiations and the maintenance of a lasting peace depend on previous withdrawal of the Viet Cong armed units and political cadres.

3: Even if the preconditions set by the Republic of Viet Nam are fulfilled, the government of the Republic of Viet Nam can only negotiate with recognized representatives of the opponent.

---

* Source: B. Translation from the Vietnamese of a leaflet published in Saigon and air-dropped over North Vietnam shortly after President Johnson's Baltimore speech of April 7, 1965. The Vietnamese text was obtained from the United States Information Agency office, Saigon.

The government of the Republic of Viet Nam has never, and at the present time, does not, recognize the so-called "South Viet Nam Liberation Front" which is only an instrument created by the Communist North Vietnamese with a view to carrying out their criminal schemes and imperialist aims. In fact it has been established that the Communist Viet Cong have not ceased to direct and supply this Front with armed units, political cadres, weapons and ammunition. They have even, through a noisy propaganda, supported the claims and promoted the so-called exploits of this front.

Saigon, April 11, 1965

Appendix 14[*]

HANOI'S FOUR POINTS

The unswerving policy of the DRV Government is to respect strictly the 1954 Geneva agreements on Vietnam and to implement correctly their basic provisions as embodied in the following points:

1—Recognition of the basic national rights of the Vietnamese people—peace, independence, sovereignty, unity, and territorial integrity. According to the Geneva agreements, the U.S. Government must withdraw from South Vietnam U.S. troops, military personnel, and weapons of all kinds, dismantle all U.S. military bases there, and cancel its military alliance with South Vietnam. It must end its policy of intervention and aggression in South Vietnam. According to the Geneva agreements, the U.S. Government must stop its acts of war against North Vietnam and completely cease all encroachments on the territory and sovereignty of the DRV.

2—Pending the peaceful reunification of Vietnam, while Vietnam is still temporarily divided into two zones the military provisions of the 1954 Geneva agreements on Vietnam must be strictly respected. The two zones must refrain from entering into any military alliance with foreign countries and there must be no foreign military bases, troops, or military personnel in their respective territory.

3—The internal affairs of South Vietnam must be settled by the South Vietnamese people themselves in accordance with the program of the NFLSV without any foreign interference.

4—The peaceful reunification of Vietnam is to be settled by the Vietnamese people in both zones, without any foreign interference.

This stand of the DRV Government unquestionably enjoys the approval and support of all peace and justice-loving governments

---

[*] SOURCE: Excerpt from report of Premier Pham Van Dong, April 8, 1965, as given on Hanoi Radio, April 13, 1965.

and peoples in the world. The government of the DRV is of the view that the stand expounded here is the basis for the soundest political settlement of the Vietnam problem.

If this basis is recognized, favorable conditions will be created for the peaceful settlement of the Vietnam problem, and it will be possible to consider the reconvening of an international conference along the pattern of the 1954 Geneva conference on Vietnam.

The DRV Government declares that any approach contrary to the aforementioned stand is inappropriate; any approach tending to secure U.N. intervention in the Vietnam situation is also inappropriate. Such approaches are basically at variance with the 1954 Geneva agreements on Vietnam.

Appendix 15 [*]

REPUBLIC OF VIETNAM DECREE LAW ON PRO-COMMUNIST ACTIVITIES, MAY, 1965

Chief of State Phan Khac Suu on Monday proclaimed Decree Law 004/65 amending Decree Law 093-SL/CT of February 1, 1964, which outlawed Communism and pro-Communist neutralism. The Decree Law, whose contents are as follows, had been favourably voted by the National Legislative Council.

Article 1

The following actions are deemed as actions specified and punished by Decree Law 093-SL/CT of February 1, 1964:

(a) All direct or indirect actions aimed at spreading Communist policies, slogans and instructions by any individual or group of individuals influenced or controlled by the Communists.

(b) All moves which weaken the national anti-Communist effort and are harmful to the anti-Communist struggle of the people and the Armed Forces. All plots and actions under the false name of peace and neutrality according to a Communist policy and similar plots and actions are considered as belonging to the category of such moves as mentioned above.

(c) The diffusion, circulation, distribution, sale, display in public places, and the keeping of these above mentioned aims, either in printed form, drawings, photographic, or otherwise, with the same effects as stated in paragraphs *a* and *b* (Article 1).

Article 2

All associations, agencies, and organizations violating Article 1

---

[*] SOURCE: *Saigon Daily News,* May 20, 1965, reprinted in American Friends Service Committee, *Peace in Vietnam* (New York: Hill and Wang, 1966). Used by permission.

shall be disbanded and their properties confiscated.

The Prime Minister will decide on procedures to liquidate the properties of these organizations by decrees.

Article 3

Except in cases where the "Du" No. 47 of August 21, 1956, on external security can be applied, all violations against this Decree incur a penalty of imprisonment from one to five years. Besides, the court can apply additional penalties mentioned in Art. 42 of the Modified Penal Code of Article 27 of the Penal Code (Viet Nam's ancient codes).

Article 4

The Corps Area Field Military Court, during the emergency situation, has the competence to judge all violations said in this Decree, which are caught *flagrante delicto* within the territory of the Corps Area, according to procedures contained in Decree 11-62 of May 21, 1962, on the setting up of the Field Military Court.

If not caught *flagrante delicto,* or if perpetrated in normal national situation, the perpetrations shall be tried by the military court.

Article 5

This Decree Law is promulgated according to the emergency procedure.

Appendix 16[*]

WASHINGTON'S FOURTEEN POINTS

January 7, 1966

The following statements are on the public record about elements which the United States believes can go into peace in Southeast Asia:

1. The Geneva Agreements of 1954 and 1962 are an adequate basis for peace in Southeast Asia;
2. We would welcome a conference on Southeast Asia or on any part thereof;
3. We would welcome "negotiations without preconditions" as the 17 nations put it;
4. We would welcome unconditional discussions as President Johnson put it;
5. A cessation of hostilities could be the first order of business at a conference or could be the subject of preliminary discussions;
6. Hanoi's four points could be discussed along with other points which others might wish to propose;
7. We want no U.S. bases in Southeast Asia;
8. We do not desire to retain U.S. troops in South Viet-Nam after peace is assured;
9. We support free elections in South Viet-Nam to give the South Vietnamese a government of their own choice;
10. The question of reunification of Viet-Nam should be determined by the Vietnamese through their own free decision;
11. The countries of Southeast Asia can be non-aligned or neutral if that be their option;

---

* SOURCE: *Department of State Bulletin* (Washington, February 14, 1966).

12. We would much prefer to use our resources for the economic reconstruction of Southeast Asia than in War. If there is peace, North Viet-Nam could participate in a regional effort to which we would be prepared to contribute at least one billion dollars;

13. The President has said "The Viet Cong would not have difficulty being represented and having their views represented if for a moment Hanoi decided she wanted to cease aggression. I don't think that would be an unsurmountable problem."

14. We have said publicly and privately that we could stop the bombing of North Viet-Nam as a step toward peace although there has not been the slightest hint or suggestion from the other side as to what they would do if the bombing stopped.

Appendix 17*

THE TEN POINTS OF
THE NATIONAL LIBERATION FRONT
MAY 8, 1969

(*EXCERPTS*)

Proceeding from a desire to reach a political solution with a view to ending the U.S. imperialists' war of aggression in South Viet Nam and helping restore peace in Viet Nam;

On the basis of the guarantee of the fundamental national rights of the Vietnamese people;

Proceeding from the fundamental principles of the 1954 Geneva Agreements on Viet Nam and the actual situation in Viet Nam;

On the basis of the Political Programme and the 5-point position of the South Viet Nam National Front for Liberation, which keep with the 4-point stand of the Government of the Democratic Republic of Viet Nam;

The South Viet Nam National Front for Liberation sets forth the principles and main content of an overall solution to the South Viet Nam problem to help restore peace in Viet Nam as follows:

---

* SOURCE: "Principles and Main Content of an Overall Solution to the South Viet Nam Problem to Help Restore Peace in Viet Nam." The text of this translation was provided to the authors by the NLF's delegation in Paris.

1—To respect the Vietnamese people's fundamental national rights, i.e. independence, sovereignty, unity and territorial integrity, as recognized by the 1954 Geneva Agreements on Viet Nam.

2—The U.S. Government must withdraw from South Viet Nam all U.S. troops, military personnel, arms and war materiel, and all troops, military personnel, arms and war materiel of the other foreign countries of the U.S. camp without posing any condition whatsoever; liquidate all U.S. military bases in South Viet Nam; renounce all encroachments on the sovereignty, territory and security of South Viet Nam and the Democratic Republic of Viet Nam.

3—The Vietnamese people's right to fight for the defence of their Fatherland is the sacred, inalienable right to self-defence of all peoples. The question of the Vietnamese armed forces in South Viet Nam shall be resolved by the Vietnamese parties among themselves.

4—The people of South Viet Nam settle themselves their own affairs without foreign interference. They decide themselves the political regime of South Viet Nam through free and democratic general elections. Through free and democratic general elections, a Constituent Assembly will be set up, a Constitution worked out, and a coalition Government of South Viet Nam installed, reflecting national concord and the broad union of all social strata.

5—During the period intervening between the restoration of peace and the holding of general elections, neither party shall impose its political regime on the people of South Viet Nam.

The political forces representing the various social strata and political tendencies in South Viet Nam, that stand for peace, independence and neutrality, including those persons who, for political reasons, have to live abroad, will enter into talks to set up a provisional coalition government based on the principle of equality, democracy and mutual respect with a view to achieving a peaceful, independent, democratic and neutral South Viet Nam.

The provisional coalition government is to have the following tasks:

a) To implement the agreements on the withdrawal of the troops of the United States and the other foreign countries of the American camp, etc.

b) To achieve national concord, and a broad union of all social strata, political forces, nationalities, religious communities, and all persons, no matter what their political beliefs and their past may be, provided they stand for peace, independence and neutrality.

c) To achieve broad democratic freedoms—freedom of speech, freedom of the press, freedom of gathering, freedom of belief, freedom to form political parties and organizations, freedom to demonstrate, etc.; to set free those persons jailed on political grounds; to prohibit all acts of terror, reprisal and discrimination against people having collaborated with either side, and who are now in the country or abroad, as provided for in the 1954 Geneva Agreements on Viet Nam.

d) To heal the war wounds, to restore and develop the economy, to restore the normal life of the people, and to improve the living conditions of the labouring people.

e) To hold free and democratic general elections in the whole of South Viet Nam with a view to achieving the South Viet Nam people's right to self-determination, in accordance with the content of point 4 mentioned above.

6—South Viet Nam will carry out a foreign policy of peace and neutrality:

To carry out a policy of good neighbourly relations with the Kingdom of Cambodia on the basis of respect for her independence, sovereignty, neutrality and territorial integrity within her present borders; to carry out a policy of good neighbourly relations with the Kingdom of Laos on the basis of respect for the 1962 Geneva Agreements on Laos.

To establish diplomatic, economic and cultural relations with all countries, irrespective of political and social regime, including the United States, in accordance with the five principles of peaceful coexistence: mutual respect for the independence, sovereignty and territorial integrity, non-aggression, non-interference in the internal affairs, equality and mutual benefit, peaceful coexistence; to accept economic and technical aid with no political conditions attached from any country.

7—The reunification of Viet Nam will be achieved step by step, by peaceful means, through discussions and agreement between the two zones, without foreign interference.

Pending the peaceful reunification of Viet Nam, the two zones reestablish normal relations in all fields on the basis of mutual respect.

The military demarcation line between the two zones at the 17th parallel, as provided for by the 1954 Geneva Agreements, is only of a provisional character and does not constitute in any way a political or territorial boundary. The two zones reach agreement on the statute of the Demilitarized Zones, and work out modalities for movements across the provisional military demarcation line.

8—As provided for in the 1954 Geneva Agreements on Viet Nam, pending the peaceful reunification of Viet Nam, the two zones North and South of Viet Nam undertake to refrain from joining any military alliance with foreign countries, not to allow any foreign country to maintain military bases, troops and military personnel on their respective soil, and not to recognize the protection of any country or military alliance or bloc.

9—To resolve the aftermath of the war:

a) The parties will negotiate the release of the armymen captured in war.

b) The U.S. Government must bear full responsibility for the losses and devastations it has caused to the Vietnamese people in both zones.

10—The parties shall reach agreement on an international supervision about the withdrawal from South Viet Nam of the troops, military personnel, arms and war materiel of the United States and the other foreign countries of the American camp.

The principles and content of the overall solution expounded above form an integrated whole. On the basis of these principles and content, the parties shall reach understanding to the effect of concluding agreements on the abovementioned questions with a view to ending the war in South Viet Nam, and contributing to restore peace in Viet Nam.

Appendix 18*

PRESIDENT NIXON'S REPORT

ON VIETNAM

MAY 14, 1969

(*EXCERPTS*)

. . . We can have honest debate about whether we should have entered the war. We can have honest debate about the past conduct of the war. But the urgent question today is what to do now that we are there, not whether we should have entered on this course, but what is required of us today.

Against that background, let me discuss, first, what we have rejected, and second, what we are prepared to accept.

We have ruled out attempting to impose a purely military solution on the battlefield.

We have also ruled out either a one-sided withdrawal from Viet-Nam or the acceptance in Paris of terms that would amount to a disguised defeat.

When we assumed the burden of helping defend South Viet-Nam, millions of South Vietnamese men, women, and children placed their trust in us. To abandon them now would risk a massacre that would shock and dismay everyone in the world who values human life.

Abandoning the South Vietnamese people, however, would jeopardize more than lives in South Viet-Nam. It

---

* SOURCE: *Department of State Bulletin* (Washington, June 2, 1969).

would threaten our longer term hopes for peace in the world. A great nation cannot renege on its pledges. A great nation must be worthy of trust.

When it comes to maintaining peace, "prestige" is not an empty word. I am not speaking of false pride or bravado—they should have no place in our policies. I speak rather of the respect that one nation has for another's integrity in defending its principles and meeting its obligations.

If we simply abandoned our effort in Viet-Nam, the cause of peace might not survive the damage that would be done to other nations' confidence in our reliability.

Another reason stems from debates within the Communist world between those who argue for a policy of confrontation with the United States and those who argue against it. If Hanoi were to succeed in taking over South Viet-Nam by force—even after the power of the United States had been engaged—it would greatly strengthen those leaders who scorn negotiation, who advocate aggression, who minimize the risks of confrontation. It would bring peace now, but it would enormously increase the danger of a bigger war later.

If we are to move successfully from an era of confrontation to an era of negotiation, then we have to demonstrate—at the point at which confrontation is being tested—that confrontation with the United States is costly and unrewarding.

Almost without exception, the leaders of non-Communist Asia have told me that they would consider a one-sided American withdrawal from Viet-Nam to be a threat to the security of their own nations.

In determining what choices would be acceptable, we have to understand our essential objective: We seek the opportunity for the South Vietnamese people to determine their own political future without outside interference.

Let me put it plainly: What the United States wants for

South Viet-Nam is not the important thing. What North Viet-Nam wants for South Viet-Nam is not the important thing. What is important is what the people of South Viet-Nam want for themselves.

The United States has suffered over 1 million casualties in four wars in this century. Whatever faults we may have as a nation, we have asked nothing for ourselves in return for these sacrifices. We have been generous toward those whom we have fought, helping former foes as well as friends in the task of reconstruction. We are proud of this record, and we bring the same attitude to our search for a settlement in Viet-Nam.

In this spirit, let me be explicit about several points:

—We seek no bases in Viet-Nam.

—We insist on no military ties.

—We are willing to agree to neutrality if that is what the South Vietnamese people freely choose.

—We believe there should be an opportunity for full participation in the political life of South Viet-Nam by all political elements that are prepared to do so without the use of force or intimidation.

—We are prepared to accept any government in South Viet-Nam that results from the free choice of the South Vietnamese people themselves.

—We have no intention of imposing any form of government upon the people of South Viet-Nam, nor will we be a party to such coercion.

—We have no objection to reunification, if that turns out to be what the people of South Viet-Nam and the people of North Viet-Nam want; we ask only that the decision reflect the free choice of the people concerned. . . .

In pursuing our limited objective, we insist on no rigid diplomatic formula. Peace could be achieved by a formal negotiated settlement. Peace could be achieved by an informal understanding, provided that the understanding is clear and that there were adequate assurances that it would be observed. Peace on paper is not as important as peace in fact.

This brings us, then, to the matter of negotiations.

We must recognize that peace in Viet-Nam cannot be achieved overnight. A war which has raged for so many years will require detailed negotiations and cannot be settled at a single stroke.

What kind of a settlement will permit the South Vietnamese people to determine freely their own political future? Such a settlement will require the withdrawal of all non-South Vietnamese forces from South Viet-Nam and procedures for political choice that give each significant group in South Viet-Nam a real opportunity to participate in the political life of the nation.

To implement these principles, I reaffirm now our willingness to withdraw our forces on a specified timetable. We ask only that North Viet-Nam withdraw its forces from South Viet-Nam, Cambodia, and Laos into North Viet-Nam, also in accordance with a timetable.

We include Cambodia and Laos to ensure that these countries would not be used as bases for a renewed war. The Cambodian border is only 35 miles from Saigon; the Laotian border is only 25 miles from Hue.

Our offer provides for a simultaneous start on withdrawal by both sides; agreement on a mutually acceptable timetable; and for the withdrawal to be accomplished quickly.

If North Viet-Nam wants to insist that it has no forces in South Viet-Nam, we will no longer debate the point— provided that its forces cease to be there and that we have reliable assurances that they will not return.

The North Vietnamese delegates have been saying in Paris that political issues should be discussed along with military issues and that there must be a political settlement in the South. We do not dispute this, but the military withdrawal involves outside forces and can therefore be properly negotiated by North Viet-Nam and the United States, with the concurrence of its allies. The political settlement is an internal matter which ought to be decided among the South Vietnamese themselves and not imposed by outside powers. However, if our presence at these political negotiations would be helpful, and if the South Vietnamese concerned agreed, we would be willing to participate, along with the representatives of Hanoi if that were also desired.

Recent statements by President Thieu have gone far toward opening the way to a political settlement. He has publicly declared his government's willingness to discuss a political solution with the National Liberation Front and has offered free elections. This was a dramatic step forward, a reasonable offer that could lead to a settlement. The South Vietnamese Government has offered to talk without preconditions. I believe that the other side should also be willing to talk without preconditions.

The South Vietnamese Government recognizes, as we do, that a settlement must permit all persons and groups that are prepared to renounce the use of force to participate freely in the political life of South Viet-Nam. To be effective, such a settlement would require two things: first, a process that would allow the South Vietnamese people to express their choice; and second, a guarantee that this process would be a fair one.

We do not insist on a particular form of guarantee. The important thing is that the guarantees should have the confidence of the South Vietnamese people and that they should be broad enough and strong enough to protect the interests of all major South Vietnamese groups.

This, then, is the outline of the settlement that we seek to negotiate in Paris. Its basic terms are very simple: mutual withdrawal of non-South Vietnamese forces from South Viet-Nam and free choice for the people of South Viet-Nam. I believe that the long-term interests of peace require that we insist on no less and that the realities of the situation require that we seek no more.

To make very concrete what I have said, I propose the following measures, which seem to me consistent with the principles of all parties. These proposals are made on the basis of full consultation with President Thieu.

—As soon as agreement can be reached, all non-South Vietnamese forces would begin withdrawals from South Viet-Nam.

—Over a period of 12 months, by agreed-upon stages, the major portions of all U.S., Allied, and other non-South Vietnamese forces would be withdrawn. At the end of this 12-month period, the remaining U.S., Allied, and other non-South Vietnamese forces would move into designated base areas and would not engage in combat operations.

—The remaining U.S. and Allied forces would move to complete their withdrawals as the remaining North Vietnamese forces were withdrawn and returned to North Viet-Nam.

—An international supervisory body, acceptable to both sides, would be created for the purpose of verifying withdrawals and for any other purposes agreed upon between the two sides.

—This international body would begin operating in accordance with an agreed timetable and would participate in arranging supervised cease-fires.

—As soon as possible after the international body was functioning, elections would be held under agreed procedures and under the supervision of the international body.

—Arrangements would be made for the earliest possible release of prisoners of war on both sides.

—All parties would agree to observe the Geneva accords of 1954 regarding Viet-Nam and Cambodia, and the Laos accords of 1962.

I believe this proposal for peace is realistic and takes account of the legitimate interests of all concerned. It is consistent with President Thieu's six points. It can accommodate the various programs put forth by the other side. We and the Government of South Viet-Nam are prepared to discuss its details with the other side. Secretary Rogers is now in Saigon and will be discussing with President Thieu how, together, we may put forward these proposed measures most usefully in Paris. He will, as well, be consulting with our other Asian allies on these measures while on his Asian trip. However, I would stress that these proposals are not offered on a take-it-or-leave-it basis. We are quite willing to consider other approaches consistent with our principles.

We are willing to talk about anybody's program—Hanoi's four points, the NLF's 10 points—provided it can be made consistent with the few basic principles I have set forth here.

Despite our disagreement with several of its points, we welcome the fact that the NLF has put forward its first comprehensive program. We are continuing to study it carefully. However, we cannot ignore the fact that immediately after the offer, the scale of enemy attacks stepped up and American casualties increased.

Let me make one point very clear. If the enemy wants peace with the United States, that is not the way to get it.

I have set forth a peace program tonight which is generous in its terms. I have indicated our willingness to consider other proposals. No greater mistake could be made than to confuse flexibility with weakness or being reasonable with lack of resolution. I must make clear, in all candor, that if the needless suffering continues, this will affect other decisions. Nobody has anything to gain by delay.

Reports from Hanoi indicate that the enemy has given up hope for a military victory in South Viet-Nam but is counting on a collapse of American will in the United States. They could make no greater error in judgment.

Let me be quite blunt. Our fighting men are not going to

be worn down; our negotiators are not going to be talked down; our allies are not going to be let down. . . .

In my campaign for the Presidency, I pledged to end this war in a way that would increase our chances to win true and lasting peace in Viet-Nam, in the Pacific, and in the world. I am determined to keep that pledge. If I fail to do so, I expect the American people to hold me accountable for that failure. . . .

Selected Bibliography

(Note: Particularly useful items are marked with an asterisk.)

AMERICAN FRIENDS SERVICE COMMITTEE, *Peace in Vietnam: A New Approach in Southeast Asia.* New York: Hill and Wang, 1967. New enlarged ed.

AZEAU, HENRI, *Ho Chi Minh, dernière chance: La conférence franco-vietnamienne de Fontainebleau, juillet 1946.* Paris: Flammarion, 1968.

BATOR, VICTOR, *Vietnam, A Diplomatic Tragedy: Origins of U.S. Involvement.* Dobbs Ferry, N.Y.: Oceana Publications, 1965.

BODARD, LUCIEN, *La guerre d'Indochine,* 3 vols. Paris: Gallimard, 1963–1967.

BODARD, LUCIEN, *The Quicksand War: Prelude to Vietnam.* Boston: Little, Brown, 1967.

BURCHETT, WILFRED G., *Vietnam: Inside Story of the Guerrilla War.* New York: International Publishers, 1965.

BUTTINGER, JOSEPH, *The Smaller Dragon: A Political History of Vietnam.* New York: Praeger, 1958.

*BUTTINGER, JOSEPH, *Vietnam: A Dragon Embattled,* 2 vols. New York: Praeger, 1967. Vol. I. From Colonialism to the Vietminh. Vol. II. Vietnam at War.

CAMERON, JAMES, *Here Is Your Enemy.* New York: Holt, Rinehart and Winston, 1966.

CHAFFARD, GEORGES, *Indochine: Dix ans d'indépendance.* Paris: Calmann-Lévy, 1964.

CHILD, FRANK C., *Essays on Economic Growth, Capital Formation, and Public Policy in Viet-Nam.* Saigon: Michigan State University Viet-Nam Advisory Group, May 1961.

COLE, ALLAN B., ed., *Conflict in Indo-China and International*

Repercussions: A Documentary History, 1945–1955. Ithaca, N.Y.: Cornell University Press, 1956.

CORSON, WILLIAM R., *The Betrayal*. New York: Norton, 1968.

DANG, NGHIEM, *Viet-Nam: Politics and Public Administration*. Honolulu: East-West Center Press, 1966.

*DEVILLERS, PHILIPPE, *Histoire du Viet-Nam de 1940 à 1952*. Paris: Editions du Seuil, 1952. 3rd ed.

*DEVILLERS, PHILIPPE AND JEAN LACOUTURE, *End of a War: Indochina, 1954*. New York: Praeger, 1969.

DOYON, JACQUES, *Les Vietcong*. Paris: Editions Denoël, 1968.

DUNCANSON, DENNIS J., *Government and Revolution in Vietnam*. New York and London: Oxford University Press, 1968.

EDEN, SIR ANTHONY, *Full Circle*. London: Cassell, 1960.

FALK, RICHARD A., ed., *The Vietnam War and International Law*. Princeton: Princeton University Press, 1967.

FALL, BERNARD B., *Hell in a Very Small Place: The Siege of Dien Bien Phu*. New York: Vintage, 1966.

*FALL, BERNARD B.,ed., *Ho Chi Minh on Revolution: Selected Writings, 1920–66*. New York: Praeger, 1967.

FALL, BERNARD B., *Last Reflections on a War*. Garden City, N.Y.: Doubleday, 1967.

FALL, BERNARD B., *Street Without Joy: From the Indochina War to the War in Viet-Nam*. Harrisburg, Pa.: The Stackpole Company, 1961.

*FALL, BERNARD B., *The Two Viet-Nams: A Political and Military Analysis*. New York: Praeger, 1967. 2nd rev. ed.

FALL, BERNARD B., *Viet-Nam Witness, 1953–66*. New York: Praeger, 1966.

FISHEL, WESLEY R., ed., *Problems of Freedom: South Vietnam Since Independence*. Glencoe, Ill. and East Lansing, Mich.:

The Free Press and Michigan State University Bureau of Social and Political Research, 1961.

FULBRIGHT, J. WILLIAM, *The Vietnam Hearings*. New York: Vintage, 1966.

*GETTLEMAN, MARVIN E., *Vietnam: History, Documents, and Opinions on a Major World Crisis*. New York: Fawcett, 1965.

GIAP, VO NGUYEN, *"Big Victory, Great Task": North Viet-Nam's Minister of Defense Assesses the Course of the War*. New York: Praeger, 1968.

GOODWIN, RICHARD N., *Triumph or Tragedy: Reflections on Vietnam*. New York: Vintage, 1966.

GRUENING, ERNEST AND HERBERT W. BEASER, *Vietnam Folly*. Washington: National Press, 1968.

GURTOV, MELVIN, *The First Vietnam Crisis: Chinese Communist Strategy and United States Involvement*. New York: Columbia University Press, 1967.

HALBERSTAM, DAVID, *The Making of a Quagmire*. New York: Random House, 1965.

*HAMMER, ELLEN J., *The Struggle for Indochina*. Stanford, Cal.: Stanford University Press, 1954.

HANH, THICH NHAT, *Vietnam: The Lotus in the Sea of Fire*. New York: Hill and Wang, 1967.

HARTKE, VANCE, *The American Crisis in Vietnam*. Indianapolis, Ind.: Bobbs-Merrill, 1968.

HENDRY, JAMES B., *The Small World of Khanh Hau*. Chicago: Aldine, 1964.

*HICKEY, GERALD CANNON, *Village in Vietnam*. New Haven, Conn.: Yale University Press, 1964.

*HILSMAN, ROGER, *To Move a Nation*. Garden City, N.Y.: Doubleday, 1967.

HONEY, P. J., ed., *North Vietnam Today*. New York: Praeger, 1962.

ISOART, PAUL, *Le phénomène national vietnamien: De l'indépendance unitaire à l'indépendance fractionnée*. Paris: Librairie Générale de Droit et de Jurisprudence, 1961.

JUMPER, ROY AND MARJORIE WEINER NORMAND, "Vietnam." In *Governments and Politics of Southeast Asia*, ed. by George McT. Kahin. Ithaca, N.Y.: Cornell University Press, 1964. 2nd ed.

JUST, WARD, *To What End: Report from Vietnam*. Boston: Houghton Mifflin, 1968.

KASTENMEIER, ROBERT W., *Vietnam Hearings: Voices from the Grass Roots*. Garden City, N.Y.: Doubleday, 1966.

*KHOI, LE THANH, *Le Viet-Nam: Histoire et civilisation*. Paris: Les Editions de Minuit, 1955.

KISSINGER, HENRY A., "The Viet Nam Negotiations." *Foreign Affairs*, 42, 2 (January 1969), 211–234.

KNOEBL, KUNO, *Victor Charlie: The Face of War in Vietnam*. New York: Praeger, 1967.

KRASLOW, DAVID AND STUART H. LOORY, *The Secret Search for Peace in Vietnam*. New York: Random House, 1968.

*LACOUTURE, JEAN, *Ho Chi Minh: A Political Biography*. New York: Random House, 1968.

LACOUTURE, JEAN, *Vietnam: Between Two Truces*. New York: Random House, 1966.

LAM, TRUONG BUU, *Patterns of Vietnamese Response to Foreign Intervention: 1858–1900*. New Haven, Conn.: Yale University, Southeast Asia Studies, 1967.

*LANCASTER, DONALD, *The Emancipation of French Indochina*. London: Oxford University Press, 1961.

LUCE, DON AND JOHN SOMMER, *Vietnam: The Unheard Voices*. Ithaca, N.Y.: Cornell University Press, 1969.

McAleavy, Henry, *Black Flags in Vietnam: The Story of a Chinese Intervention, The Tonkin War of 1884–85*. New York: Macmillan, 1968.

McAlister, John T., Jr., *Viet Nam: The Origins of Revolution*. New York: Knopf, 1969.

Mecklin, John, *Mission in Torment*. Garden City, N.Y.: Doubleday, 1965.

Morgenthau, Hans, *Vietnam and the United States*. Washington: Public Affairs Press, 1965.

Murti, B. S. N., *Vietnam Divided: The Unfinished Struggle*. New York: Asia Publishing House, 1964.

Mus, Paul, *Viet-Nam: Sociologie d'une guerre*. Paris: Editions du Seuil, 1952.

Nixon, Richard M., "Asia After Viet Nam." *Foreign Affairs,* 46, 1 (October 1967), 111–125.

Osborne, Milton E., *Strategic Hamlets in South Viet-Nam: A Survey and a Comparison* (Data Paper 55). Ithaca, N.Y.: Cornell Southeast Asia Program, 1965.

Pfeffer, Richard M., ed., *No More Vietnams: The War and the Future of American Foreign Policy*. New York: Harper and Row, 1968.

Pike, Douglas, *Viet Cong: The Organization and Techniques of the National Liberation Front*. Cambridge, Mass.: M.I.T. Press, 1966.

Pike, Douglas, *War, Peace, and the Viet Cong: A Study of Current Communist Strategy in Vietnam*. Cambridge, Mass.: M.I.T. Press, 1969.

*Raskin, Marcus G. and Bernard B. Fall, *The Viet-Nam Reader: Articles and Documents on American Foreign Policy and the Viet-Nam Crisis*. New York: Vintage, 1965.

Reischauer, Edwin O., *Beyond Vietnam: The United States and Asia*. New York: Knopf, 1967.

ROBEQUAIN, CHARLES, *The Economic Development of French Indo-China*. London: Oxford University Press, 1944.

ROY, JULES, *The Battle of Dienbienphu*. New York: Harper and Row, 1965.

SALISBURY, HARRISON E., *Behind the Lines—Hanoi: December 23–January 7*. New York: Harper and Row, 1967.

SCHELL, JONATHAN, *The Military Half: An Account of Destruction in Quang Ngai and Quang Tin*. New York: Knopf, 1968.

SCHELL, JONATHAN, *The Village of Ben Suc*. New York: Knopf, 1967.

SCHLESINGER, ARTHUR M., JR., *The Bitter Heritage: Vietnam and American Democracy*. Boston: Houghton Mifflin, 1966.

SCHLESINGER, ARTHUR M., JR., *A Thousand Days*. Boston: Houghton Mifflin, 1965.

SCHOENBRUN, DAVID, *Vietnam: How We Got In. How to Get Out*. New York: Atheneum, 1968.

SCHURMANN, FRANZ, ET AL., *The Politics of Escalation in Vietnam*. Boston: Beacon Press, 1966.

*SCIGLIANO, ROBERT, *South Vietnam: Nation Under Stress*. Boston: Houghton Mifflin, 1963.

SCIGLIANO, ROBERT AND GUY H. FOX, *Technical Assistance in Vietnam: The Michigan State University Experience*. New York: Praeger, 1965.

*SHAPLEN, ROBERT, *The Lost Revolution*. New York: Harper and Row, 1965.

SORENSEN, THEODORE C., *Kennedy*. New York: Harper and Row, 1965.

TANHAM, GEORGE K., *Communist Revolutionary Warfare*. New York: Praeger, 1967. Rev. ed.

TANHAM, GEORGE K., ET AL., *War Without Guns*. New York: Praeger, 1966.

THAI, NGUYEN, *Is South Vietnam Viable?* Manila: Carmelo and Bauermann, 1962.

THOMPSON, SIR ROBERT, *Defeating Communist Insurgency.* New York: Praeger, 1966.

U.S. SENATE, COMMITTEE ON FOREIGN RELATIONS, *Background Information Relating to Southeast Asia and Vietnam.* Washington: U.S. Government Printing Office, 1969. 5th rev. ed.

WEINSTEIN, FRANKLIN B., *Vietnam's Unheld Elections: The Failure to Carry Out the 1956 Reunification Elections and the Effect on Hanoi's Present Outlook.* Ithaca, N.Y.: Cornell Southeast Asia Program, 1966.

ZAGORIA, DONALD S., *Vietnam Triangle: Moscow, Peking, Hanoi.* New York: Pegasus, 1967.

ZINN, HOWARD, *Vietnam: The Logic of Withdrawal.* Boston: Beacon Press, 1967.

Index

Abrams, Creighton, 389, 391

Aggression and aggressors, 120, 127, 131, 171, 184, 244, 245, 273, 300–301, 303*n.*, 309, 315, 328, 335, 337 and *n.*, 339, 455, 477, 479, 490, 491, 495, 498, 506, 518

Agrarian problems. *See* Land Policies

Aid, communist military and economic, to Hanoi, 30*n.*, 88, 90, 92, 109, 189–190, 227–228, 271, 282, 283, 285*n.*, 289

Aid, U.S. military and economic
  to Diem, 67, 68, 70, 72, 73, 74, 77–80, 92, 106, 130*n.*
  to the French, 32, 35, 38
  to Saigon (post-Diem), 152, 154, 166, 239, 256, 328, 331, 335, 336, 493

Aiken, George D., 398

Air strikes, 158, 170, 175, 182, 186, 191, 193, 207, 213–214, 217, 224, 229–231, 238, 283, 298, 317–318, 330, 339, 368, 377, 378, 391

Aleo, Ybih, 134

Algeria, 28, 406*n.*

All-Religions Citizen's Front, 383

Alliance of National, Democratic and Peace Forces, 374*n.*, 382, 396, 405*n.*

Alliances, military, 44, 50, 59, 61–63, 118–119, 130*n.*, 215*n.*, 271–272, 277, 279, 299–303, 326, 432, 442

Alsop, Joseph, 144*n.*

American Friends of Vietnam, 66*n.*

Annam, 8, 9, 11, 13, 18, 20, 26, 28, 35, 109*n.*

Armed forces, 185, 520–521, 522. *See also* Specific actions, forces
  Australian, 184–185
  Chinese, 23, 25, 190, 289
  Diem's Special Forces, 143, 144
  French. *See* French Union, forces of
  New Zealand, 184–185
  People's Army of Vietnam (PAVN), 49, 55, 130*n.*, 182, 187–189, 221, 231*n.*, 338, 370–373, 384, 386, 391, 395, 399–401, 422, 423, 424, 429, 440, 446, 520–521
  South Korean, 184–186, 221, 362, 363*n.*
  South Vietnamese Army (ARVN), 68, 69, 71, 72, 77, 79, 109, 117, 128, 131, 144, 153, 166–167, 184–186, 189, 242, 244–245, 251, 256, 329, 330, 331*n.*–332*n.*, 333, 336, 362, 363, 366*n.*, 367, 368, 372, 373, 374, 402, 404–405, 470. *See also* Specific actions
  U.K., 23, 24, 25
  U.S., 128, 130*n.*, 137, 139, 156, 183–185, 188, 189, 194, 201, 215, 217*n.*, 218, 221, 329, 330, 333, 335–336, 337, 343*n.*, 362–364, 365, 366, 375, 376, 391, 395, 398, 399–400, 401–402, 403–404, 489,